THE COMPLETE WORKS OF
JOHN WEBSTER

VOLUME II

THE COMPLETE WORKS
OF
JOHN WEBSTER

Edited by

F. L. LUCAS

FELLOW OF KING'S COLLEGE
CAMBRIDGE

Volume II
The Duchess of Malfi
The Devil's Law-Case

NEW YORK

GORDIAN PRESS, INC.

1966

Originally Published 1927
Reprinted 1966

Published by arrangement with
Chatto and Windus, London
Library of Congress Catalog Card No. 66-20023

Printed in U.S.A. by
EDWARDS BROTHERS, INC.
Ann Arbor, Michigan

This edition published in 1966 is a facsimile of that published by Chatto and Windus, London, in 1927.

CONTENTS

PLAYS

THE DUCHESS OF MALFI
THE DEVIL'S LAW-CASE

THE DUCHESS OF MALFI

DATE

THE play must have been produced before Dec. 16th 1614: for on that day died William Ostler, who acted Antonio (cf. Wallace's letters to *The Times*, Oct. 2nd and 4th 1909). Our other limit is rather less easy to fix; for it depends on the always risky evidence of metrical tests and parallel passages. But the metre certainly seems later than that of *The White Devil* (see Metrical Appendix); and it is striking that *The Duchess of Malfi* should show repeated parallels with two works first published in 1612—Chapman's *Petrarch's Seven Penitential Psalms* and Donne's *An Anatomy of the World*, both the first part which had appeared in 1611 and its sequels of 1612 (for details see Commentary).

Further the frequent resemblances between the play and *A Monumental Column* (registered Dec. 25th 1612) and the quite extraordinary indebtedness visible in both to Sidney's *Arcadia* (this influence appears much less clearly in *The White Devil* and indeed has been denied there altogether; a new edition of the *Arcadia* appeared in 1613) make it natural to suppose that the two works were written fairly close together. It is perhaps just worth recording that of the most marked parallels between the elegy and the tragedy, Act I contains two, Act II two, Act III five, Act IV one, and Act V none; so that it would agree very prettily if Webster turned out to have been about half-way through *The Duchess of Malfi* when he wrote *A Monumental Column*. But of course such an indication is too slight to be taken seriously.

There are also some significant parallels with the "Overbury" *Characters*—not only with the *New Characters* of 1615, which are probably Webster's own work, but also, in two places (I. I. 380–1; V. 2. 244: see Commentary), with the original *Characters* published as Overbury's in May 1614. But here again the evidence cannot be pressed too far. For the *Characters* are very likely to have circulated in MS; Webster may well have known Overbury; the passages in *The Duchess of Malfi* might

be later insertions; and it is even possible that Webster might
have had a hand in the 1614 collection of *Characters*, which
were not exclusively by Overbury.

As for the suggested borrowing in Act IV from Campion's
Lords' Masque (Feb. 14th 1613) which also contains a dance
of madmen, the resemblance seems to me too vague and Elizabethan lunatics too common.

Still we may say that such evidence as there is points to the
conclusion that *The Duchess of Malfi* was written after, though
not very long after, the sister-tragedy it so much resembles, in
1613–4[1].

Something must however be said of that fearful warning
against rash and dogmatic dating—the Concini allusion which
opens the play. The first scene begins with a desultory discussion between Antonio and Delio of a recent salutary purging
of the French Court by its King; and in this Vaughan first
saw a reference to the dramatic murder of Concino Concini,
Maréchal d'Ancre, on April 24th[2] 1617, which sent a wave
of excitement over all Western Europe. His suggestion has since
found general acceptance; and there is no reason to question its
accuracy (see on I. I. 8). Of course, however, critics pounced
on the passage as proof positive that the whole play must be
dated 1617–8 (Burbage, the original Ferdinand, having died
on March 13th, 1619). Doubt was no more: and Professor
Schelling wrote: "This puts to rest, once and for all, former
surmises on the subject". In fact, however, as Rupert Brooke
observes, "This eternal rest lasted nearly five[3] years"—until the
discovery, that is, of the date of Ostler's death. It is simply a

---

[1] See also on IV. 2. 60.

[2] Stoll makes a most extraordinary attempt (p. 25) to disprove this date
of April 24th, on the bare evidence of two entries in the *Stationers' Register*
and in the teeth of all the historians of the period, backed by contemporary
records so precise that we know almost the exact minute when the fatal shots
were fired. It is perfectly true that pamphlets on the murder are entered in
the Register on April 17th and 23rd. But the explanation is the very simple
one that England, not having adopted the Gregorian calendar, was ten days
behind, so that April 24th (French) = April 14th (English) and the whole
discrepancy vanishes.

For an admirable account of the Concini murder see Batiffol, *Louis XIII
à Vingt Ans*, ch. I.

[3] Really, thirteen. The suggestion was first made, not by Sampson (1904),
but by Vaughan (1896).

case of a topical allusion being interpolated in a play at a later revival. The Elizabethans must have done this wholesale, though only the rarest coincidences, as here, enable us to detect them in the act; and yet plays still go on being dated with childish reliance on exactly similar evidence. It is so human to prefer certainty to truth.

A revival, then, of *The Duchess of Malfi* must be supposed to have taken place in 1617, though it is frivolous to identify Webster's play with the "enterlude concerning the late Marquesse d'Ancre" of June 22nd 1617 (see Collier, *Annals of the Stage*, I. 391). Still this revival must in any case have occurred while the excitement was still high enough to make the allusion intelligible and interesting: probably, that is, not later than the end of 1617. The stream of English pamphlets on the subject in the *Stationers' Register* dries up in June; and interest must have waned after the execution of the Maréchal's wife in July 1617. This performance of *The Duchess* may be the one described by Orazio Busino (Feb. 7th 1618—see on *D.M.* III. 4) as if fairly recent[1].

A second revival is indicated by the second Actor-list to have occurred at some time after Taylor's replacement of Burbage (who died on March 13th 1619) and, probably, before Towley's death (June 1623); certainly, at all events, before the end of 1623, the year when the First Quarto was printed.

---

[1] He does not say he saw it himself, as Brooke asserts (p. 247): so that we cannot base any argument on the date of his arrival in England, Oct. 1617.

HISTORICAL INTRODUCTION
WEBSTER'S SOURCES

In the diary of Giacomo the Notary, of Naples, among the records of battles, bread-riots, pestilences, and births of eight-legged cats, occurs this entry:

On Sunday November 17th, 1510, it was common talk throughout the city of Naples, that the illustrious Signora Joanna of Aragon, daughter of the late illustrious Don Enrico of Aragon, and sister of the most Reverend Monsignore the Cardinal of Aragon, having given out that she wished to make a pilgrimage to Santa Maria de Loreto, had gone thither with a retinue of many carriages and thence departed with Antonio de Bologna, son of Messer Antonino de Bologna, and gone with the aforesaid, saying that he was her husband, to Ragusa, leaving behind her one male child of ten, who was Duke of Amalfi[1].

Giacomo says no more; in the next year his record suddenly ends. But there is a strange thrill in coming on this dry contemporary confirmation of Webster's romantic story. For the true relation of the fate of the Duchess of Malfi has been curiously neglected by English scholarship despite its passion for sources. When it had been recorded that the story of the Duchess was derived from Bandello, because Bandello wrote fiction, it seemed to be assumed that he could not have written fact[2]. As it is, much more is known of the Duchess's life than of Webster's own.

---

[1] Notar Giacomo, *Cronica di Napoli* (printed at Naples, 1845), p. 331: "Adi. 17. de novembro 1510 dedomenica puplice perla Cita denapoli era fama como (*sic*) la illustre Signora Ioanna de aragonia duchessa de amalfe figliola del quondam illustre signore don herrico de aragonia et sorella carnale del Reuerendissimo Monsignore lo cardinale de aragonia hauendo data fama de volere andare ad sancta maria deloreto per deuocione nce (*sic*) ando con multi carriagi et dalla se partio con Antonio debolognia figliolo de messere Antonino debologna et andosene con el predicto con dire che era suo marito in ragosa laxando vno figliolo mascolo de eta de anni x quale era duca de amalfe scopis ornatus." (What the last two words mean I cannot say.)

[2] Thus Kiesow suggests that Bandello dated the story in his own time to lend it extra interest. And even Sugden's excellent *Topographical Dictionary to the Works of Shakespeare* as recently as 1925 makes the amazing statement that the Duchess's Malfi is on the east coast of the Adriatic, seven miles N.W. of Ragusa. For the historical facts the main authority is D. Morellini, *Giovanna d' Aragona* (Cesena, 1906).

She was the grand-daughter of Ferdinand or Ferrante I of Naples, the second of her kings of the house of Aragon, a man half fox, half wolf, who kept his enemies in cages and, as a Machiavellian masterpiece, poisoned a guest after feasting him royally for twenty-seven days. His enemies indeed asserted that he was really no true scion of Aragon, but his mother's bastard by a Moor of Valentia. One of his many mistresses, Diana Guardati of Sorrento, bore Ferdinand a son, Enrico d' Aragona, who in 1465 married Polissena Centelles and in 1473 was created by his father Marchese di Gerace, a small town on the underside of the Calabrian toe of Italy. Five years later, in 1478, he died, together with his major-domo and others of his household, from eating poisonous fungi; and was lamented in a naïve and curious poem which is the earliest known composition in the Calabrian dialect:

> Piangi, Cosenza, giniralimente,
> et tu, Calabria, a dirite ritorno
> a donni Arrichu, benigno e clemente,
> Ch' è mortu e trapassato, notte e iorno,
> coll' occhi corporali, amara mente,
> pir sin che sonarà l' ultimu cornu.

So runs one stanza; though whether the son of Ferdinand and brother of Alfonso II of Naples, "the Abominable", was indeed "benigno e clemente" we do not know. He left four children, one of them born only after his death. Lodovico, the eldest, is Webster's Cardinal; Caterina is out of our story; Carlo is Webster's Ferdinand; and Giovanna, the future Duchess of Amalfi.

Lodovico's career was typical of the precocity common in that age[1]. Proclaimed Marchese di Gerace as a child, in his early teens (1489) he was astonishing the ambassadors of France, Castile, Venice, Florence, and Milan by the skill by which he broke four lances in the tilt. Three years later he wedded the grand-daughter of Innocent VIII in the presence of the Pope at Rome; and by the time he was twenty he was already a widower and, renouncing his title in favour of his younger brother Carlo, had become Cardinal of Aragon (1494). Two years after, warlike as in the play, he was fighting the French invaders at the side of the Great Captain, Gonsalvo di Cordova[2];

---

[1] See *Archivio Storico per le provincie Napoletane*, XIII. 130 ff.
[2] Notar Giacomo, pp. 201, 203.

but, unlike Webster's Cardinal, he died peacefully in Rome in
1519 and was richly interred in Santa Maria sopra la Minerva.

His sister Giovanna was married in 1490[1], as a girl of twelve
or so, to Alfonso Piccolomini, son and heir of Antonio Piccolomini, first Duke of Amalfi, with great rejoicings—"*fu
facta festa grande con danze et soni et farse*". Antonio Piccolomini,
nephew of Pius II, had been sent years before to help Ferdinand
against the Angevins, and received in reward the Duchy of
Amalfi, to which his son, the young Alfonso, succeeded in 1493.
But Giovanna's husband did not long enjoy his dukedom, for
he died of gout in 1498, the year of the burning of Savonarola.
He left his Duchess with a daughter Caterina, who died in
childbed, and a son not born till the next year, the future
Alfonso II of Amalfi. Meanwhile she ruled the Duchy as
Regent for her child and though there now began, with the
French and Spanish invasions, what Guicciardini calls "*gli anni
miserabili*", she is said to have prospered and paid off the heavy
debts her husband had incurred[2]. So all went well for years.
But she was young—a girl of nineteen or twenty at her husband's
death; and she had remained unmarried, whether for her child's
sake, or because she cared for none of her own rank, or because
it suited her brothers' ends to keep her so. At this point Antonio
Bologna crossed her path.

Antonio Bologna, son of Antonino Bologna, came of a reputable
house. Of his forbears Vannino Beccadelli had migrated from
Bologna (whence their name) to Palermo in the fourteenth
century: Vannino's son, Enrico, had been first magistrate at
Palermo in the last decade of that century; and his grandson
Antonio Beccadelli ("il Panormita"), our hero's grandfather,
was one of the most distinguished literary figures of fifteenth
century Italy, honoured in turn at the courts of Filippo Maria
Visconti, the Emperor Sigismund, and Alfonso I of Naples,
for whom his eloquence obtained from Padua that precious relic,
an arm of Livy the historian[3].

[1] Leostello, *Effemeridi* in *Documenti per la storia* by G. Filangieri (Naples,
1883) p. 352.
[2] See M. Camera, *Memorie storico-diplomatiche di Amalfi* (Salerno, 1881),
II. 28, 69, 78–82. C. needs checking: but gives some interesting details and
documents.
[3] It is perhaps of some interest to Webster's fellow-countrymen that the
learned "Panormita" knew a legend of his family's descent, 800 years before,

For details of the tragedy that followed we have to depend on Bandello (*Novelle*, 1. 26), whose faithfulness is borne out by the Corona manuscripts and Filonico, by Giacomo the Notary and the *Register of Deaths* at Milan.

Antonio Bologna, brought up at the Court of Naples and long major-domo of Federico, the last of its Aragonese dynasty, had followed his master to his exile in France. For in 1501 Federico, his Kingdom partitioned between his enemy Louis XII and his treacherous ally Ferdinand the Catholic, threw himself on the mercy of Louis, was given the Duchy of Anjou, and died at Tours towards the end of 1504. Returning after this to Naples, Antonio was offered the office of major-domo by the Duchess of Amalfi; devoted still to the house of Aragon, he willingly accepted it. Before long he and his mistress had fallen passionately in love and, dreading her brothers' anger, went through a secret marriage witnessed only by her waiting-woman. For years their relations were successfully concealed. Even the birth of a son remained undiscovered; but the birth of a second child started whispers which reached the brothers' ears, so that they set spies on the Duchess. Antonio growing alarmed withdrew with his two children to Ancona, to await the passing of the storm; but the Duchess, now expecting a third child, could not bear the loneliness of her palace. Like Bracciano seventy years later, she made a pretext of a pilgrimage to Loretto, whither she set out with a great retinue. Thence she proceeded to join Antonio in Ancona; and there threw off the mask before her astonished household. She would renounce her rank, she said, and henceforth live quietly with her husband in a private station. Her servants, foreseeing the storm, sent one of their number to the Cardinal of Aragon in Rome, and returned to Amalfi. For a little the lovers were left in peace at Ancona, where their third child was born; but the Cardinal of Aragon was putting pressure on Cardinal Gonzaga, Legate of Ancona under Julius II (who died in 1513). After "six or seven months" (summer of 1511), Antonio seeing that his efforts to combat the sentence of expulsion were bound soon to fail, obtained through a friend in Siena leave to take refuge there. Accordingly,

from an English Ambassador sent to the Pope, who was buried in San Giovanni in Monte at Bologna. It was also related that Galeazzo Beccadelli, a later ancestor, had been knighted at Forli by Edward I of England.

the moment the decree of "banishment from Ancona within fifteen days" was issued, he was able to set out for his new home before the brothers could conveniently arrange to have him way-laid and murdered. But in Siena the same relentless pressure recommenced. Through Cardinal Petrucci, his brother Borghese, head of the Signiory at Siena, was induced to expel the refugees (1512). (It is some consolation to know that five years later Cardinal Petrucci was strangled in the Castle of St Angelo for having tried to poison Leo X.)

Antonio and his family now turned (once more like Bracciano and his Duchess) to seek refuge in Venice; but in the territory of Forli they were overtaken by armed horsemen. The Duchess, pleading that her brothers would not harm her in person, per-suaded her husband to leave her and escape. So with his eldest son and four servants he rode off and reached Milan; the Duchess, with the other two children and her waiting woman, were carried off to one of the castles of her Duchy. She was never seen again.

Antonio, ignorant of her fate, lived on in Milan for more than a year, first under the protection of Silvio Savello[1] (who has lent his name to Webster's Silvio), while he was besieging the French garrison of the Citadel of Milan on behalf of Massimiliano Sforza (in the earlier part of 1513). Then, when Silvio went out to fight at Crema (August 1513)[2], Antonio attached himself to the Marchese di Bitonto, and finally to Alfonso Visconti. Although the brothers had had Antonio's property at Naples confiscated, the exile still lived in hopes of appeasing them. In vain he was warned that his life was in danger. "I had some reason to believe," says Girolamo Visconti, who tells the story in Bandello, "that he was secretly given to understand (by the brothers, who wished to keep him within reach) that he might even yet have his wife restored to him". Next, a certain Neapolitan condottiere (probably Cesare Fiera-mosca) related Antonio's history to a person whom Visconti calls "il nostro Delio", and added that he had himself been commissioned to have Antonio murdered; but, not regarding himself as a hired assassin, had warned the victim of his danger.

[1] See Guicciardini (Florence, 1919), III. pp. 67, 92, 102: Gregorovius, *Rome in the Middle Ages*, VII. 493.

[2] Cf. Marin Sanudo, *Diari* 16, col. 609: Guicciardini, III. 67.

Finally one day (in October 1513)[1] Delio and L. Scipione Attellano, who foreseeing Antonio's tragic end, had already thought of making a *novella* of his story, passed Antonio accompanied by two servants on his way to Mass at the church of S. Francesco. They noted dismay in his looks; and a few minutes later they heard an uproar. Antonio had been attacked and stabbed to death by a certain Lombard Captain, Daniel da Bozolo (Webster's Bosola), with three others. The assassins escaped unmolested from the territory of Milan.

The interest grows when it emerges that "Delio" (which is also the name assumed by Bandello in his sonnets) is probably Bandello himself, who was at this time a *protégé* of Ippolita Sforza and thus met in Milan not only Antonio[2], but another ill-fated figure of his *novelle*, the Countess of Celant. So that Webster's ultimate authority was probably one of the last persons to see his hero alive, and the Delio of the play is in origin Bandello himself. It throws, we may add, an ironic light on the standards of the day to find Bandello a few pages later (the separate *novelle* were of course only collected and published years afterwards) dedicating another of his tales with every expression of gratitude and esteem to the murderer, Lodovico Cardinal of Aragon. Yet there is, as we see, good reason to believe the story of the barbarous fate of the Duchess of Malfi to be essentially true[3].

[1] The date is established and the whole story confirmed by an entry in the *necrologio* of Milan (1450–1550), preserved in the *archivio di stato*—"Die Jovis sexto mensis Octobris 1513 Antonius de Bononia de Neapoli annorum xxx (he must surely have really been older) ex vulneribus". (Morellini, *Matteo Bandello*, p. 58 n.)

The Antonio Bologna whose epitaph at *Padua* is given in Nemeitz, *Inscriptionum singularium* (Leipzig, 1726), p. 298, is clearly a different person.

[2] Antonio is quoted as the narrator of another of the *novelle* (i. 5)—hardly the sort of story one would expect from a melancholy exile.

[3] The story is found also in the Corona MSS. of the Naples Library (so-called because a number of them are by Silvio and Ascanio Corona—*flor.* 1525: see D. Morellini in *Napoli Nobilissima*, XIV. 77). This version is apparently based mainly on Bandello, but omits items of more purely Milanese interest. According to them Antonio's surviving son was brought back to Naples and reared by his father's kin. An independent narrative, on the other hand, appears in Filonico's *Vita di Dorotea d' Avalos*, where the Duchess is said to have been taking to a religious life when she fell in love with Antonio, "vinta dalle tentazioni diaboliche". She fled to Ancona and was there poisoned with her children. (See also Ammirato, *Delle famiglie nobili napoletane* (Florence, 1651) II. "Bologna".)

The Duchess's son by her first husband became Duke of Amalfi and died in 1559, like his father, of gout. That his mother's misalliance did not rankle

From Bandello the tale passed to Belleforest, in whose second volume of *Histoires tragiques* it forms the first story[1]. Belleforest is a pedant and a prig. His characters all talk like great whales and their interminable speeches and soliloquies make even the Duchess's story dull; while the author's high moral tone compels him to pelt his unhappy heroine with a volley of references to Semiramis, Messalina, Faustina, even Pasiphae, in order to express his disgust at her shameless behaviour in marrying a man she loved. "Shall I be of opinion that a homeless servaunt oughte to sollicite, nay rather suborne the Daughter of his Lorde without punishment, or that a vyle and abject person dare to mount upon a Prynces Bed?" (Painter's translation.) At the execrable impiety of the pretended pilgrimage to Loretto, his voice rises to a scream: "and yet you see this great and mighty Duchesse trot and run after the male, like a female Wolfe or Lionesse, (when they goe to sault) and forget the noble bloud of Aragon whereof she was descended, to couple hir self almost with the simplest person of the trimmest Gentlemen of Naples". Bandello is no Boccaccio: but he belongs to a different stage of civilisation from Belleforest. The Frenchman, sermons and all, was translated by William Painter in his *Palace of Pleasure* (1566–7: II. 23) during a varied career which ranged from the headmastership of Sevenoaks School to some highly successful embezzlement as clerk of Her Majesty's Ordnance. And so through the hands of a gentleman, a fool, and a knave the tale reached Webster.

The following are the main divergences of Belleforest and Painter from their source Bandello:

(1) It is the waiting-maid who suggests the pilgrimage to Loretto. (In Bandello, the Duchess: in Webster, Bosola.)

(2) Belleforest definitely calls the story a "*tragédie*"; of the marriage he remarks "*voici le premier acte de cette tragédie*"; Antonio's departure to Ancona completes the second act, his death the last.

(3) He changes Bandello's "Petrucci" to "Castruccio" (cf. Webster's Castruchio).

violently we may gather from the fact that he called one of his sons Antonio (and see Camera, II. 95–7, 99).

[1] A first volume of eighteen tales adapted from Bandello's *Novelle* by P. Boaistuau and Belleforest had appeared in 1559; this second, containing another eighteen by Belleforest alone, in 1565.

(4) Strangling is definitely mentioned as the manner of the Duchess's murder.

On these as well as on general grounds it seems likely that Webster used Belleforest's narrative in Painter's translation[1]. But it is interesting to see how very little Webster borrows from Painter's language, considering how freely he conveys from Montaigne and Sidney.

The following alterations are made by Webster in his turn[2] (apart from his important change of general attitude towards the Duchess, from the disapproval of Belleforest to complete sympathy):

(1) The previous warnings of the brothers are added to make the wooing-scene more dramatic.

(2) The Duchess's "guilt" is discovered at the birth of the first child, not the second. The manner—by the dropping of a horoscope—is Webster's invention.

(3) The pretended peculation of Antonio is also Webster's addition. He says nothing of the stay at Siena. And the Duchess parts from Antonio before, not after, their pursuers appear.

(4) The tortures of the Duchess, the deaths of the brothers, and the manner of Antonio's murder (*i.e.* practically all IV and V) are new.

(5) Julia and her sub-plot are added. Castruchio has become her husband, instead of a Cardinal.

(6) Bosola, instead of being simply the final assassin, becomes the villain of the whole piece.

There remains however a further question—had Webster also seen the tragedy on the subject by Lope de Vega—*El Mayordomo de la Duquesa de Amalfi* (written before 1609: first printed (1618) in *Works*, vol. XI)? This play is based directly on Bandello, an edition of whom had been printed at Valladolid in 1603. It shows on the whole considerable divergences from Webster's work; whether it shows any considerable resemblances, opinion differs. The chief parallels are these—Lope's Duchess also bids Antonio "be covered", as a mark that he is now her

---

[1] For verbal indications of this see on I. 1. 73, 507–8; II. 5. 44–5, 87–91 (decisive); IV. 2. 259. It remains possible of course that Webster may also have read Bandello (see on II. 5. 46–9).

[2] Cf. Kiesow, *Die verschiedenen Bearbeitungen der Novelle von der Herzogin von Amalfi* in *Anglia* XVII. 199–258. (His attempt to reconstruct Bandello's chronology is, however, quite inaccurate.)

equal; she does so, however, in the wooing-scene. Secondly, Antonio's withdrawal to Ancona is screened in both plays by a pretence of dismissal in disgrace. In Lope he is indeed accused of a different offence—of seducing the Duchess's maid Libia, who answers to Cariola. But it is noteworthy that this stratagem has no foundation in the non-dramatic versions of the story; though of course some excuse for Antonio's departure was clearly needed by the plot. Thirdly, in Lope, the Duchess's brother Julio (Webster's Ferdinand; the pious Spaniard omits the wicked Cardinal) writes to Antonio inviting him back to a reconciliation. "Letters" of this tenour are vaguely mentioned in the prose stories; but the development of that suggestion is common to both dramatists. In Lope, however, Antonio is deceived, returns, and is poisoned by kissing Julio's hands. "Compare the death of Webster's Julia," argues Morellini, who believes in Lope's influence; but he forgets Isabella's similar death in *The White Devil*, to say nothing of the commonness of the idea in general. The Duchess herself is given poison, then a curtain is drawn revealing the heads of Antonio and her children. This certainly recalls the disclosure of the wax figures behind the traverse in Webster, which has no counterpart in Painter; though even here the influence of the *Arcadia* (see below) may be sufficient explanation. Finally, in Lope, the Duchess's son and heir, the young Duke, enters horrified at her murder and breathing vengeance[1]. This has no parallel in Webster's *Duchess of Malfi*: but it at once recalls the end of *The White Devil*[2], where Giovanni's appearance is quite contrary to the sources of that play. (The real Virginio Orsini was probably accessory to Vittoria's murder; certainly not hostile like Giovanni.)

What is the answer? It is difficult to feel sure. Coincidence and the logical necessities of the plot may be sufficient to account for the resemblances. And it is certainly asking a good deal to expect us to believe that Webster was seriously influenced by a Spanish play which had not yet appeared in print. That seems to me the real difficulty, though it has not deterred some

---

[1] A sequel called *La Venganza de la Duquesa de Amalfi* by Diego Muxet de Solis appeared in 1624.

[2] For another very slight trace of conceivable influence by Lope de Vega see on *W.D.* III. 2. 178–83.

scholars. Webster's indebtedness remains, I think, decidedly improbable; happily it remains also very unimportant.

There are also certain separate sources for various incidents in the play. The description of the Duke's lycanthropia in v. 2 is largely based on Grimeston's translation (1607: pp. 364–7) of S. Goulart's *Histoires admirables* (1600 and 1606); so that Webster had doubtless read also the same writer's brief account of the Duchess of Malfi, which has however no independent interest, being clearly based on Belleforest[1].

Again, for the tormenting of the Duchess in Act iv with wax-figures representing her husband and children as dead, Webster drew to some extent on Sidney's account in his *Arcadia* of the persecution of Philoclea and Pamela by their aunt Cecropia, who frightens each of them with the seeming death of the other —Pamela is apparently beheaded, and Philoclea's head is shown in a basin. This influence is decisively confirmed by verbal borrowings as well (see Commentary on the scene).

As for the shutting in of the Duchess with madmen, a similar idea in a comic form recurs in several Elizabethan plays, in Dekker's *Honest Whore* (Part I. iv. 3) and again in *Northward Ho!* where a character who probably represented the poet Chapman, is so treated in jest.

I may perhaps add here, not as sources, but as parallels that may well have been present in the minds of Webster and his audience, two contemporary or almost contemporary episodes of real life. I know that such supposed historical allusions are dangerous. Miss Winstanley in her pursuit of them has reached the point of finding the Porter in *Macbeth* to be really Guy Fawkes, and Ariel Henry of Navarre. And it is too easy to discover in an Elizabethan dramatist, as Taine says of La Fontaine, "des souvenirs qu'il avait et des intentions qu'il n'avait pas". But it is only with "souvenirs" that I am here concerned; and certainly in the scene of the Duchess among the madmen,

[1] Like another short *résumé* of no particular importance, which Webster may or may not have seen, in T. Beard's *Theatre of God's Judgments* (1579), II. 322 ("Of Whoredoms committed under the colour of Marriage").

There are also passing references to the story in the *Forest of Fancy* (1579), sig. N 1, in Whetstone's *Heptameron of Civil Discourses* (1582), 5th day, and in Greene's *Card of Fancy* (1584), p. 119 (the first and last of these call Antonio "Ulrico"); and some critics have, not very convincingly, conjectured "the lady of Malfy" for "the lady of the Strachey" in *Twelfth Night*, II. 5. 44.

we are strongly reminded of the story of the fate of Torquato
Tasso at the hands of another Italian duke. Tasso was shut up
in the madhouse of Sta Anna in 1579 by Alfonso d' Este,
Duke of Ferrara. The real reason was the simple and sufficient
one that the poet had become insane. But by the beginning
of the seventeenth century there had begun to grow up the
famous legend of the singer caged by the tyrant, with hints of
an unhappy romance behind. Thus in 1609 we have d'Alessandro
in his *Studio sulle Fonti della Gerusalemme* writing mysteriously:

Essendo stato tredici anni in corte del signor Duca di Ferrara, al
fine per malignità di altrui cadde in disgrazia a detto Signore, in tanto
che per ordine di quello sette anni dimorò nelle carceri di Ferrara—
nè saprei dire più la causa della sua prigione, che cagione per la quale
Ovidio fu relegato in Ponto da Cesare Augusto.

Now this is indeed *ignotum per ignotius*: for the cause of
Ovid's banishment is itself a mystery. Still, the allusion here is
clearly to a love-affair with a princess of high rank, such as
Ovid is supposed to have had with the younger Julia: and later
narrators of the story were only to tell more explicitly and in
detail the fatal passion of Tasso for Leonora d' Este, Alfonso's
sister. My only point is that here we have an Italian Court,
a Duke's sister entangled with a lover by birth beneath her, and
the imprisonment of the victim of family-pride among madmen.
The resemblance may surely have occurred to Webster, who
actually quotes a phrase of Tasso in the play.

There is also a second parallel, of Webster's own day, which
deserves passing mention. For while his audience watched *The
Duchess of Malfi*, some of them must have remembered the real
tragedy which was creeping to its close in the Tower, a few
minutes' walk away—whether Webster himself had thought of
it or not. For there in the Tower, imprisoned for the last three
years and with a mind now unhinged, lay Lady Arabella Stuart,
the cousin of the King, in punishment for her offence in wedding
Lord William Seymour. The pair had married secretly in the
summer of 1610. Seymour's birth, however, was not too low,
but too high; for he happened to be the one man in England
whom James dreaded as his cousin's husband, since he strengthened
yet further her claim to the crown. So they were both imprisoned, as soon as the secret came out, a few weeks after the
marriage. In 1611 they escaped from the Tower, but Arabella

was recaptured by her pursuers in mid-Channel, while she lingered there in her anxiety to assure herself of the safety of her husband's vessel. She was brought back to the Tower, went mad in her misery, and died in 1615: while Lord Seymour sheltered helplessly in Paris, like Antonio in Milan. I do not wish to exaggerate the resemblances, though it will be seen that there are several: but it is perhaps a little surprising that the authorities did not feel the subject of the persecuted Duchess a dangerous one for popular sympathy.

THE PLAY

"My wife and I to the Duke of York's house, to see 'The Duchesse of Malfy', a sorry play, and sat with little pleasure, for fear of my wife's seeing me look about."   S. PEPYS (Nov. 25th, 1668)[1].

"The irredeemable mediocrity of its dramatic evolution of human passion is unmistakable."   G. H. LEWES.

"Vous ne trouveriez rien de plus triste et de plus grand, de l'Edda à Lord Byron."   H. A. TAINE.

The Duchess of Malfi seems the work of a dramatist definitely older, in mind as well as in years, than the creator of *The White Devil*. There is here a sadder, tenderer, less violent mood, of which the scenes where Giovanni mourns a lost mother and Cornelia a lost son, alone give a foretaste in the earlier play. The characters of *The Duchess of Malfi* come before us less brightly coloured, in a less dazzling world. The action pulses at less of a fever heat; and instead of the sunlight a-glitter on a flashing Mediterranean, we seem to watch the cypress shadows on the hillsides of Amalfi lengthen slowly towards the coming night. It is in the shadow of night, indeed, that scene after scene takes place: and a twilight seems to lie across the characters themselves. The innocent Antonio goes shuddering like a guilty soul through that harsh world where Paolo Giordano Orsini shouldered so unhesitatingly his superb and insolent way. Antonio sheds no man's blood: he shudders at the sight of his own. And in his Duchess likewise there is a tenderness such as Vittoria never knew. Hers is a sadder and more pensive, though not less undaunted, soul; and at the last, in her prison darkness gibbered around by madmen, she sits before us silently with the sad and terrible patience of a Mater Dolorosa. Here is no heroine who starts up before the tribunal in Rome to meet her day of judgment with defiance, in the proud consciousness that upon her are the eyes of the Ambassadors of Christendom and behind them the wide theatre of the world. And while

---

[1] Perhaps Pepys's mental disturbance was partly the cause of this unfavourable judgment: for a performance of the play on Sept. 30th 1662 is much more pleasantly recorded, and he had found it "pretty good" to read (Nov. 2nd and 6th 1666).

Vittoria dies, like a Roman Emperor, standing, her gentler counterpart bows her head to the murderer's cord and kneels humbly before that cold star-lit heaven whence no hand stoops to save. The Duchess is the sister, indeed, of Isabella rather than Vittoria[1]. On the minor characters also the same twilight has fallen. Francisco Duke of Florence would never have died raving with the remorse of Duke Ferdinand, though the death of a dozen sisters lay crimson upon his soul. The bitter Monticelso toyed with no mistresses; we cannot hear him sue for mercy like the Cardinal of Aragon, or pray in death only to be laid by and forgotten. Even the black Zanche died like a queen, where the unhappy Cariola scratches and screams and lies to gain a moment longer of life. And, last of all, Bosola with his vexed refrain of "honest", his melancholy, his belated, ineffectual repentances, is but one more example, when we set him beside Flamineo, of the change of key which marks Webster's treatment of this, his second and last great work. It is not on its inferiority to *The White Devil* (though it does seem to me inferior) that I wish here to dwell; but simply on the deep difference of tone which goes together with the innumerable parallels of situation and idea to be found in these twin plays. And if *The Duchess of Malfi* is on the whole the weaker work, yet there are compensations. If the vigour is less, there is a new and gentler grace in the moments when Webster allows his tortured figures a little span of happiness. For we shall find nothing in *The White Devil* like that exquisite wooing of Antonio by the Duchess or the happy jesting of the married lovers on the eve of ruin. Here are new colours for Webster: it is as if these gleams of sudden sun cast a momentary rainbow across the driving spray of his fierce and wind-swept sea. And, again, with the relaxation of the writer's passionate energy, comes the deeper meditativeness of those passages of poetry which, far more justly than any garishness of dancing maniacs and dead men's hands, have made *The Duchess of Malfi* grow into the memories of men. There is no character in *The White Devil*

---

[1] To Kiesow the Duchess is "eine Schöpfung echt germanischen Geistes— der Typus für die Liebe germanischer Frauen." One may well object that the Duchess is not a "Typus", but a charming individual. But it illustrates the difference: not even Teutonic criticism (be it said without any disparagement of that indefatigable German scholarship which has done so much for our English drama) has yet tried to annex Vittoria.

that we can imagine brooding like Antonio over the ruined church at Milan with a sadness that recalls at once that of Hamlet over Yorick's skull and, with a strange anticipation, the *Elegy* of Gray. And similarly with the Echo-scene that follows. In itself but one instance among hundreds of a tiresome fashion of Renaissance ingenuity, in Webster's hands it becomes at once a thing apart from its tediously conceited fellows. If we ask what Webster could do that his contemporaries could not, the answer lies not in horror-scenes, but in such things as this. Yet this scene too could hardly have found a place in *The White Devil*; and if we ask what forms there its nearest counterpart, perhaps we may answer that Echo is the ghostly sister of the boy Giovanni—this Echo that cries its simple, artificial answers with the pathetic cleverness of a child, as it too laments a Duchess foully slain.

> *Del.* I told you 'twas a pretty one: You may make it
> A Huntes-man, or a Faulconer, a Musitian,
> Or a Thing of Sorrow.
> *Eccho.* *A Thing of Sorrow.*
> *Ant.* I sure: that suites it best.
> *Eccho.* *That suites it best.*

There is indeed something far ghostlier about this dream-scene than about any robust, top-booted apparition in *The White Devil*; as befits what is essentially the ghostlier play[1]. And it is as from a trance, at the end of it, that Antonio wakes to the real darkness round him, there to recall at last that essential courage which lies at the heart of both Webster's great plays alike.

And yet here too there is a difference. With the Duchess and Antonio it is the enduring courage of the martyr; not, as with Vittoria and Brachiano, the high spirit of the soldier who hews his way to death through the thickest of the battle. For, after all, what is left in such a world worth fighting for? This busy trade of life, which appears so vain only in the final moments of *The White Devil*, has the sense of its vanity, the doubt of all its values, stamped here on every page. Antonio at the very

---

[1] This quality of *The Duchess of Malfi* makes particularly happy and appropriate Mr Waley's choice of it for transposition into the ghostly form of a Nō play. See Commentary on *D.M.* III. 4.

moment when love declares itself before him, questions, even though it be half-playfully, the worth of love itself and of the life it hands on to posterity. Imagine Brachiano, with his mistress before him, playing the theorizing sceptic thus! Here are no longer those strong hearts whose covenant with the world was so hard to break, to whom the name of death was "infinitely terrible". To the Duchess death has become the best gift her brothers can give; to Antonio, the yearned-for release from his long pain.

Such is the atmosphere, I feel, of *The Duchess of Malfi*—a profound, unalterable sadness. Melancholy has shrouded it in her shadow. Her name passes perpetually like a watchword across the lips of these sentinels who gaze wanly into the hopeless night and look only for relief. Bosola is "melancholy"; and Antonio and the Duchess become so; and her brother Ferdinand goes mad with it; and the Cardinal is haunted by it with the vision of a thing armed with a rake, that seems to strike at him from the fish-ponds in his garden, as he broods on the flames of Hell. We come indeed to feel that this phantom of insane melancholia pursues, like a hereditary curse, the last generation of the House of Aragon in Amalfi. And of such a tragedy the melancholy madmen are after all a fitting chorus: they are more than a mere episode in this play whose conclusion is not only death, but madness. Unity of tone—that one unity which the Romantics at their best have continued to respect—is surely accomplished here.

The creation of this atmosphere, its poetry, and two or three supreme scenes—these are the greatness of *The Duchess of Malfi*. The characters are less outstanding: and the plot has obvious weaknesses. It is indeed ridiculous to say with Charles Kingsley of the Duchess, that she is not a "person" at all. That is mere Betsy Priggishness. Before the night closes on her, the Duchess shows vivid colours, though delicate ones. If in the gloom of the end there remains to her only the grey of fortitude, lit up at moments with the dull red of anger, there is surely no lack of reality in the charming, gay, spontaneous young sovereign of the earlier acts, whose "half-blush" so gracefully becomes her in the sudden wave of unneeded shame that follows her successful wooing. Happily we have emerged from an age when that wooing was felt to be "painful", and it was necessary to defend or excuse this figure of fresh, high-spirited youth for loving with the body as well as with the soul.

The fatal error of the Duchess—fault we cannot call it—is that she ever fell in love with Antonio. Weakness is the least dramatic of human qualities; and the play, as well as his mistress, suffers from its presence in him. We do not demand that every character shall be cast in heroic mould: but we blush uncomfortably at the scene where Antonio enters, pistol in hand, after the Duke has safely retired, only to bluster where he should have acted. The dagger left by Ferdinand has a handle, he cries to his mistress, as well as a point: but whose hand should grasp that hilt if not his own? We come to feel that Antonio is not good enough for the woman he has won. Perilous as his position was, hard as it might have been to ride out into the night after Duke Ferdinand and meet sword to sword the brother of his mistress, or to try to raise Amalfi in its Duchess's name, none the less a stouter heart would have found a better end. It is not physical cowardice: we have Bosola's word for it, in one of those Elizabethan speeches made by one character about another which are clearly meant to be taken by the audience as true, that Antonio was a good soldier. It is the initiative, the generalship that is fatally lacking. Antonio was better at managing horses than men. Because of this weakness he saves himself, always, only "by halves", until in the end his life becomes worse than death. Soldier, courtier, lover, poet—only the poet in him succeeds in not leaving us cold. If we care for him beyond that, it is for his mistress's sake. Such as he is, for all his sensitiveness, a juster and a happier fate would have wedded him, not to the Duchess, but to Cariola.

After the Duchess, the only character that holds us is Bosola. He too has some of the weakness of his victim Antonio; his soul, unlike Flamineo's, is perpetually a house of Beelzebub divided against itself, and doomed thereby to fall. Conscience is sour in his mouth: and he is more human, not more real, than the reptile Flamineo simply in this, that his conscience turns his sting upon himself. His mixture of punctilio and unscrupulousness may seem unreal to the modern reader; it is not so to those who have a better knowledge of that age when *bravi* like the assassin of Troilo Orsini, with an artist's disinterestedness, refused all reward when their work was done.

We have even the story of a cut-throat who, being hired by one Italian to kill another, was offered a higher price by the victim to go back and murder his employer: he accepted; but insisted none the less, to the victim's horror, that his original contract must first be honourably fulfilled. So Bosola, while clearly sympathising with the Duchess and to some extent with Antonio, continues to earn his pay. He would be really honest, were he sure that such a thing as honesty existed. His mouth grows bitter with a genuine anger at the vices of courts which seem to belie all human goodness. Yet though unlike Flamineo he feels pity, he remains as helpless as Hamlet, his distant kinsman in the family of Malcontents, to carry it into effect. He is cynical, yet furious against hypocrisy; his insight avails to show him only his own and the world's degradation; too proud to flatter, he stoops to be a tool; and only when it is too late he deserts the side of sin, to earn the wages of death. The curse of the Stoic poet is upon him: his vision torments him with regret for the beauty of that goodness he has flung away. He dies as he lived:

> In a mist, I know not how.

Flamineo too dies "in a mist": but he did not live in one.

As for Duke Ferdinand, he is mainly what the plot requires him to be, an angry tyrant. Only a sudden flash here and there quickens the spectator's imagination to try to fathom him more deeply. It has been suggested to me that he is really in love with his sister. This is an ingenious idea, though it seems to me out of the question that Webster meant his audience to take that view. The analysis Ferdinand gives of his own motives at the end of Act IV, though muddled, is clearly intended to be accepted as true. An Elizabethan audience was simple[1] and would certainly have swallowed it. And if we to-day are apt to feel that his alleged motives are inadequate, it is partly that Webster has failed to make us conceive vividly enough the importance of the "infinite mass of treasure", by giving it more prominence; partly, that we find it difficult to imagine the violence of family pride in a sixteenth-century Spaniard or

---

[1] Cf. Tailor, *The Hog hath lost his Pearl*, I. 1: "*Player*. I hope you have made no dark sentence in't; for, I'll assure you, our audience commonly are very simple, idle-headed people, and if they should hear what they understand not, they would quite forsake our house".

Italian. We have to realise that these things were different in an age and land in which, for instance, the six sons of Lelio Massimo, on their father's second marriage, entered the bridal-chamber next morning and shot the bride in bed, because she was a cast-off mistress of Marcantonio Colonna.

I do not believe, then, that Webster meant us to hunt for more motives in Ferdinand's heart than he has set in Ferdinand's mouth. And yet, when one reads *The Fair Maid of the Inn*, with its brother confessedly half-enamoured of his sister and passionately jealous of her lover[1], and then turns back to the frenzies with which Ferdinand (unlike the Cardinal) hears of his sister's seduction, the agonized remorse with which he sees her dead, it is hard to be positive that some such motive had never crossed Webster's own mind. It is merely a suggestion, and an inessential one; it can be taken or left; but it does not seem to me impossible in the part-author of *The Fair Maid of the Inn*, the friend and collaborator of John Ford.

The weakness of the play, however, lies clearly in its plot. It lives too long, when it outlives the heroine. Imagine if in *The White Devil* Vittoria had died before Brachiano; and yet even that would have been less fatal. The play goes well enough at first. The opening Act contains the exposition and then the fatal wooing; Act II the discovery of the Duchess's "guilt"; Act III the discovery also of Antonio's, followed by the lovers' flight; and Act IV the death of the Duchess. So far so good; unfortunately, as William Archer suavely puts it, "the play still drags its festering length through another Act", which consists of Antonio's murder, followed by the necessary poetic justice on the brothers and Bosola in their turn. Thus though there is less sub-plot, less irrelevant complication than in *The White Devil*, the plot of *The Duchess of Malfi* has the far worse defect of reaching its natural end before the play. And yet, despite *longueurs*, even here Webster retains his gift of putting his most living poetry in the mouths of dying men. Its plot as a whole has added nothing to the greatness of *The Duchess of Malfi*: but neither can it destroy it. We turn back from the critics, from Lamb with his outcries of admiration, from Archer with his nibbling pedantries, from Stoll and Kiesow with their vision of

[1] Mainly in Ford and Massinger's part of the play: but cf. II. 4, which is Webster's; and again *D.L.* v. 2. 36.

the play as a warning of the awful results of marrying beneath one, to the poet himself.

> 'Tis weakenesse,
> Too much to thinke what should have bin done.

Let us be thankful for what has been—for this picture of a spirit that faces the cold shining of the stars with none of Pascal's terror before their infinite silence, and the mopping and mowing of the demented world around it with a calm that prosperity could not give, nor disaster take away.

THE TRAGEDY
OF THE DVTCHESSE
OF MALFY

THE
TRAGEDY

OF THE DVTCHESSE
Of Malfy.

As it was Prefented priuatly, at the Black-
Friers; and publiquely at the Globe, By the
Kings Maiefties Seruants.

The perfeƈt and exaƈt Coppy, with diuerfe
things Printed, that the length of the Play would
not beare in the Prefentment.

VVritten by *John Webfter*.

Hora.———*Si quid*———
———*Candidus Imperti fi non his vtere mecum.*

LONDON:

Printed by Nɪᴄʜᴏʟᴀs Oᴋᴇs, for Iᴏʜɴ
Wᴀᴛᴇʀsᴏɴ, and are to be fold at the
figne of the Crowne, in *Paules*
Church-yard, 1 6 2 3.

The Actors Names.

BOSOLA, *J. Lowin.*

FERDINAND, 1 *R. Burbidge.* 2 *J. Taylor.*

CARDINALL, 1 *H. Cundaile.* 2 *R. Robinson.*

ANTONIO, 1 *W. Ostler.* 2 *R. Benfeild.*

DELIO, *J. Underwood.*

FOROBOSCO, *N. Towley.*

MALATESTE.

The Marquesse of Pescara, *J. Rice.*

SILVIO, *T. Pollard.*

[CASTRUCHIO.]

[RODERIGO.]

[GRISOLAN.]

The severall mad men, *N. Towley. J. Underwood, &c.*

The DUTCHESSE, *R. Sharpe.*

The CARDINALS Mis. *J. Tomson.*

The DOCTOR,
CARIOLA, } *R. Pallant.*
COURT OFFICERS. }

[*Old Lady.*]

Three young Children.

Two Pilgrimes.

[*Ladies, Executioners, and Attendants.*]

TO THE RIGHT HONORABLE, *GEORGE*

HARDING, *Baron* Barkeley, *of* Barkeley
Castle and Knight of the Order of the *Bathe*
To the Illustrious Prince CHARLES.

My Noble Lord,

*T*HAT *I may present my excuse, why, (being a stranger to your Lordshippe) I offer this Poem to your Patronage, I plead this warrant; Men (who never saw the Sea, yet desire to behold that regiment of waters,) choose some eminent River, to guide them thither; and make that as it were, their Conduct, or* Postilion: *By the like ingenious meanes, has your* fame *arrived at my knowledge, receiving it from some of worth, who both in* contemplation, *and* practise, *owe to your* Honor *their clearest service. I do not altogether looke up at your* Title: *The ancien'st* Nobility, *being but a* rellique *of time past, and the truest* 10 Honor *indeede beeing for a man to conferre* Honor *on himselfe, which your* Learning *strives to propagate, and shall make you arrive at the* Dignity *of a great* Example. *I am confident this worke is not unworthy your* Honors *perusal for by such* Poems *as this,* Poets *have kist the hands of* Great Princes, *and drawne their gentle eyes to looke downe upon their sheetes of paper, when the* Poets *themselves were bound up in their winding-sheetes. The like curtesie from your* Lordship, *shall make you live in your grave, and* laurell *spring out of it; when the ignorant scorners of the* Muses *(that like wormes in* Libraries, *seeme to live onely to destroy* 20 learning) *shall wither, neglected, and forgotten. This worke and my selfe I humbly present to your approved censure. It being the utmost of my wishes, to have your Honorable selfe my weighty and perspicuous* Comment: *which grace so done me, shall ever be acknowledged*

By your Lordships
in all duty and
Observance,

John Webster.

In the just Worth, of that well Deserver,
M^r. JOHN WEBSTER, *and Upon this*
Maister-peece of Tragœdy.

IN this Thou imitat'st one Rich, and Wise,
That sees His Good Deedes done before he dies;
As He by Workes, Thou by this Worke of Fame,
Hast well provided for thy Living Name;
To trust to others Honorings, is Worth's Crime,
Thy Monument is rais'd in thy Life Time;
And 'tis most just; for every Worthy Man
Is his owne Marble; and his Merit can
Cut Him to any Figure, and expresse
More Art, then Deaths Cathedrall Pallaces,
Where Royall Ashes keepe their Court: thy Note
Be ever Plainnes, 'tis the Richest Coate:
Thy Epitaph onely the Title *bee,*
Write, Dutchesse, *that will fetch a teare for thee,*
For who e're saw this Dutchesse *live, and dye,*
That could get off under a Bleeding Eye?

In Tragædiam.

Ut Lux *ex Tenebris ictu percussa* TONANTIS;
Illa, (*Ruina Malis*) *claris fit vita Poetis.*

Thomas Middletonus,
Poëta & Chron:
Londinensis.

To his friend Mr. *John Webster*
Upon his Dutchesse
of *Malfy*.

I Never saw thy Dutchesse, till the day,
That She was lively body'd in thy Play;
How'ere she answer'd her low-rated Love,
Her brothers anger did so fatall proove,
Yet my opinion is, she might speake more;
But never (in her life) so well before.

WIL: ROWLEY.

To the Reader of the Authour,
and his Dutchesse of *Malfy*.

CRowne Him a Poet, whom nor Rome, *nor* Greece,
Transcend in all theirs, for a Master-peece:
In which, whiles words and matter change, and Men
Act one another; Hee, from whose cleare Pen
They All tooke life, To Memory hath lent
A lasting Fame, to raise his Monument.

JOHN FORD

Actus Primus. Scena Prima.

[Amalfi. The Palace of the Duchess.]

[Enter Antonio and Delio.]

DELIO.

YOU are wel-come to your Country (deere *Antonio*)
You have bin long in *France*, and you returne
A very formall French-man, in your habit.
How doe you like the French Court?
  ANT. I admire it—
In seeking to reduce both State, and People
To a fix'd Order, the[ir] juditious King
Begins at home: Quits first his Royall Pallace
Of flattring Sicophants, of dissolute,
And infamous persons—which he sweetely termes   10
His Masters Master-peece (the worke of Heaven)
Considring duely, that a Princes Court
Is like a common Fountaine, whence should flow
Pure silver-droppes in generall: But if 't chance
Some curs'd example poyson't neere the head,
"Death, and diseases through the whole land spread.
And what is't makes this blessed government,
But a most provident Councell, who dare freely
Informe him the corruption of the times?
Though some oth'Court hold it presumption   20
To instruct Princes what they ought to doe,
It is a noble duety to informe them
What they ought to fore-see: Here comes *Bosola* *[Enter Bosola.]*
The onely Court-Gall: yet I observe his rayling
Is not for simple love of Piety:
Indeede he rayles at those things which he wants,
Would be as leacherous, covetous, or proud,
Bloody, or envious, as any man,
If he had meanes to be so: Here's the Cardinall. *[Enter Cardinall.]*
  Bos. I doe haunt you still.   30
  CAR. So.

Bos. I have done you better service then to be slighted thus:
miserable age, where onely the reward of doing well, is the doing
of it!

Car. You inforce your merrit to[o] much.

Bos. I fell into the Gallies in your service, where, for two
yeares together, I wore two Towells in stead of a shirt, with a
knot on the shoulder, after the fashion of a Romaine Mantle:
Slighted thus? I will thrive some way: black-birds fatten best
40 in hard weather: why not I, in these dogge dayes?

Car. Would you could become honest—

Bos. With all your divinity, do but direct me the way to it—I
have knowne many travell farre for it, and yet returne as arrant
knaves, as they went forth; because they carried themselves
always along with them; [Exit Cardinal.] Are you gon? Some
fellowes (they say) are possessed with the divell, but this great
fellow, were able to possesse the greatest Divell, and make him
worse.

Ant. He hath denied thee some suit?

50 Bos. He, and his brother, are like Plum-trees (that grow
crooked over standing-pooles) they are rich, and ore-laden with
Fruite, but none but Crowes, Pyes, and Catter-pillers feede on
them: Could I be one of their flattring Panders, I would hang
on their eares like a horse-leach, till I were full, an[d] then droppe
off: I pray leave me.

Who wold relie upon these miserable dependances, in expectation to be advanc'd to-morrow? what creature ever fed worse,
then hoping *Tantalus*? nor ever di[e]d any man more fearefully,
then he that hop'd for a p[ar]don: There are rewards for hawkes,
60 and dogges, ∧ when they have done us service; but for a
Souldier, that hazards his Limbes in a battaile, nothing but a
kind of Geometry, is his last Supportation.

Del. Geometry?

Bos. I, to hang in a faire paire of slings, take his latter-swinge
in the world, upon an honorable pare of Crowtches, from
hospitall to hospitall—fare ye well Sir. And yet do not you
scorne us, for places in the Court, are but [like] beds in the
hospitall, where this mans head lies at that mans foote, and so
lower, and lower.   [Exit.]

70 Del. I knew this fellow (seaven yeares) in the Gallies,
For a notorious murther, and 'twas thought

The Cardinall suborn'd it: he was releas'd
By the French Generall (*Gaston de Foux*)
When he recover'd *Naples.*
   A N T. 'Tis great pitty
He should be thus neglected—I have heard
He's very valiant: This foule mellancholly
Will poyson all his goodnesse, for (i'le tell you)
If too immoderate sleepe be truly sayd
To be an inward rust unto the soule;   80
It then doth follow want of action
Breeds all blacke male-contents, and their close rearing
(Like mothes in cloath) doe hurt for want of wearing.

     [*Enter Silvio, Castruchio, Roderigo, & Grisolan.*]

   D E L. The Presence 'gins to fill, you promis'd me
To make me the partaker of the natures
Of some of your great Courtiers.
   A N T. The Lord Cardinall's
And other strangers', that are now in Court?—
I shall: here comes the great *Calabrian* Duke. [*Enter Ferdinand.*]
   F E R D. Who tooke the Ring oftnest?   90
   S I L. *Antoni*[o] *Bologna* (my Lord.)
   F E R D. Our Sister Duchesse' great Master of her houshold?
Give him the Jewell: when shall we leave this sportive-action,
and fall to action indeed?
   C A S T. Me thinkes (my Lord) you should not desire to go to
war, in person.
   F E R. Now, for some gravity: why (my Lord?)
   C A S T. It is fitting a Souldier arise to be a Prince, but not
necessary a Prince descend to be a Captaine.
   F E R D. Noe?   100
   C A S T. No, (my Lord) he were far better do it by a Deputy.
   F E R D. Why should he not as well sleepe, or eate, by a Deputy?
This might take idle, offensive, and base office from him, whereas
the other deprives him of honour.
   C A S T. Beleeve my experience: that Realme is never long in
quiet, where the Ruler, is a Souldier.
   F E R D. Thou toldst me thy wife could not endure fighting.
   C A S T. True (my Lord.)

F[ER]D. And of a jest, she broke of a Captaine she met, full
110 of wounds: I have forgot it.

CAST. She told him (my Lord) he was a pittifull fellow, to
lie, like the Children of *Ismael*, all in Tents.

FERD. Why, there's a wit were able to undoe all the Chyr-
urgeons o'the City, for although Gallants should quarrell, and
had drawne their weapons, and were ready to goe to it; yet her
perswasions would make them put up.

CAST. That she would (my Lord)—How doe you like my
Spanish Gennit?

ROD. He is all fire.

120 FERD. I am of *Pliney's* opinion, I thinke he was begot by
the wind, he runs, as if he were ballass'd with Quick-silver.

SIL. True (my Lord) he reeles from the Tilt often.

ROD. GRIS. Ha, ha, ha.

FERD. Why do you laugh? Me thinks you that are Courtiers
should be my touch-wood, take fire, when I give fire; that is,
laugh when I laugh, were the subject never so wity—

CAST. True (my Lord) I my selfe have heard a very good
jest, and have scorn'd to seeme to have so silly a wit, as to understand it.

130 FERD. But I can laugh at your Foole (my Lord.)

CAST. He cannot speake (you know) but he makes faces, my
lady cannot abide him.

FERD. Noe?

CAST. Nor endure to be in merry Company: for she saies
too much laughing, and too much Company, fils her too full of
the wrinckle.

FERD. I would then have a Mathematicall Instrument made
for her face, that she might not laugh out of compasse: I shall
shortly visit you at *Millaine* (Lord *Silvio*.)

140 SIL. Your Grace shall arrive most wel-come.

FERD. You are a good Horse-man (*Antonio*) you have excellent Riders in *France*—what doe you thinke of good Horse-
man-ship?

ANT. Noblely (my Lord)—as out of the Grecian-horse,
issued many famous Princes: So, out of brave Horse-man-ship,
arise the first Sparkes of growing resolution, that raise the minde
to noble action.

FERD. You have be-spoake it worthely.

SIL. Your brother, the Lord Cardinall, and sister Dutchesse.

[*Enter Cardinal, Duchess, Cariola, & Julia.*]

CARD. Are the Gallies come about?   150

GRIS. They are (my Lord.)

FERD. Here's the Lord *Silvio*, is come to take his leave.

DEL. Now (Sir) your promise: what's that Cardinall?
I meane his Temper? they say he's a brave fellow,
Will play his five thousand crownes, at Tennis, Daunce,
Court Ladies, and one that hath fought single Combats.

ANT. Some such flashes superficially hang on him, for forme:
but observe his inward Character: he is a mellancholly Churchman: The Spring in his face, is nothing but the Ingendring of
Toades: where he is jealous of any man, he laies worse plots 160
for them, then ever was impos'd on *Hercules*: for he strewes
in his way Flatter[er]s, Panders, Intelligencers, Athiests, and a
thousand such politicall Monsters: he should have beene Pope:
but in stead of comming to it by the primative decensie of the
church, he did bestow bribes, so largely, and so impudently, as
if he would have carried it away without heavens knowledge.
Some good he hath done.

DEL. You have given too much of him: what's his brother?

ANT. The Duke there? a most perverse, and turbulent
         Nature—
What appeares in him mirth, is meerely outside,   170
If he laugh hartely, it is to laugh
All honesty out of fashion.

DEL. Twins?

ANT. In qualitie:
He speakes with others Tongues, and heares mens suites,
With others Eares: will seeme to sleepe o'th bench
Onely to intrap offenders, in their answeres;
Doombes men to death, by information,
Rewards, by heare-say.

DEL. Then the Law to him   180
Is like a fowle blacke cob-web, to a Spider—
He makes it his dwelling, and a prison
To entangle those shall feede him.

ANT. Most true:
He nev'r paies debts, unlesse they be [shrewd] turnes,
And those he will confesse that he doth owe.

Last: for his brother, there, (the Cardinall)
They that doe flatter him most, say Oracles
Hang at his lippes: and verely I beleeve them:
190 For the Divell speakes in them.
　　　But for their sister, (the right noble Duchesse)
You never fix'd you[r] eye on three faire Meddalls,
Cast in one figure, of so different temper:
For her discourse, it is so full of Rapture,
You onely will begin, then to be sorry
When she doth end her speech: and wish (in wonder)
She held it lesse vaine-glory, to talke much,
Then your pennance, to heare her: whilst she speakes,
She throwes upon a man so sweet a looke,
200 That it were able raise one to a Galliard
That lay in a dead palsey; and to doate
On that sweete countenance: but in that looke,
There speaketh so divine a continence,
As cuts off all lascivious, and vaine hope.
Her dayes are practis'd in such noble vertue,
That sure her nights (nay more her very Sleepes)
Are more in Heaven, then other Ladies Shrifts.
Let all sweet Ladies breake their flattring Glasses,
And dresse themselves in her.
210 　Del. Fye *Antoni*[o],
You play the wire-drawer with her commendations.
　　　Ant. I'll case the picture up: onely thus much—
All her particular worth growes to this somme:
She staines the time past: lights the time to come—
　　　Cariola. You must attend my Lady, in the gallery,
Some halfe an houre hence.
　　　Ant. I shall.　　　　　[*Exeunt Antonio & Delio.*]
　　　Ferd. Sister, I have a suit to you:
　　　Duch. To me, Sir?
220 　Ferd. A Gentleman here: *Daniel de Bosola:*
One, that was in the Gallies.
　　　Duch. Yes, I know him:
　　　Ferd. A worthy fellow h'is: pray let me entreat for
The provisorship of your horse.
　　　Duch. Your knowledge of him,
Commends him, and prefers him.

FERD. Call him heither,   [*Exit Servant.*]
Wee [are] now upon parting: Good Lord *Silvio*
Do us commend to all our noble friends
At the League[r].   230
  SIL. Sir, I shall.
  [DUCH.] You are for *Millaine*?
  SIL. I am:
  DUCH. Bring the Carroches: we'll bring you down to the
    Haven.   [*Exeunt, except Card. & Ferd.*
  CAR. Be sure you entertaine that *Bosola*
For your Intelligence: I would not be seene in't.
And therefore many times I have slighted him,
When he did court our furtherance: as this Morning.
  FERD. *Antonio*, the great Master of her houshold
Had beene farre fitter: 240
  CARD. You are deceiv'd in him,
His Nature is too honest for such businesse,
He comes: I'll leave you: [*Exit. Enter Bosola.*]
  BOS. I was lur'd to you.
  FERD. My brother here (the Cardinall) could never abide you.
  BOS. Never since he was in my debt.
  FERD. May be some oblique character in your face,
Made him suspect you?
  BOS. Doth he study Phisiognomie?
There's no more credit to be given to th'face,   250
Then to a sicke mans uryn, which some call
The Physitians whore, because she cozens him:
He did suspect me wrongfully:
  FERD. For that
You must give great men leave to take their times:
Distrust, doth cause us seldome be deceiv'd;
You see, the oft shaking of the Cedar-Tree
Fastens it more at roote.
  BOS. Yet take heed:
For to suspect a friend unworthely,   260
Instructs him the next way to suspect you,
And prompts him to deceive you.
  [F]ERD. There's gold.
  BOS. So:
What followes? (Never raind such showres as these

Without thunderbolts i'th taile of them;) whose throat must I cut?

FERD. Your inclination to shed blood rides post
Before my occasion to use you: I give you that
To live i'th Court, here: and observe the Duchesse,
270 To note all the particulars of her haviour:
What suitors doe sollicite her for marriage
And whom she best affects: she's a yong widowe,
I would not have her marry againe.

Bos. No, Sir?

FERD. Doe not you aske the reason: but be satisfied,
I say I would not.

Bos. It seemes you would create me
One of your familiars.

FERD. Familiar? what's that?

280 Bos. Why, a very quaint invisible Divell, in flesh:
An Intelligencer.

FERD. Such a kind of thriving thing
I would wish thee: and ere long, thou maist arrive
At a higher place by't.

Bos. Take your Divels
Which Hell calls Angels: these curs'd gifts would make
You a corrupter, me an impudent traitor,
And should I take these, they'll'd take me [to] Hell.

FER. Sir, I'll take nothing from you, that I have given:
290 There is a place, that I procur'd for you
This morning: (the Provisor-ship o'th' horse)—
Have you heard o[n']t?

Bos. Noe.

FER. 'Tis yours, is't not worth thankes?

Bos. I would have you curse your selfe now, that your bounty
(Which makes men truly noble) ere should make
Me a villaine: oh, that to avoid ingratitude
For the good deed you have done me, I must doe
All the ill man can invent: Thus the Divell
300 Candies all sinnes [o'er]: and what Heaven termes vild,
That names he complementall.

FER. Be your selfe:
Keepe your old garbe of melencholly: 'twill expresse
You envy those that stand above your reach,
Yet strive not to come neere'em: This will gaine

Accesse, to private lodgings, where your selfe
May (like a pollitique dormouse—
    Bos. As I have seene some,
Feed in a Lords dish, halfe asleepe, not seeming
To listen to any talke: and yet these Rogues   310
Have cut his throat in a dreame: whats my place?
The Proviso[r]-ship o'th horse? say then my corruption
Grew out of horse-doong: I am your creature.
    Ferd. Away!
    Bos. Let good men, for good deeds, covet good fame,
Since place, and riches oft are bribes of shame—
Sometimes the Divell doth preach.   *Exit Bosola.*
                    [*Enter Cardinal, Duchess, & Cariola.*]
    Card. We are to part from you: and your owne discretion.
Must now be your director.
    Ferd. You are a Widowe: 320
You know already what man is: and therefore
Let not youth...high promotion, eloquence—
    Card. No, nor any thing without the addition, *Honor*,
Sway your high blood.
    Ferd. Marry? they are most luxurious,
Will wed twice.
    Card. O fie!
    Ferd. Their livers are more spotted
Then *Labans* sheepe.
    Duch. Diamonds are of most value   330
They say, that have past through most Jewellers hands.
    Ferd. Whores, by that rule, are precious:
    Duch. Will you heare me?
I'll never marry:
    Card. So most Widowes say:
But commonly that motion lasts no longer
Then the turning of an houreglasse—the funeral Sermon,
And it, end both together.
    Ferd. Now heare me:
You live in a ranke pasture here, i'th Court—   340
There is a kind of honney-dew, that's deadly:
'Twill poyson your fame; looke [to]'t: be not cunning:
For they whose faces doe belye their hearts,
Are Witches, ere they arrive at twenty yeeres,

I: and give the divell sucke.

DUCH. This is terrible good councell:

FERD. Hypocrisie is woven of a fine small thred,
Subtler, then *Vulcans* Engine: yet (beleev't)
Your darkest actions: nay, your privat'st thoughts,
350 Will come to light.

CARD. You may flatter your selfe,
And take vour owne choice: privately be married
Under the E[a]ves of night . . .

FERD. Think't the best voyage
That ere you made; like the irregular Crab,
Which though't goes backward, thinkes that it goes right,
Because it goes its owne way: but observe;
Such weddings, may more properly be said
To be executed, then celibrated.

360 CARD. The marriage night
Is the entrance into some prison.

FERD. And those joyes,
Those lustfull pleasures, are like heavy sleepes
Which doe fore-run mans mischiefe.

CARD. Fare you well.
Wisdome begins at the end: remember it.   [*Exit.*]

DUCH. I thinke this speech betweene you both was studied,
It came so roundly off.

FERD. You are my sister,
370 This was my Fathers poyniard: doe you see,
I'll'd be loth to see't looke rusty, 'cause 'twas his:
I would have you to give ore these chargeable Revels;
A Vizor, and a Masque are whispering roomes
That were nev'r built for goodnesse: fare ye well:
And woemen like that part, which (like the Lamprey)
Hath nev'r a bone in't.

DUCH. Fye Sir!

FERD. Nay,
I meane the Tongue: varietie of Courtship;
380 What cannot a neate knave with a smooth tale,
Make a woman beleeve? farewell, lusty Widowe.   [*Exit.*]

DUCH. Shall this move me? if all my royall kindred
Lay in my way unto this marriage:
I'll'd make them my low foote-steps: And even now,

Even in this hate (as men in some great battailes
By apprehending danger, have atchiev'd
Almost impossible actions: I have heard Souldiers say so),
So I, through frights, and threatnings, will assay
This dangerous venture: Let old wives report
I wincked, and chose a husband: *Cariola*,   390
To thy knowne secricy, I have given up
More then my life, my fame:
  CAR[IOL]A. Both shall be safe:
For I'll conceale this secret from the world
As warily as those that trade in poyson,
Keepe poyson from their children.
  DUCH. Thy protestation
Is ingenious, and hearty: I beleeve it.
Is *Antonio* come?
  CARIOLA. He attends you: 400
  DUCH. Good deare soule,
Leave me: but place thy selfe behind the Arras,
Where thou maist over-heare us: wish me good speed [*Cariola*
For I am going into a wildernesse,   *withdraws behind*
Where I shall find nor path, nor friendly clewe   *the arras.*
To be my guide—I sent for you, Sit downe: *The Duchess*
Take Pen and Incke, and write: are you ready?   *draws the*
  ANT. Yes: *traverse*
  DUCH. What did I say?   *revealing Antonio.*]
  ANT. That I should write some-what.   410
  DUCH. Oh, I remember:
After [these] triumphs, and this large expence
It's fit (like thrifty husbands) we enquire
What's laid up for to-morrow:
  ANT. So please your beauteous Excellence.
  DUCH. Beauteous?
Indeed I thank you: I look yong for your sake.
You have tane my cares upon you.
  ANT. I'le fetch your Grace
The particulars of your revinew, and expence.   420
  DUCH. Oh, you are an upright treasurer: but you mistooke,
For when I said I meant to make enquiry,
What's layd up for to-morrow: I did meane
What's layd up yonder for me.

ANT. Where?

DUCH. In Heaven,
I am making my will, (as 'tis fit Princes should
In perfect memory) and I pray Sir, tell me
Were not one better make it smiling, thus?
430 Then in deepe groanes, and terrible ghastly lookes,
As if the guifts we parted with, procur'd
That violent distr[a]ction?

ANT. Oh, much better.

DUCH. If I had a husband now, this care were quit:
But I intend to make yo[u] Over-seer;
What good deede, shall we first remember? say.

ANT. Begin with that first good deed began i'th'world,
After mans creation, the Sacrament of marriage—
I'ld have you first provide for a good husband,
440 Give him all.

DUCH. All?

ANT. Yes, your excellent selfe.

DUCH. In a winding sheete?

ANT. In a cople.

DUCH. St. *Win[i]frid*, that were a strange will.

ANT. 'Twere strange
If there were no will in you to marry againe.

DUCH. What doe you thinke of marriage?

ANT. I take't, as those that deny Purgatory,
450 It locally containes, or heaven, or hell,
There's no third place in't.

DUCH. How doe you affect it?

ANT. My banishment, feeding my mellancholly,
Would often reason thus.

DUCH. Pray let's heare it.

ANT. Say a man never marry, nor have children,
What takes that from him? onely the bare name
Of being a father, or the weake delight
To see the little wanton ride a cocke-horse
460 Upon a painted sticke, or heare him chatter
Like a taught Starling.

DUCH. Fye, fie, what's all this?
One of your eyes is blood-shot, use my Ring to't,
They say 'tis very soveraigne, 'twas my wedding Ring,

And I did vow never to part with it,
But to my second husband.
A N T. You have parted with it now.
D U C H. Yes, to helpe your eye-sight.
A N T. You have made me starke blind.
D U C H. How?   470
A N T. There is a sawcy, and ambitious divell
Is dauncing in this circle.
D U C H. Remoove him.
A N T. How?
D U C H. There needs small conjuration, when your finger
May doe it: thus, is it fit?
A N T. What sayd you?   *he kneeles*
D U C H. Sir,
This goodly roofe of yours, is too low built,
I cannot stand upright in't, nor discourse,   480
Without I raise it higher: raise your selfe,
Or if you please, my hand to helpe you: so.
A N T. Ambition (Madam) is a great mans madnes,
That is not kept in chaines, and close-pent-roomes,
But in faire lightsome lodgings, and is girt
With the wild noyce of pratling visitan[t]s,
Which makes it lunatique, beyond all cure—
Conceive not, I am so stupid, but I ayme
Whereto your favours tend: But he's a foole
That (being a-cold) would thrust his hands i'th'fire   490
To warme them.
D U C H. So, now the ground's broake,
You may discover what a wealthy Mine,
I make you Lord [of].
A N T. Oh my unworthinesse.
D U C H. You were ill to sell your selfe,
This darkning of your worth, is not like that
Which trades-men use i'th'City—their false lightes
Are to rid bad wares off: and I must tell you
If you will know where breathes a compleat man,   500
(I speake it without flattery) turne your eyes,
And progresse through your selfe.
A N T. Were there nor heaven, nor hell,
I should be honest: I have long serv'd vertue,

And nev'r tane wages of her.

DUCH. Now she paies it—
The misery of us, that are borne great!—
We are forc'd to wo[o], because none dare wo[o] us:
And as a Tyrant doubles with his words,
510 And fearefully equivocates: so we
Are forc'd to expresse our violent passions
In ridles, and in dreames, and leave the path
Of simple vertue, which was never made
To seeme the thing it is not: Goe, go brag
You have left me heartlesse—mine is in your bosome,
I hope 'twill multiply love there: You doe tremble:
Make not your heart so dead a peece of flesh
To feare, more then to love me: Sir, be confident,
What is't distracts you? This is flesh, and blood, (Sir,)
520 'Tis not the figure cut in Allablaster
Kneeles at my husbands tombe: Awake, awake (man)
I do here put of[f] all vaine ceremony,
And onely doe appeare to you a yong widow
That claimes you for her husband, and like a widow,
I use but halfe a blush in't.

ANT. Truth speake for me,
I will remaine the constant Sanctuary
Of your good name.

DUCH. I thanke you (gentle love)
530 And 'cause you shall not come to me in debt,
(Being now my Steward) here upon your lippes
I signe your *Quietus est*: This you should have beg'd now,
I have seene children oft eate sweete-meates thus,
As fearefull to devoure them too soone.

ANT. But for your Brothers?

DUCH. Do not thinke of them,
All discord, without this circumference,   [*she puts her arms*
Is onely to be pittied, and not fear'd: *about him.*]
Yet, should they know it, time will easily
540 Scatter the tempest.

ANT. These words should be mine,
And all the parts you have spoke, if some part of it
Would not have savour'd flattery.

DUCH. Kneele.   [*Cariola shows herself.*]

ANT. Hah?

DUCH. Be not amaz'd, this woman's of my Councell,
I have heard Lawyers say, a contract in a Chamber,
(*Per verba [de] presenti*) is absolute marriage:
Blesse (Heaven) this sacred Gordian, which let violence
Never untwine.   550

ANT. And may our sweet affections, (like the Sphears)
Be still in motion.

DUCH. Quickning, and make
The like soft Musique.

ANT. That we may imitate the loving Palmes
(Best Embleme of a peacefull marriage)
That nev'r bore fruite devided.

DUCH. What can the Church force more?

ANT. That Fortune may not know an accident
Either of joy, or sorrow, to devide   560
Our fixed wishes.

DUCH. How can the Church build faster?
We now are man, and wife, and 'tis the Church
That must but eccho this: Maid, stand apart,
I now am blinde.

ANT. What's your conceit in this?

DUCH. I would have you leade your Fortune by the hand,
Unto your marriage bed:
(You speake in me this, for we now are one)
We'll onely lie, and talke together, and plot   570
T'appease my humorous kindred; and if you please
(Like the old tale, in *Alexander* and *Lodowicke*)
Lay a naked sword betweene us, keepe us chast:
Oh, let me shrowd my blushes in your bosome,
Since 'tis the treasury of all my secrets.

CAR. Whether the spirit of greatnes, or of woman
Raigne most in her, I know not, but it shewes
A fearefull madnes. I owe her much of pitty.   *Exeunt.*

ACTUS II. SCENA I.

[*The Same.*]

[*Enter Bosola & Castruchio.*]

Bos. You say you would faine be taken—for an eminent
Courtier?

CAST. 'Tis the very maine of my ambition.

Bos. Let me see, you have a reasonable good face for't
already, and your night-cap expresses your eares sufficient largely
—I would have you learne to twirle the strings of your band
with a good grace; and in a set speech, (at th'end of every
sentence,) to hum, three, or foure times, or blow your nose (till
it smart againe,) to recover your memory—when you come to
10 be a president in criminall causes, if you smile upon a prisoner,
hang him, but if you frowne upon him, and threaten him, let
him be sure to scape the Gallowes.

CAST. I would be a very merrie president—

Bos. Do not sup a nights, 'twill beget you an admirable wit.

CAST. Rather it would make me have a good stomake to
quarrel, for they say, your roaring-boyes eate meate seldome,
and that makes them so valiant: but how shall I know whether
the people take me for an eminent fellow?

Bos. I will teach a tricke to know it—give out you lie a-
20 dying, and if you heare the common people curse you, be sure
you are taken for one of the prime night-caps— [*Enter Old Lady.*]
You come from painting now?

OLD LADY. From what?

Bos. Why, from your scurvy face-physicke—to behold thee
not painted enclines somewhat neere a miracle: These. . . in thy
face here, were deepe rutts, and foule sloughes the last progresse:
There was a Lady in *France*, that having had the small pockes,
flead the skinne off her face, to make it more levell; and whereas
before she look'd like a Nutmeg-grater, after she resembled an
30 abortive hedge-hog.

OLD LADY. Do you call this painting?

Bos. No, no, but [I] call [it] carreening of an old morphew'd
Lady, to make her disembogue againe—There's rough-cast
phrase to your plastique.

OLD LADY. It seemes you are well acquainted with my
closset?

BOS. One would suspect it for a shop of witch-craft, to finde
in it the fat of Serpents; spawne of Snakes, Jewes spittle, and
their yong children['s] ordures—and all these for the face: I
would sooner eate a dead pidgeon, taken from the soles of the 40
feete of one sicke of the plague, then kisse one of you fasting:
here are two of you, whose sin of your youth is the very patrimony
of the Physition, makes him renew his foote-cloth with the
Spring, and change his high-priz'd curtezan with the fall of the
leafe: I do wonder you doe not loath your selves—observe my
meditation now:
What thing is in this outward forme of man
To be belov'd? we account it ominous,
If Nature doe produce a Colt, or Lambe,
A Fawne, or Goate, in any limbe resembling   50
A Man; and flye from't as a prodegy.
Man stands amaz'd to see his deformity,
In any other Creature but himselfe.
But in our owne flesh, though we beare diseases
Which have their true names onely tane from beasts,
As the most ulcerous Woolfe, and swinish Meazeall;
Though we are eaten up of lice, and wormes,
And though continually we beare about us
A rotten and dead body, we delight
To hide it in rich tissew—all our feare,   60
(Nay all our terrour) is, least our Phisition
Should put us in the ground, to be made sweete.
Your wife's gone to *Rome*: you two cople, and get you
To the wels at *Leuca*, to recover your aches. [*Exeunt Castruchio*
I have other worke on foote: I observe our Duchesse   *& Old*
Is sicke a dayes, she puykes, her stomacke seethes,   *Lady.*]
The fins of her eie-lids looke most teeming blew,
She waines i'th'cheeke, and waxes fat i'th'flanke;
And (contrary to our *Italian* fashion,)
Weares a loose-bodied Gowne—there's somewhat in't,   70
I have a tricke, may chance discover it
(A pretty one)—I have bought some Apricocks,
The first our Spring yeelds.   [*Enter Delio & Antonio.*]
DEL. And so long since married?

You amaze me.

ANT. Let me seale your lipps for ever,
For did I thinke, that any thing but th'ayre
Could carry these words from you, I should wish
You had no breath at all: [to Bosola] Now Sir, in your contem-
plation?
80 You are studdying to become a great wise fellow?

BOS. Oh Sir, the opinion of wisedome is a foule tettor, that
runs all over a mans body: if simplicity direct us to have no
evill, it directs us to a happy being: For the subtlest folly proceedes from the subtlest wisedome: Let me be simply honest.

ANT. I do understand your in-side.

BOS. Do you so?

ANT. Because you would not seeme to appeare to th'world
Puff'd up with your preferment: You continue
This out of [f]ashion mellancholly—leave it, leave it.
90 BOS. Give me leave to be honest in any phrase, in any complement whatsoever—shall I confesse my selfe to you? I looke
no higher then I can reach: they are the gods, that must ride
on winged horses, a Lawyers mule of a slow pace will both suit
my disposition, and businesse: For (marke me) when a mans
mind rides faster then his horse can gallop, they quickly both
tyre.

ANT. You would looke up to Heaven, but I thinke
The Divell, that rules i'th'aire, stands in your light.

BOS. Oh (Sir) you are Lord of the ascendant, chiefe man
100 with the Duchesse, a Duke was your cosen German, remov'd:
Say you were lineally descended from King *Pippin*, or he himselfe,
what of this? search the heads of the greatest rivers in the World,
you shall finde them but bubles of water: Some would thinke
the soules of Princes were brought forth by some more weighty
cause, then those of meaner persons—they are deceiv'd, there's
the same hand to them: The like passions sway them, the same
reason, that makes a Vicar goe to Law for a tithe-pig, and undoe
his neighbours, makes them spoile a whole Province, and batter
downe goodly Cities, with the Cannon. [*Enter Duchess & Ladies.*]
110 DUCH. Your arme *Antonio*, do I not grow fat?
I am exceeding short-winded: *Bosola*,
I would have you (Sir) provide for me a Littor,
Such a one, as the Duchesse of *Florence* roade in.

Bos. The Duchesse us'd one, when she was great with childe.

Duch. I thinke she did: come hether, mend my ruffe—
Here, when? thou art such a tedious Lady; and
Thy breath smells of Lymmon pils, would thou hadst done—
Shall I sound under thy fingers? I am so troubled
With the mother.

Bos. [aside] I feare to[o] much.   120

Duch. I have heard you say, that the French Courtie[r]s
Weare their hats on fore the King.

Ant. I have seene it.

Duch. In the Presence?

Ant. Yes:

[Duch.] Why should not we bring up that fashion?
'Tis ceremony more then duty, that consists
In the remooving of a peece of felt:
Be you the example to the rest o'th' Court,
Put on your hat first.   130

Ant. You must pardon me:
I have seene, in colder countries then in *France*,
Nobles stand bare to th'Prince; and the distinction
M[e]thought show'd reverently.

Bos. I have a present for your Grace.

Duch. For me sir?

Bos. Apricocks (Madam.)

Duch. O sir, where are they?
I have heard of none to yeare.

Bos. [aside] Good, her colour rises.   140

Duch. Indeed I thanke you: they are wondrous faire ones:
What an unskilfull fellow is our Gardiner!
We shall have none this moneth.

Bos. Will not your Grace pare them?

Duch. No, they tast of muske (me thinkes) indeed they doe:

Bos. I know not: yet I wish your Grace had parde 'em:

Duch. Why?

Bos. I forgot to tell you the knave Gardner,
(Onely to raise his profit by them the sooner)
Did ripen them in horse-doung.   150

Duch. O you jest:
You shall judge: pray tast one.

Ant. Indeed Madam,

I doe not love the fruit.

DUCH. Sir, you are loath
To rob us of our dainties: 'tis a delicate fruit,
They say they are restorative?

BOS. 'Tis a pretty
Art: this grafting.

160 DUCH. 'Tis so: a bettring of nature.

BOS. To make a pippin grow upon a crab,
A dampson on a black thorne: [aside] how greedily she eats them!
A whirlewinde strike off these bawd-farthingalls,
For, but for that, and the loose-bodied gowne,
I should have discover'd apparently
The young spring-hall cutting a caper in her belly.

DUCH. I thanke you (Bosola:) they were right good ones,
If they doe not make me sicke.

ANT. How now Madame?

170 DUCH. This greene fruit . . . and my stomake are not friends—
How they swell me!

BOS. [aside] Nay, you are too much swell'd already.

DUCH. Oh, I am in an extreame cold sweat.

BOS. I am very sorry: [Exit.]

DUCH. Lights to my chamber: O, good Antonio,
I feare I am undone.   Exit Duchesse

DEL. Lights there, lights!

ANT. O my most trusty Delio, we are lost:
I feare she's falne in labour: and ther's left
180 No time for her remove.

DEL. Have you prepar'd
Those Ladies to attend her? and procur'd
That politique safe conveyance for the Mid-wife
Your Duchesse plotted?

ANT. I have:

DEL. Make use then of this forc'd occasion:
Give out that Bosola hath poyson'd her,
With these Apricocks: that will give some colour
For her keeping close.

190 ANT. Fye, fie, the Physitians
Will then flocke to her.

DEL. For that you may pretend
She'll use some prepar'd Antidote of her owne,

Least the Physitians should repoyson her.

ANT. I am lost in amazement: I know not what to think on't.

Ex.

SCENA II.

[*The Same.*]

[*Enter Bosola & old Lady.*]

BOS. [*aside*] So, so: ther's no question but her teatchi[n]es and most vulterous eating of the Apricocks, are apparant signes of breeding—[*to the old Lady*] now?

OLD LADY. I am in hast (Sir.)

BOS. There was a young wayting-woman, had a monstrous desire to see the Glasse-house.

OLD LA. Nay, pray let me goe:

BOS. And it was onely to know what strange instrument it was, should swell up a glasse to the fashion of a womans belly.

OLD LA. I will heare no more of the Glasse-house—you 10 are still abusing woemen?

BOS. Who—I? no, onely (by the way now and then) mention your fraileties. The Orrenge tree bear[s] ripe and greene fruit, and blossoms altogether: And some of you give entertainment for pure love: but more, for more precious reward. The lusty Spring smels well: but drooping Autumne tasts well: If we have the same golden showres, that rained in the time of *Jupiter* the Thunderer: you have the same *Dan[a]es* still, to hold up their laps to receive them: didst thou never study the *Mathematiques*?

OLD LA. What's that (Sir?)   20

BOS. Why, to know the trick how to make a many lines meete in one center: Goe, goe; give your foster-daughters good councell: tell them, that the Divell takes delight to hang at a womans girdle, like a false rusty watch, that she cannot discerne how the time passes.   [*Exit Old Lady. Enter Antonio, Delio,*

ANT. Shut up the Court gates: *Roderigo, & Grisolan.*]

ROD. Why sir? what's the danger?

ANT. Shut up the Posternes presently: and call All the Officers o'th' Court.

GRIS. I shall instantly: [*Exit.*] 30

ANT. Who keepes the key o'th' Parke-gate?

ROD. *Forobosco.*

Ant. Let him bring't presently.

[Re-enter Grisolan with Servants.]

Servant. Oh, Gentlemen o'th' Court, the fowlest treason.

Bos. *[aside]* If that these Apricocks should be poysond, now;
Without my knowledge!

Serv. There was taken even now
A Switzer in the Duchesse Bed-chamber.

2. Serv. A Switzer?

40   Serv. With a Pistoll in his great cod-piece.

Bos. H[a], ha, ha.

Serv. The cod-piece was the case for't.

2. Ser. There was a cunning traitor.
Who would have search'd his cod-piece?

Serv. True, if he had kept out of the Ladies chambers:
And all the mowldes of his buttons, were leaden bullets.

2. Serv. Oh wicked Caniball: a fire-lock in's cod-piece?

Serv. 'Twas a French plot, upon my life.

2. Ser. To see what the Divell can doe!

50   Ant. All the Office[r]s here?

Serv. We are:

Ant. Gentlemen,
We have lost much Plate you know; and but this evening
Jewels, to the value of foure thousand Duckets
Are missing in the Du[tc]hesse Cabinet—
Are the Gates shut?

Ser. Yes.

Ant. 'Tis the Duchesse pleasure
Each Officer be lock'd into his chamber

60   Till the Sun-rysing: and to send the keyes
Of all their chests, and of their outward doores
Into her bed-chamber: She is very sicke.

Rod. At her pleasure.

Ant. She intreates you take't not ill: The Innocent
Shall be the more approv'd by it.

Bos. Gentleman o'th' Wood-yard, where's your Switzer now?

Serv. By this hand, 'twas creadably reported by one o'th'
Black-guard.   *[Exeunt except Antonio & Delio.]*

Del. How fares it with the Dutchesse?

Ant. She's expos'd

70   Unto the worst of torture, paine, and feare;

DEL. Speake to her all happy comfort.

ANT. How I do play the foole with mine own danger!
You are this night (deere friend) to poast to Rome,
My life lies in your service.

DEL. Doe not doubt me—

ANT. Oh, 'Tis farre from me: and yet feare presents me
Somewhat that look[s] like danger.

DEL. Beleeve it,
'Tis but the shadow of your feare, no more:
How superstitiously we mind our evils!　　　　　　　　80
The throwing downe salt, or crossing of a Hare;
Bleeding at nose, the stumbling of a horse:
Or singing of a Criket, are of powre
To daunt whole man in us: Sir, fare you well:
I wish you all the joyes of a bless'd Father;
And (for my faith) lay this unto your brest,
Old friends (like old swords) still are trusted best. [*Exit. Enter*

CARIOLA. Sir, you are the happy father of a sonne,　　*Car.*
Your wife commends him to you.　　　　　　　*with a child.*]

ANT. Blessed comfort:　　　　　　　　　　　　　　90
For heaven-sake tend her well: I'll presently
Goe set a figure for's Nativitie.　　　　　　　*Exeunt.*

SCENA III.

[*The Same. Outside the Palace.*]

[*Enter Bosola, with a dark lanthorn.*]

BOS. Sure I did heare a woman shreike: list, hah!
And the sound came (if I receiv'd it right)
From the Dutchesse lodgings: ther's some stratagem
In the confyning all our Courtiers
To their severall wards: I must have part of it,
My Intelligence will freize else: List againe—
It may be 'twas the mellencholly bird,
(Best friend of silence, and of solitarines)
The Oowle, that schream'd so: hah? *Antonio?*

[*Enter Antonio with a candle, his sword drawn.*]

ANT. I heard some noyse: [who's] there? what art thou?
　　speake.　　　　　　　　　　　　　　　　　　10

Bos. *Antonio?* Put not your face; nor body
To such a forc'd expression of feare—
I am *Bosola*; your friend.
    Ant. *Bosola?*
(This Moale do's undermine me) heard you not
A noyce even now?
    Bos. From whence?
    Ant. From the *Duchesse* lodging.
    Bos. Not I: did you?
20   Ant. I did: or else I dream'd.
    Bos. Let's walke towards it.
    Ant. No: It may be, 'twas
But the rising of the winde:
    Bos. Very likely:
Me thinkes 'tis very cold, and yet you sweat.
You looke wildly.
    Ant. I have bin setting a figure
For the Dutchesse Jewells;
    Bos. Ah: and how falls your question?
30 Doe you find it radicall?
    Ant. What's that to you?
'Tis rather to be question'd what designe
(When all men were commanded to their lodgings)
Makes you a night-walker.
    Bos. In sooth I'll tell you:
Now all the Court's asleepe, I thought the Divell
Had least to doe here; I came to say my prayers,
And if it doe offend you I doe so,
You are a fine Courtier.
40   Ant. [*aside*] This fellow will undoe me;
You gave the Dutchesse Apricocks to-day,
Pray heaven they were not poysond?
    Bos. Poysond? a spanish figge
For the imputation.
    Ant. Traitors are ever confident,
Till they are discover'd: There were Jewels stolne too—
In my conceit, none are to be suspected
More then your selfe.
    Bos. You are a false steward.
50   Ant. Sawcy slave! I'll pull thee up by the rootes;

Bos. May be the ruyne will crush you to peeces.
Ant. You are an impudent snake indeed (sir)—
Are you scarce warme, and doe you shew your sting?
[Bos.]   .   .   .   .
Ant. You Libell well (sir.)
Bos. No (sir,) copy it out:
And I will set my hand to't.
Ant. My nose bleedes:
One that were superstitious, would count
This ominous: when it meerely comes by chance.   60
Two letters, that are wrought here, for my name
Are drown'd in blood:
Meere accedent: for you (sir) I'll take order:
I'th morne you shall be safe: [aside] 'tis that must colour
Her lying-in: sir, this doore you passe not:
I doe not hold it fit, that you come neere
The Dutchesse lodgings, till you have [quit] your selfe;
[aside] *The Great are like the Base; nay, they are the same,*
When they seeke shamefull waies, to avoid shame.   *Ex.*
Bos. *Antonio* here about, did drop a Paper—   70
Some of your helpe (falce-friend)—oh, here it is:
What's here? a childes Nativitie calculated!
    The Dutchesse was deliver'd of a Sonne, 'tweene the houres
twelve, and one, in the night: Anno Dom: 1504. *(that's this*
yeere) decimo nono Decembris, *(that's this night)* taken ac-
cording to the Meridian of Malfy (that's our Dutchesse: happy
discovery!). The Lord of the first house, being combust in the
ascendant, signifies short life: and Mars *being in a human signe,*
joyn'd to the taile of the Dragon, in the eight house, doth threaten
a violent death; Cæte[r]a non scrutantur.   80
Why now 'tis most apparant: This precise fellow
Is the Dutchesse Bawde: I have it to my wish:
This is a parcell of Intelligency
Our Courtiers were [cas'de-up] for? It needes must follow,
That I must be committed, on pretence
Of poysoning her: which I'll endure, and laugh at:
If one could find the father now! but that
Time will discover; Old *Castruchio*
I'th morning poasts to Rome; by him I'll send
A Letter, that shall make her brothers Galls   90

Ore-flowe their Livours—this was a thrifty way.
Though Lust doe masque in ne['e]r so strange disguise,
She's oft found witty, but is never wise.   [*Exit.*]

SCENA IIII.

[*Rome. The Cardinal's Palace.*]

[*Enter Cardinal and Julia.*]

CARD. Sit: thou art my best of wishes—pre-thee tell me
What tricke didst thou invent to come to Rome,
Without thy husband?
    JUL. Why, (my Lord) I told him
I came to visit an old Anchorite
Heare, for devotion.
    CARD. Thou art a witty false one:
I meane to him.
    JUL. You have prevailed with me
10 Beyond my strongest thoughts: I would not now
Find you inconstant.
    CARD. Doe not put thy selfe
To such a voluntary torture: which proceedes
Out of your owne guilt.
    JUL. How (my Lord?)
    CARD. You feare
My constancy, because you have approov'd
Those giddy and wild turning[s] in your selfe.
    JUL. Did you ere find them?
20   CARD. Sooth generally for woemen,
A man might strive to make glasse male-able,
Ere he should make them fixed.
    JUL. So, (my Lord)!—
    CARD. We had need goe borrow that fantastique glasse
Invented by *Galileo* the Florentine,
To view another spacious world i'th' Moone,
And looke to find a constant woman there.
    JUL. This is very well (my Lord.)
    CARD. Why do you weepe?
30 Are teares your justification? the selfe-same teares
Will fall into your husbands bosome, (Lady)

With a loud protestation, that you love him
Above the world: Come, I'll love you wisely,
That's jealously, since I am very certaine
You cannot me make cuckould.
    JUL. I'll go home
To my husband.
    CARD. You may thanke me, (Lady)
I have taken you off your mellancholly pearch,
Boare you upon my fist, and shew'd you game,   40
And let you flie at it: I pray the[e] kisse me—
When thou wast with thy husband, thou wast watch'd
Like a tame Ellephant: (still you are to thanke me)
Thou hadst onely kisses from him, and high feeding,
But what delight was that? 'twas just like one
That hath a little fingring on the Lute,
Yet cannot tune it: (still you are to thanke me.)
    JUL. You told me of a piteous wound i'th'heart,
And a sicke livour, when you woed me first,
And spake like one in physicke.   50
    CARD. Who's that?   [Enter Servant.]
Rest firme, for my affection to thee,
Lightning mooves slow to't.
    SER. (Madam) a Gentleman
That's come post from _Malfy_, desires to see you.
    CAR. Let him enter, I'll with-draw.   _Exit._
    SER. He sayes,
Your husband (old _Castruchio_) is come to _Rome_,
Most pittifully tyr'd with riding post.   [_Exit. Enter Delio._]
    JUL. Signior _Delio_? 'tis one of my old Suitors.   60
    DEL. I was bold to come and see you.
    JUL. Sir, [you] are wel-come.
    DEL. Do you lie here?
    JUL. Sure, your owne experience
Will satisfie you no—our Romane Prelates
Do not keepe lodging, for Ladies.
    DEL. Very well:
I have brought you no comendations from your husband,
For I know none by him.
    JUL. I heare he's come to _Rome_?   70
    DEL. I never knew man, and beast, of a horse, and a knight,

So weary of each other—if he had had a good backe,
He would have undertooke to have borne his horse,
His breech was so pittifully sore.
    JUL. Your laughter,
Is my pitty.
    DEL. Lady, I know not whether
You want mony, but I have brought you some.
    JUL. From my husband?
80   DEL. No, from mine owne allowance.
    JUL. I must heare the condition, ere I be bound to take it.
    DEL. Looke on't, 'tis gold, hath it not a fine colour?
    JUL. I have a Bird more beautifull.
    DEL. Try the sound on't.
    JUL. A Lute-string far exceedes it,
It hath no smell, like Cassia, or Cyvit,
Nor is it phisicall, though some fond Doctors
Perswade us seeth'[t] in Cullisses—I'le tell you,
This is a Creature bred by——   [*Enter Servant.*]
90   SER. Your husband's come,
Hath deliver'd a letter to the Duke of *Calabria*,
That, to my thinking hath put him out of his wits.   [*Exit.*]
    JUL. Sir, you heare,
'Pray let me know your busines, and your suite,
As briefely as can be.
    DEL. With good speed, I would wish you
(At such time, as you are non-resident
With your husband) my mistris.
    JUL. Sir, I'le go aske my husband if I shall,
100 And straight returne your answere.   *Exit.*
    DEL. Very fine—
Is this her wit, or honesty that speakes thus?
I heard one say the Duke was highly mov'd
With a letter sent from *Malfy*: I doe feare
Antonio is betray'd: how fearefully
Shewes his ambition now, (unfortunate Fortune)!—
"They passe through whirle-pooles, and deepe woes doe shun,
Who the event weigh, ere the action's done.   *Exit.*

SCENA V.

[The Same.]

[Enter] Cardinall, and Ferdinand, with a letter.

FERD. I have this night dig'd up a man-drake.

CAR. Say you?

FERD. And I am growne mad with't.

CAR. What's the pro[deg]y?

FERD. Read there—a sister dampn'd—she's loose i'th'hilts:
Growne a notorious Strumpet.

CAR. Speake lower.

FERD. Lower?
Rogues do not whisper't now, but seeke to publish't,
(As servants do the bounty of their Lords)
Aloud; and with a covetuous searching eye,   10
To marke who note them: Oh confusion sease her,
She hath had most cunning baudes to serve her turne,
And more secure conveyances for lust,
Then Townes of garrison, for Service.

CARD. Is't possible?
Can this be certaine?

FERD. Rubarbe, oh, for rubarbe
To purge this choller—here's the cursed day
To prompt my memory, and here'it shall sticke   20
Till of her bleeding heart, I make a spunge
To wipe it out.

CARD. Why doe you make your selfe
So wild a Tempest?

FERD. Would I could be one,
That I might tosse her pallace 'bout her eares,
Roote up her goodly forrests, blast her meades,
And lay her generall territory as wast,
As she hath done her honors.

CARD. Shall our blood   30
(The royall blood of *Arragon*, and *Castile*)
Be thus attaincted?

FERD. Apply desperate physicke—
We must not now use Balsamum, but fire,
The smarting cupping-glasse, for that's the meane

To purge infected blood, (such blood as hers:)
There is a kind of pitty in mine eie,
I'll give it to my hand-kercher; and now 'tis here,
I'll bequeath this to her Bastard.

40   CARD. What to do?

FERD. Why, to make soft lint for his mother['s] wounds,
When I have hewed her to peeces.

CARD. Curs'd creature—
Unequall nature, to place womens hearts
So farre upon the left-side!

FERD. Foolish men,
That ere will trust their honour in a Barke,
Made of so slight, weake bull-rush, as is woman,
Apt every minnit to sinke it!

50   CAR. Thus Ignorance, when it hath purchas'd honour,
It cannot weild it.

FERD. Me thinkes I see her laughing,
Excellent *Hyenna*—talke to me somewhat, quickly,
Or my imagination will carry me
To see her, in the shamefull act of sinne.

CARD. With whom?

FERD. Happily, with some strong-thigh'd Bargeman;
Or one [o']th'wood-yard, that can quoit the sledge,
Or tosse the barre, or else some lovely Squire

60 That carries coles up, to her privy lodgings.

CARD. You flie beyond your reason.

FERD. Goe to (Mistris.)
'Tis not your whores milke, that shall quench my wild-fire,
But your whores blood.

CARD. How idlely shewes this rage!—which carries you,
As men convai'd by witches, through the ayre,
On violent whirle-windes—this intemperate noyce,
Fitly resembles deafe-mens shrill discourse,
Who talke aloud, thinking all other men

70 To have their imperfection.

FERD. Have not you,
My palsey?

CARD. Yes—I can be angry
Without this rupture—there is not in nature
A thing, that makes man so deform'd, so beastly,

As doth intemperate anger: chide your selfe—
You have divers men, who never yet exprest
Their strong desire of rest, but by unrest,
By vexing of themselves: Come, put your selfe
In tune.   80

    FERD. So—I will onely study to seeme
The thing I am not: I could kill her now,
In you, or in my selfe, for I do thinke
It is some sinne in us, Heaven doth revenge
By her.

    CARD. Are you starke mad?

    FERD. I would have their bodies
Burn't in a coale-pit, with the ventage stop'd,
That their curs'd smoake might not ascend to Heaven:
Or dippe the sheetes they lie in, in pitch or sulphure,   90
Wrap them in't, and then light them like a match:
Or else to boile their Bastard to a cullisse,
And give't his leacherous father, to renew
The sinne of his backe.

    CARD. I'll leave you.

    FERD.   Nay, I have done,
I am confident, had I bin damn'd in hell,
And should have heard of this, it would have put me
Into a cold sweat: In, in, I'll go sleepe—
Till I know who leapes my sister, i'll not stirre: 100
That knowne, i'll finde Scorpions to string my whips,
And fix her in a generall ecclipse.   *Exeunt.*

ACTUS III. SCENA I.

[Amalfi. The Palace of the Duchess.]

[Enter Antonio and Delio.]

    ANT. Our noble friend (my most beloved *Delio*)
Oh, you have bin a stranger long at Court,
Came you along with the Lord *Ferdinand*?

    DEL. I did Sir, and how faires your noble *Duchesse*?

    ANT. Right fortunately well: She's an excellent
Feeder of pedegrees: since you last saw her,
She hath had two children more, a sonne, and daughter.

DEL. Me thinkes 'twas yester-day: Let me but wincke,
And not behold your face, which to mine eye
10 Is somewhat leaner, verily I should dreame
It were within this halfe houre.

ANT. You have not bin in Law, (friend *Delio*)
Nor in prison, nor a Suitor at the Court
Nor beg'd the reversion of some great mans place,
Nor troubled with an old wife, which doth make
Your time so inse[n]cibly hasten.

DEL. 'Pray Sir tell me,
Hath not this newes arriv'd yet to the eare;
Of the Lord *Cardinall*?

20 ANT. I feare it hath,
The Lord *Ferdinand*, (that's newly come to Court,)
Doth beare himselfe right dangerously.

DEL. Pray why?

ANT. He is so quiet, that he seemes to sleepe
The tempest out (as Dormise do in Winter)—
Those houses, that are haunted, are most still,
Till the divell be up.

DEL. What say the common people?

ANT. The common-rable, do directly say
30 She is a Strumpet.

DEL. And your graver heades,
(Which would [b]e pollitique) what censure they?

ANT. They do observe, I grow to infinite purchase
The leaft-hand way, and all suppose the Duchesse
Would amend it, if she could: For, say they,
Great Princes, though they grudge their Officers
Should have such large, and unconfined meanes
To get wealth under them, will not complaine
Least thereby they should make them odious
40 Unto the people—for other obligation
Of love, or marriage, betweene her and me,
They never dreame [of]. [*Enter Ferdinand, Duchess, & Bosola.*]

DEL. The Lord *Ferdinand*
Is going to bed.

FERD. I'll instantly to bed,
For I am weary: I am to ∧ be-speake
A husband for you.

Duch. For me (Sir?)—'pray who is't?

Ferd. The great Count *Malateste*.

Duch. Fie upon him,   50
A Count! he's a meere sticke of sugar-candy,
(You may looke quite thorough him)—when I choose
A husband, I will marry for your honour.

Ferd. You shall do well in't: How is't (worthy *Antonio*?)

Duch. But (Sir) I am to have private conference with you,
About a scandalous report, is spread
Touching mine honour.

Ferd. Let me be ever deafe to't:
One of Pasquils paper-bullets, court calumney,
A pestilent ayre, which Princes pallaces   60
Are seldome purg'd [of]: Yet, say that it were true,
I powre it in your bosome, my fix'd love
Would strongly excuse, extenuate, nay deny
Faults, [were] they apparant in you: Goe be safe
In your owne innocency.

Duch. [aside] Oh bless'd comfort—
This deadly aire is purg'd.   *Exeunt, [except Ferdinand & Bosola]*.

Ferd. Her guilt treads on
Hot burning cultures: Now *Bosola*,
How thrives our intelligence?   70

Bos. (Sir) uncertainly—
'Tis rumour'd she hath had three bastards, but
By whom, we may go read i'th'Starres.

Ferd. Why some
Hold opinion, all things are written there.

Bos. Yes, if we could find Spectacles to read them—
I do suspect, there hath bin some Sorcery
Us'd on the Duchesse.

Ferd. Sorcery?—to what purpose?

Bos. To make her doate on some desertles fellow,   80
She shames to acknowledge.

Ferd. Can your faith give way
To thinke there's powre in potions, or in Charmes,
To make us love, whether we will or no?

Bos. Most certainely.

Ferd. Away, these are meere gulleries, horred things
Invented by some cheating mounte-banckes

To abuse us: Do you thinke that hearbes, or charmes
Can force the will? Some trialls have bin made
90 In this foolish practise; but the ingredients
Were lenative poysons, such as are of force
To make the patient mad; and straight the witch
Sweares (by equivocation) they are in love.
The witch-craft lies in her rancke b[l]ood: this night
I will force confession from her: You told me
You had got (within these two dayes) a false key
Into her Bed-chamber.
          Bos. I have.
          Ferd. As I would wish.
100   Bos. What doe you intend to doe?
          Ferd. Can you ghesse?
          Bos. No:
          Ferd. Doe not aske then:
He that can compasse me, and know my drifts,
May say he hath put a girdle 'bout the world,
And sounded all her quick-sands.
          Bos. I doe not
Thinke so.
          Ferd. What doe you thinke then, pray?
110   Bos. That you
Are your owne Chronicle too much: and grosly
Flatter your selfe.
          Ferd. Give me thy hand, I thanke thee:
I never gave Pention but to flatterers,
Till I entertained thee: farewell,
That Friend a Great mans ruine strongely checks,
Who railes into his beliefe, all his defects.   *Exeunt*

SCENA II.

[The Bed-chamber of the Duchess.]

[Enter Duchess, Antonio, & Cariola.]

          Dutch. Bring me the Casket hither, and the Glasse;
You get no lodging here, to-night (my Lord.)
          Ant. Indeed, I must perswade one:
          Duch. Very good!

I hope in time 'twill grow into a custome,
That Noblemen shall come with cap, and knee,
To purchase a nights lodging, of their wives.

    ANT. I must lye here.

    DUTCH. Must? you are a Lord of Misse-rule.

    ANT. Indeed, my Rule is onely in the night.   10

    DUTCH. To what use will you put me?—

    ANT. Wee'll sleepe together:

    DUTCH. Alas, what pleasure can two Lovers find in sleepe?

    CAR. My Lord, I lye with her often: and I know
She'll much disquiet you:

    ANT. See, you are complain'd of.

    CAR. For she's the sprawlingst bedfellow.

    ANT. I shall like her the better for that

    CAR. Sir, shall I aske you a question?

    ANT. I pray thee *Cariola*.   20

    CAR. Wherefore still when you lie with my Lady
Doe you rise so early?

    ANT. Labouring men
Count the Clocke oftnest *Cariola*,
Are glad when their task's ended.

    DUCH. I'll stop your mouth.   [*kisses him.*]

    ANT. Nay, that's but one, *Venus* had two soft Doves
To draw her Chariot: I must have another: [*kisses her.*]
When wilt thou marry, *Cariola*?

    CAR. Never (my Lord.)   30

    ANT. O fie upon this single life: forgoe it:
We read how *Daphne*, for her peevish [f]light
Became a fruitlesse Bay-tree: *Siri[n]x* turn'd
To the pale empty Reede: *Anaxar[e]te*
Was frozen into Marble: whereas those
Which married, or prov'd kind unto their friends
Were, by a gracious influence, transhap'd
Into the Oliffe, Pomgranet, Mulbery:
Became Flowres, precious Stones, or eminent Starres.

    CAR. This is a vaine Poetry: but I pray you tell me,   40
If there were propos'd me, Wisdome, Riches, and Beauty,
In three severall young men, which should I choose?

    ANT. 'Tis a hard question: This was *Paris*' case
And he was blind in't, and there was great cause:

For how was't possible he could judge right,
Having three amorous Goddesses in view,
And they starcke naked? 'twas a Motion
Were able to be-night the apprehention
Of the seveerest Counsellor of Europe.
50 Now I looke on both your faces, so well form'd,
It puts me in mind of a question, I would aske.
    CAR. What is't?
    ANT. I doe wonder why hard-favour'd Ladies
For the most part, keepe worse-favour'd waieting women,
To attend them, and cannot endure faire-ones.
    DUCH. Oh, that's soone answer'd.
Did you ever in your life know an ill Painter
Desire to have his dwelling next doore to the shop
Of an excellent Picture-maker? 'twould disgrace
60 His face-making, and undoe him: I pre-thee
When were we so merry? my haire tangles.
    ANT. 'Pray-thee (*Cariola*) let's steale forth the roome,
And let her talke to her selfe: I have divers times
Serv'd her the like—when she hath chafde extreamely:
I love to see her angry: softly *Cariola. Exeunt* [*Antonio & Cariola*].
    DUCH. Doth not the colour of my haire 'gin to change?
When I waxe gray, I shall have all the Court
Powder their haire, with Arras, to be like me:
You have cause to love me, I entred you into my heart   [*Enter*
70 Before you would vouchsafe to call for the keyes.   *Ferdinand*
We shall one day have my brothers take you napping: *unseen.*]
Me thinkes his Presence (being now in Court)
Should make you keepe your owne Bed: but you'll say
Love mixt with feare, is sweetest: I'll assure you
You shall get no more children till my brothers
Consent to be your Ghossips: have you lost your tongue? [*She*
'Tis welcome: *turns & sees Ferdinand.*]
For know whether I am doomb'd to live, or die,
I can doe both like a Prince.   *Ferdinand gives*
80   FERD. Die then, quickle: *her a ponyard.*
Vertue, where art thou hid? what hideous thing
Is it, that doth ecclipze thee?
    DUCH. 'Pray sir heare me:
    FERD. Or is it true, thou art but a bare name,

And no essentiall thing?
    DUCH. Sir!
    FERD. Doe not speake.
    DUCH. No sir:
I will plant my soule in mine eares, to heare you.
    FERD. Oh most imperfect light of humaine reason,   90
That mak'st [us] so unhappy, to foresee
What we can least prevent: Pursue thy wishes:
And glory in them: there's in shame no comfort,
But to be past all bounds, and sence of shame.
    DUCH. I pray sir, heare me: I am married—
    FERD. So!
    DUCH. Happily, not to your liking: but for that
Alas: your sheeres doe come untimely now
To clip the birds wings, that's already flowne:
Will you see my Husband?   100
    FERD. Yes, if I could change
Eyes with a Basilisque:
    DUCH. Sure, you came hither
By his con[fe]deracy.
    FERD. The howling of a Wolfe
Is musicke to the[e] (schrech-Owle) pre'thee peace:
What ere thou art, that hast enjoy'd my sister,
(For I am sure thou hearst me) for thine owne sake
Let me not know thee: I came hither, prepar'd
To worke thy discovery: yet am now perswaded   110
It would beget such violent effects
As would damp[n]e us both: I would not for ten Millions
I had beheld thee: therefore use all meanes
I never may have knowledge of thy name;
Enjoy thy lust still, and a wret[c]hed life,
On that condition: And for thee (vilde woman,)
If thou doe wish thy Leacher may grow old
In thy Embracements, I would have thee build
Such a roome for him, as our Anchorites
To holier use enhabite: Let not the Sunne   120
Shine on him, till he's dead: Let Dogs, and Monkeys
Onely converse with him, and such dombe things
To whom Nature denies use to sound his name.
Doe not keepe a Paraqueto, least she learne it;

If thou doe love him, cut out thine owne tongue
Least it bewray him.
    DUCH. Why might not I marry?
I have not gone about, in this, to create
Any new world, or custome.
130   FERD. Thou art undone:
And thou hast ta'ne that massiy sheete of lead
That hid thy husbands bones, and foulded it
About my heart.
    DUTCH. Mine bleedes for't.
    FERD. Thine? thy heart?
What should I nam't, unlesse a hollow bullet
Fill'd with unquenchable wild-fire?
    DUTCH. You are, in this
Too strict: and were you not my Princely brother
140   I would say to[o] wilfull: My reputation
Is safe.
    FERD. Dost thou know what reputation is?
I'll tell thee—to small purpose, since th'instruction
Comes now too late:
Upon a time Reputation, Love, and Death,
Would travell ore the world: and [i]t was concluded
That they should part, and take three severall wayes:
Death told them, they should find him in great Battailes:
Or Cities plagu'd with plagues: Love gives them councell
150   To enquire for him 'mongst unambitious shepheards,
Where dowries were not talk'd of: and sometimes
'Mongst quiet kindred, that had nothing left
By their dead Parents: stay (quoth Reputation)
Doe not forsake me: for it is my nature
If once I part from any man I meete,
I am never found againe: And so, for you:
You have [shooke] hands with Reputation,
And made him invisible: So fare you well.
I will never see you more.
160   DUTCH. Why should onely I,
Of all the other Princes of the World
Be cas'de-up, like a holy Relique? I have youth,
And a litle beautie.
    FERD. So you have some Virgins,

That are Witches: I will never see thee more.   *Exit. Enter*
                Antonio with a Pistoll, [*& Cariola.*]

DUTCH. You saw this apparition?

ANT. Yes: we are
Betraid; how came he hither? I should turne   [*he points the*
This, to thee, for that.   *pistol at Cariola.*]

CAR. Pray sir doe: and when   170
That you have cleft my heart, you shall read there,
Mine innocence:

DUTCH. That Gallery gave him entrance.

ANT. I would this terrible thing would come againe,
That (standing on my Guard) I might relate
My warrantable love: ha, what meanes this?

DUTCH. He left this with me: *she shewes the*

ANT. And it seemes, did wish   *poniard.*
You would use it on your selfe?

DUTCH. His Action seem'd   180
To intend so much.

ANT. This hath a handle to't,
As well as a point—turne it towards him, and
So fasten the keene edge, in his rancke gall: [*Knocking within.*]
How now? who knocks? more Earthquakes?

DUTCH. I stand
As if a Myne, beneath my feete, were ready
To be blowne up.

CAR. 'Tis *Bosola*:

DUTCH. Away!—   190
Oh misery, me thinkes unjust actions
Should weare these masques, and curtaines; and not we:
You must instantly part hence: I have fashion'd it already.
                 Ex. Ant. [*Enter Bosola.*]

BOS. The Duke your brother is ta'ne up in a whirlewind—
Hath tooke horse, and's rid poast to Rome.

DUTCH. So late?

BOS. He told me, (as he mounted into th'sadle,)
You were undone.

DUTCH. Indeed, I am very neere it.

BOS. What's the matter?   200

DUTCH. *Antonio*, the master of our house-hold
Hath dealt so falsely with me, in's accounts:

My brother stood engag'd with me for money
Ta'ne up of certaine Neopolitane Jewes,
And *Antonio* lets the Bonds be forfeyt.

BOS. S[t]range: [*aside*] this is cunning:

DUTCH. And hereupon
My brothers Bills at Naples are protested
Against: call up our Officers.

210 BOS. I shall.   *Exit.* [*Enter Antonio.*]

DUTCH. The place that you must flye to, is *Ancona*—
Hire a house there. I'll send after you
My Treasure, and my Jew[e]lls: our weake safetie
Runnes upon engenous wheeles: short sillables,
Must stand for periods: I must now accuse you
Of such a fained crime, as *Tasso* calls
Magnanima Mensogna: a Noble Lie,
'Cause it must shield our honors: harke they are comming.
                    [*Enter Bosola & Officers.*]

ANT. Will your Grace heare me?

220 DUTCH. I have got well by you: you have yeelded me
A million of losse; I am like to inherit
The peoples curses for your Stewardship:
You had the tricke, in Audit time to be sicke,
Till I had sign'd your *Quietus*; and that cur'de you
Without helpe of a Doctor. Gentlemen,
I would have this man be an example to you all:
So shall you hold my favour: I pray let him;
For h'as done that (alas) you would not thinke of,
And (because I intend to be rid of him)

230 I meane not to publish: use your fortune else-where.

ANT. I am strongly arm'd to brooke my over-throw,
As commonly men beare with a hard yeere:
I will not blame the cause on't; but doe thinke
The necessitie of my malevolent starre
Procures this, not her humour: O the inconstant,
And rotten ground of service, you may see:
'Tis ev'n like him, that in a winter night
Takes a long slumber, ore a dying fire;
[As] loth to part from't: yet parts thence as cold,

240 As when he first sat downe.

DUTCH. We doe confi[s]cate

(Towards the satisfying of your accounts)
All that you have.

   ANT. I am all yours: and 'tis very fit
All mine should be so.

   DUTCH. So, sir; you have your Passe.

   ANT. You may see (Gentlemen) what 'tis to serve
A Prince with body, and soule.   *Exit.*

   BOS. Heere's an example, for extortion; what moysture is
drawne out of the Sea, when fowle weather comes, powres downe, 250
and runnes into the Sea againe.

   DUTCH. I would know what are your opinions
Of this *Antonio.*

   2. OFFI. He could not abide to see a Pigges head gaping—
I thought your Grace would finde him a Jew:

   3. OFFI. I would you had bin his Officer, for your owne
sake.

   4. OFFI. You would have had more money.

   1. OFFI. He stop'd his eares with blacke wooll: and (to those
came to him for money) said he was thicke of hearing.   260

   2. OFFI. Some said he was an hermophrodite, for he could
not abide a woman.

   4. OFFI. How scurvy prowd he would looke, when the
Treasury was full: Well, let him goe:

   1. OFFI. Yes, and the chippings of the Buttrey fly after
him, to scowre his gold Chaine.

   DUTCH. Leave us: what doe you thinke of these?   *Exeunt*

   BOS. That these are Rogues; that in's prosperitie, [*Officers*].
But to have waited on his fortune, could have wish'd
His durty Stirrop rivited through their noses: 270
And follow'd after's Mule, like a Beare in a Ring.
Would have prostituted their daughters, to his Lust:
Made their first-borne ∧ Intelligencers: thought none happy
But such as were borne under his bless'd Plannet
And wore his Livory: and doe these Lyce drop off now?
Well, never looke to have the like againe;
He hath left a sort of flattring rogues behind him,
Their doombe must follow: Princes pay flatterers,
In their owne money: Flatterers dissemble their vices,
And they dissemble their lies, that's Justice: 280
Alas, poore gentleman!—

DUCH. Poore! he hath amply fill'd his cofers.

BOS. Sure he was too honest: *Pluto* the god of riches,
When he's sent (by *Jupiter*) to any man
He goes limping, to signifie that wealth
That comes on god's name, comes slowly, but when he's sent
[On] the divells arrand, he rides poast, and comes in by scuttles:
Let me shew you, what a most unvalu'd jewell,
You have (in a wanton humour) throwne away,
290 To blesse the man shall find him: He was an excellent
Courtier, and most faithfull, a souldier, that thought it
As beastly to know his owne value too little,
As devillish to acknowledge it too much,
Both his vertue, and forme, deserv'd a farre better fortune:
His discourse rather delighted to judge it selfe, then shew it selfe.
His breast was fill'd with all perfection,
And yet it seem'd a private whispring roome.
It made so little noyse of't.

DUCH. But he was basely descended.

300   BOS. Will you make your selfe a mercinary herald,
Rather to examine mens pedegrees, then vertues?
You shall want him,
For know an honest states-man to a Prince,
Is like a Cedar, planted by a Spring,
The Spring bathes the trees roote, the gratefull tree
Rewards it with his shadow: you have not done so—
I would sooner swim to the *Bermoothes* on
Two Politisians' rotten bladders, tide
Together with an Intelligencers hart-string
310 Then depend on so changeable a Princes favour.
Fare-thee-well (*Antonio*) since the mallice of the world
Would needes downe with thee, it cannot be sayd yet
That any ill happened unto thee,
Considering thy fall was accompanied with vertue.

DUCH. Oh, you render me excellent Musicke.

BOS. Say you?

DUCH. This good one that you speake of, is my husband.

BOS. Do I not dreame? can this ambitious age
Have so much goodnes in't, as to prefer
320 A man, meerely for worth: without these shadowes
Of wealth and painted honors? possible?

DUCH. I have had three children by him.

BOS. Fortunate Lady,

For you have made your private nuptiall bed
The humble, and faire Seminary of peace,
No question but: many an unbenific'd Scholler
Shall pray for you, for this deed, and rejoyce
That some preferment in the world can yet
Arise from merit. The virgins of your land
(That have no dowries) shall hope your example   330
Will raise them to rich husbands: Should you want
Souldiers 'twould make the very *Turkes* and *Moores*
Turne Christians, and serve you for this act.
Last, the neglected Poets of your time,
In honour of this trophee of a man,
Rais'd by that curious engine, (your white hand)
Shall thanke you, in your grave, for't; and make that
More reverend then all the Cabinets
Of living Princes: For *Antonio*—
His fame shall likewise flow from many a pen,   340
When Heralds shall want coates, to sell to men.

DUCH. As I taste comfort, in this friendly speech,
So would I finde concealement.

BOS. O the secret of my Prince,
Which I will weare on th'in-side of my heart.

DUCH. You shall take charge of all my coyne, and jewels,
And follow him, for he retires himselfe
To *Ancona*.

BOS. So.

DUCH. Whither, within few dayes,   350
I meane to follow thee.

BOS. Let me thinke:
I would wish your Grace, to faigne a Pilgrimage
To our Lady of *Loretto*, (scarce seaven leagues
From faire *Ancona*)—so may you depart
Your Country, with more honour, and your flight
Will seeme a Princely progresse, retaining
Your usuall traine about you.

DUCH. Sir, your direction
Shall lead me, by the hand.   360

CAR. In my opinion,

She were better progresse to the bathes at *Leuca*,
Or go visit the *Spaw*
In *Germany*, for (if you will beleeve me)
I do not like this jesting with religion,
This faigned Pilgrimage.
    Duch. Thou art a superstitious foole,
Prepare us instantly for our departure:
Past sorrowes, let us moderately lament them,
370 For those to come, seeke wisely, to prevent them. *Exit* [*Duchess,*
    Bos. A Polititian is the divells quilted anvell,   *with*
He fashions all sinnes on him, and the blowes   *Cariola*].
Are never heard—he may worke in a Ladies Chamber,
(As here for proofe)—what rests, but I reveale
All to my Lord? oh, this base quality
Of Intelligencer! why, every Quality i'th'world
Preferres but gaine, or commendation:
Now for this act, I am certaine to be rais'd,
"And men that paint weedes, (to the life) are prais'd.   *Exit.*

SCENA III.

[Rome. The Cardinal's Palace.]

[Enter] Cardinall, Ferdinand, Mallateste, Pescara, Silvio, Delio.

    Card. Must we turne Souldier then?
    Mal. The Emperour,
Hearing your worth that way, (ere you attain'd
This reverend garment,) joynes you in commission
With the right fortunate souldier, the Marquis of *Pescara*,
And the famous *Lanoy*.
    Card. He that had the honour
Of taking the *French* King Prisoner?
    Mal. The same—
10 Here's a plot drawne, for a new Fortification,
At *Naples*.
    Ferd. This great Count *Mala*[*teste*], I perceive
Hath got employment?
    Del. No employment (my Lord)—
A marginall note in the muster-booke, that he is
A voluntary Lord.

FERD. He's no Souldier?

DEL. He has worne gun-powder, in's hollow tooth,
For the tooth-ache.

SIL. He comes to the leaguer, with a full intent,   20
To eate fresh beefe, and garlicke, meanes to stay
Till the sent be gon, and straight returne to Court.

DEL. He hath read all the late service,
As the City Chronicle relates it,
And keepe[s] two [Painters] going, onely to expresse
Battailes in modell.

SIL. Then he'l fight by the booke.

DEL. By the Almanacke, I thinke,
To choose good dayes, and shun the Criticall.
That's his mistris' skarfe.   30

SIL. Yes, he protests
He would do much for that taffita—

DEL. I thinke he would run away from a battaile
To save it from taking prisoner.

SIL. He is horribly afraid,
Gun-powder will spoile the perfume on't—

DEL. I saw a Duch-man breake his pate once
For calling him pot-gun—he made his head
Have a boare in't, like a musket.

SIL. I would he had made a touch-hole to't.   40
He is indeede a guarded sumpter-cloath
Onely for the remoove of the Court.   [*Enter Bosola.*]

PES. *Bosola* arriv'd? what should be the businesse?
Some falling out amongst the Cardinalls.
These factions amongst great men, they are like
Foxes—when their heads are devided
They carry fire in their tailes, and all the Country
About them, goes to wracke for't.

SIL. What's that *Bosola*?

DEL. I knew him in *Padua*, a fantasticall scholler,   50
Like such, who studdy to know how many knots
Was in *Hercules* club, of what colour *Achilles* beard was,
Or whether *Hector* were not troubled with the tooth-ach—
He hath studdied himselfe halfe bleare-ei'd, to know
The true semitry of *Cæsars* nose by a shooing-horne,
And this he did

To gaine the name of a speculative man.
    PES. Marke Prince *Ferdinand*,
A very *Salamander* lives in's eye,
60 To mocke the eager violence of fire.
     SIL. That Cardinall hath made more bad faces with his op-
      pression
Then ever *Michael Angelo* made good ones,
He lifts up's nose, like a fowle Por-pisse before
A storme—
    PES. The Lord *Ferdinand* laughes.
    DEL. Like a deadly Cannon,
That lightens ere it smoakes.
    PES. These are your true pangues of death,
The pangues of life, that strugle with great states-men—
70 DEL. In such a deformed silence, witches whisper
Their charmes.
    CARD. Doth she make religion her riding hood
To keepe her from the sun, and tempest?
     FERD. That: that damnes her: Me thinkes her fault, and
      beauty
Blended together, shew like leaprosie—
The whiter, the fowler: I make it a question
Whether her beggerly brats were ever christned.
    CARD. I will instantly sollicite the state of *Ancona*
To have them banish'd.
80   FERD. You are for *Loretto*?
I shall not be at your Ceremony: fare you well,
Write to the Duke of *Malfy*, my yong Nephew,
She had by her first husband, and acquaint him,
With's mothers honesty.
    BOS. I will.
    FERD. *Antonio!*
A slave, that onely smell'd of yncke, and coumpters,
And nev'r in's lirfje, look'd like a Gentleman,
But in the audit time—go, go presently,
90 Draw me out an hundreth and fifty of our horse,
And meete me at the fort-bridge.   *Exeunt.*

SCENA IIII.

[*Loretto.*]

[Enter] Two Pilgrimes to the Shrine of our Lady of Loretto.

1. PILG. I have not seene a goodlier Shrine then this,
Yet I have visited many.
2. PILG. The Cardinall of *Arragon*
Is, this day, to resigne his Cardinals hat,
His sister Duchesse likewise is arriv'd
To pay her vow of Pilgrimage—I expect
A noble Ceremony.
1. PILG. No question:——They come.

Here the Ceremony of the Cardinalls enstalment, in the habit
[of] a Souldier: perform'd in delivering up his Crosse, Hat,
Robes, and Ring, at the Shrine; and investing him with
Sword, Helmet, Sheild, and Spurs: Then Antonio, *the*
Duchesse, *and their Children, (having presented themselves*
at the Shrine) are (by a forme of Banishment in dumbe-shew,
expressed towards them by the Cardinall, and the State of
Ancona) *banished: During all which Ceremony, this Ditty*
is sung (to very sollemne Musique) by divers Church-men;
and then Exeunt.

Armes, and Honors, decke thy story,
To thy Fames eternall glory,　　　　　　　　　　　　10
Adverse Fortune ever flie-thee,　　　The Au-
No disastrous fate come nigh-thee.　　thor dis-
　　　　　　　　　　　　　　　　　claimes
I alone will sing thy praises,　　　　this Ditty
Whom to honour vertue raises;　　　to be his.
And thy study, that divine-is,
Bent to Marshiall discipline-is:
Lay aside all those robes lie by thee,
Crown thy arts, with armes: they'll beutifie thee.

O worthy of worthiest name, adorn'd in this manner,
Lead bravely thy forces on, under wars warlike banner:　　20
O mayst thou prove fortunate, in all Marshiall courses,
Guide thou still, by skill, in artes, and forces:

Victory attend thee nigh, whilst fame sings loud thy powres,
Triumphant conquest crowne thy head, and blessings powre
    downe showres.

    1. PILG. Here's a strange turne of state—who would have
        thought
So great a Lady, would have match'd her selfe
Unto so meane a person? yet the Cardinall
Beares himselfe much too cruell.
    2. PILG. They are banish'd.
30   1. PILG. But I would aske what power hath this state
Of *Ancona*, to determine of a free Prince?
    2. PILG. They are a free state sir, and her brother shew'd
How that the Pope fore-hearing of her loosenesse,
Hath seaz'd into th'protection of the Church
The Dukedome, which she held as dowager.
    1. PIL. But by what justice?
    2. PILG. Sure I thinke by none,
Only her brothers instigation.
    1. PILG. What was it, with such violence he tooke
40 Of[f] from her finger?
    2. PIL. 'Twas her wedding ring,
Which he vow'd shortly he would sacrifice
To his revenge.
    1. PILG. Alasse *Antonio*,
If that a man be thrust into a well,
No matter who sets hand to't, his owne weight
Will bring him sooner to th'bottome: Come, let's hence.
Fortune makes this conclusion generall,
"All things do helpe th'unhappy man to fall.   *Exeunt.*

SCENA V.

[Near Loretto.]

[*Enter*] *Antonio, Duchesse, Children, Cariola, Servants.*

    DUCH. Banish'd *Ancona*!
    ANT. Yes, you see what powre
Lightens in great mens breath.
    DUCH. Is all our traine
Shrunke to this poore remainder?

ANT. These poore men,
(Which have got little in your service) vow
To take your fortune: But your wiser buntings
Now they are fledg'd, are gon.
　　DUCH. They have done wisely——　　　　　　　　10
This puts me in minde of death, Physitians thus,
With their hands full of money, use to give ore
Their Patients.
　　ANT. Right the fashion of the world——
From decaide fortunes, every flatterer shrinkes,
Men cease to build, where the foundation sinkes.
　　DUCH. I had a very strange dreame to-night.
　　ANT. What was't?
　　DUCH. Me thought I wore my Coronet of State,
And on a sudaine all the Diamonds　　　　　　　20
Were chang'd to Pearles.
　　ANT. My Interpretation
Is, you'll weepe shortly, for to me, the pearles
Doe signifie your teares:
　　DUTCH. The Birds, that live i'th field
On the wilde benefit of Nature, live
Happier then we; for they may choose their Mates,
And carroll their sweet pleasures to the Spring:　　[Enter Bosola
　　BOS. You are happily ore-ta'ne.　　　　　　　with a letter.]
　　DUCH. From my brother?　　　　　　　　　　30
　　BOS. Yes, from the Lord *Ferdinand*...your brother,
All love, and safetie——
　　DUTCH. Thou do'st blanch mischiefe——
Wouldst make it white: See, see; like to calme weather
At Sea, before a tempest, false hearts speake faire
To those they intend most mischiefe.
　　　　[*Reads*] A Letter.
Send Antonio *to me; I want his head in a busines:*
A politicke equivocation——
He doth not want your councell, but your head;
That is, he cannot sleepe till you be dead.　　　　40
And here's annother Pitfall, that's strew'd ore
With Roses: marke it, 'tis a cunning one.
I stand ingaged for your husband, for severall debts at Naples: *let
not that trouble him, I had rather have his heart, then his mony.*

And I beleeve so too.

    Bos. What doe you beleeve?

    Dutch. That he so much distrusts my husbands love,
He will by no meanes beleeve his heart is with him
Untill he see it: The Divell is not cunning enough
50 To circumvent us in Ridles.

    Bos. Will you reject that noble, and free league
Of amitie, and love which I present you?

    Dutch. Their league is like that of some politick Kings
Onely to make themselves of strength, and powre
To be our after-ruine: tell them so;

    Bos. And what from you?

    Ant. Thus tell him: I will not come.

    Bos. And what of this?

    Ant. My brothers have dispers'd
60 Blood-hounds abroad; which till I heare are muzell'd,
No truce, though hatch'd with nere such politick skill
Is safe, that hangs upon our enemies will.
I'll not come at them.

    Bos. This proclaimes your breeding.
Every small thing drawes a base mind to feare:
As the Adamant drawes yron: fare you well sir,
You shall shortly heare from's.   *Exit.*

    Dutch. I suspect some Ambush:
Therefore by all my love...I doe conjure you
70 To take your eldest sonne, and flye towards *Millaine*;
Let us not venture all this poore remainder
In one unlucky bottom.

    Ant. You councell safely:
Best of my life, farewell: Since we must part,
Heaven hath a hand in't: but no otherwise,
Then as some curious Artist takes in sunder
A Clocke, or Watch, when it is out of frame
To bring't in better order.

    Dutch. I know not which is best,
80 To see you dead, or part with you: Farewell Boy.
Thou art happy, that thou hast not understanding
To know thy misery: For all our wit
And reading, brings us to a truer sence
Of sorrow: In the eternall Church, Sir,

I doe hope we shall not part thus.

ANT. Oh, be of comfort,
Make Patience a noble fortitude:
And thinke not how unkindly we are us'de:
"Man (like to *Cassia*) is prov'd best, being bruiz'd.

DUTCH. Must I like to a slave-borne Russian, 90
Account it praise to suffer tyranny?
And yet (O Heaven) thy heavy hand is in't.
I have seene my litle boy oft scourge his top,
And compar'd my selfe to't: naught made me ere
Go right, but Heavens scourge-sticke.

ANT. Doe not weepe:
Heaven fashion'd us of nothing: and we strive,
To bring our selves to nothing: farewell *Cariola*,
And thy sweet armefull: if I doe never see thee more,
Be a good Mother to your litle ones, 100
And save them from the Tiger: fare you well.

DUCH. Let me looke upon you once more: for that speech
Came from a dying father: your kisse is colder
Then that I have seene an holy Anchorite
Give to a dead mans skull.

ANT. My heart is turnde to a heavy lumpe of lead,
With which I sound my danger: fare you well. *Exit,* [with son.]

DUCH. My Laurell is all withered.

CAR. Looke (Madam) what a troope of armed men
Make toward us. *Enter Bosola with a Guard,* [with Vizards.] 110

DUCH. O, they are very welcome:
When Fortunes wheele is over-charg'd with Princes,
The waight makes it move swift. I wo[u]ld have my ruine
Be sudden: I am your adventure, am I not?

BOS. You are, you must see your husband no more—

DUCH. What Divell art thou, that counterfeits heavens
    thunder?

BOS. Is that terrible? I would have you tell me whether
Is that note worse, that frights the silly birds
Out of the corne; or that which doth allure them
To the nets? you have hearkned to the last too much. 120

DUCH. O misery: like to a rusty ore-char[g]'d Cannon,
Shall I never flye in peeces? come: to what Prison?

BOS. To none:

DUCH. Wh[i]ther then?

BOS. To your Pallace.

DUCH. I have heard that *Charons* boate serves to convay
All ore the dismall Lake, but brings none backe againe.

BOS. Your brothers meane you safety, and pitie.

DUTCH. Pitie!

130 With such a pitie men preserve alive
Pheasants, and Quailes, when they are not fat enough
To be eaten.

BOS. These are your children?

DUTCH. Yes:

BOS. Can they pratle?

DUTCH. No:
But I intend, since they were borne accurs'd;
Cursses shall be their first language.

BOS. Fye (Madam)

140 Forget this base, low-fellow.

DUTCH. Were I a man:
I'll'd beat that counterfeit face, into thy other—

BOS. One of no Birth.

DUTCH. Say that he was borne meane...
Man is most happy, when's owne actions
Be arguments, and examples of his Vertue.

BOS. A barren, beggerly vertue.

DUTCH. I pre-thee who is greatest, can you tell?
Sad tales befit my woe: I'll tell you one.

150 A Salmon, as she swam unto the Sea,
Met with a Dog-fish; who encounters her
With this rough language: why art thou so bold
To mixe thy selfe with our high state of floods
Being no eminent Courtier, but one
That for the calmest, and fresh time o'th' yeere
Do'st live in shallow Rivers, rank'st thy selfe
With silly Smylts, and Shrympes? and darest thou
Passe by our Dog-ship, without reverence?
O (Quoth the Salmon) sister, be at peace:

160 Thanke *Jupiter*, we both have pass'd the Net—
Our value never can be truely knowne,
Till in the Fishers basket we be showne,
I'th' Market then my price may be the higher,

Even when I am neerest to the Cooke, and fire.
So, to Great men, the Morrall may be stretched.
"Men oft are valued high, when th'are most wretch[e]d.
But come: wh[i]ther you please: I am arm'd 'gainst misery:
Bent to all swaies of the Oppressors will.
There's no deepe Valley, but neere some great Hill.   Ex.

ACTUS IIII. SCENA I.

[*Amalfi. The Palace of the Duchess.*]

[*Enter Ferdinand & Bosola.*]

FERD. How doth our sister Dutchesse beare her selfe
In her imprisonment?
    Bos. Nobly: I'll describe her:
She's sad, as one long us'd to't: and she seemes
Rather to welcome the end of misery
Then shun it: a behaviour so noble,
As gives a majestie to adversitie:
You may discerne the shape of lovelinesse
More perfect, in her teares, then in her smiles;
She will muse foure houres together: and her silence,   10
(Me thinkes) expresseth more, then if she spake.
    FERD. Her mellancholly seemes to be fortifide
With a strange disdaine.
    Bos. 'Tis so: and this restraint
(Like English Mastiffes, that grow feirce with tying)
Makes her too passionately apprehend
Those pleasures she's kept from.
    FERD. Curse upon her!
I will no longer study in the booke
Of anothers heart: informe her what I told you. *Exit.* [*Enter*   20
    Bos. All comfort to your Grace;   *Duchess & Attendants.*]
    DUTCH. I will have none:
'Pray-thee, why do'st thou wrap thy poysond Pilles
In Gold, and Sugar?
    Bos. Your elder brother the Lord *Ferdinand*
Is come to visite you: and sends you word,
'Cause once he rashly made a solemne vowe

Never to see you more; he comes i'th' night:
And prayes you (gently) neither Torch, nor Taper
30 Shine in your Chamber: he will kisse your hand:
And reconcile himselfe: but, for his vowe,
He dares not see you:
    DUCH. At his pleasure:
Take hence the lights: he's come. [*Exeunt Servants with lights;*
FERD. Where are you? DUTCH. Here sir: *enter Ferd.*]
FERD. This darkenes suites you well.
    DUTCH. I would aske you pardon:
    FERD. You have it;
For I account it the honorabl'st revenge
40 Where I may kill, to pardon: where are your Cubbs?
    DUCH. Whom! FERD. Call them your children;
For though our nationall law distinguish Bastards
From true legitimate issue: compassionate nature
Makes them all equall.
    DUCH. Doe you visit me for this?
You violate a Sacrament o'th' Church
Shall make you howle in hell for't.
    FERD. It had bin well,
Could you have liv'd thus alwayes: for indeed
50 You were too much i'th' light: But no more—
I come to seale my peace with you: here's a hand,   *gives her*
To which you have vow'd much love: the Ring upon't   *a dead*
You gave.   *mans*
    DUCH. I affectionately kisse it: *hand.*
    FERD. 'Pray doe: and bury the print of it in your heart:
I will leave this Ring with you, for a Love-token:
And the hand, as sure as the ring: and doe not doubt
But you shall have the heart too: when you need a friend,
Send it to him, that ow'de it: you shall see
60 Whether he can ayd you.
    DUTCH. You are very cold.
I feare you are not well after your travell:
Hah? lights: oh horrible!
    FERD. Let her have lights enough.   *Exit.* [*Re-enter*
                                     Servants with lights.]
    DUTCH. What witch-craft doth he practise, that he hath left
A dead-mans hand here?————*Here is discover'd, (behind a*

Travers;) the artificiall figures of Antonio, *and his children; appearing as if they were dead.*

Bos. Looke you: here's the peece, from which 'twas ta'ne;
He doth present you this sad spectacle,
That now you know directly they are dead,
Hereafter you may (wisely) cease to grieve   70
For that which cannot be recovered.

Duch. There is not betweene heaven, and earth one wish
I stay for after this: it wastes me more,
Then were't my picture, fashion'd out of wax,
Stucke with a magicall needle, and then buried
In some fowle dung-hill: and yond's an excellent property
For a tyrant, which I would account mercy—

Bos. What's that?

Dutch. If they would bind me to that liveles truncke,
And let me freeze to death.   80

Bos. Come, you must live.

Dutch. That's the greatest torture soules feele in hell,
In hell: that they must live, and cannot die:
Portia, I'll new kindle thy Coales againe,
And revive the rare, and almost dead example
Of a loving wife.

Bos. O fye: despaire? remember
You are a Christian.

Dutch. The Church enjoynes fasting:
I'll starve my selfe to death.   90

Bos. Leave this vaine sorrow;
Things being at the worst, begin to mend: the Bee
When he hath shot his sting into your hand
May then play with your eye-lyd.

Dutch. Good comfortable fellow
Perswade a wretch that's broke upon the wheele
To have all his bones new set: entreate him live,
To be executed againe: who must dispatch me?
I account this world a tedious Theatre,
For I doe play a part in't 'gainst my will.   100

Bos. Come, be of comfort, I will save your life.

Dutch. Indeed I have not leysure to tend so small a busines.

Bos. Now, by my life, I pitty you.

Dutch. Thou art a foole then,

To wast thy pitty on a thing so wretch'd
As cannot pitty it[self]: I am full of daggers:
Puffe: let me blow these vipers from me.
What are you?   [*she turns suddenly to a Servant.*]
    SER. One that wishes you long life.
110   DUCH. I would thou wert hang'd for the horrible curse
Thou hast given me: I shall shortly grow one
Of the miracles of pitty: I'll goe pray: No,
I'll goe curse:
    BOS. Oh fye!
    DUTCH. I could curse the Starres.
    BOS. Oh fearefull!
    DUTCH. And those three smyling seasons of the yeere
Into a Russian winter: nay the world
To its first Chaos.
120   BOS. Looke you, the Starres shine still:
    DUTCH. Oh, but you must remember, my curse hath a great
        way to goe:
Plagues, (that make lanes through largest families)
Consume them!
    BOS. Fye Lady!
    DUTCH. Let them like tyrants
Never be remembred, but for the ill they have done:
Let all the zealous prayers of mortefied
Church-men forget them—
    BOS. O uncharitable!
130   DUTCH. Let heaven, a little while, cease crowning Martirs
To punish them:
Goe, howle them this: and say I long to bleed—
"It is some mercy, when men kill with speed.
               Exit, [*with Servants: re-enter Ferdinand.*]
    FERD. Excellent; as I would wish: she's plagu'd in Art.
These presentations are but fram'd in wax,
By the curious Master in that Qualitie,
Vincentio Lauriola, and she takes them
For true substantiall Bodies.
    BOS. Why doe you doe this?
140   FERD. To bring her to despaire.
    BOS. 'Faith, end here:
And go no farther in your cruelty—

Send her a penetentiall garment, to put on,
Next to her delicate skinne, and furnish her
With beades, and prayer bookes.
    FERD. Damne her, that body of hers,
While that my blood ran pure in't, was more worth
Then that which thou wouldst comfort, (call'd a soule)—
I will send her masques of common Curtizans,
Have her meate serv'd up by baudes, and ruffians,   150
And ('cause she'll needes be mad) I am resolv'd
To remove forth the common Hospitall
All the mad-folke, and place them neere her lodging:
There let them practise together, sing, and daunce,
And act their gambols to the full o'th'moone:
If she can sleepe the better for it, let her,
Your worke is almost ended.
    BOS. Must I see her againe?
    FERD. Yes.   BOS. Never.
    FERD. You must.   160
    BOS. Never in mine owne shape,
That's forfeited, by my intelligence,
And this last cruell lie: when you send me next,
The businesse shalbe comfort.
    FERD. Very likely!—
Thy pity is nothing of kin to thee: *Antonio*
Lurkes about *Millaine*, thou shalt shortly thither,
To feede a fire, as great as my revenge,
Which nev'r will slacke, till it have spent his fuell—
"Intemperate agues, make Physitians cruell.   *Exeunt.*   170

SCENA II.

[The Same.]

[Enter Duchess & Cariola.]

    DUCH. What hideous noyse was that?
    CARI. 'Tis the wild consort
Of Mad-men (Lady) which your Tyrant brother
Hath plac'd about your lodging: This tyranny,
I thinke was never practis'd till this howre.
    DUCH. Indeed I thanke him: nothing but noyce, and folly

Can keepe me in my right wits, whereas reason
And silence, make me starke mad: Sit downe,
Discourse to me some dismall Tragedy.
10 CARI. O 'twill encrease your mellancholly.
  DUCH. Thou art deceiv'd,
To heare of greater griefe, would lessen mine—
This is a prison? CARI. Yes, but you shall live
To shake this durance off. DUCH. Thou art a foole,
The Robin red-brest, and the Nightingale,
Never live long in cages. CARI. Pray drie your eyes.
What thinke you of, Madam? DUCH. Of nothing:
When I muse thus, I sleepe.
  CARI. Like a mad-man, with your eyes open?
20 DUCH. Do'st thou thinke we shall know one another,
In th'other world? CARI. Yes, out of question.
  DUCH. O that it were possible we might
But hold some two dayes conference with the dead,
From them, I should learne somewhat, I am sure
I never shall know here: I'll tell thee a miracle—
I am not mad yet, to my cause of sorrow.
Th'heaven ore my head, seemes made of molt[e]n brasse,
The earth of flaming sulphure, yet I am not mad:
I am acquainted with sad misery,
30 As the tan'd galley-slave is with his Oare,
Necessity makes me suffer constantly,
And custome makes it easie—who do I looke like now?
  CARI. Like to your picture in the gallery,
A deale of life in shew, but none in practise:
Or rather like some reverend monument
Whose ruines are even pittied. DUCH. Very proper:
And Fortune seemes onely to have her eie-sight,
To behold my Tragedy:
How now, what noyce is that?   [Enter Servant.
40 SERVANT. I am come to tell you,
Your brother hath entended you some sport:
A great Physitian, when the Pope was sicke
Of a deepe mellancholly, presented him
With severall sorts of mad-men, which wilde object
(Being full of change, and sport,) forc'd him to laugh,
And so th'impost-hume broke: the selfe same cure,

The Duke intends on you.

    DUCH. Let them come in.

    SER. There's a mad Lawyer, and a secular Priest,
A Doctor that hath forfeited his wits   50
By jealousie: an Astrologian,
That in his workes, sayd such a day o'th'moneth
Should be the day of doome; and fayling of't,
Ran mad: an English Taylor, crais'd i'th'braine,
With the studdy of new fashion: a gentleman usher
Quite beside himselfe, with care to keepe in minde,
The number of his Ladies salutations,
Or "how do you", she employ'd him in each morning:
A Farmer too, (an excellent knave in graine)
Mad, 'cause he was hindred transportation,   60
And let one Broaker (that's mad) loose to these,
You'ld thinke the divell were among them.

    DUCH. Sit *Cariola*: let them loose when you please,
For I am chain'd to endure all your tyranny.   [*Enter Madmen.*]

> *Here (by a Mad-man) this song is sung, to a dismall
> kind of Musique.*
>
> *O let us howle, some heavy note,*
>   *some deadly-dogged howle,*
> *Sounding, as from the threatning throat,*
>   *of beastes, and fatall fowle,*
> *As Ravens, Schrich-owles, Bulls, and Beares,*
>   *We'll b[e]ll, and bawle our parts,*   70
> *Till yerk-some noyce have cloy'd your eares,*
>   *and corasiv'd your hearts.*
> *At last when as our quire wants breath,*
>   *our bodies being blest,*
> *We'll sing like Swans, to welcome death,*
>   *and die in love and rest.*

    1. MAD-MAN. [*Astrologer.*] Doomes-day not come yet? I'll
draw it neerer by a perspective, or make a glasse, that shall set
all the world on fire upon an instant: I cannot sleepe, my pillow
is stuff't with a littour of Porcupines.   80

    2. MAD. [*Lawyer.*] Hell is a meere glasse-house, where the
divells are continually blowing up womens soules, on hollow
yrons, and the fire never goes out.

3. MAD. [*Priest.*] I will lie with every woman in my parish the tenth night: I will tithe them over, like hay-cockes.

4. MAD. [*Doctor.*] Shall my Pothecary out-go me, because I am a Cuck-old? I have found out his roguery: he makes allom of his wives urin, and sells it to Puritaines, that have sore throates with over-strayning.

90   1. MAD. I have skill in Harroldry.

2. Hast?

1. You do give for your creast a wood-cockes head, with the Braines pickt out on't, you are a very ancient Gentleman.

3. Greeke is turn'd Turke, we are onely to be sav'd by the Helvetian translation.

1. Come on Sir, I will lay the law to you.

2. Oh, rather lay a corazive—the law will eate to the bone.

3. He that drinkes but to satisfie nature is damn'd.

4. If I had my glasse here, I would shew a sight should make
100 all the women here call me mad Doctor.

1. What's he, a rope-maker?   [*pointing at the Priest.*]

2. No, no, no, a snufling knave, that while he shewes the tombes, will have his hand in a wenches placket.

3. Woe to the Caroach, that brought home my wife from the Masque, at three a clocke in the morning, it had a large Feather-bed in it.

4. I have paired the divells nayles forty times, roasted them in Ravens egges, and cur'd agues with them.

3. Get me three hundred milch bats, to make possets, to
110 procure sleepe.

4. All the Colledge may throw their caps at me, I have made a Soape-boyler costive, it was my master-peece:——*Here the Daunce consisting of* 8. *Mad-men, with musicke answerable thereunto, after which,* Bosola (*like an old man*) *enters.*

DUCH. Is he mad to[o]?

SER. 'Pray question him: I'll leave you. [*Exeunt Servant &*

BOS. I am come to make thy tombe.   *Madmen.*]

DUCH. Hah, my tombe?
Thou speak'st, as if I lay upon my death bed,
Gasping for breath: do'st thou perceive me sicke?

BOS. Yes, and the more dangerously, since thy sicknesse is
120 insensible.

DUCH. Thou art not mad sure, do'st know me?

Bos. Yes.   Duch. Who am I?

Bos. Thou art a box of worme-seede, at best, but a salvatory
of greene mummey: what's this flesh? a little cruded milke,
phantasticall puffe-paste: our bodies are weaker then those paper
prisons boyes use to keepe flies in: more contemptible: since ours
is to preserve earth-wormes: didst thou ever see a Larke in a
cage? such is the soule in the body: this world is like her little
turfe of grasse, and the Heaven ore our heades, like her looking
glasse, onely gives us a miserable knowledge of the small com- 130
passe of our prison.

Duch. Am not I, thy Duchesse?

Bos. Thou art some great woman sure, for riot begins to sit
on thy fore-head (clad in gray haires) twenty yeares sooner, then
on a merry milkemaydes. Thou sleep'st worse, then if a mouse
should be forc'd to take up her lodging in a cats eare: a little
infant, that breedes it's teeth, should it lie with thee, would crie
out, as if thou wert the more unquiet bed-fellow.

Duch. I am Duchesse of *Malfy* still.

Bos. That makes thy sleepes so broken: 140
"Glories (like glowe-wormes) afarre off, shine bright,
But look'd to neere, have neither heate, nor light.

Duch. Thou art very plaine.

Bos. My trade is to flatter the dead, not the living—
I am a tombe-maker.

Duch. And thou com'st to make my tombe?

Bos. Yes.

Duch. Let me be a little merry—
Of what stuffe wilt thou make it?

Bos. Nay, resolve me first, of what fashion?   150

Duch. Why, do we grow phantasticall in our death-bed?
Do we affect fashion in the grave?

Bos. Most ambitiously: Princes images on their tombes
Do not lie, as they were wont, seeming to pray
Up to heaven: but with their hands under their cheekes,
(As if they died of the tooth-ache)—they are not carved
With their eies fix'd upon the starres; but as
Their mindes were wholy bent upon the world,
The selfe-same way they seeme to turne their faces.

Duch. Let me know fully therefore the effect   160
Of this thy dismall preparation,

This talke, fit for a charnell?

Bos. Now, I shall——   [*Enter Executioners with*]
Here is a present from your Princely brothers,   *a Coffin,*
And may it arrive wel-come, for it brings   *Cords, and*
Last benefit, last sorrow.   *a Bell.*

Duch. Let me see it——
I have so much obedience, in my blood,
I wish it in ther veines, to do them good.

170   Bos. This is your last presence Chamber.

Cari. O my sweete Lady.

Duch. Peace, it affrights not me.

Bos. I am the common Bell-man,   [*Takes up the Bell.*]
That usually is sent to condemn'd persons
The night before they suffer:

Duch. Even now thou said'st,
Thou wast a tombe-maker?

Bos. 'Twas to bring you
By degrees to mortification: Listen.   [*Rings his bell.*]

180 *Hearke, now every thing is still——*
The Schritch-Owle, and the whistler shrill,
Call upon our Dame, aloud,
And bid her quickly don her shrowd:
Much you had of Land and rent,
Your length in clay's now competent.
A long war disturb'd your minde,
Here your perfect peace is sign'd——
Of what is't fooles make such vaine keeping?
Sin their conception, their birth, weeping:
190 *Their life, a generall mist of error,*
Their death, a hideous storme of terror——
Strew your haire, with powders sweete:
Don cleane linnen, bath your feete,
And (the foule feend more to checke)
A crucifixe let blesse your necke,
'Tis now full tide, 'tweene night, and day,
End your groane, and come away.

Cari. Hence villaines, tyrants, murderers: alas!
What will you do with my Lady? call for helpe.

200   Duch. To whom, to our next neighbours? they are mad-
folkes.

Bos. Remoove that noyse.

Duch. Farwell *Cariola*,
In my last will, I have not much to give—
A many hungry guests have fed upon me,
Thine will be a poore reversion.

Cari. I will die with her.

Duch. I pray-thee looke thou giv'st my little boy
Some sirrop, for his cold, and let the girle
Say her prayers, ere she sleepe. Now what you please, [*Cariola*
What death?   *is forced off.*] 210

Bos. Strangling, here are your Executioners.

Duch. I forgive them:
The apoplexie, cathar, or cough o'th'loongs,
Would do as much as they do.

Bos. Doth not death fright you?

Duch. Who would be afraid on't?
Knowing to meete such excellent company
In th'other world.

Bos. Yet, me thinkes,
The manner of your death should much afflict you,   220
This cord should terrifie you? Duch. Not a whit—
What would it pleasure me, to have my throate cut
With diamonds? or to be smothered
With Cassia? or to be shot to death, with pearles?
I know death hath ten thousand severall doores
For men, to take their *Exits*: and 'tis found
They go on such strange geometricall hinges,
You may open them both wayes: any way, (for heaven sake)
So I were out of your whispering: Tell my brothers,
That I perceive death, (now I am well awake)   230
Best guift is, they can give, or I can take—
I would faine put off my last womans-fault,
I'ld not be tedious to you.

Exec. We are ready.

Duch. Dispose my breath, how please you, but my body
Bestow upon my women, will you? Exec. Yes.

Duch. Pull, and pull strongly, for your able strength,
Must pull downe heaven upon me:
Yet stay, heaven gates are not so highly arch'd
As Princes pallaces—they that enter there   240

Must go upon their knees: Come violent death,   *[She kneels.]*
Serve for *Mandragora*, to make me sleepe;
Go tell my brothers, when I am laid out,   *They*
They then may feede in quiet.   *strangle her.*
    Bos. Where's the waiting woman?
Fetch her: Some other strangle the children: *[Re-enter Execu-*
Looke you, there sleepes your mistris.   *tioner with Cariola.]*
    CARI. Oh you are damn'd
Perpetually for this: My turne is next,
250 Is't not so ordered? Bos. Yes, and I am glad
You are so well prepar'd for't.
    CARI. You are deceiv'd Sir,
I am not prepar'd for't, I will not die,
I will first come to my answere; and know
How I have offended. Bos. Come, dispatch her:
You kept her counsell, now you shall keepe ours.
    CARI. I will not die, I must not, I am contracted
To a young Gentle-man.
    EXEC. Here's your wedding Ring.
260   CAR. Let me but speake with the Duke: I'll discover
Treason to his person.
    Bos. Delayes: throttle-her.
    EXEC. She bites: and scratches:
    CAR. If you kill me now
I am damn'd: I have not bin at Confession
This two yeeres: Bos. When!
    CAR. I am quicke with child.
    Bos. Why then,
Your credit's sav'd: beare her into th' next roome:
    [They strangle her, and bear her away. Enter Ferdinand.]
270 Let this lie still. FERD. Is she dead?
    Bos. Shee is what
You'll'd have her: But here begin your pitty—   *Shewes the*
Alas, how have these offended?   *children strangled.*
    FERD. The death
Of young Wolffes, is never to be pittied.
    Bos. Fix your eye here: FERD. Constantly.
    Bos. Doe you not weepe?
Other sinnes onely speake; Murther shreikes out:
The Element of water moistens the Earth,

But blood flies upwards, and bedewes the Heavens. 280
    FERD. Cover her face: Mine eyes dazell: she di'd yong.
    BOS. I thinke not so: her infelicitie
Seem'd to have yeeres too many.
    FERD. She, and I were Twinnes:
And should I die this instant, I had liv'd
Her Time to a Mynute.
    BOS. It seemes she was borne first:
You have bloodely approv'd the auncient truth,
That kindred commonly doe worse ag[r]ee
Then remote strangers. 290
    FERD. Let me see her face againe;
Why didst not thou pitty her? what an excellent
Honest man might'st thou have bin
If thou hadst borne her to some Sanctuary!
Or (bold in a good cause) oppos'd thy selfe
With thy advanced sword above thy head,
Betweene her Innocence, and my Revenge!
I bad thee, when I was distracted of my wits,
Goe kill my dearest friend, and thou hast don't.
For let me but examine well the cause; 300
What was the meanenes of her match to me?
Onely I must confesse, I had a hope
(Had she continu'd widow) to have gain'd
An infinite masse of Treasure by her death:
And that was the mayne cause; her Marriage—
That drew a streame of gall quite through my heart;
For thee, (as we observe in Tragedies
That a good Actor many times is curss'd
For playing a villaines part) I hate thee for't:
And (for my sake) say thou hast done much ill, well: 310
    BOS. Let me quicken your memory: for I perceive
You are falling into ingratitude: I challenge
The reward due to my service.
    FERD. I'll tell thee,
What I'll give thee— BOS. Doe:
    FERD. I'll give thee a pardon
For this murther:
    BOS. Hah? FERD. Yes: and 'tis
The largest bounty I can studie to doe thee.

320 By what authority did'st thou execute
    This bloody sentence? Bos. By yours—
        Ferd. Mine? was I her Judge?
    Did any ceremoniall forme of Law,
    Doombe her to not-Being? did a compleat Jury
    Deliver her conviction up i'th Court?
    Where shalt thou find this [j]udgement registerd
    Unlesse in hell? See: like a bloody foole
    Th'hast forfeyted thy life, and thou shalt die for't.
        Bos. The Office of Justice is perverted quite
330 When one Thiefe hangs another: who shall dare
    To reveale this? Ferd. Oh, I'll tell thee:
    The Wolfe shall finde her Grave, and scrape it up:
    Not to devoure the corpes, but to discover
    The horrid murther.
        Bos. You; not I, shall quake for't.
        Ferd. Leave me:
        Bos. I will first receive my Pention.
        Ferd. You are a villaine:
        Bos. When your Ingratitude
340 Is Judge, I am so. Ferd; O horror!
    That not the feare of him, which bindes the divels
    Can prescribe man obedience.
    Never looke upon me more. Bos. Why fare thee well:
    Your brother, and your selfe, are worthy men;
    You have a paire of hearts, are hollow Graves,
    Rotten, and rotting others: and your vengeance,
    (Like two chain'd bullets) still goes arme in arme—
    You may be Brothers: for treason, like the plague,
    Doth take much in a blood: I stand like one
350 That long hath ta'ne a sweet, and golden dreame.
    I am angry with my selfe, now that I wake.
        Ferd. Get thee into some unknowne part o'th' world
    That I may never see thee. Bos. Let me know
    Wherefore I should be thus neglected? sir,
    I serv'd your tyranny: and rather strove,
    To satisfie your selfe, then all the world;
    And though I loath'd the evill, yet I lov'd
    You that did councell it: and rather sought
    To appeare a true servant, then an honest man.

FERD. I'll goe hunt the Badger, by Owle-light: 360
'Tis a deed of darkenesse.   *Exit.*
    BOS. He's much distracted: Off my painted honour!—
While with vaine hopes, our faculties we tyre,
We seeme to sweate in yce, and freeze in fire;
What would I doe, we[r]e this to doe againe?
I would not change my peace of conscience
For all the wealth of Europe: She stirres; here's life:
Returne (faire soule) from darkenes, and lead mine
Out of this sencible Hell: She's warme, she breathes:
Upon thy pale lips I will melt my heart   370
To store them with fresh colour: who's there?
Some cordiall drinke! Alas! I dare not call:
So, pitty would destroy pitty: her Eye opes,
And heaven in it seemes to ope, (that late was shut)
To take me up to mer[c]y.
    DUTCH. *Antonio.*
    BOS. Yes (Madam) he is living,
The dead bodies you saw, were but faign'd statues;
He's reconcil'd to your brothers: the Pope hath wrought
The attonement.   380
    DUTCH. Mercy!   *she dies.*
    BOS. Oh, she's gone againe: there the cords of life broake:
Oh sacred Innocence, that sweetely sleepes
On Turtles feathers: whil'st a guilty conscience
Is a blacke Register, wherein is writ
All our good deedes, and bad: a Perspective
That showes us hell; that we cannot be suffer'd
To doe good when we have a mind to it!
This is manly sorrow:
These teares, I am very certaine, never grew   390
In my Mothers Milke. My estate is suncke below
The degree of feare: where were these penitent fountaines,
While she was living?
Oh, they were frozen up: here is a sight
As direfull to my soule, as is the sword
Unto a wretch hath slaine his father: Come,
I'll beare thee hence,
And execute thy last will; that's deliver
Thy body to the reverend dispose

400 Of some good women: that the cruell tyrant
Shall not denie me: Then I'll poast to *Millaine*,
Where somewhat I will speedily enact
Worth my dejection.   *Exit* [*with the body*].

ACTUS V. SCENA I.

[*Milan.*]

[*Enter Antonio & Delio.*]

ANT. What thinke you of my hope of reconcilement
To the *Aragonian* brethren? DEL. I misdoubt it,
For though they have sent their letters of safe conduct
For your repaire to *Millaine*, they appeare
But Nets, to entrap you: The Marquis of *Pescara*
Under whom you hold certaine land in Cheit,
Much 'gainst his noble nature, hath bin mov'd
To ceize those lands, and some of his dependants
Are at this instant, making it their suit
10 To be invested in your Revenewes.
I cannot thinke, they meane well to your life,
That doe deprive you of your meanes of life,
Your living. ANT. You are still an heretique
To any safety, I can shape my selfe.
      DEL. Here comes the Marquis: I will make my selfe
Petitioner for some part of your land,
To know wh[i]ther it is flying. ANT. I pray doe.
                    [*Enter Pescara: Antonio withdraws.*]
      DEL. Sir, I have a suit to you. PESC. To me?
      DEL. An easie one:
20 There is the Cittadell of St. *Bennet*,
With some demeasnes, of late in the possession
Of *Antonio Bologna*—please you bestow them on me?
      PESC. You are my friend: But this is such a suit,
Nor fit for me to give, nor you to take.
      DEL. No sir?
      PESC. I will give you ample reason for't,
Soone in private: Here's the Cardinalls Mistris.   [*Enter Julia.*]
      JUL. My Lord, I am growne your poore Petitioner,
And should be an ill begger, had I not

A Great mans letter here, (the Cardinalls)   30
To Court you in my favour.   *[gives letter.]*
    P E S C. *[reads]* He entreates for you
The Cittadell of Saint *Bennet*, that belong'd
To the banish'd *Bologna*. J U L. Yes:
    P E S C. I could not have thought of a friend I could
Rather pleasure with it: 'tis yours:
    J U L. Sir, I thanke you:
And he shall know how doubly I am engag'd
Both in your guift, and speedinesse of giving,
Which makes your graunt, the greater.   *Exit.* 40
    A N T. *[aside]* How they fortefie
Themselves with my ruine! D E L. Sir: I am
Litle bound to you: P E S C. Why?
    D E L. Because you denide this suit, to me, and gav't
To such a creature.
    P E S C. Doe you know what it was?
It was *Antonios* land: not forfeyted
By course of lawe; but ravish'd from his throate
By the Cardinals entreaty: it were not fit
I should bestow so maine a peece of wrong   50
Upon my friend: 'tis a gratification
Onely due to a Strumpet: for it is injustice;
Shall I sprinckle the pure blood of Innocents
To make those followers, I call my friends
Looke ruddier upon me? I am glad
This land, (ta'ne from the owner by such wrong)
Returnes againe unto so fowle an use,
As Salary for his Lust. Learne, (good *Delio*)
To aske noble things of me, and you shall find
I'll be a noble giver. D E L. You instruct me well: 60
   A N T. *[aside]* Why, here's a man, now, would fright im-
            pudence
From sawciest Beggers.
    P E S C. Prince *Ferdinand's* come to *Millaine*
Sicke (as they give out) of an Appoplexie:
But some say, 'tis a frenzie; I am going
To visite him.   *Exit.*
    A N T. 'Tis a noble old fellow:
    D E L. What course doe you meane to take, *Antonio*?

ANT. This night, I meane to venture all my fortune
70 (Which is no more then a poore lingring life)
To the Cardinals worst of mallice: I have got
Private accesse to his chamber: and intend
To visit him, about the mid of night.
(As once his brother did our noble Dutchesse.)
It may be that the sudden apprehension
Of danger (for I'll goe in mine owne shape)
When he shall see it fraight with love, and dutie,
May draw the poyson out of him, and worke
A friendly reconcilement; if it faile...
80 Yet, it shall rid me of this infamous calling,
For better fall once, then be ever falling.
    DEL. I'll second you in all danger: and (how ere)
My life keepes rancke with yours.
    ANT. You are still my lov'd, and best friend.   *Exeunt.*

SCENA II.

[*Milan. The Palace of the Cardinal and Ferdinand.*]

[*Enter Pescara and Doctor.*]

PESC. Now Doctor; may I visit your Patient?
    DOCTOR. If't please your Lordship: but he's instantly
To take the ayre here in the Gallery,
By my direction.
    PESC. 'Pray-thee, what's his disease?
    DOC. A very pestilent disease (my Lord)
They call *Licanthropia.* PESC. What's that?
I need a Dictionary to't. DOC. I'll tell you:
In those that are possess'd with't there ore-flowes
10 Such mellencholy humour, they imagine
Themselves to be transformed into Woolves,
Steale forth to Church-yards in the dead of night,
And dig dead bodies up: as two nights since
One met the Duke, 'bout midnight in a lane
Behind St. *Markes* Church, with the leg of a man
Upon his shoulder; and he howl'd fearefully:
Said he was a Woolffe: onely the difference

Was, a Woolffes skinne was hairy on the out-side,
His on the In-side: bad them take their swords,
Rip up his flesh, and trie: straight I was sent for,   20
And having ministerd to him, found his Grace
Very well recovered. Pesc. I am glad on't.

Doc. Yet not without some feare
Of a relaps: if he grow to his fit againe,
I'll goe a neerer way to worke with him
Then ever *Parac[el]sus* dream'd of: If
They'll give me leave, I'll buffet his madnesse out of him.
Stand aside: he comes.

[*Enter Ferdinand, Malateste, Cardinal & Bosola.*]

Ferd. Leave me.

Mal. Why doth your Lordship love this solitarines?   30

Ferd. Eagles commonly fly alone: They are Crowes, Dawes,
and Sterlings that flocke together: Looke, what's that, followes
me? Mal. Nothing (my Lord).

Ferd. Yes: Mal. 'Tis your shadow.

Ferd. Stay it, let it not haunt me.

Mal. Impossible; if you move, and the Sun shine:

Ferd. I will throtle it.   [*Throws himself on the ground.*]

Mal. Oh, my Lord: you are angry with nothing.

Ferd. You are a foole: How is't possible I should catch my
shadow unlesse I fall upon't? When I goe to Hell, I meane to   40
carry a bribe: for looke you good guifts ever-more make way,
for the worst persons.

Pesc. Rise, good my Lord.

Ferd. I am studying the Art of Patience.

Pesc. 'Tis a noble Vertue;

Ferd. To drive six Snailes before me, from this towne to
Mosco; neither use Goad, nor Whip to them, but let them take
their owne time: (the patientst man i'th' world match me for
an experiment) and I'll crawle after like a sheepe-biter.

Card. Force him up.   50

Ferd. Use me well, you were best:
What I have don, I have don: I'll confesse nothing.

Doctor. Now let me come to him: Are you mad (my Lord?)
Are you out of your Princely wits?

Ferd. What's he? Pesc. Your Doctor.

FERD. Let me have his beard saw'd off, and his eye-browes
Fil'd more civill.

DOCT. I must do mad trickes with him,
For that's the onely way on't. I have brought
60 Your grace a Salamanders skin, to keepe you
From sun-burning.

FERD. I have cruell sore eyes.

DOCT. The white of a Cockatrixes-egge is present remedy.

FERD. Let it be a new-layd one, you were best:
Hide me from him: Phisitians are like Kings,
They brooke no contradiction.

DOCT. Now he begins
To feare me, now let me alone with him.   *[takes off his gown.]*

CARD. How now, put off your gowne?

70 DOCT. Let me have some forty urinalls fill'd with Rose-
water: He, and I'll go pelt one another with them—now he
begins to feare me: Can you fetch a friske, sir? Let him go, let
him go, upon my perrill: I finde by his eye, he stands in awe of
me, I'll make him—as tame as a Dormouse.

FERD. Can you fetch your friskes, sir? I will stamp him into
a Cullice: Flea off his skin, to cover one of the An[a]tomies, this
rogue hath set i'th'cold yonder, in Barber-Chyrurgeons hall:
Hence, hence, you are all of you, like beasts for sacrifice, *[Throws
the doctor down & beats him]* there's nothing left of you, but
80 tongue, and belly, flattery, and leachery.   *[Exit.]*

PES. Doctor, he did not feare you throughly.

DOCT. True, I was somewhat to[o] forward.

BOS. Mercy upon me, what a fatall judgement
Hath falne upon this *Ferdinand*!

PES. Knowes your grace
What accident hath brought unto the Prince
This strange distraction?

CARD. *[aside]* I must faigne somewhat: Thus they say it
    grew.
You have heard it rumor'd for these many yeares,
90 None of our family dies, but there is seene
The shape of an old woman, which is given
By tradition, to us, to have bin murther'd
By her Nephewes, for her riches: Such a figure
One night (as the Prince sat up late at's booke)

Appear'd to him—when crying out for helpe,
The gentlemen of's chamber, found his grace
All on a cold sweate, alter'd much in face
And language: Since which apparition,
He hath growne worse, and worse, and I much feare
He cannot live.   100
    Bos. Sir, I would speake with you.
    Pes. We'll leave your grace,
Wishing to the sicke Prince, our noble Lord,
All health of minde, and body.
    Card. You are most welcome:
                [*Exeunt. Manent Cardinal and Bosola.*]
Are you come? so: [*aside*] this fellow must not know
By any meanes I had intelligence
In our Duchesse death: For (though I counsell'd it,)
The full of all th'ingagement seem'd to grow
From *Ferdinand*: [*to Bosola*] Now sir, how fares our sister?   110
I do not thinke but sorrow makes her looke
Like to an oft-di'd garment: She shall now
Tast comfort from me: why do you looke so wildely?
Oh, the fortune of your master here, the Prince
Dejects you—but be you of happy comfort:
If you'll do on[e] thing for me I'll entreate,
Though he had a cold tombe-stone ore his bones,
[I'll] make you what you would be.
    Bos. Any thing—
Give it me in a breath, and let me flie to't: 120
They that thinke long, small expedition win,
For musing much o'th'end, cannot begin.   [*Enter Julia.*]
    Jul. Sir, will you come in to Supper?
    Card. I am busie, leave me.
    Jul. [*aside*] What an excellent shape hath that fellow! *Exit.*
    Card. 'Tis thus: *Antonio* lurkes here in *Millaine*,
Enquire him out, and kill him: while he lives,
Our sister cannot marry, and I have thought
Of an excellent match for her: do this, and stile me
Thy advancement.   130
    Bos. But by what meanes shall I find him out?
    Card. There is a gentleman, call'd *Delio*
Here in the Campe, that hath bin long approv'd

His loyall friend: Set eie upon that fellow,
Follow him to Masse—may be *Antonio*,
Although he do account religion
But a Schoole-name, for fashion of the world,
May accompany him—or else go enquire out
Delio's Confessor, and see if you can bribe
140 Him to reveale it: there are a thousand wayes
A man might find to trace him: As to know,
What fellowes haunt the Jewes, for taking up
Great summes of money, for sure he's in want,
Or else to go to th'Picture-makers, and learne
Who [bought] her Picture lately—some of these
Happily may take——
    Bos. Well, I'll not freeze i'th'businesse,
I would see that wretched thing, *Antonio*
Above all sightes i'th'world.
150   Card. Do, and be happy.   *Exit.*
    Bos. This fellow doth breed Bazalisques in's eies,
He's nothing else, but murder: yet he seemes
Not to have notice of the Duchesse death:
'Tis his cunning: I must follow his example,
There cannot be a surer way to trace,
Then that of an old Fox. [*Enter Julia, pointing a pistol at him.*]
    Jul. So, sir, you are well met. Bos. How now?
    Jul. Nay, the doores are fast enough:
Now, Sir, I will make you confesse your treachery.
160   Bos. Treachery? Jul. Yes, confesse to me
Which of my women 'twas you hyr'd, to put
Love-powder into my drinke?
    Bos. Love-powder?
    Jul. Yes, when I was at *Malfy*—
Why should I fall in love with such a face else?
I have already suffer'd for thee so much paine,
The onely remedy to do me good,
Is to kill my longing.
    Bos. Sure your Pistoll holds
170 Nothing but perfumes, or kissing comfits: excellent Lady,
You have a pritty way on't to discover
Your longing: Come, come, I'll disarme you,
And arme you thus—yet this is wondrous strange. [*Embraces her.*]

JUL. Compare thy forme, and my eyes together,
You'll find my love no such great miracle:
Now you'll say,
I am wanton: This nice modesty, in Ladies
Is but a troublesome familiar,
That haunts them.

BOS. Know you me, I am a blunt souldier. JUL. The better, 180
Sure, there wants fire, where there are no lively sparkes
Of roughnes. BOS. And I want complement.

JUL. Why, ignorance in court-ship cannot make you do amisse,
If you have a heart to do well.

BOS. You are very faire.

JUL. Nay, if you lay beauty to my charge,
I must plead unguilty. BOS. Your bright eyes
Carry a Quiver of darts in them, sharper
Then Sun-beames.

JUL. You will mar me with commendation,   190
Put your selfe to the charge of courting me,
Whereas now I wo[o] you.

BOS. [aside] I have it, I will worke upon this Creature—
Let us grow most amorously familiar:
If the great Cardinall now should see me thus,
Would he not count me a villaine?

JUL. No, he might count me a wanton,
Not lay a scruple of offence on you:
For if I see, and steale a Diamond,
The fault is not i'th'stone, but in me the thiefe,   200
That purloines it: I am sudaine with you—
We that are great women of pleasure, use to cut off
These uncertaine wishes, and unquiet longings,
And in an instant joyne the sweete delight
And the pritty excuse together: had you bin in'th'streete,
Under my chamber window, even there
I should have courted you.

BOS. Oh, you are an excellent Lady.

JUL. Bid me do somewhat for you presently,
To expresse I love you.   210

BOS. I will, and if you love me,
Faile not to effect it:
The Cardinall is growne wondrous mellancholly,

Demand the cause, let him not put you off,
With faign'd excuse, discover the maine ground on't.
  JUL. Why would you know this?
  Bos. I have depended on him,
And I heare that he is falne in some disgrace
With the Emperour—if he be, like the mice
220 That forsake falling houses, I would shift
To other dependance.
  JUL. You shall not neede follow the warres,
I'll be your maintenance.
  Bos. And I your loyall servant,
But I cannot leave my calling.
  JUL. Not leave an
Ungratefull Generall, for the love of a sweete Lady?
You are like some, cannot sleepe in feather-beds,
But must have blockes for their pillowes.
230   Bos. Will you do this? JUL. Cunningly.
  Bos. To-morrow I'll expect th'intelligence.
  JUL. To-morrow! get you into my Cabinet,
You shall have it with you: do not delay me,
No more then I do you: I am like one
That is condemn'd: I have my pardon promis'd.
But I would see it seal'd: Go, get you in,
You shall see me winde my tongue about his heart,
Like a skeine of silke.
                    [*Exit Bosola, into her cabinet. Enter Cardinal.*]
  CARD. Where are you? [*Enter Servants.*] SERV. Here.
240   CARD. Let none, upon your lives,
Have conference with the Prince *Ferdinand*,
Unlesse I know it: [*aside*] In this distraction   [*Exeunt Serv.*]
He may reveale the murther:
Yond's my lingring consumption:
I am weary of her; and by any meanes
Would be quit off. JUL. How now, my Lord?
What ailes you? CARD. Nothing.
  JUL. Oh, you are much alterd:
Come, I must be your Secretary, and remove
250 This lead from off your bosome, what's the matter?
  CARD. I may not tell you.
  JUL. Are you so farre in love with sorrow,

You cannot part with part of it? or thinke you
I cannot love your grace, when you are sad,
As well as merry? or do you suspect
I, that have bin a secret to your heart,
These many winters, cannot be the same
Unto your tongue?

    CARD. Satisfie thy longing,
The onely way to make thee keepe my councell,   260
Is not to tell thee. JUL. Tell your eccho this,
Or flatterers, that (like ecchoes) still report
What they heare (though most imperfect), and not me:
For, if that you be true unto your selfe,
I'll know. CARD. Will you racke me?

    JUL. No, judgement shall
Draw it from you: It is an equall fault,
To tell ones secrets, unto all, or none.

    CARD. The first argues folly.

    JUL. But the last tyranny.   270

    CARD. Very well; why, imagine I have committed
Some secret deed, which I desire the world
May never heare of.

    JUL. Therefore may not I know it?
You have conceal'd for me, as great a sinne
As adultery: Sir, never was occasion
For perfect triall of my constancy
Till now: Sir, I beseech you.

    CARD. You'll repent it. JUL. Never.

    CARD. It hurries thee to ruine: I'll not tell thee—   280
Be well advis'd, and thinke what danger 'tis
To receive a Princes secrets: they that do,
Had neede have their breasts hoop'd with adamant
To containe them: I pray thee yet be satisfi'd,
Examine thine owne frailety, 'tis more easie
To tie knots, then unloose them: 'tis a secret
That (like a lingring poyson) may chance lie
Spread in thy vaines, and kill thee seaven yeare hence.

    JUL. Now you dally with me.

    CARD. No more—thou shalt know it.   290
By my appointment, the great Duchesse of *Malfy*,
And two of her yong children, foure nights since

Were strangled.

    JUL. Oh heaven! (sir) what have you done?

    CARD. How now? how setles this? thinke you your bosome
Will be a grave, darke and obscure enough
For such a secret?

    JUL. You have undone your selfe (sir.)

    CARD. Why? JUL. It lies not in me to conceale it. CARD. No?

300 Come, I will sweare you to't upon this booke.

    JUL. Most religiously. CARD. Kisse it.
Now you shall never utter it, thy curiosity
Hath undone thee: thou'rt poyson'd with that booke—
Because I knew thou couldst not keepe my councell,
I have bound the[e] to't by death.   [*Enter Bosola.*]

    BOS. For pitty sake, hold. CARD. Ha, *Bosola?*

    JUL. I forgive you
This equall peece of Justice you have done:
For I betraid your councell to that fellow,
310 He overheard it; that was the cause I said
It lay not in me, to conceale it.

    BOS. Oh foolish woman,
Couldst not thou have poyson'd him?

    JUL. 'Tis weakenesse,
Too much to thinke what should have bin done—I go,
I know not wh[i]ther.   [*Dies.*]

    CARD. Wherefore com'st thou hither?

    BOS. That I might finde a great man, (like your selfe,)
Not out of his wits (as the Lord *Ferdinand*)
320 To remember my service.

    CARD. I'll have thee hew'd in peeces.

    BOS. Make not your selfe such a promise of that life
Which is not yours, to dispose of.

    CAR. Who plac'd thee here?

    BOS. Her lust, as she intended.

    CARD. Very well,
Now you know me for your fellow murderer.

    BOS. And wherefore should you lay faire marble colours,
Upon your rotten purposes to me?
330 Unlesse you imitate some that do plot great Treasons,
And when they have done, go hide themselves i'th'graves
Of those were Actors in't? CARD. No more,

There is a fortune attends thee.

Bos. Shall I go sue to fortune any longer?
'Tis the fooles Pilgrimage.

Card. I have honors in store for thee.

Bos. There are a many wayes that conduct to seeming
Honor, and some of them very durty ones.

Card. Throw to the divell
Thy mellancholly—the fire burnes well,   340
What neede we keepe a-stirring of't, and make
A greater smoother? thou wilt kill *Antonio*?

Bos. Yes. Card. Take up that body.

Bos. I thinke I shall
Shortly grow the common B[ie]re, for Church-yards?

Card. I will allow thee some dozen of attendants,
To aide thee in the murther.

Bos. Oh, by no meanes—Phisitians that apply horse-leiches
to any rancke swelling, use to cut of[f] their tailes, that the
blood may run through them the faster: Let me have no traine, 350
when I goe to shed blood, least it make me have a greater, when
I ride to the Gallowes.

Card. Come to me
After midnight, to helpe to remove that body
To her owne Lodging: I'll give out she dide o'th' Plague;
'Twill breed the lesse enquiry after her death.

Bos. Where's *Castruchio*, her husband?

Card. He's rod[e] to *Naples* to take possession
Of *Antonio's* Cittadell.

Bos. Beleeve me, you have done a very happy turne.   360

Card. Faile not to come: There is the Master-key
Of our Lodgings: and by that you may conceive
What trust I plant in you.

Bos. You shall find me ready.   *Exit* [*Cardinal*].
Oh poore *Antonio*, though nothing be so needfull
To thy estate, as pitty, Yet I finde
Nothing so dangerous: I must looke to my footing;
In such slippery yce-pavements, men had neede
To be frost-nayld well: they may breake their neckes else.
The Pre[ce]dent's here afore me: how this man   370
Beares up in blood!—seemes feareles!—why, 'tis well:
Securitie some men call the Suburbs of Hell,

Onely a dead wall betweene. Well (good *Antonio*)
I'll seeke thee out; and all my care shall be
To put thee into safety from the reach
Of these most cruell biters, that have got
Some of thy blood already. It may be,
I'll joyne with thee, in a most just revenge.
The weakest Arme is strong enough, that strikes
380 With the sword of Justice: Still me thinkes the Dutchesse
Haunts me: there, there!. . .'tis nothing but my mellancholy.
O Penitence, let me truely tast thy Cup,
That throwes men downe, onely to raise them up.   *Exit.*

SCENA III.

[*Milan. Part of the fortifications of the city.*]

[*Enter Antonio & Delio. There is an*] *Eccho, (from the*
Dutchesse Grave.)

DEL. Yond's the Cardinall's window: This fortification
Grew from the ruines of an auncient Abbey:
And to yond side o'th' river, lies a wall
(Peece of a Cloyster) which in my opinion
Gives the best Eccho, that you ever heard;
So hollow, and so dismall, and withall
So plaine in the destinction of our words,
That many have supposde it is a Spirit
That answeres.
10   ANT. I doe love these auncient ruynes:
We never tread upon them, but we set
Our foote upon some reverend History.
And questionles, here in this open Court
(Which now lies naked to the injuries
Of stormy weather) some men lye Enterr'd
Lov'd the Church so well, and gave so largely to't,
They thought it should have canopide their Bones
Till Doombes-day: But all things have their end:
Churches, and Citties (which have diseases like to men)
20 Must have like death that we have.
ECCHO. *Like death that we have.*
DEL. Now the *Echo* hath caught you:

ANT. It groan'd (me thought) and gave
A very deadly Accent?

ECCHO. *Deadly Accent.*

DEL. I told you 'twas a pretty one: You may make it
A Huntes-man, or a Faulconer, a Musitian,
Or a Thing of Sorrow.

ECCHO. *A Thing of Sorrow.*

ANT. I sure: that suites it best.

ECCHO. *That suites it best.*   30

ANT. 'Tis very like my wi[f]es voyce.

ECCHO. *I, wifes-voyce.*

DEL. Come: let's ∧ walke farther from't:
I would not have you go to th' *Cardinalls* to-night:
Doe not.

ECCHO. *Doe not.*

DEL. Wisdome doth not more moderate wasting Sorrow
Then time: take time for't: be mindfull of thy safety.

ECCHO. *Be mindfull of thy safety.*   40

ANT. Necessitie compells me:
Make scruteny throughout the pass[ag]es
Of your owne life; you'll find it impossible
To flye your fate.

[ECCHO.] *O flye your fate.*

DEL. Harke: the dead stones seeme to have pitty on you
And give you good counsell.

ANT. *Eccho*, I will not talke with thee;
For thou art a dead Thing.

ECCHO. *Thou art a dead Thing.*   50

ANT. My Dutchesse is asleepe now,
And her litle-Ones, I hope sweetly: oh Heaven
Shall I never see her more?

ECCHO. *Never see her more:*

ANT. I mark'd not one repetition of the *Eccho*
But that: and on the sudden, a cleare light
Presented me a face folded in sorrow.

DEL. Your fancy; meerely.

ANT. Come: I'll be out of this Ague;
For to live thus, is not indeed to live: 60
It is a mockery, and abuse of life—
I will not henceforth save my selfe by halves,

Loose all, or nothing.

DEL. Your owne vertue save you!
I'll fetch your eldest sonne; and second you:
It may be that the sight of his owne blood
Spred in so sweet a figure, may beget
The more compassion.

[ANT.] How ever, fare you well:
70 Though in our miseries, Fortune have a part,
Yet, in our noble suffrings, she hath none—
Contempt of paine, that we may call our owne.   *Exe.*

SCENA IIII.

[*Milan. The Palace of the Cardinal and Ferdinand.*]

[*Enter Cardinal, Pescara, Malateste, Roderigo, Grisolan.*]

CARD. You shall not watch to-night by the sicke Prince,
His Grace is very well recover'd.

MAL. Good my Lord suffer us.

CARD. Oh, by no meanes:
The noyce, and change of object in his eye,
Doth more distract him: I pray, all to bed,
And though you heare him in his violent fit,
Do not rise, I intreate you.

PES. So, sir; we shall not—
10 CARD. Nay, I must have you promise
Upon your honors, for I was enjoyn'd to't
By himselfe; and he seem'd to urge it sencibly.

PES. Let ou[r] honors bind this trifle.

CARD. Nor any of your followers.

MAL. Neither.

CARD. It may be, to make triall of your promise,
When he's asleepe, my selfe will rise, and faigne
Some of his mad trickes, and crie out for helpe,
And faigne my selfe in danger.

20 MAL. If your throate were cutting,
I'll'd not come at you, now I have protested against it.

CARD. Why, I thanke you.   [*withdraws a little.*]

GRIS. 'Twas a foule storme to-night.

ROD. The Lord *Ferdinand's* chamber shooke like an Ozier.

MAL. 'Twas nothing but pure kindnesse in the Divell,
To rocke his owne child.   *Exeunt, [except Cardinal.]*

CARD. The reason why I would not suffer these
About my brother, is, because at midnight
I may with better privacy, convay
Julias body to her owne Lodging: O, my Conscience!   30
I would pray now: but the Divell takes away my heart
For having any confidence in Praier.
About this houre, I appointed *Bosola*
To fetch the body: when he hath serv'd my turne,
He dies.   *Exit. [Enter Bosola.]*

BOS. Hah? 'twas the Cardinalls voyce: I heard him name,
Bosola, and my death: listen, I heare ones footing.   *[Enter*

FERD. Strangling is a very quie[t] death.   *Ferdinand.]*

BOS. Nay then I see, I must stand upon my Guard.

FERD. What say' to that? whisper, softly: doe you agree to't? 40
So—it must be done i'th' darke: the Cardinall
Would not for a thousand pounds, the Doctor should see it. *Exit.*

BOS. My death is plotted; here's the consequence of murther.
"We value not desert, nor Christian breath,
When we know blacke deedes must be cur'de with death.
     [Enter Antonio & Servant.]

SER. Here stay Sir, and be confident, I pray:
I'll fetch you a darke Lanthorne.   *Exit.*

ANT. Could I take him
At his prayers, there were hope of pardon.

BOS. Fall right my sword: *[Strikes him.]* 50
I'll not give thee so much leysure, as to pray.

ANT. Oh, I am gone: Thou hast ended a long suit,
In a mynut.

BOS. What art thou?

ANT. A most wretched thing,
That onely have thy benefit in death,
To appeare my selfe.   *[Re-enter Servant, with light.]*

SER. Where are you Sir?

ANT. Very neere my home: *Bosola?*

SER. Oh misfortune!   60

BOS. *[to the Servant]* Smother thy pitty, thou art dead else:
     Antonio?
The man I would have sav'de 'bove mine owne life!

We are meerely the Starres tennys-balls (strooke, and banded
Which way please them)—oh good *Antonio*,
I'll whisper one thing in thy dying eare,
Shall make thy heart breake quickly: Thy faire Dutchesse
And two sweet Children...
  A N T. Their very names
Kindle a litle life in me.
70 B o s. Are murderd!
  A N T. Some men have wish'd to die,
At the hearing of sad tydings: I am glad
That I shall do't in sadnes: I would not now
Wish my wounds balm'de, nor heal'd: for I have no use
To put my life to: In all our Quest of Greatnes...
(Like wanton Boyes, whose pastime is their care)
We follow after bubbles, blowne in th'ayre.
Pleasure of life, what is't? onely the good houres
Of an Ague: meerely a preparative to rest,
80 To endure vexation: I doe not aske
The processe of my death: onely commend me
To *Delio*.
  B o s. Breake heart!
  A N T. And let my Sonne, flie the Courts of Princes. [*Dies.*]
  B o s. Thou seem'st to have lov'd *Antonio*?
  S E R. I brought him hether,
To have reconcil'd him to the Cardinall.
  B o s. I doe not aske thee that:
Take him up, if thou tender thine owne life,
90 And beare him, where the Lady *Julia*
Was wont to lodge: Oh, my fate moves swift.
I have this Cardinall in the forge already,
Now I'll bring him to th'hammer: (O direfull misprision:)
I will not Imitate things glorious,
No more then base: I'll be mine owne example.
On, on: and looke thou represent, for silence,
The thing thou bear'st.   *Exeunt.*

SCENA V.

[*The same.*]

[*Enter*] *Cardinall* (*with a Booke*).

CARD. I am puzzell'd in a question about hell:
He saies, in hell, there's one materiall fire,
And yet it shall not burne all men alike.
Lay him by: How tedious is a guilty conscience!
When I looke into the Fish-ponds, in my Garden,
Me thinkes I see a thing, arm'd with a Rake
That seemes to strike at me:
　　　　　　　　[*Enter Bosola & Servant bearing Antonio's body.*]
Now? art thou come? thou look'st ghastly:
There sits in thy face, some great determination,
Mix'd with some feare.　　　　　　　　　　　　　　　　　10
　BOS. Thus it lightens into Action:
I am come to kill thee.
　CARD. Hah? helpe! our Guard!
　BOS. Thou art deceiv'd:
They are out of thy howling.
　CARD. Hold: and I will faithfully devide
Revenewes with thee.
　BOS. Thy prayers, and proffers
Are both unseasonable.
　CARD. Raise the Watch:　　　　　　　　　　　　　　　20
We are betraid.
　BOS. I have confinde your flight:
I'll suffer your retreyt to *Julias* Chamber,
But no further.
　CARD. Helpe: we are betraid!　[*Enter Malateste, Roderigo,*
　MAL. Listen:　　　　　　　　　*Pescara, Grisolan, above.*]
　CARD. My Dukedome, for rescew!
　ROD. Fye upon his counterfeyting!
　MAL. Why, 'tis not the Cardinall.
　ROD. Yes, yes, 'tis he:　　　　　　　　　　　　　　　30
But I'll see him hang'd, ere I'll goe downe to him.
　CARD. Here's a plot upon me, I am assaulted: I am lost,
Unlesse some rescew.
　GRIS. He doth this pretty well:

But it will not serve; to laugh me out of mine honour!

CARD. The sword's at my throat:

ROD. You would not bawle so lowd then.

MAL. Come, come: ⌈let⌉'s goe to bed: he told us thus much
　　aforehand.

PESC. He wish'd you should not come at him: but beleev't,

40 The accent of the voyce sounds not in jest.
I'll downe to him, howsoever, and with engines
Force ope the doores.　　　　　　　　　　　　[*Exit above.*]

ROD. Let's follow him aloofe,
And note how the Cardinall will laugh at him. [*Exeunt above.*]

BOS. There's for you first: 'cause you shall not unbarracade
The doore to let in rescew.　　　　*He kills the Servant.*

CARD. What cause hast thou
To pursue my life?

BOS. Looke there:

50 CARD. *Antonio?*

BOS. Slaine by my hand unwittingly:
Pray, and be sudden: when thou kill'dst thy sister,
Thou tookst from Justice her most equall ballance,
And left her naught but her sword.

CARD. O mercy!

BOS. Now it seemes thy Greatnes was onely outward:
For thou fall'st faster of thy selfe, then calamitie
Can drive thee: I'll not wast longer time: There. [*Wounds him.*]

CARD. Thou hast hurt me:

60 BOS. Againe:

CARD. Shall I die like a Levoret
Without any resistance? helpe, helpe, helpe:
I am slaine.　　　　　　　　　　　　　　[*Enter Ferdinand.*]

FERD. Th'allarum? give me a fresh horse:
Rally the vaunt-guard: or the day is lost:
Yeeld, yeeld: I give you the honour of Armes,
Shake my Sword over you—will you yeilde?

CARD. Helpe me, I am your brother.

FERD. The divell?

70 My brother fight upon the adverse party? *He wounds the Cardinall,*
There flies your ransome.　　　　*and (in the scuffle) gives*
　　　　　　　　　　　　　　　　Bosola his death wound.

CARD. Oh Justice:
I suffer now, for what hath former bin:

"Sorrow is held the eldest child of sin.

FERD. Now you're brave fellowes: *Cæsars* Fortune was
harder then *Pompeys*: *Cæsar* died in the armes of prosperity,
Pompey at the feete of disgrace: you both died in the field—
the paine's nothing: paine many times is taken away with the
apprehension of greater, (as the tooth-ache with the sight of a
Barbor, that comes to pull it out) there's Philosophy for you.   80

BOS. Now my revenge is perfect: sinke (thou maine cause
Of my undoing)—the last part of my life,
Hath done me best service.   *He kills Ferdinand.*

FERD. Give me some wet hay, I am broken-winded—
I do account this world but a dog-kennell:
I will vault credit, and affect high pleasures,
Beyond death.

BOS. He seemes to come to himselfe,
Now he's so neere the bottom.

FERD. My sister, oh! my sister, there's the cause on't.   90
"Whether we fall by ambition, blood, or lust,
"Like Diamonds, we are cut with our owne dust.   [*Dies.*]

CARD. Thou hast thy payment too.

BOS. Yes, I hold my weary soule in my teeth,
'Tis ready to part from me: I do glory
That thou, which stood'st like a huge Piramid
Begun upon a large, and ample base,
Shalt end in a little point, a kind of nothing.
                    [*Enter Pescara, Malateste, Roderigo & Grisolan.*]

PES. How now (my Lord?)

MAL. Oh sad disastre!   100

ROD. How comes this?

BOS. Revenge, for the Duchesse of *Malfy*, murdered
By th'*Aragonian* brethren: for *Antonio*,
Slaine by [t]his hand: for lustfull *Julia*,
Poyson'd by this man: and lastly, for my selfe,
(That was an Actor in the maine of all,
Much 'gainst mine owne good nature, yet i'th'end
Neglected.)

PES. How now (my Lord?)

CARD. Looke to my brother: 110
He gave us these large wounds, as we were strugling
Here i'th' rushes: And now, I pray, let me

Be layd by, and never thought of. [*Dies.*]

P es. How fatally (it seemes) he did withstand
His owne rescew!

M al. Thou wretched thing of blood,
How came *Antonio* by his death?

B os. In a mist: I know not how,
Such a mistake, as I have often seene
120 In a play: Oh, I am gone—
We are onely like dead wals, or vaulted graves,
That ruin'd, yeildes no eccho: Fare you well—
It may be paine: but no harme to me to die,
In so good a quarrell: Oh this gloomy world,
In what a shadow, or deepe pit of darknesse,
Doth (womanish, and fearefull) mankind live!
Let worthy mindes nere stagger in distrust
To suffer death, or shame, for what is just—
Mine is another voyage. [*Dies.*]
130 P es. The noble *Delio*, as I came to th'Pallace,
Told me of *Antonio's* being here, and shew'd me
A pritty gentleman his sonne and heire.

[*Enter Delio with Antonio's Son.*]

M al. Oh Sir, you come to[o] late.

D el. I heard so, and
Was arm'd for't ere I came: Let us make noble use
Of this great ruine; and joyne all our force
To establish this yong hopefull Gentleman
In's mothers right. These wretched eminent things
Leave no more fame behind 'em, then should one
140 Fall in a frost, and leave his print in snow—
As soone as the sun shines, it ever melts,
Both forme, and matter: I have ever thought
Nature doth nothing so great, for great men,
As when she's pleas'd to make them Lords of truth:
    "*Integrity of life, is fames best friend,*
    Which noblely (beyond Death) shall crowne the end.   Exeunt.

FIN IS.

COMMENTARY

THE DUCHESS OF MALFI

C = Crawford, *Collectanea*.
H.D.S. = H. Dugdale Sykes.

TITLE-PAGE

priuatly, at the Black-Friers: not "privately" in any modern sense. It is merely that Blackfriars was a "private" house as contrasted with "public" theatres like The Globe. It has been suggested by W. J. Lawrence that a "private house" was originally one where payment was made in advance, not at the door, in order to evade restrictions like those of the Act of Common Council of Dec. 6th 1574, where an exception is made in favour of "any plays, interludes, comedies, tragedies, or shows to be played in the private house, dwelling, or lodgings of any nobleman, citizen, or gentleman... *without public or common collection of money of the auditory*". (Cf. the performances of the modern Stage Society and others.) But in any case, if this distinction about the method of payment ever existed, it had ceased by the time Dekker wrote, in his *Gull's Horn-Book* (1609), "whether therefore the gatherers of the public *or private* Playhouses stand to receive the afternoon's rent". And it seems more probable that the private theatres of Blackfriars, Whitefriars, and St Paul's really owed their name to the fiction that the performances of the boy-companies who first played there, were mere rehearsals of the plays they were to act before the Queen; to "*a private view*" of which a select audience was thus admitted, but without any flying of flags or beating of drums through the streets. (Cf. J. Q. Adams, *Shakespearian Playhouses*, 93–4.)

At all events after 1608, when the Blackfriars Theatre was taken over from the Children of the Revels by R. Burbage as a winter-house for the King's Men, the distinction between public and private theatres became very shadowy: though there remained the important structural difference between the public playhouse, derived from the inn-yard, which was open to the sky and lit by daylight; and the private house, in origin a large room, which was roofed and artificially illuminated.

Kings Maiefties Seruants: see Chambers, *Eliz. Stage*, ii. 192 ff.
diuerfe things Printed...not...in the Prefentment. For "cuts" thus restored in the published text, cf. Jonson, *Ev. Man out of h. H.* (1600), advertised as "containing more than hath been publiquely spoken or acted"; Barnes, *Devil's Charter* (1607), "Corrected and

augmented". (See Chambers, *Eliz. Stage*, III. 192–3; where it is suggested that Q_2 of *Hamlet* was perhaps similarly enlarged.)

Hora: Horace, *Epistles*, I. 6. 67–8. The full sentence runs:

> Si quid novisti rectius istis,
> Candidus imperti: si non, his utere mecum.

"If you know wiser precepts than these of mine, be kind (*not* 'candid') and tell me them: if you know none, then practise mine with me."

As usual, Webster's application of his Latin tag is obscure in the extreme: the only possible meaning here seems to be—"If you know a better play, let's hear it; if not, hear mine". The inappropriateness of the quotation makes one suspect borrowing by Webster: and, sure enough, I have found the tag at the end of Dekker's *Lanthorn and Candle-light* (1609).

Nicholas Okes: see on *W.D.*, title-page.

John Waterson: bookseller 1620–? 1641: died 1656.

THE ACTORS NAMES

Where there are two names to a part, the first would appear to belong to the original performance. Ostler, at all events, died in Dec. 1614. We may suppose that there was a revival in 1617–8, to account for the topical allusion to the Concini murder, inserted in I. 1 (see on I. 1. 8 ff.); this might be the performance referred to, as if fairly recent, by Orazio Busino in Feb. 1618 (see p. 172). Then there seems to have been another revival after Burbage's replacement by Taylor in 1619; and it is probably to this last that the other names numbered "2", like Taylor, Robinson, and Benfeild belong. The same applies to Rice, who was one of the Lady Elizabeth's Men in 1611 and does not appear in any King's lists before 1620; and perhaps to Pollard, Sharpe and Tomson, who only appear in them about 1617. (See J. T. Murray, *Eng. Dram. Companies*, II. 147.)

J. Lowin (1576–1659 or 1669), whose portrait is in the Ashmolean at Oxford, is said to have acted Falstaff, Volpone, Sir Epicure Mammon, Melantius (in *The Maid's Tragedy*), and Hamlet; and as the original Henry VIII to have "had his instruction from Mr Shakespeare himself". He made money and became one of the two managers of the King's Men about 1623. But the Civil War brought him hard times. It was in vain that in 1648 he and J. Taylor attempted to revive acting at The Cockpit; after three or four days the players were seized by soldiers while acting *The Bloody Brother*, carried off to Hatton House, then a prison, and only released after being despoiled of their stage-clothes. In 1652 Fletcher's *Wild Goose Chase* was published in folio for his and Taylor's benefit. But the benefit was little or short-lived; for when the old man died as host of "The Three Pigeons" at Brentford, "his poverty was as great as his age".

R. Burbidge, son of James, the founder of the first Elizabethan public theatre, was born about 1565, and long before his death in 1619 had become the most distinguished actor of his day. An Elegy records some of his chief parts:

> No more young Hamlett, ould Heironymoe.
> Kind Leer, the greved Moore, and more beside
> That lived in him, have now for ever died.

Richard III and many of the chief parts in Jonson and Beaumont and Fletcher were also his: and a special link between him and Webster is perhaps to be found in the "Character of an Excellent Actor", printed in "Overbury's" *Characters*, 6th ed., 1615. For its allusion to his skill in painting makes it probable that Richard Burbage was the model; and its style, that Webster was the author. (See vol. IV., p. 57.)

J. Taylor (? 1586–? 1653) appears to have left the Prince's company for the King's Men in 1619, as successor to Burbage. He is said to have played Hamlet "incomparably well"; also Iago, Mosca (*Volpone*), Face (*The Alchemist*), and Truewit (*Epicoene*). Later we find him one of the two managers, with Lowin, of the King's Men. In the lean years of the Commonwealth he was one of the ten actors who tried to raise a little money by publishing the First Folio of Beaumont and Fletcher in 1647.

H. Cundaile or *Condell* is best known as one of the editors (1623) of the First Folio of Shakespeare, who had bequeathed him 26s. 8d. to buy a ring. He seems to have ceased acting in 1619; and died in 1627.

R. Robinson (d. 1648). Praised by Jonson in *The Devil is an Ass*, II. 3. for his skill in acting as a woman.

W. Ostler is mainly important for having opportunely died in 1614 and thereby disproved the older theories which assigned this play to 1617–8. He began as one of the child-actors of Q. Elizabeth's Chapel in 1601, taking women's parts; then married Hemmings's daughter Thomasine and was admitted to partnership in the Globe in 1611–2. He must have been about twenty-five at this time; making perhaps, still, a rather feminine young Antonio.

J. Underwood (? 1587–1624): a contemporary of Ostler's, having been likewise one of the Children of the Chapel in 1601.

N. Towley (d. June 1623).

DEDICATION

George Harding, thirteenth Baron Berkeley, was now twenty-two and took his M.A. at Oxford in this year. He had a family connection with the stage and with the King's Men in particular; for his mother's grandfather and father, the first and second Lords Hunsdon, held the office of Lord Chamberlain and were patrons of the most famous of Elizabethan companies, the Lord Chamberlain's Men, whom James I made the King's Majesty's Servants. Indeed it has been suggested that *A Midsummer Night's Dream* was written for the wedding of George Harding's parents (Chambers, *Eliz. Stage*, II. 194). Two years before, in 1621, Burton had brought to this youthful patron the sombre offering of *The Anatomy of Melancholy*, and was rewarded in 1630 with the living of Segrave in Leicestershire; in which year Massinger in his turn dedicated *The Renegado* to "George Harding, Baron Barkeley".

Knight...to...Prince Charles: *i.e.* he had been made a Knight of the Bath at the creation of the Prince on Nov. 3rd 1616.

3–5. *Sea...River, to guide.* Cf. *W.D.* I. 2. 342–3.

10. *Nobility...rellique.* Cf. Overbury, *Wife*, xx. 3: "Gentry is but a relique of time past". (H.D.S.)

12. *which*: *i.e.* a practice which.

19–21. *scorners of the Muses...forgotten.* Cf. Sappho's famous expression of the same idea, addressed to a wealthy, but Philistine woman-friend. Bergk, *Poet. Lyr. Graeci* (1843), Fr. 73:

> κατθάνοισα δὲ κείσεαι οὐδέ ποτα μναμοσύνα σέθεν
> ἔσσετ' οὐδέποτ' εἰς ὕστερον· οὐ γὰρ πεδέχεις βρόδων
> τῶν ἐκ Πιερίας· ἀλλ' ἀφάνης κἠν Ἀίδα δόμοις
> φοιτάσεις πεδ' ἀμαύρων νεκύων ἐκπεποταμένα.

When thou art not, thou shalt lie forgot, all memories of thee
Shall be lost and dumb through the years to come. Since now from the Muses' Tree
Thou hast plucked no rose, a wraith none knows, that none remembereth,
Thou shalt drift 'mid the hosts of nameless ghosts that haunt the House of Death.

COMMENDATORY VERSES

MIDDLETON'S.

Middleton had been collaborating with Webster about two years before, in *A.Q.L.* (*c.* 1621); Rowley and Ford were to collaborate with him about two years later, in *C.C.* and *F.M.I.* (Ford also in a lost play of 1624).

In Tragœdiam.

To Tragedy.
As light at the Thunderer's stroke from darkness springs,
To the wicked, doom, to the poet, life she brings.

Chron: Londinensis. Middleton received this office of City Chronologer in 1620. For its duties see on III. 3. 24.

ROWLEY'S.

3–6. "However eloquently in her real life the Duchess may have defended that misalliance *which* her brothers' anger made so fatal, though she may have spoken more, she can never have spoken so well as in your play." Cf. Margaret, Duchess of Newcastle, *Sociable Letters*, cxxiii (of Shakespeare): "Certainly *Julius Caesar, Augustus Caesar*, and *Antonius* did never Really Act their parts Better, if so Well, as he hath Described them, and I believe that *Antonius* and *Brutus* did not Speak Better to the People, than he hath Feign'd them".

For *answer* = "justify" cf. Beveridge, *Sermons* (1729), I. 307: "How they will answer it. . . at the last day I know not".

FORD'S.

1–2. Perhaps ultimately modelled on Propertius' tribute to Virgil's *Aeneid* (II. 34. 65–6):

> Cedite Romani scriptores, cedite Grai:
> Nescio quid maius nascitur Iliade.

3. *whiles words and matter change*: seems to mean—"while things are put into words", "while literature lasts".

I. I.

Outer stage, probably, till 406; then whole stage.

1. The *W.D.* begins with "Banisht!" (cf. III. 5 below); this, Webster's next play, with a return from banishment—"You are wel-come to your country".

2. *long in France.* Antonio had followed the deposed Federico, the last Aragonese king of Naples, into his French exile, which lasted from 1501 to his death at Tours in Nov. 1504.

4 ff. Contrast the description of the French court at the opening of Chapman's *Bussy d'Ambois*.

8 ff. *Quits. . . Sicophants.* Vaughan first pointed out that this, and indeed the whole speech, is an allusion to the assassination of the Maréchal d'Ancre on April 24th 1617.

Concino Concini, son of a Florentine notary, after spending a dissolute youth came to France in the train of Marie de' Medici, the queen of Henri IV; and there married her *femme de chambre*, Leonora Galigai. This woman had an extraordinary influence over her mistress, and when the Queen became Regent after Henry's murder, the Regent herself was still ruled by Leonora; while Concini, though not liked by the Queen and perpetually at feud with his wife, in some strange way contrived to use the two women to make himself the chief power in France. The greater his influence became, the greater he made it, by pretending that it was even greater than it was, so that a sycophantic court flocked to the feet of this supreme dispenser of favours. In his hands the boy Louis XIII, already crushed by an indifferent mother, became a mere *roi fainéant* at the mercy of his Mayor of the Palace; whole armies were maintained in the usurper's pay; and some sudden stroke, whether arrest or assassination, was the only weapon left to the young king. On the morning of April 24th 1617, Concini in the midst of his enormous suite was confronted by de Vitry, captain of the royal guard, and a few followers at the entrance to the Louvre; and, at the first sign of resistance to arrest, riddled with bullet and sword-thrust. The hated corpse was torn limb from limb in the streets of Paris; and throughout France, already partly in rebellion, the news roused wild enthusiasm. The old counsellors of Henri IV, Villeroi, Jeannin, du Vair, de Sillery were recalled (cf. 18–9), the Queen-Mother and Concini's tools disgraced or imprisoned (cf. 8–10). Marie de' Medici had been the friend of Spain; and accordingly there were great rejoicings throughout Protestant Europe, so that in England not to share the general joy was to brand oneself as "more than half Spanish". (Cf. *Cal. Venet. State-Papers*, 1615–7, 510 *n*.) A dozen or more pamphlets in the British Museum still testify to the popular interest which occasioned this insertion in our play.

Now since Ostler died in Dec. 1614, this cannot have been the original opening. Has something been displaced? We might imagine the play beginning with Bosola's "I doe haunt you still"; followed by the entrance of Antonio and Delio behind. But the Duke's reference to Antonio's having been in France (142) would be obscure without the first three lines of the present text to explain it. And something must have linked these lines to "Here comes Bosola" in 23 or "I doe haunt you still" in 30.

10. *which he sweetely termes*, etc.: the antecedent to *which* has troubled editors. *Pallace* (Vaughan and Allen) makes little sense; *persons* (Sampson—"man being the chief work of the creator") makes even less; while *Order*, his other suggestion, is too far away. But there is no difficulty if *which* is taken to refer to *the whole previous sentence* (cf. Lat. *id quod*), *i.e.* his policy of cleansing his court. Then *Considering*, etc., in 12 follows quite naturally to explain *why* he terms his action a heavenly piece of work. For this use of *which* cf. the Dedication of the Play, 12.

11. *Masters Master-peece*: crowning master-piece. Krusius ingeniously sees an allusion to Christ's cleansing of the Temple: I am inclined to think, however, that if Webster had meant this, he would have made it clearer. No suspicion of it seems to have occurred to any of his editors.

14. *in generall*: *not* "as a rule", but "universally", "without exception". Cf. *Troil. and Cress.* IV. 5. 21: "Twere better she were kiss'd in general" (*i.e.* by everyone).

17–23. Cf. Louis XIII's words to the Assembly of Notables at Rouen summoned in October, 1617: "que sans autres respect ni considération quelquonque, crainte ou désir de plaire ou complaire à personne, ils nous donnent en toutes franchise et sincérité les conseils qu'ils jugeront en leurs consciences les plus salutaires et convenables". (Stoll: from Isambert et Decrusy, *Recueil Général des Anciennes Lois Françaises* (1829), XVI. 108.)

24. *Court-Gall*: "gall" primarily in the sense of "sore place". So Spenser, *State of Ireland* (Globe ed. 654/1), speaks of the Irish as being "a gall and inconvenience". So Pericles called hostile Aegina "the eyesore of the Peiraeus", and Augustus described his degenerate posterity as his "sores and cancers" (Sueton. *Aug.* 65). The association with the *bitterness* of the gall-bladder is, however, doubtless meant to be present here as well.

33. *onely the reward*: i.e. the only reward. Cf. Caxton, *Golden Legend*, 333 b/₁: "Luke is only with me".

For the idea, cf. Montaigne II. 16 (a rendering of Seneca): "The reward of well-doing is the doing and the fruit of our duty is our duty". (C.)

37. *two Towells in stead of a shirt*. Cf. 1 *Hen. IV*, IV. 2. 47 (Vaughan).

39. *black-birds...hard weather*: a medieval idea, perhaps due to the birds fluffing out their feathers. Cf. *Hortus Sanitatis*, III. 74 (of the ousel): "and in the winter for fatness it can scarcely fly".

40. *dogge dayes*: evil days. See on *W.D.* III. 3. 67.

43-5. Cf. Montaigne I. 38: "It was told Socrates that one was no whit amended by his travell: I believe it wel (said he) for he carried him-selfe with him". Similarly the famous tag of Horace (*Ep.* I. 11. 27):

Caelum, non animum mutant qui trans mare currunt.

So in the *Characters* the "Improvident Young Gallant" comes back from abroad "never the more mended in his conditions, cause he carried himselfe along with him".

51. *standing-pooles*: stagnant pools with green scum. Cf. *Lear*, III. 4. 137: "the green mantle of the standing pool".

58-9. *di[e]d...p[ar]don*: we may recall Tourneur, *Revenger's Tragedy*, III. 3.

59. *rewards*: a technical hunting term. See on *W.D.* IV. 2. 193.

62-5. *Geometry...Crowtches*. "To hang by geometry" is a curious idiom used to describe clothes hanging awkwardly and angularly. *E.g.* Fletcher, *Span. Curate*, III. 2: "and the old Cut-worke Cope, that hangs by Gymitrie". So Swift, *Pol. Convers.* I. 85: "Lord! my Petticoat! how it hangs by Jommetry".

Here the obvious resemblance between a man on crutches and a pair of compasses must come in, as well as the idea of hanging stiffly and awkwardly. But it would no doubt be fanciful to press further the original meaning of "geometry"—"earth-measurement"—and to imagine the cripple, as he swings over the countryside, to be compared with a pair of dividers traversing a map (cf. Donne's likening of his mistress and himself to a pair of compasses). Webster's mind runs on such "mystical Mathematicks"; cf. *W.D.* I. 2. 93; *D.M.* I. 1. 137; II. 2. 19; IV. 2. 227; *D.L.* I. 1. 72.

73. *Gaston de Foux*: Gaston de Foix (1489–1512), "whose fame," says Guicciardini, "will last as long as the world", both made his name and lost his life in the space of those two months of 1512 which

culminated in the victory of Ravenna over the Spanish and Papal armies. There the young leader of twenty-four fell in the moment of his success, after having revealed to the world the marching power of French infantry and how to make full use of it. He had, however, nothing to do with the taking of Naples in 1501, at which date he was, indeed, a mere child.

The allusion was clearly suggested to Webster by Painter, who quite correctly uses the victory "of that notable Capitayne Gaston de Foix...at the Journey of Ravenna" to date the misfortunes of the Duchess.

80. *rust unto the soule*. Cf. *Characters*, "A Fayre and happy Milke-mayde", 9 ff. For the general idea H.D.S. quotes Burton, *Anat.* I. 2. 2. 7.

82–3. *Breeds all blacke male-contents, and their close rearing*
      (*Like mothes in cloath*) *doe hurt for want of wearing.*

Sampson explains—"*is* like moths *which* do hurt". But it is surely impossible to supply *is* and ignore the brackets in this way. Fortunately there is an exactly parallel construction in *D.L.* IV. 2. 131–3:

<blockquote>
a kind of sawcy <i>pride</i>,
Which <i>like to Mushromes</i>, ever <i>grow</i> most ranke,
When they do spring from dung-hills.
</blockquote>

Here we have exactly the same confusion in the simile, which causes *grow* to be in the plural, though its subject *Which* is singular, owing to the attraction of the plural *Mushromes*. So here, we should expect *does hurt*, not *doe hurt*, since the subject is clearly *close rearing*; but the plural *mothes* led Webster to write *doe*. "The secret breeding of these discontents is so harmful (like moths in clothes) just for want of stirring up". Only *wearing* is much more appropriate to the clothes than the discontents; just as the *dung-hills* in the *D.L.* passage really belong to the *Mushromes* rather than to *pride*. Webster telescopes together his main sentence and his simile.

It has also to be remembered that plural verbs with singular subjects, and *vice versa*, were in any case less startling in the looser English of the Elizabethans. Cf. 2 *Hen. VI*, III. 1. 301:

<blockquote>
Men's <i>flesh</i> preserv'd so whole <i>do</i> seldom win.
</blockquote>

I.e. "men whose flesh is preserv'd"; so here *their close rearing* = "they, closely reared". It is the exact opposite of the Latin idiom in which *Caesar occisus* = "Caesar's murder".

83–4. S.D. *Silvio*: the name was doubtless suggested by Silvio Savello (see Hist. Introd. p. 10).

Castruchio is similarly derived from the historic Petrucci, Cardinal of Siena, in Bandello, whose name Belleforest, followed by Painter, changes to "Castruccio".

90. *the Ring*: running at the ring (*i.e.* trying to carry off on the point of one's lance a ring suspended in the air) was tending under James I to replace the more dangerous jousting of the previous reign; though

James himself was a poor hand even at this and was much talked of for the inferiority he showed compared with his brother-in-law, Christian of Denmark, when the latter visited England in 1606.

95–6. *go to war, in person.* Cf. *W.D.* II. I. 119 ff.

107. *fighting*: probably with a *double entendre*.

112. *all in Tents*: *Tents* being used (1) in the ordinary sense; (2) = "rolls of lint", not so much, here, for "searching a wound" (Dyce), as for keeping it open, like the rubber tubes of modern surgery; they were left to plug the wound. Hence "*lie* in Tents".

For the pun, cf. Middleton, *More Dissemblers besides Women*, II. 3. 103:

                              lies you all in tents

       Like your camp-vict'lers. (Dyce.)

H.D.S. quotes also *Troil. and Cress.* v. I. 11–3.

115–6. With a double sense.

118. *Spanish Gennit*: a light, but valuable, breed of horse. The Spanish *ginete* (perhaps from the Gk. γυμνήτης, light-armed soldier) meant originally a horse*man* riding *à la gineta*, *i.e.* "with the legs trussed up in short stirrups, with a target and a ginnet launce".

120. *Pliney's opinion*: Pliny VIII. 42 (Holland's transl.): "In Portugall, along the river Tagus, and about Lisbon, certaine it is, that when the West wind bloweth, the mares set up their tailes, and turn them full against it, and so conceive that genitall aire in steed of naturall seed: in such sort as they become great withall, and quicken in their time, and bring forth foles as swift as the wind, but they live not above three yeares". It was a widely spread idea. Cf. Aristotle, *Hist. Anim.* VI. 18; Varro, *Re Rust.* II. 1; Virg. *Georg.* III. 273; Sil. Ital. III. 381; Justin XLIV. 3; Augustine, *Civ. Dei.* XXI. 5. D. W. Thompson in his note on the Aristotle passage in the Oxford transl. (1910) suggests that the idea may be traced back to Homer, *Il.* XX. 223 ff., where we hear how Boreas loved the mares of Erichthonios, King of Troy, and begat on them colts so light of foot that they could run over the waves of the sea. But this is rather one instance, than the origin, of so common an idea; the transition is natural enough from "swift as the wind" to "son of the wind".

The notion recurs in Fletcher's *Woman's Prize*, II. 5:

       They are a genealogy of jennets, gotten

       And born thus, by the boisterous breath of husbands.

And among other "Vulgar Errors" Sir T. Browne duly discusses also (III. 21) these "subventaneous conceptions from the Western wind".

122. *reeles from the Tilt.* Such tilting phrases seem to be used in a metaphorical and wider sense in the current speech of the period. Thus Chamberlain writes to Carleton (Jan. 5th 1607–8), of a certain Fuller who has got into trouble in ecclesiastical controversy: "he hath...feigned himself sick in bed when he should come to the tilt"

—(*i.e.* "face the music" as we might say). It seems possible, then, that Silvio means here that the horse has a trick of jibbing and refusing in general.

138. *laugh out of compasse*: beyond bounds, out of measure. So Hall in his *Characters*, of the Unthrift: "He ranges beyond his pale, and lives without compasse". There is perhaps also the sense of "laughing *impertinently*". Cf. the story in Bacon's *Apophthegms* (6) (*Wks.* ed. Spedding, VII. 125): "Pace, the bitter Fool, was not suffered to come at the Queen, because of his bitter humour. Yet at one time some persuaded the Queen that he should come to her; undertaking for him that he should *keep compass* (*v.l.* within compass). So he was brought to her, and the Queen said: 'Come on, Pace; now we shall hear of our faults'. Saith Pace: 'I do not use to talk of that that all the town talks of'".

141–2. *excellent Riders in France*. Cf. *W.D.* IV. 3. 99; Ford, *Love's Sacrifice*, I. 2. The French were held the best horsemen in Europe. It is an interesting coincidence, at least, that a certain Monsieur St Anthoine was sent over by Henri IV in 1603 to be Prince Henry's riding-master and was known in England as "St Anthony the rider". On the prince's death in 1612 St Anthoine led a *cheval de deuil* in the funeral procession; and subsequently became equerry of Prince Charles, whose helmet he holds in the equestrian portrait by Vandyke. The Duchess of Newcastle speaks of him as accounted the best master of his art. (W. B. Rye, *England as seen by Foreigners*, 253.) So it is possible that Webster may have thought of St Anthoine here; though, independently of this, he had the authority of Painter for the horsemanship of Antonio—"for riding and managing of greate horse, he had not his fellow in Italy".

144–5. *Grecian-horse... Princes*. Cf. Cicero's remark on the school of Isocrates (*De orat.* II. 22. 94): "From his school, as from the Trojan horse, came forth only men of sovereign rank".

155. *five thousand crownes, at Tennis*. Cf. *W.D.* II. 1. 185.

157. *flashes*: pieces of showy behaviour. Cf. Jonson's character, Sir Petronel Flash.

159–60. *Spring in his face... Toades*. Cf. Chapman, *Bussy d'Ambois*, III. 2. 452:

That toad-pool that stands in thy complexion.

Camille Cé in his version (1922) renders *Spring* by *printemps*: but the parallel from Chapman is decisive. Cf., too, *Merch. of Ven.* I. 1. 88–9:

There are a sort of men whose visages
Do cream and mantle like a standing-pond.

For the engendering of toads as a type of supreme loathsomeness, cf. *Troil. and Cress.* II. 3. 170–1: "I do hate a proud man, as I hate the engendering of toads"; and *Othello*, IV. 2. 56 ff.

179. *Rewards, by heare-say*: at random, without troubling to discover

the real deservers? Or does it mean: "Rewards with mere words, hearsay recompenses"? This makes better sense: but loses the apparent antithesis between "by information" and "by heare-say". It is supported however by *D.L.* III. 3. 425: the poem "To Master H. Cockeram", 3; and *Char.* "A Worthy Commander", 4–5.

180–1. *Law...cob-web...Spider.* Cf. Massinger and Fletcher, *Spanish Curate*, IV. 5:

> A lawyer that entangles all men's honesties,
> And lives like a spider in a cob-web lurking,
> And catching at all flies that pass his pit-falls.

The simile is more commonly used to illustrate the fact that there is one law for the strong, another for the weak; just as large flies break through the cobweb which holds the small ones. Dyce (p. xx) quotes examples of this from Field (*A Woman's a Weathercock*, 1612, sig. E), Braithwaite's *Honest Ghost* (1658), p. 79, etc.

185–6. Cf. *Char.* "An Intruder into favour", 20–1.

195–8. A difficult passage, ignored by editors. It is indeed one of those sentences which seem to be quite easy till one tries to analyse them. The words *might* mean: "You wish she thought, not so much that it was vanity of her to talk, as that it was your appointed penance to hear her, (like some fair Father-confessor)". But I think this scarcely possible: and would rather read *And* for *Then.* See Text. Note.

200. *Galliard*: a particularly lively, capering dance. Cf. the description in Sir J. Davies, *Orchestra* (quoted in *Sh.'s Eng.* II. 448):

> A gallant dance that lively doth bewray
> A spirit and a virtue masculine;
> Impatient that her house on earth should stay,
> Since she herself is fiery and divine,
> Oft does she make her body upward fine,
> With lofty turns and capriols in the air
> Which with the lusty tunes accordeth fair.

202–3. *countenance...continence*: probably an intentional jingle.

206–7. Cf. Donne, *Of the Progress of the Soul* (1612), 463–4:

> Whose twilights were more cleare, then our mid-day;
> Who dreamt devoutlier, then most use to pray. (C.)

208–9. Cf. *Char.* "A vertuous Widdow", 20–2.

208. *flattring Glasses.* Cf. *Char.* "An Intruder", 22; and H. King, *Elegy on Gustavus Adolphus*:

> Here then break your false glasses, which present
> You greater than your Maker ever meant.
> Make Truth your Mirrour now.

So Burton curiously records (*Anat.* I. 2. 4. 7): "Acco, an old woman, seeing by chance her face in a true glass (for she used false flattering glasses belike at other times, as most gentlewomen do), *animi dolor̃t in insaniam delapsa est*, ran mad".

211. *wire-drawer*: one who draws out and distorts the truth.

212. *case the picture up*: put it away. Cf. III. 2. 162. (H.D.S.)

214. Repeated in *Mon. Col.* 278.

    Staines—not in the modern sense, but "deprives of lustre" (the oldest meaning being "to deprive of colour", *not* "to colour"). Hence a perfect antithesis to "lights". Cf. *Histrio-mastix*, III. 138:

> As glorious Titan stains a silly Star.

Hence "stain" comes to mean simply "surpass" and in the *Arcadia* we have: "O voice that doth the Thrush in shrilnesse staine".

230. *Leaguer*: camp (Germ. *Lager*).

244. *lur'd*: met. of hawking. See on *W.D.* IV. I. 139.

257. H.D.S. quotes Chapman, *Bussy d'Ambois*, I. I. 5–6:

> As cedars beaten with continual storms,
> So great men flourish.

260–2. From Montaigne III. 9: "*Multi fallere docuerunt, dum timent falli, et aliis jus peccandi suspicando fecerunt* (Cic.): Many have taught others to deceive, while themselves feare to be deceived, and have given them just cause to offend by suspecting them unjustly". (C.)

265–6. With reference to the legend of Jupiter's finding access to Danae in her brazen tower in the shape of a shower of gold. Cf. II. 2. 18 below.

278. *familiars*: a word with sinister associations for an Elizabethan; being applied not only to evil spirits, but to servants of the Pope or Roman bishops and to officers of the Holy Inquisition, charged with making arrests.

280. *quaint*: cunning (Lat. *comptus*). So Gavin Douglas (*Aen.* II. I. 59) speaks of "quent Ulexes".

281. *An Intelligencer*: another word with hateful associations to Elizabethan ears. The name was given to the special correspondents employed by ambassadors or great men to keep them posted with regular intelligence in the absence of newspapers. Chamberlain's letters to Carleton are an outstanding example. Naturally the methods by which their information was procured were not always above suspicion: and the *Camb. Hist. of Eng. Lit.* (VII. 193) quotes Francis Osborne's *Advice to a Son*: "It is an office unbecoming a Gentleman to be an Intelligencer, which in real Truth is no better than a Spie". Nash couples them with Judas.

286. *Angels*: the Angel-Noble, first coined by Edward IV, was so-called from having on it, like our sovereign, a design of St Michael killing the dragon.

300. *Candies...[o'er]*: sugars over. Cf. *W.D.* v. 6. 60–1.

301. *complementall*: *i.e.* a polite accomplishment.

307. *dormouse*. Cf. III. I. 25.

308–13. Bosola, like an old blood-hound, kindles to excitement as the Duke brings back to his imagination the details of the hunt of intrigue.

315. *covet good fame*: *i.e.* good fame *only*, not those more material rewards which are the price of base services.

325. *luxurious*: wanton.

326. *wed twice*. Cf. Chapman's *Widow's Tears*, II. 4. 27 ff.: "open and often detestations of that incestuous life (as she termed it) of widows' marriages; as being but a kind of lawful adultery; like usury, permitted by the law, but not approved".

329. *Labans sheepe*: *Genesis* xxx. 31–42.

335–8. Cf. Chapman, *Widow's Tears*, I. I. 106 ff.; *W.D.* v. 6. 155 ff.

336. *motion*: resolve.

341. *honney-dew*: a sweet, sticky substance found on plants and now supposed to be excreted by aphides.

345. *give the divell sucke*: one of the most recurrent details in witch-trials is the supposed suckling of animal familiars, either with the witch's blood or more often from a supernumerary nipple (one of the best established physical signs of a witch). See M. A. Murray, *Witchcult in Western Europe*, 90–6.

348. *Vulcans Engine*. Cf. Homer, *Od.* VIII. 266 ff., where Demodocus the minstrel tells how Hephaestus contrived an invisible engine to trap the guilty Ares in the arms of his wife Aphrodite.

353. *Under the E[a]ves of night*: a vivid phrase, doubtless helped by the similarity of "eve" in the sense of "evening". For hiding under eaves, cf. "to eavesdrop", which is "to lurk within the 'eaves-drop' of a house" (*i.e.* the space where fall the droppings from the eaves).

355. *Crab*. Cf. *Arcadia*, II. (*Wks.* I. 164): "A Crab-fish which...lookes one way and goes another"; so *Hortus Sanitatis*: "The Crab goes backward, and has never known how to follow his nose".

359. *executed*, apart from its sinister associations with punishment, is a regular ecclesiastical word for performing a religious service.

366. *begins at the end*: considers the final view first. Cf. the Gk. saw, "σκόπει τέλος"—"Consider the end".

372. *chargeable*: "expensive", not "accusable", "compromising".

373. *whispering roomes*: privy closets for secret interviews.

375–6. *Lamprey...nev'r a bone*: so Sir T. Browne, *Pseudodoxia*, III. 19, speaks of its "defect of bones, whereof it hath not one".

379. *the Tongue*. Cf. Chambers and Sidgwick, *Early English Lyrics*, p. 191:

> Wikked tungë breketh bone
> Thow the tungës self have none.

380–1. Cf. "Overbury", *Characters*, "A Good Woman": "She leaves the neat youth, telling his lushious tales". For the bearing of this parallel (cf. v. 2. 244) on the date of the play, see p. 3. H.D.S. points out another borrowing by N. Richards, in "The Flesh" (*Poems Sacred and Satirical*, 1641):

> As what cannot a spruce Queane with a smooth Tale
> Make him believe?

384. *foote-steps*: *i.e.* not in our sense, but steps to tread on, or rungs of a ladder. Thus Latimer speaks (*6th Sermon before Edw. VI*) of "the footsteps of the ladder of heaven".

386. *apprehending danger*: not "fearing", but "grasping" it, taking the bull by the horns.

390. *wincked, and chose a husband*: not "gained a husband by bold encouragement" (Allen), but "shut my eyes and blindly chose". Thus Topsell says that female goats "never wink in their sleep". Cf. III. 1. 8; *A.V.* IV. 1. 312; Middleton, *Roaring Girl*, II. 2. 15:

> I know that man
> Ne'er truly loves—if he gainsay't, he lies—
> That winks and marries with his father's eyes.
> I'll keep mine own wide open.

H.D.S. quotes from Ray's *Proverbs* the expression "you may wink and choose". It recurs in Ford, *Lady's Trial*, II. 1.

398. *ingenious*: "ingenuous", the two words being interchangeable in the English of the time.

404–6. *wildernesse...guide*: imitated by Shirley (*The Brothers*, II. 1):

> Sir, with your pardon
> You lead me to a wilderness and take
> Yourself away, that should be guide.

406. s.d. *The Duchess draws the traverse*: the Quarto has no directions: *Enter Antonio* is usually supplied. The fact however that Antonio is not told to enter—"He attends", says Cariola, who then conceals herself behind the arras—makes my arrangement slightly easier. His sitting down to write implies the use of the inner stage with its properties; and there is something more dramatic in the idea of the Duchess taking the initiative in this also. With the cry "I am going into a wilderness" she turns and stepping to the curtain reveals the lover who is to be her ruin. The action then proceeds on the whole stage (there would be no lack of hangings round the stage, as far as one can gather, to hide Cariola). Then at the end of the scene the curtain is drawn again upon the lovers and the next act begins on the outer stage.

412. *triumphs*: festivities.

413. *husbands*: a significant and ambiguous word. Cf. the play on the double sense of "husbandry" in Chapman, *All Fools*, I. 1. 141: Valerio seeing his wife Gratiana cries, weary of his household economies:

> And see, bright heaven, here comes my husbandry.

417. *I look yong for your sake*: (1) "thanks to you". Cf. Tindall, *Genesis* iii. 17: "Cursed be the erth for thy sake". (2) "For love of you".

435. *Over-seer*: a technical term, overseers being appointed to oversee and assist executors. However, as usual, *Quis custodes custodiet ipsos?* Judging, at least, by the fifteenth-century proverb "Too

secutours and an overseere make thre theves", overseers were only
too capable of oversights.

443. *In a winding sheete*: since her husband is dead.

444. *In a cople*: *i.e.* of sheets, with also the inevitable *double entendre*.

445. *St. Win[i]frid* lived in the seventh century and was the daughter
of the Welsh Tenyth ap Eylud. She had her head struck off by
Caradoc ap Alauc whose advances she had rejected; but was restored
to life by St Bruno. From the spring which bubbled up where her
blood was shed, the town of Holywell in Flint takes its name; and
the stones in it are still streaked as with blood. (See Baring-Gould,
Lives of the Saints, November, I. 69–72.)

St Winfrid, on the other hand, in case that should be the right
reading, is Boniface the missionary of Germany who was born, also
in the seventh century, at Crediton in Devon.

449–51. It seems to me possible that these lines were suggested to
Webster by a note on two lines of Tofte's Ariosto, *Satire IV* (from which
he certainly copies a whole passage in II. I), although the sense is
exactly opposite. The note runs: "The Poet compareth marriage
to Purgatory, where, as they say, they continue in paine but for a
certaine time. But the Batchellors life he termeth hell, because he
thinkes that none perhaps live honest untill they be married; & therefore in greater danger if they die not maides". (The lines of Ariosto
are:

> Yet better 'tis in Purgatory dwell
> A little space than always live in hell.)

456–61. One of those general gnomic passages to which Webster, like
Euripides (who was similarly much exercised about this particular
question of children), is too prone to sacrifice strict dramatic relevance.
Cf. II. 45 and Bosola's bald "Observe my meditation now"—followed
by fifteen lines clearly based on Webster's commonplace-book; *D.L.*
II. 3. 110, where Romelio similarly launches into a "meditation" in
couplets; and again the obscurely apposite parables of the Crocodile
in *W.D.*, of the Salmon and of Reputation later in this play. Too
often Ariosto's comment in *The Devil's Law-Case* is justified of
Webster in general: "Very fine words, I assure you, if they were to
any purpose".

472. *in this circle*: the necromancer would, of course, be in extreme
danger once the devil got *inside* his circle.

479. *roofe...low built.* Cf. Hall, *Characters*, "Humble Man": "a
true temple of God built with a low roofe".

483 ff. Almost prophetic: cf. IV. 2. 44 ff.

498. *trades-men...i'th'City*: for this dishonest darkening of shops,
a perpetual accusation in the writings of the time, cf. *W. Ho!* I. I (p. 73):
"politic penthouses, which commonly make the shop of a mercer or
a linen-draper as dark as a room in Bedlam"; *A.Q.L.* II. 2, 51–2;
Beaum. and Fl., *Philaster*, V. 3: "May their false lights undo them,

and discover presses, holes, stains, and oldness in their stuffs". In Middleton's *Michaelmas Term*, again, Quomodo the draper has a satellite pointedly named Falselight:

> Go, make my coarse commodities look sleek...
> Be near to my trap-window, cunning Falselight.

502. *progresse*: the word appropriate to a prince surveying his kingdom.

504–5. An echo, with a difference, of Bosola's words above, 33–4.

506. *paies it*: "repays it", "rewards your conduct" rather than "pays your wages", which would need *them*, not *it*.

507–8. Cf. Painter: "'Alas,' sayd shee, 'am I happed into so straunge misery, that with mine owne mouth I must make request to him, which with all humility ought to offer mee hys service!'"

514–5. Cf. *W.D.* IV. 2. 119–20.

520–1. *figure cut in Allablaster...husbands tombe*: an ominous comparison, with its suggestions both of death and her forgetfulness of the dead. Cf. *Merch. of Ven.* I. I. 83–4:

> Why should a man, whose blood is warm within,
> Sit like his grandsire cut in alabaster?

(There too "Alablaster" in the original spelling.)

532. *Quietus est*: (medieval Lat.) = "he is quit, acquitted of his obligations". Cf. Massinger, *Gt. Duke of Flor.* v. 3. The phrase easily became applied (helped perhaps by its resemblance to "quiet") to "death", as being the final payment of nature's debt. Cf. *Haml.* III. I. 75: *Mon. Col.* 220. And though that sense is not present here, the word may help to create that atmosphere of mortality which broods over all this love-scene.

533–4. Repeated in *A.V.* I. I. 20–1. A similar phrase occurs in *Arcadia*, I. (*Wks.* I. 96): "*Zelmane's* eyes were (like children afore sweet meate) eager but fearefull of their ill-pleasing governors".

535, 541–3. Antonio's characteristic hesitancy (cf. above) is almost painfully lifelike. His gentle, uncertain character is never in danger of distracting our attention from the heroine his mistress.

548. *Per verba [de] presenti*. By the canon law *sponsalia de presenti*, in which the pair recognized each other as wife and husband at the time of speaking, were valid; as contrasted with *sponsalia de futuro*, which were only an undertaking to enter into that relationship at some future time and were not binding unless followed by intercourse. The Council of Trent (1563) insisted on all marriages taking place henceforward *in facie ecclesiae*; but in Protestant countries the canon law remained in force (it had been abolished in England by Henry VIII, but was restored under Edward VI) though such a union had to be consecrated subsequently by a religious service, under pain of certain penalties. Thus it was by *sponsalia de presenti* that the first Duke of Amalfi, our heroine's father-in-law, wedded Maria d'Aragona; the historic Bracciano, Vittoria; and Shakespeare's Claudio, his Juliet (*Meas. for Meas.* I. 2. 155 ff.).

549. *Gordian.* Gordius was a Phrygian peasant. One day as he was ploughing, an eagle alighted on the yoke of his oxen and sat there till evening; going to the Telmissians to ask the meaning of this portent, he met outside one of their villages a young prophetess who bade him sacrifice to Zeus βασιλεύς (the King). In return for this counsel he wedded her and so she became the mother of the notorious Midas. When her son grew up dissensions broke out in Phrygia; and an oracle bade the people take as king him whom a chariot should bring them. At this vital moment Gordius appeared in a chariot with his wife and son; and either he or Midas—accounts differ—was raised to the throne. In memory of this the car of Gordius and the yoke of his oxen were dedicated to Zeus at Gordium; and another oracle declared that whoever untied the cunning knot with which the yoke was fastened, would become lord of all Asia. Centuries later Alexander, after trying in vain to disentangle it, sundered it with his sword.

So here the phrase is again ominous, when we remember that final severance by the sword. Cf. *D.L.* II. 4, end:

With Gordi[a]n knots, of such a strong threed spun,
They cannot *without violence* be undone.

Similarly Chapman, *Bussy d'Ambois,* IV. I. 227:

To cut a gordian when he could not loose it.

552. *still*: always.

555. *the loving Palmes.* Holland's Pliny (XIII. 4), has a charming passage: "The females be naturally barrein, and will not beare fruit without the company of the males among them to make them for to conceive;...and verily a man shall see many of the femals stand about one male, bending and leaning in the head full kindly toward him, yeelding their braunches that way as if they courted him for to win his love. But contrariwise he, a grim sir and a coy, carrieth his head aloft, beareth his bristled and rough arms upright on high, and yet what with his very lookes, what with his breathing and exhalations upon them, or else with a certain dust that passeth from him, he doth the part of an husband, insomuch as all the females about him, conceive and are fruitfull with his onely presence. It is said moreover, that if this male tree be cut downe, his wives will afterwards become barrein and beare no more Dates, as if they were widdowes". Dyce quotes a similar passage to Webster's from Glapthorne, *Argalus and Parthenia*; there is another in Du Bartas, *Oeuvres* (1593), II. 63, describing the loving palms embracing across a river. Cf. *Char.* "A Vertuous Widdow", I.

563–4. *the Church...must but eccho this. Sponsalia de presenti,* though valid by themselves, had to be completed ceremonially by a marriage *in facie ecclesiae*; and a refusal to obey the injunction of an ecclesiastical judge to do this was punishable with excommunication and imprisonment.

565. *I now am blinde*: like Love, as well as Fortune? Blind, also, to the consequences—there is surely here an intentional tragic irony.

570 ff. The sudden revulsion of the Duchess to womanly shame, which Fletcher, say, might easily have made hateful, is naturally and charmingly drawn.

571. *humorous*: full of humours, difficult-tempered.

572. *Alexander and Lodowicke.* There is a ballad on this subject from the Pepys collection (printed in Th. Evans, *Old Ballads*, 1810, I. 77): "The Two Faithful Friends, the pleasant History of Alexander and Lodwicke, who were so like one another, that none could know them asunder; wherein is declared how Lodwicke married the Princesse of Hungaria, in Alexander's name, and how each night he layd a naked sword betweene him and the Princesse, because he would not wrong his friend". The ballad is poor enough doggerel, of the style—

> But every night between them twain
> His naked sword he'd lay,
> Such constant friendship at that time
> His heart and thoughts did sway.

Henslowe in his *Diary* (p. 79) mentions a play by Martin Slaughter on the subject. And there are references to the tale in Dekker's *Satiromastix* (*Wks.* 1873, I. 235) and Cooke's *Greene's Tu Quoque* and a partial adaptation in Heywood's *A Challenge for Beauty*.

The commentators here have omitted however to point out that the tale is itself a variant of one of the most famous stories of the Middle Ages, which perhaps came from the East through Byzantium —*Amis and Amiloun.* The version of it, in which the friends are Alexandre and Loys (Louis, Lodowick), is to be found in *L'Ystoire des Sept Sages de Rome* (ed. by G. Paris, *Soc. des Anc. Textes Franç.,* 1876, pp. 167 ff. Also in Latin in Buchner, *Historia Septem Sapientium,* 1889, p. 71).

Alexandre persuaded Florentine, the daughter of the Emperor, to become the mistress of his friend Loys; after a time, however, the intrigue was suspected and Loys challenged to an ordeal by battle. Being weak in body and dreading defeat, he went in search of Alexandre and found him on the point of mounting the throne of Egypt. Now the two friends were exactly alike in appearance; and so Alexandre agreed to impersonate his friend in the lists. Since, however, Alexandre could not openly leave Egypt, they decided that Loys should at the same time impersonate Alexandre with the Egyptians and with the Queen his bride. So Alexandre departed and defeated the challenger; while Loys lay night after night with a sword between him and his friend's wife. When Alexandre returned, however, the woman, resenting her treatment, poisoned him so that he became a leper. Then followed the episode, famous in *Amis and Amiloun*, of the father (Loys) killing his own sons to cure his friend's leprosy; and the children's miraculous restoration to life. (See W. Pater, *Renaissance*, "Two Early French Stories".) The impersonation of one friend by another and the naked sword curiously recall Sigurd's winning of Brynhild for Gunnar in the *Volsunga Saga*.

574. *shrowd*: shelter. See on *W.D.* 1. 2. 33. H.D.S. quotes Middleton's *Changeling* (acted 1623), III. 4. 167:

> Come, rise and shroud your blushes in my bosom.

576–8. These forebodings of Cariola's correspond to the gloomy anticipations expressed by the author in Belleforest-Painter at this point.

II. I.

Outer stage.

3. *maine*: not "main part", but "goal", "objective" ("perhaps originally a term of archery". *N.E.D.*). Cf. Jonson's *Tale of a Tub*, III. 4:

> That was all the main I aimed at.

Similarly *Arcadia*, I. (*Wks.* I. 89): "I thought nothing could shoot righter at the *mark* of my desires".

5. *night-cap*: lawyer's coif. See on 21 below.

6. *strings of your band*: Elizabethan sergeants already wore the white bands or tabs familiar to-day.

7–9. Cf. *Char.* "A Fellow of an House", 12–3: "Hee hath learn't to cough, and spit, and blow his nose at every period, to recover his memory". And for the *hum*, cf. "Overbury's" Character of "An Hypocrite" with his "endless tongue", "the motion whereof, when matter and words faile, must be patched up…with long & fervent hummes".

9–12. For Webster's obvious and inveterate hatred of lawyers, cf. the trial-scenes in *W.D.*, *D.L.*, and *A.V.*

16. *roaring-boyes*: the regular Elizabethan slang-word for "bullies", "rowdies". See *Char.* "A Roaring Boy"; and there is a scene in a mock-school for training them in Middleton, *Fair Quarrel*, IV. I.

21. *night-caps*: "lawyers", not here "bullies", as *N.E.D.* suggests. Indeed it ignores the first sense altogether. But "lawyer" is certainly the meaning in a number of passages, including this one: cf. *D.L.* II. I. 43; IV. I. 73; *A.V.* IV. I. 121, where the Nurse calls the advocate "the fellow i'th' nightcap".

Vaughan first suggested that lawyers were meant here: but he missed the true explanation, in which however I later found I had been anticipated by Mr Sykes. The nickname "nightcap" is simply due to the white coif or skull-cap of lawn or silk worn by Sergeants at Law (who ceased to exist at the end of the nineteenth century, but corresponded to the modern K.C.). It was of immemorial antiquity— seven centuries old, said Selden—and only disappeared with the coming of the large wig, at the end of the seventeenth century.

Even then a relic of it survived in the shape of a small hole cut in the top of the wig, as if to show the coif, but really filled up with a black patch edged with white. Cf. Pulling, *Order of the Coif* (1884), pp. 13 ff. and Plates I–IV and VII: *Sh.'s Eng.* I. 396. Jonson makes similar references to the "nightcap" in *Staple of News*, v. 1; *Magnetic Lady*, I. I.

21. *Old Lady*: this personage appears to be the same as the midwife of 183.

25. *These...*: a word like "dimples" may have dropped out; or Bosola may simply point.

26. *sloughes*: (1) "bogs"; (2) "dead tissue" to be sloughed off.

27–30. *Lady in France*. Cf. Montaigne I. 40: "Who hath not heard of her at Paris who only to get a fresher hew of a new skin, endured to have her face flead all over?" (C.)

    The Secretes of Maister Alexis (transl. by W. Warde, 1558, p. 69) gives an actual recipe for a composition which, applied to the face for eight days, purports to fetch off the old skin and leave new.

32. *carreening*: *i.e. lit.* "turning a ship on one side to scrape the paint, etc."; hence "scraping clean". Cf. Fletcher, *A Wife for a Month*, II. 4: "a weather-beaten lady new-careen'd".

32. *morphew'd*: scurfy, tettered.

33. *disembogue*: "'empty', properly of a river, here figuratively" (Sampson). But what then is the meaning? "To disembogue" is *lit.* "to come out of the mouth of a river into the open sea". Hence, here, "to put to sea in search of fresh prizes after careening and re-fitting". The Old Lady is to be on the war-path again, in Massinger's words (*Guardian*, v. 4):

>   as the pirate
> Who, from a narrow creek, puts off for prey
> In a small pinnace.

For "disembogue" of ships, cf. Fletcher and Massinger, *Knight of Malta*, I. 3:

>   My ships ride in the bay
> Ready to disembogue.

And for the metaphor, cf. Massinger, *Old Law*, v. 1 (Gnotho, of his aged wife): "She's going to sea...; she has a strong wind with her, it stands full in her poop; when you please, let her disembogue"— (though here it is into another world that she is to sail).

    Similarly Jonson, *Magnetic Lady*, II. 1:

> And maidens are young ships that would be sailing
> When they be rigged; wherefore is all their trim else?

And we may recall the description of Dalila in *Samson Agonistes*.

33. *rough-cast*: a rough mixture of lime and gravel for cheap plastering of walls. Cf. Mabbe's transl. of Aleman's *Guzman d'Alfarache* (1622 ed.), I. 39: "The face of her looked like an old wall all to bedawbed with rough-cast". There is of course a play on this and the sense of harsh home-truths.

34. *plastique*: modelling.

37–9. Sampson quotes Tofte's version of Ariosto's *Satires* (1608) IV:

> Knew *Herculan* but where those lips of his
> He layeth when his *Lidia* he doth kisse,
> He would disdaine and loath himselfe as much
> As if the loathsom'st ordure he did touch.
> He knows not, did he know it he would spewe,
> That painting's made with spettle of a Jewe…
> Little thinks he that with the filthy doung
> Of their small circumcised children young,
> The fat of hideous serpents, spaune of snakes,
> Which slaves from out their poisonous bodies takes.

(*I.e.* that the paint is made with these.)

Similarly Lyly, *Euphues*, 116: "Looke in their closettes, and there shalt thou finde an Appoticaryes shop of sweete confections, a surgions boxe of sundry salves, a Pedlers packe of newe fangles"; and Massinger, *Bondman*, IV. 4.

40–1. *dead pidgeon…plague*: a regular treatment, of which however there seem to be two forms. In one the birds are applied to the feet in order "to draw the vapors from the Head", as here; while in the other they are applied directly to the plague-sore with the idea of extracting its poisonous matter. This approaches the general treatment of devouring ulcers with flesh to feed them, as in *W.D.* v. 3. 55–6.

For the first method cf. *The English Huswife* (1615), quoted by Sampson, which recommends the application of hot bricks to the feet—"then to the same apply a live Pidgeon cut in two parts". Donne (*Devotions*, 12) characteristically compares such pigeons to the Dove of the Holy Spirit, which draws down the vapours of sin to be trodden under our feet. Cf. Congreve, *Love for Love*, IV. 3: "Ha! ha! ha! that a man should have a stomach to a wedding-supper when the pigeons ought rather to be laid to his feet, ha! ha! ha!"

For the second method, see T. Lodge, *Treatise of the Plague* (1603): "It is likewise very allowable, to draw out the venime from the sore, to take a chicken or cocke, and to pull the feathers from his taile, and to apply him to the soare, for by this meanes he drives out the venome, and when he is dead, apply another: Instead of this remedy, some use to take great pullets, and pigeons, and cutting them in two along the backe, apply them hote as they are upon the tumor or carbuncle".

Thus of Prince Henry's last illness (1612) we hear: "The extremity of his disease seemed to lie in his head, for remedy whereof they shaved him, and applied warm cocks, and pigeons newly killed, but with no success". See also *N.Q.*, CLI. 136 and 175.

41. *kisse one of you fasting*: *i.e.* when *you* are fasting and the offensiveness therefore at its worst. Cf. Massinger, *A Very Woman*, I. I:

> strong perfumes to stifle
> The sourness of our breaths as we are fasting.

43. *foote-cloth*: housings of his horse or mule, and the regular mark of the eminent physician. Cf. *D.L.* III. 2. 155–6; Massinger, *Bondman*, II. 3:

> Your lord that feels no ache in his chine at twenty,
> Forfeits his privilege; how should their surgeons build else
> Or ride on their footcloths?

Nares (*s.v.* "footcloth") quotes Howell's *Parly of Beasts* (1660), 73: "Nor are the fees which belong to that profession anything considerable; where doctors of physic use to attend a patient, with their mules and foot-cloths, in a kind of state, yet they receive but two shillings for their fee, for all their gravity and pains".

45–6. *observe my meditation.* See on I. 1. 456.

56. *Woolfe*: lupus, ulcer. See on *W.D.* v. 3. 55–6.

56. *Meazeall*: there is no real connection, only a confusion of popular etymology, between common human measles (O.H.G. *masala*, blood-blister) and the older English use of "mesel" to mean "leprosy" or "leprous" (O.F. *mesel*, Lat. *misellus*). It was on the analogy of the latter that "measle" or "measles" became applied to a skin-disease of swine, really caused by tape-worm.

64. *wels at Leuca*: warm springs in the Val di Lima, containing carbonic acid gas, unknown to the Romans, but frequented from the thirteenth century to the present day. They were visited by Montaigne, but he remained as sceptical about their value as about most other things. Cf. *W.Ho!* I. 2 (p. 79).

67. *fins of her eie-lids*: *N.E.D.* gives "fins" = "eye-lids". But "eyelids of her eyelids"? It must mean here "rims, edges". Dyce quotes Marston, *Malcontent*, I. 1. 103: "Till the fin of his eyes look as blue as the welkin".

67. *teeming blue*: blue like those of a pregnant woman.

69–70. *contrary to our Italian fashion..loose-bodied Gowne*: on the other hand Sampson quotes from Montaigne's *Italian Journey* (Hazlitt's transl. p. 574): "but their (Roman women's) custom of having the waist exceeding loose gives them all the appearance of being with child". Such gowns in Elizabethan England were regularly associated with prostitutes. Cf. Middleton, *Michaelmas Term*, I. 2. 14.

71. *tricke*: for Bosola's trick with the Apricocks, cf. Donne, *Elegies* IV, where his mistress's "immortall mother", in her suspicion,

> To trie if thou long, doth name strange meates
> And notes thy palenesse, blushing, sighs, and sweats.

79 ff. After baiting Castruchio and the Old Lady, Bosola is now baited in his turn.

81–2. From Montaigne II. 12: "the opinion of wisdome is the plague of man". (C.)

81. *tettor*: skin-disease.

82–3. *if simplicity...happy being.* From Montaigne II. 12: "If simplicitie directeth us to have no evill, it also addresseth us according to our condition to a most happy estate". (C.)

83–4. *subtlest folly...subtlest wisedome*: from the same essay of Montaigne as the previous borrowing, though separated by many pages: "Whence proceeds the subtilest follie but from the subtilest wisedome?" (C.)

92–3. From Montaigne I. 42: "It is for Gods to mount winged horses, and to feed on Ambrosia". (C.)

98. Repeated in *D.L.* v. 4. 222.

that rules i'th'aire. Cf. *Ephesians* ii. 2: "the prince of the power of the air" (the air being supposed full of spirits, largely evil). Webster is however certainly closer to the rendering of the Bishops' Bible (which Shakespeare also used)—"the governour that ruleth in the ayre".

99. *Lord of the ascendant.* In astrology the heavens are divided into twelve "houses" or sections (six above, six below, the horizon) by imaginary lines drawn through the north and south points of the horizon. The "first house" or "house of the ascendant" is that part of the sky which is at the moment rising above the horizon, and extends from 5° above the east horizon to 25° below. From it the other houses were numbered in order eastwards. (There are, however, other rival and more complicated methods of marking out the houses: see Wilson, *Dict. of Astrology, s.v.* "Figure".) Each planet is associated with some one or two signs of the zodiac; and the "lord of the first house" or "of the ascendant" at a given moment is that planet whose sign is entering the first house. Thus the sign Pisces is the mansion of Jupiter: when Pisces are entering the "house of the ascendant", Jupiter is "lord of the ascendant". And accordingly Pisces and Jupiter will be dominating factors in the nativity of a child born at that moment. For the first house is the "House of Life".

102–9. Again from Montaigne II. 12: "The soules of Emperours and Coblers are all cast in one same mould. Considering the importance of Princes actions, and their weight, wee perswade ourselves that they are brought forth by some as weighty and important causes; wee are deceived: They are moved, stirred and removed in their motions by the same springs and wards that we are in ours. The same reason that makes us chide and braule and fall out with any of our neighbours, causeth a warre to follow betweene Princes; the same reason that makes us whip or beat a lackey maketh a Prince (if hee apprehend it) to spoyle and waste a whole Province". And later in the same essay, speaking of laws, Montaigne says: "In rowling on they swell and grow greater and greater, as doe our rivers: follow them upward into their source, and you shall find them but a bubble of water". (C.)

It will be noticed that the picturesque "tithe-pig" (l. 107) is Webster's addition; but for that cf. *Rom. and Jul.* I. 4. 80 (Mercutio of Q. Mab):

> And sometimes comes she with a tithe-pig's tail,
> Tickling a parson's nose as a' lies asleep,
> Then dreams he of another benefice.

117. *Lymmon pils*: Sampson doubts whether "pills" or "peels" is meant; by the spelling it might equally well be either. It is, however, certainly lemon-*peel* that is intended here. Cf. Wycherley, *Love in a Wood*, III. 2: "Warrant her breath with some Lemmon Peil"; L'Estrange, *Fables*, CXXXVI: "Never without Lemmon Pill in her Mouth to correct an unsavoury Vapour of her Own". Sampson supports "pills" by a passage from the *Secretes of Maister Alexis* mentioning "orenge pilles": but the context shows, on the contrary, that "peel" is meant even there, for it is a recipe for *candying* it.

118. *sound*: swoon.

118–9. *troubled With the mother*: *i.e.* with hysteria. Cf. *D.L.* III. 3. 256–7; *Lear*, II. 4. 56:

> O! how this mother swells up toward my heart;
> *Hysterica passio!* down, thou climbing sorrow.

On which W. J. Craig in the *Arden* edition quotes from E. Jordan's *A Brief Discourse of a Disease called the Suffocation of the Mother* (1605), where the commonest symptom is said to be a choking in the throat.

122. *hats on fore the King*: Grandees of Spain had this same privilege, and the ceremony of their creation consisted simply in the King saying "Cobrese por Grande"—"Cover yourself for a Grandee". (Howell, *Letters* (1890), I. 263.)

126. *Why should not we bring up that fashion?* This rash caprice of the Duchess is doubtless meant as another symptom of her hysterical condition.

132. *in colder countries then* (*than*) *in France*: clearly an allusion to English loyalty.

139. *to yeare*: this year; like "to-day".

144. *pare*: peel.

145. *muske*: an esteemed flavour in fruit. Cf. Parkinson, *Paradise* (1629 ed.), 583: "The Muske Nectorin...both smelleth and eateth as if the fruit were steeped in Muske".

148–50. It is hard to be sure whether this is mere Elizabethan nastiness for its own sake, or whether Bosola's mind is running on the dirty work connected with his provisorship of the horse (cf. I. I. 312: "say then my corruption Grew out of horse-doong"). Or is he testing the violence of the Duchess's craving by suggesting obstacles to it? Both of these last possibilities seem quite probable.

159. *this grafting*: editors and the *N.E.D.* have ignored the *double entendre* with which this word is sometimes used. Cf. the fuller phrase "graft the forked tree", copied from Montaigne (II. 12) by Marston (*Fawn*, IV. I. 104).

163. *-farthingalls*: a hooped petticoat, cf. the crinoline (O.F. *vertugall*, Span. *verdugado* from *verdugo*, a rod).

165. *apparently*: clearly, manifestly.

166. *spring-hall*: springal, stripling.

178 ff. It is just like Antonio to be "lost in amazement"; and like Delio to keep his head and think for both.

II. 2.

Outer stage: no break is needed.

1. *teatchi[n]es*: irritability. (Fr. *tache*, "spot"; and thence "bad habit, blemish of character".)

2. *apparant*: manifest.

6. *Glasse-house*: for this favourite topic of Webster's see on *W.D.* I. 2. 134.

13–4. *The Orrenge tree beare[s] ripe and greene fruit, and blossoms altogether.* The point is apparently that the race of women, like the orange-tree, produces all sorts together—women that love for love's sake, women that love for a price.

     Cf. *Mon. Col.* 45–6; Bacon, *Sylva Sylvarum* (pub. 1627), VI. 581: "There be divers fruit trees in the hot countries, which have blossoms, and young fruit, and ripe fruit, almost all the year succeeding one another. And it is said the orange hath the like with us for a great part of summer, and so also hath the fig". (C.)

18. *Dana[e]s*: see on I. I. 265–6. This heroine, whose lover appeared in the shape of a shower of gold, had already in antiquity become the ironic type of mercenary love. Cf. the inscription in Buecheler's *Carmina Latina Epigraphica* (Teubner), No. 938:

> Pulveris aurati pluvia sit sparsa papyrus:
>   Rescribet Danae sollicitata "Veni".

> Shower gold-dust on the note, when you address
>   Your love; and Danaë will answer "Yes".

21–2. *lines meete in one center*: *double entendre*. Cf. Montaigne III. 5: "(love) is a matter everywhere infused, and a centre whereto all lines come, all things looke". Similarly Marston, *Dutch Courtezan*, II. I. 121: "love is the centre in which all lines close".

24. *false rusty watch*. Cf. Middleton, *Roaring Girl*, II. 2. 111–2:

> his watch ne'er goes right
> That sets his dial by a rusty clock.

32. *Forobosco*: the name recurs in Webster's part of *F.M.I.* and was perhaps suggested by Alphonso Ferrabosco or Ferabosco of Bologna (d. 1628), who like his father and his son served the gaieties of the English court, and provided airs for many of Jonson's Masques from 1606 to 1611. In 1605 he had been appointed musical instructor to Prince Henry. The name had however already been used by Marston for a character in *Antonio's Revenge*.

38. *Switzer*: Swiss mercenary soldiers were common then, as for centuries to come.

40. *Pistoll in his great cod-piece*. For the great cod-piece see on *W.D.*

v. 3. 101: and for its use as a receptacle H.D.S. quotes Herrick, "Upon Shark", who eats so modestly when asked to dinner,

> When if the servants search, they may descry
> In his wide codpeece, dinner being done,
> Two napkins cramm'd up, and a silver spoone.

47. *Caniball*: blood-thirsty savage.

48. *French*: possibly with a play on the *morbus Gallicus*.

67. *Black-guard*: scullions and turnspits. See on *W.D.* I. 2. 128.

73. *poast to Rome*: to keep watch on the Duchess's brothers there.

80. *mind*: pay heed to.

81 ff. Cf. Montaigne II. 12: "A gust of contrarie winds, the croking of a flight of Ravens, the false pace of a Horse, the casual flight of an Eagle...are enough to overthrowe, sufficient to overwhelme and able to pull him (man) to the ground". (H.D.S.) Similarly Wither, *Abuses Stript and Whipt* (1613):

> For worthlesse matters some are wondrous sad
> Whom if I call vaine I must terme mad.
> If that their Noses bleede some certaine Drops,
> And then againe upon the suddaine stops,
> Or if the babling Foule we call the Jay,
> A Squirrell, or a Hare, but crosse their way,
> Or if the Salt fall toward them at the Table,
> Or any such like superstitious Bable,
> Their mirth is spoil'd, because they hold it true
> That some mischance must thereupon ensue.

There is an allusion to the title of this book, it may be noted, in *A.Q.L.* II. 2. 181–2.

81. *throwing downe salt*: a superstition probably connected with the feeling that salt, with its preservative qualities, was the symbol of enduring friendship and faith.

81. *crossing of a Hare*. From S. Africa to Scotland this is held an evil omen; perhaps because the animal was a favourite disguise of witches, but more probably because it is a weak timorous creature, whereas the savage wolf has been regarded as lucky to meet (Grimm, *Teut. Mythology* (Eng. transl.), III. 1126; Brand, *Pop. Antiq.* 689–90). The crossing of the hare was supposed also to disorder the senses. Cf. "Beaum. & Fl.", *Wit at Sev. Weapons*, II. 3 (where a clown is behaving fantastically): "I'll lay my life some hare has crossed him".

82. *Bleeding at nose*: as Antonio fears when his bleeds in II. 3. 58. Cf. *Merch. of Ven.* II. 5. 24: and the alarm of Charles II's servants when his nose bled during his hiding at Boscobel House.

82. *stumbling of a horse*. Cf. *Rich. III*, III. 4. 83:

> Three times to-day my foot-cloth horse did stumble.

Similarly in the *Ballad of Lord Derwentwater* (Child's *Engl. and Scott. Ballads*, IV. 120):

> He set his foot in the level stirrup,
>   And mounted his bonny grey steed;
> The gold rings from his fingers did break
>   And his nose began for to bleed.

> He had not ridden past a mile or two,
>   When his horse stumbled over a stone.
> "There are tokens enough," said my Lord Derwentwater,
>   "That I shall never return."

83. *Criket*: for this omen see on *W.D.* v. 4. 79.
84. *To daunt whole man in us*: all our manhood. Cf. *W.D.* 1. 1. 44;
"Beaum. & Fl.", *Bonduca*, iv. 3:

> 'Tis loss of whole man in me.

Double Marriage, iii. 3:

> For sure there is no taste of right man in it.

Middleton, *Fair Quarrel*, iv. 3. 111–2:

> Being his soul's wish to depart absolute man,
> In life a soldier, death a christian.

92. *a figure for's Nativitie*: a typical first step for Antonio to take immediately after a lecture from his friend against superstition. It is a
curious piece of irony, whether intended by Webster or no, that
though the infant turns out in the next scene to have the most appalling
horoscope, it is eventually the one member of the family to survive.

II. 3.

Outer stage: Bosola's lantern would suffice to imply night to the audience
in the public theatre.
15. *This Moale do's undermine me*: see on *D.L.* iv. 2. 322–4.
25. Cf. ii. 5. 97–9; iv. 2. 364.
27–8. For this recourse to astrology for the discovery of lost goods cf.
Donne, *Elegies* xi, where the poet imagines going to "some dread
Conjurer", who is in league with thief and murderer, to recover his
mistress's lost bracelet; and the "Character of a Quack-Astrologer"
(1673), quoted in Brand, *Pop. Antiq.* 623—"to help people to what
they have lost, he picks their pockets afresh. Not a ring or spoon is
nim'd away but pays him twelve pence toll". Cf. *F.M.I.* ii. 2. 85.
30. *radicall*: not, here, "going to the root of the matter", "conclusive"
(Sampson): it is a technical term in astrology, meaning "fit to be
judged or decided". Cf. Lilly, *Chr. Astrol.* (1647 ed.), 121: "The
question then shall be taken for radicall, or fit to be judged, when as
the Lord of the hour at the time of proposing the question...and
the Lord of the Ascendant or First House, are of one Triplicity or
be one". (The twelve signs of the zodiac were divided into four
triplicities.) So Wilson (a fiery believer, who regards Newton with
his gravitation as a superstitious bigot) in his *Dict. of Astrol.* (1819)

explains "radical" as "a term used of horary questions to signify that the question is fit and may be resolved".

37. *I came to say my prayers*: there is a disinterested sense of humour and irony about Bosola which helps to raise his villainy almost to an art.

43. *spanish figge*: there has been great confusion about the Elizabethan use of "fig". For the fruit is associated (1) with the poison often administered in it; (2) with an indecent gesture based on its appearance; (3) with contempt, on account of its cheapness.

For (1) cf. *W.D.* IV. 2. 63 and note.

(2) In several European languages the fig is associated with an offensive gesture as old, at least, as Rome itself (cf. Span. *dar una higa* (*higo*, fig); Ital. *far le fiche* (plural for both hands); Fr. *faire la figue*; Germ. *die Feigen zeigen*; Eng. "to give the fig" or "to fig" a person). The gesture consisted in thrusting the thumb between fore-finger and middle-finger (or into the mouth), with a phallic implication, from which the name is perhaps derived owing to the resemblance between the opening fig and the *vulva*. Both in ancient Rome and in Spain and Portugal up to the last century amulets resembling a hand in this position were hung on children and beasts of burden to avert the evil eye. Villani relates that the men of a neighbouring town set up a statue in the thirteenth century, making this gesture in the direction of Florence. The practice was prohibited altogether by Paul II on pain of a fine of 20 soldi: but clearly with little effect. (There is a ridiculous account of the origin of the name quoted in Littré's *French Dict. s.v. figue*—see *N.Q.* 9. 11. 185; Douce, *Illustrat. of Shakesp.* (1807), 1. 492.)

(3) There is, lastly, a second contemptuous use, perhaps really derived from (2) by misunderstanding or bowdlerization, in such phrases as "not worth a fig", figs being abundant in the south.

Here, at all events, Bosola doubtless makes the indecent gesture as he speaks.

52-3. *snake...warme...sting*: with allusion to the fable of the countryman and the snake. "Scarce warme" because of the newness of Bosola's provisorship of the horse. So Spenser in his *State of Ireland* says of an O'Neale favoured by the Queen: "now hee playeth like the frozen snake, who being for compassion releived of the husband-man, soone after he was warme began to hisse, and threaten danger even to him and his".

54-7. An obscure passage (see Text. Note) neglected by editors. Allen indeed suggests that Antonio hands Bosola the horoscope about the stolen jewels with the intention that he should copy it, "adding at the same time the propitiatory remark 'you libel well'". Bosola however refuses the paper and offers as proof of his innocence to sign a copy of the horoscope drawn up by Antonio. But it is ridiculous to suppose that Antonio had really written out also an astrological figure for the theft. That figure was merely invented as an excuse,

on the spur of the moment: it did not actually exist. In any case why
should it be copied, or signed, by Bosola? Sampson remarks: "Bosola's
speech is tantamount to saying 'As I am innocent, I will sign a statement you have made concerning the jewels'". But what sort of
statement? And why sign it? What would that prove?

It seems probable that a line has dropped out (the Quarto repeats
"*Ant.*" as the speaker in 55, though no intervening speech appears),
in which Bosola repeated some such charge as "You are a false
steward" (cf. 49)—perhaps accused Antonio of being himself the thief.
"You are a fine slanderer," replies Antonio. Now "to libell" can
mean not only "to defame", but also "to bring a suit with a *libel,
i.e. a formal charge in writing*". And so Bosola plays on this second
sense and rejoins, "No, but write out yourself the charge (libel) I
bring against you and I will sign it with pleasure". It is merely a
rather pointless, quibbling thrust in their verbal fencing-match.

This seems a possible explanation; though it is not a very satisfactory one.

61. *Two letters*: initials worked in his handkerchief; *not*, as has been
suggested, in the copy of the horoscope—in which the letters were not
wrought, and Antonio's initials would not occur.

71. *falce-friend*: the dark-lantern, a thing of sinister association for
Webster's audience. For Barrington, *Observations on the Antient
Statutes* (quoted in Brand, *Pop. Antiq.* 781), mentions a vulgar error
that their use was unlawful,—a notion which may have arisen from
Guy Fawkes's use of one a few years before this.

77–8. *Lord of the first house...ascendant*: see on II. I. 99.

77. *combust*: *lit.* "burnt up", means within $8\frac{1}{2}°$ of the sun, whereby
a planet's influence was supposed to be destroyed.

78. *human signe*: Aquarius, Gemini, Virgo, or Sagittarius.

79. *the Dragon*: the apparent path of the sun, or ecliptic, is intersected in
two places by the path of the moon. (It is simplest to imagine the two
lines drawn on the sky above one.) That part of the moon's path
which lies to the south of the ecliptic was called "the Dragon". The
Dragon's Head lay where the moon in its ascent crossed the ecliptic,
the Tail where it re-crossed the ecliptic in its descent. The influence
of the former was auspicious, that of the latter sinister. The names
were due to the fact that these two points of intersection are the only
places where eclipses occur; and eclipses all the world over have been
associated with the efforts of a dragon to swallow the sun and moon.
Cf. Chaucer, *Astrolabe*, II. 4: "a fortunat assendent clepen they
whan that no wykkid planet, as Saturne or Mars, or elles the tail
of the dragoun, is in the hous of the assendent". Thus Edmund in
King Lear was begotten under it (I. 2. 144).

79. *the eight house*: regularly signifies the manner of death, just as the
first is the "House of Life": *eight* is quite common for "eighth".

80. *Caete[r]a non scrutantur*: "the rest is not investigated". (*Scrutor*, a

deponent verb in classical Latin, is used as a passive, as here, in later writers, *e.g. Ammianus Marcellinus.*)

81. *apparant*: evident.

81. *precise*—puritanical: "Precisians" was another name for the Puritans.

II. 4.

Inner stage (cf. "Sit" in l. 1). With the drawing back of its curtain the audience would be prepared for a change of scene. The second line tells them whither—"to Rome".

7. *witty*: note this echo of the warning last line of the previous scene.

21. *glasse male-able*: malleable. It is conceivable that a pun on "male" is intended. At all events this idea of malleability was doubtless suggested by the well-known story of the inventor who came to Tiberius with an actual specimen of malleable glass he had made: and was put to death for his pains because the Emperor was jealous, says Dio (LVII. 21). Pliny, more plausibly, suggests economic reasons, *i.e.* consideration for the glass-makers. Albertus Magnus in his *Of the Virtues of Animals* actually gives a recipe: "If Goat's blood be taken warm, with vinegar and the juice of hay, and the like be boiled with glass, it makes the glass soft like paste, and it may be thrown against a wall, and will not break". Sir T. Browne (*Pseud.* II. 5. 2) is eloquently sceptical of the possibility of such a thing: our age has however at last really invented it.

24–5. *fantastique glasse...Galileo.* The first practical telescope (though the idea seems to occur in Roger Bacon) was constructed by the Dutch spectacle-maker Nippershey about 1608. In 1609 Galileo, hearing in Venice that some such instrument had been devised, solved the problem independently and with considerable improvements. This anachronism of Webster's worried the precise Theobald. In his preface to *The Fatal Secret* (1735) he complains of our poet: "Nor has he been less licentious in another respect (*i.e.* in addition to infringing the Unities): he makes mention of Galileo and Tasso, neither of whom were born till near half a century after the Dutchess of Malfy was murthered". These lines of Webster will recall to many those of a greater poet on the same theme:

the Moon whose Orb
Through Optic Glass the Tuscan Artist views
At Ev'ning, from the top of Fesole
Or in Valdarno, to descry new Lands,
Rivers or Mountains in her spotty Globe.

26–7. *Moone...constant woman*: this can hardly be a reminiscence of Lyly's *Woman in the Moon*, for *she* is placed in that sphere because her inconstancy and its changeableness go well together:

Forgetfull, foolish, fickle, franticke, madde;
These be the humors that content me best
And therefore will I stay with Cynthia.

34. *since*: either the Cardinal is being paradoxical, or "though" would be more natural: for the fact that he is not Julia's husband and so cannot be cuckolded by her, is a reason for *not* being jealous.

42–3. *watch'd Like a tame Ellephant.* Does this mean "watched like an Elephant being tamed by being kept awake"? Cf. *A.Q.L.* I. I. 158–60: "she rail'd upon me when I should sleep, And that's, you know, intollerable; for indeed 'Twill tame an Elephant". This parallel is, I think, strong evidence: hawks also were regularly tamed in this way (*Sh.'s Eng.* II. 357), and the idea may have come into Webster's mind by association with the hawking metaphors of the previous lines. Cf., too, *A.V.* v. I. 146–51, of taming lions by sleeplessness. Or does *watch'd* refer to the staring of a crowd of spectators at the animal? There was a famous exhibition of an Elephant in London (*c.* 1594), alluded to in literature for years after—cf. Basse (d. 1653?), *Metam. of the Walnut Tree*, "in our youth we saw the Elephant". It is sometimes coupled with Banks's horse (see on *W.D.* II. 2. 14). Cf. Jonson, *Ev. Man out of his H.* IV. 4: "He keeps more ado with this monster than ever Banks did with his horse, or the fellow with the elephant". Grierson in a note on the date of Donne's *Satires* quotes Sir J. Davies, "In Titum" (about 1594—whence the date given above):

> Titus the brave and valorous young gallant
> Three years together in the town hath beene,
> Yet my Lo. Chancellors tombe he hath not seene,
> Nor the new water-worke, nor the Elephant.
> I cannot tell the cause without a smile:
> He hath been in the Counter all the while.

On the whole, however, though an allusion to this elephant would be quite possible, the passages from *A.Q.L.* and *A.V.* seem to me stronger evidence.

46–7. *a little fingring on the Lute, Yet cannot tune it.* Cf. *Haml.* III. 2. 387–94; Chapman, *Seven Penitential Psalms* (1612), "To Young Imaginaries" (quoted on II. 5. 50–1).

The sense seems to demand that *tune* should here mean "play". *N.E.D.* quotes no example of this sense before 1701: but *N.E.D.* is not at all reliable for fixing earliest dates (for instance, it gives no example before 1675 of "intelligency" as used in II. 3. 83; nor before 1810 of "Alastor", which appears in *F.M.I.* III. I. 68). At all events "tuner" = "singer", "player" is found as early as *c.* 1580.

53. *Lightning mooves slow to't*: in comparison with it. Lightning is a dubious symbol for a constant affection; as perhaps the Cardinal is well aware. It is certainly a formidable, almost menacing one. For the image cf. Donne, *Of the Progress of the Soul*, "Harbinger to the Progresse" (1612), 11–2:

> Thy flight which doth our thoughts outgoe
> So fast, that now the lightning moves but slow.

72. *if he had had a good backe*: with a *double entendre*. Cf. II. 5. 94. Castruchio belongs to the same type of impotent nincompoop as Camillo in *The White Devil*.

80. *allowance* seems almost to mean "income", "revenue". Cf. J. Ward, *Diary* (1662: publ. 1839), 183: "Mr Shakespeare…had an allowance so large that he spent at the rate of 1,000 l. a-year". Otherwise the phrase must mean "(The gold is) allowed you by me".

86. *Cassia*: a coarser kind of cinnamon.

87. *phisicall*: good for the health, restorative. Cf. *W.D.* v. 4. 23–4 and note.

88. *Cullisses*: strengthening broths. See on *W.D.* v. 4. 23–4.

89. *Creature bred by*——: Julia was doubtless going to add "unnatural means" (cf. *Char.* "A Divellish Usurer", 6: "unnaturall Act of generation"), with allusion to the time-worn comparison of usury to an unnatural breeding of gold, which is older than Aristotle himself (*Politics* I. 10—cf. the Greek word for "interest", τόκος, *lit.* "offspring"; and *Merch. of Ven.* I. 3. 135, "breed of barren metal").

98. *my mistris*. It would seem, though it is far from clear and no one appears to have suggested it, that Delio means to use Julia as a means of extracting information about the Cardinal's intentions, just as Bosola actually does use her, and as Francisco uses Zanche in *W.D.* This would make the present scene somewhat less irrelevant: but it looks almost as if Webster, after starting with this idea, had then failed to develop it.

107–8. Cf. the Cardinal's similar maxim in I. I. 366. And for the inverted commas, used merely to mark a striking saying, see on *W.D.* II. I. 278–9.

II. 5.

Inner stage as before, though the Outer, of course, may have been used as well.

1. *dig'd up a man-drake*: for the madness supposed to ensue see on *W.D.* III. I. 54.

5. *loose i'th'hilts*: unchaste. Cf. Fletcher, *The Chances*, II. 4. The phrase might simply be a metaphor of an untrustworthy weapon: or, since the basket-hilt used with wooden cudgels was changeable from one stick to another, it might mean too ready to change. But it seems more likely that there was a general sexual association with the screwing of hilt into blade: this would explain the applicability of the phrase to venereal disease in Fletcher's *Maid of the Mill*, I. 3:

> And this is a 'pothecary's: I have lain here many times
> For a looseness in my hilts.

11. *covetuous*: because hoping for hush-money.

15. *Service*: sexual indulgence? See *N.E.D. s.v.* "service¹" 6 c and 36; "serve" v^1. 52.

18–9. *rubarbe...choller*: see on *W.D.* v. 1. 193–4.

19. *here's the cursed day*: presumably, the horoscope, giving the date, which Bosola had picked up in II. 3 and has now forwarded to Rome.

20. *here'it shall sticke.* With these words the Duke must be imagined to thrust back the paper into his bosom, next his heart, whence he had taken it in the preceding line. Perhaps if he makes this gesture, the emphasis should be laid on "*her* bleeding heart" in the next line. *here'it*: the apostrophe, if correct, merely signifies that the preceding syllable is spoken shortly.

35. *cupping-glasse*: see on *W.D.* v. 6. 105.

44–5. *womens hearts...left-side.* Vaughan refers to Browne, *Pseudo-doxia*, IV. 2, which in turn quotes *Ecclesiastes* x. 2: "A wise man's heart is at his right hand; but a fool's heart at his left" (the Hebrew really means "A wise man's will is *for the right*; but a fool's desire is *for the left*, *i.e.* tends in the wrong direction"). Here too, as in *Ecclesiastes*, *left* is really figurative. Cf. "sinister" and "*gauche*"; and III. 1. 33–4 below:

> I grow to infinite purchase
> The leaft-hand way.

For the general sentiment cf. Painter, where, in the corresponding passage, the Duchess's brother exclaims of women: "they seem to be procreated and borne againste all order of Nature, and to live withoute Lawe, whych governeth al other things indued with some reason and understanding".

46–9. Cf. the sentiment of Bandello's preface to his narrative of the Duchess: "E nel vero grave sciocchezza quella degli uomini mi pare che vogliono che l' onor loro e di tutta la casata consista ne l' appetito d' una donna".

I do not see anything equivalent in Painter: and it suggests the possibility that Webster had also read Bandello. He had, we know, at all events enough Italian to quote Tasso.

50. *purchas'd*: obtained (Fr. *pour-chasser*). The meaning "pay for" is only secondary: the original sense being of violent or wrongful acquisition, as in hunting or theft or war. Thence it came to mean "acquire" in general. It might seem, none the less, that the meaning here was "bought", with a reference to the sale of honours. But cf. Otway, *Orphan*, I. 1:

> The honours he has gain'd are justly his;
> He *purchas'd* them in war.

There is a neat combination of the old sense and the new in Shirley, *Bird in a Cage*, IV. 2:

> *Rol.* And when I have put a girdle 'bout the world,
>   This purchase will reward me. (*I.e.* the *gain* of Eugenia's love.)
> *Eug.* Purchase! I am not bought
>   And sold, I hope.

50–1. Cf. Chapman, *Seven Penitential Psalms* (1612), "To Young
Imaginaries":

> Terms, tongues, reading, all
> That can within a man, call'd learned, fall,
> Whose life is led yet like an ignorant man's,
> Are but as tools to gouty artisans
> That cannot use them. (C.)

58. *quoit the sledge*: throw the hammer. Cf. Nash, *Have with you to
Saffron Walden* (Grosart), p. 52 (he is laughing at the ponderousness
of a pamphlet of Gabriel Harvey's): "Credibly it was once rumord
about the Court, that the Guard meant to trie masteries with it before
the Queene, and, in stead of throwing the sledge or the hammer, to
hurle it foorth at the armes ende for a wager".

77–9. One of Webster's deepest themes (cf. the knell of *W.D.* v. 6.
273–4)—the cry of the world-weariness of the later Renaissance.

87–91. This might seem a reminiscence of the Neronian *tunica molesta*
or shirt smeared with combustibles in which condemned criminals
were burned as illuminants. Cf. Juvenal VIII. 235—and J. B. Mayor's
note.

It was, however, clearly suggested to Webster by a hitherto un-
noticed passage in Painter's story of the Duchess (*Palace of Pleasure*,
ed. Jacobs, III. 38): "We may confesse also these brutall brethren
to be more butcherly than ever Otho Erle of Monferrato, and prince
of Urbin was, who caused a yeoman of his chamber to be wrapped
in a sheete poudred with sulpher and brimstone, and afterwards
kindled with a Candle,...bicause he waked not at an hour by him
appointed".

97–9. Cf. *W.D.* II. 1. 252–3.

101. *Scorpions*: see on *W.D.* II. 1. 247.

102. *generall ecclipse*: total.

III. 1.

Outer stage.

18. *eare;*—if the semi-colon is right, we must suppose it to imply an
awed hush before pronouncing the Cardinal's name.

25. *Dormise.* Cf. I. 1. 307.

33. *purchase*: aggrandisement. See on II. 5. 50 above.

33–42. An agreeable piece of irony at the expense of club-politicians
with their profoundly subtle explanations of non-existent facts.

51. *sticke of sugar-candy*: *i.e.* cheap, sugary, and easily seen-through?
Cf. *D.L.* II. 1. 153–5: "You are a foole, a precious one—you are a
meere sticke of Sugar Candy, a man may looke quite thorow you".
Similarly *Much Ado*, IV. 1. 322: "a goodly Count Comfect; a sweet
gallant, surely".

59. *Pasquils paper-bullets.* Pasquino or Pasquillo was a sharp-tongued
Roman schoolmaster or cobbler of the fifteenth century, whose name
was subsequently given to a mutilated statue excavated in 1501 (close

to his shop, says one account) and set up opposite the palace of Cardinal Caraffa. Under the Cardinal's patronage the statue used to be dressed up every St Mark's Day and Latin verses affixed to it by students of the New Learning. Naturally these *pasquinate* tended to become satirical; and the "pasquinade" spread to France and across the Channel, so that Nash, for instance, took to signing himself "Pasquil of England".

These satires generally took the form of dialogues between Pasquillo and another statue from the Forum called Marforio. Thus under Sixtus V Pasquillo appeared in a dirty shirt. "Why?" asked Marforio. "I have no laundress," replied Pasquillo, "since the Pope's sister became a princess". Then Pasquillo took to hastily turning and returning the shirt. "Why such haste?"—"Before they start a tax on sunlight!" Sixtus wanted to throw Pasquillo into the Tiber; but Tasso wrote on his behalf: "Do not drown him or on the bank of the river there will spring up from his dust innumerable frogs that will croak in derision night and day".

paper-bullets: Sampson quotes *Much Ado*, II. 3. 249: "paper bullets of the brain".

64. *apparant*: evident.

67. *This deadly aire is purg'd*: referring to the *pestilent ayre* of l. 60 above. Cf. Montaigne II. 3: "And God be thanked, since this good advertisement, our ayre is infinitely purged of them". (Not in C.)

69. *burning cultures*: coulters. The coulter is the iron blade in front of the plough-share which makes the vertical cut in the soil. The ordeal by red-hot plough-shares is familiar in old English and German law, nine shares being the usual number. Emma, mother of Edward the Confessor, for instance, is related to have passed through it successfully when accused of an intrigue with the Bishop of Winchester (Freeman, *Norman Conq.* II. Append. Note H); similarly St Cunigund, consort of the Emperor Henry II. Burton (*Anat.* III. 3. 2) has a characteristically recondite list of such cases.

73. *go read i'th' Starres*: an ironic reminiscence of Antonio's horoscope?

82–4. Perhaps an echo of *Othello*, I. I. 172:

> Is there not charms
> By which the property of youth and maidhood
> May be abused?

91. *lenative*: "soothing, but insidious" (Allen). Other editors have not even turned in their sleep over this strange epithet. But if *lenative* = "lenitive", it must mean simply "soothing"; and it is odd to be driven mad with soothing-syrup. It looks as if Webster's learning might have led him into either a false etymology or a new coinage of his own. "Lenitive" comes from "*lenire*, to soothe"; might not "*lenative*" be derived from "*lenare*, to prostitute" (cf. *lena*, bawd; *lenocinium*, meretricious attraction)? Then "*lenative* poisons" would be some such violent aphrodisiac as is said to have driven Lucretius

mad, when administered by his wife as a love-philtre. Cf. Ovid, *Ars Amat.* II. 105–6:

> Nec data profuerint pallentia philtra puellis:
> Philtra nocent animis vimque furoris habent.

If Webster really did mean "lenitive" ("lenatively" is certainly used in its normal sense in *A.Q.L.* I. I. 91; and "primitive" spelt "primative" elsewhere in *D.M.*) we can only explain—"poisons purporting to soothe the passion of the lover who administers the philtre". But this is very forced. Or simply "slow poisons"?

93. *by equivocation*: by some quibble, *e.g.* that love is a madness.

105. *girdle 'bout the world*: a favourite Elizabethan metaphor, usually to describe a literal journey round the world, like Drake's (cf. *Mids. Night's Dream*, II. I. 175; Chapman, *Bussy d'Ambois*, I. I. 23; Massinger, *Maid of Honour*, I. I; Middleton, *Sun in Aries* (Bullen), p. 342, etc.); but it is used sometimes to express having done and seen everything, encompassed all knowledge, as here and in the character of "A noble and retir'd Housekeeper", 19–20: "he hath as it were, put a gird about the whole world and sounded all her *quicksandes*".

Parrott, on the Chapman passage, suggests that the phrase may have been suggested by a device in Whitney's *Choice of Emblems* (Leyden, 1586, p. 203) celebrating Drake's circumnavigation of 1577–80, in which the hand of Providence emerges from a cloud and holds the globe by a girdle. But it is unlikely that we can give so precise an origin to so general an idea. Indeed the print might equally well be based on the current phrase.

111. *your owne Chronicle.* Cf. *W.D.* v. 1. 100–1.

III. 2.

Inner stage: the curtain may well have been drawn and disclosed the Duchess already untiring herself. In the latter part of the scene doubtless the whole stage was brought into use.

6. *with cap, and knee*: a regular phrase for "with cap in hand and bended knee". Cf. Marbeck, *Book of Notes*, 1189 (1581): "they shall have cappe and knee, and many gaye goodmorrowes in this lyfe".

9. *Lord of Misse-rule*: an unusual spelling. It *may*, one fears, be intended to suggest a play on "Misse" = "kept mistress" (cf. Evelyn, *Diary*, June 1645: "The com'on misses...go abroad bare-fac'd"). The Lord of Mis-rule, perhaps a survival of the old Fertility King, used to be appointed to reign over the Christian revels at Court, the Universities, the Inns of Court, and in the houses of the great. (See Frazer, *Golden Bough*, IX. 331 ff.; Chambers, *Medieval Stage*, I. 403 ff.)

31 ff. Antonio's panegyric of marriage is a charmingly ironic contrast to his very different view of it in I. I. 456 ff.

32. *Daphne*: wooed by Apollo (Ovid, *Met.* 1. 452).
32. *peevish*: not "foolish" (Dyce), but "froward", "perverse". Cf. *Ralph Roister Doister*, III. 3:

> These women be all such mad peevish elves
> They will not be won, except to please themselves.

33. *Siri[n]x*: a nymph vainly beloved by Pan, who made his Pan-pipe of the whispering reed into which she was changed (Ovid, *Met.* 1. 689).

34. *Anaxar[e]te*. Her rejected lover Iphis hanged himself at his stony mistress's door. As she was watching, still unmoved, his body on its journey to the grave, Venus in just anger changed her to a stone figure, which was thenceforth preserved in the goddess's temple at Salamis in Cyprus (Ovid, *Met.* xIV. 698).

38. *The Oliffe* was the gift to Athens of the virgin-goddess Athene; and so not a very happy instance from Antonio's point of view.

38. *Pomgranet*: I do not know of any woman turned into a pomegranate, though Robert Browning was to turn the pomegranate flower (βαλαύστιον) into a woman.

38. *Mulbery*: this tree changed the colour of its fruit to red from the blood of Pyramus, when he slew himself, thinking Thisbe dead (Ovid, *Met.* IV. 55).

39. *Flowres*: such as Clytie who loved Apollo and became a sun-flower.

39. *eminent Starres*: e.g. Callisto, a nymph of Diana, loved by Jupiter and changed by the jealous Juno into the Great Bear (Ovid, *Met.* II. 409); Andromeda the bride of Perseus; the Pleiades, the seven daughters of Atlas, of whom one, Sterope, was fabled to shine faintly and almost invisibly because she alone gave herself to a mortal lover, but her sisters to gods.

47. *Motion*: show, spectacle (often of puppets). Cf. Jonson, *Ev. Man out of his H.* II. 1: "They say there's a new Motion of the city of Nineveh, with Jonas, and the whale, to be seen at Fleet-bridge"; Marston, *Dutch Courtezan*, III. 1. 134: "A motion, sister".— "Nineveh, Julius Caesar, Jonas, or the destruction of Jerusalem?"

48–9. Cf. Archilochus' description of his love:

$$\text{ἐσμυρισμένας κόμας}$$
$$\text{καὶ στῆθος, ὡς ἂν καὶ γέρων ἠράσσατο}$$

(so that even an old man would have fallen in love with her); and J. M. Synge's rendering of Villon's "Regrets de la belle Heaulmière": "Where is the round forehead I had, and the two eyebrows, and the eyes with a big gay look out of them would bring folly from a great scholar?"

57. *Painter*: with, of course, an allusion to the painting of faces as well as of portraits.

61. *When were we so merry?* Cf. the "feyness" often supposed to

precede disaster: as when the suitors in the *Odyssey* laugh on the eve of their slaying "with alien lips". So Romeo says (*Romeo and Juliet*, v. 3. 88):

> How oft when men are at the point of death
> Have they been merry! which their keepers call
> A lightning before death.

The phrase was proverbial. Sir T. More, again, in Holinshed, describing the mood of Lord Hastings just before his sudden execution by Richard III, says: "he was never merier, nor never so full of good hope in his life; which selfe thing is oft seene a signe of change".

68. *Arras*: powdered orris- (iris-) root, a white powder with a smell of violets. Cf. *W.D.* v. 3. 118. The reader may perhaps recall this passage later on, at IV. 2. 134, 192.

69–70. *entred you into my heart...keyes.* From *Arcadia*, I. (*Wks.* I. 69): "His fame had so framed the way to my mind that his presence...had entred there before he vouchsafed to call for the keyes". (C.)

76. *Ghossips*: god-parents to your children.

77–9. A typical utterance of Webster's cardinal virtue of courage in despair. (Cf. *D.L.* I. 2. 259–60; *Char.* "Housekeeper", 22–3.) Equally typically, he borrowed it, from the *Arcadia*, I. (*Wks.* I. 25): "Lastly, whether your time call you to live or die, doo both like a prince".

It is a curious coincidence to find these words again in some of the verses written by Frederick the Great amid the disasters of the Seven Years War, which are better than his poetry usually is:

> Pour moi, menacé du naufrage,
> Je dois, en affrontant l'orage,
> Penser, vivre, et mourir en roi.

The situation may remind us of the first of the *Sonnets from the Portuguese*. There the poetess feels a presence behind her—Death it seems; but it proves to be Love. Here the Duchess looks round for Love, and sees Death standing before her.

81–5. *Vertue...a bare name, And no essentiall thing.* From *Arcadia*, II. (*Wks.* I. 146): "O Vertue, where doost thou hide thy selfe? or what hideous thing is this which doth eclips thee? or is it true that thou weart never but a vaine name, and no essentiall thing?" (C.) Cf. too Chapman, *Byron's Tragedy*, v. 3. 199 ff.; Massinger, *Bashful Lover*, IV. I: "Virtue's but a word, Fortune makes all.—We are her tennis-balls".

But the ultimate source of all these in their turn has not, I think, been pointed out; it is the account in Dio Cassius (XLVII. 49) of the last utterance of Brutus at Philippi, which consists of two iambic lines (they might well be from some lost play of Euripides):

ὦ τλῆμον ἀρετή, λόγος ἄρ' ἦσθ' ἐγὼ δέ σε
ὡς ἔργον ἤσκουν· σὺ δ' ἄρ' ἐδούλευες τύχῃ.
Poor Virtue, so thou wast but a mere word!
I held thee real, that art but Fortune's slave.

Whence also Lord Chesterfield's acid summary of Henry Fox—"He lived, as Brutus died, calling virtue a name".

90–4. *reason...foresee...prevent...shame.* From *Arcadia*, II. (*Wks.* I. 146): "O imperfect proportion of reason which can too much forsee, and too little prevent!...In shame there is no comfort but to be beyond all bounds of shame". (C.)

98–9. *sheeres...flowne.* From *Arcadia*, II. (*Wks.* I. 177): "Alas, thought *Philoclea* to her selfe, your sheeres come to[o] late to clip the birds wings that already is flowne away". (C.)

102. *Basilisque*: the same as the cockatrice, a fabulous king of the serpents, with the body of a cock, the tail of a viper, and a crown-like crest on its head whence its name (βασιλίσκος, royal). "The Basilisk," says the *Hortus Sanitatis*, III. 13, "is sometimes gendered from a cock; for towards the end of the summer the cock lays an egg from which the Basilisk is hatched. Also the opinion of some is that a viper or toad sits on that cock's egg—but this is doubtful." Its breath, even the sight of it, was fatal (Pliny VIII. 21); hence Topsell's story of the man who caused a great mortality among cockatrices by going about enclosed in mirrors so that they saw their own faces; Topsell, however, judiciously questions the truth of this, on the ground that the man would assuredly have been killed by their breath. Their only successful enemy was the weasel, which fortified itself against their poisonous exhalations by eating rue. For the repartee cf. *Rich. III*, I. 2. 150:

> *Glouc.* Thine eyes, sweet lady, have infected mine.
> *Anne.* Would they were basilisks, to strike thee dead!

106. *musicke to the[e]*: *i.e.* compared to thee.

119–20. *Such a roome...as our Anchorites*: *i.e.* walled up in a cell with only a small aperture, like Thais, for instance, after her conversion in Hroswitha's play; or, only a little before Webster wrote, the nun Virginia Maria de Leyva who was sentenced for unchastity to be "inclosed within a little dungeon, the door of which shall be walled up with stones and mortar, so that the said Virginia Maria shall abide there for the term of her natural life, immured both day and night, never to issue thence, but shall receive food and other necessaries through a small hole in the wall of the said chamber, and light and air through an aperture". (J. A. Symonds, *The Catholic Reaction* (1886), I. 353.) Crawford quotes Donne, *Of the Progress of the Soul*, 169:

> Thinke that no stubborne sullen Anchorit,
> Which fixt to a pillar, or a grave, doth sit
> Bedded, and bathed in all his ordures, dwels
> So fowly as our Soules in their first-built Cels.

There is an interesting likeness and difference between the two
writers. Both dwell lovingly on the physically loathsome; but at least
Webster never put it on an altar and grovelled before it like the
Dean of St Paul's.

124. *Paraqueto.* Cf. the popinjay (or pyet) who betrays the murder
in some versions of the Ballad of "Young Hunting" and the hawk
who reveals the wife's infidelity in "The Bonny Birdy".

131–3. *sheete of lead...my heart.* Cf. *W.D.* III. 2. 343; H. King,
Poems, "The Departure":

> Might all your crosses in that sheet of lead
> Which folds my heavy heart lie buried.

136. *hollow bullet*: *i.e.* cannon-ball, Fr. *boulet.* The explosive shell, as
an improvement on the solid cannon-ball, was first introduced about
the middle of the sixteenth century.

145 ff. *Reputation, Love, and Death.* This fable is the basis of a poem
"Love, Death, and Reputation", generally (and, no doubt, rightly)
assigned to Charles Lamb, in *Poetry for Children,* a joint-volume
written by him and his sister Mary (1809):

> Once on a time, Love, Death, and Reputation,
> Three travellers, a tour together went;
> And, after many a long perambulation,
> Agreed to part by mutual consent.
>
> Death said: "My fellow tourists, I am going
> To seek for harvests in the embattled plain;
> Where drums are beating, and loud trumpets blowing,
> There you'll be sure to meet with me again.
>
> Love said: "My friends, I mean to spend my leisure
> With some young couple, fresh in Hymen's bands;
> Or 'mongst relations, who in equal measure
> Have had bequeathéd to them house or lands."
>
> But Reputation said: "If once we sever,
> Our chance of future meeting is but vain:
> Who parts from me, must look to part for ever,
> For *Reputation lost comes not again.*"

The third verse is the most altered from Webster and very much
for the worse: we can ill exchange the shepherds for Hymen or the
utter absence of legacies for that dubious source of affection, their
equal division.

I have searched in vain for the source of this apologue. It looks
as if it might be based ultimately on some popular saying. For
Mr Robin Flower has kindly pointed out to me a recurrence of the
essential idea in T. D. MacDonald's *Gaelic Proverbs and Proverbial
Sayings,* p. 42:

> "She asked of the wind—'If I lost you where could I find you?'
> The wind—'On the top of the cairns.'
> She asked of the mist—'If I lost you where could I find you?'
> The mist—'On the top of the mountains.'

She asked of fame—'If I lost you where could I find you?'
Fame—'Lose me once, and you will never find me again'".

149–50. *Love...unambitious shepheards.* Cf. Wordsworth's "Love
had he found in huts where poor men lie". Note the irony of the
contrast between the Duke's idyllic vision of an Arcadia with no
dowries and no heirlooms, and that avarice which, as much as
wounded pride, is at this very moment driving him to destroy the
sister he preaches at and the family whose honour he upholds.

157. *[shooke] hands with.* Cf. the Greek χαίρειν λέγειν to a thing:
Lyly, *Euphues*, p. 75: "Were I not over charie of mine honestie,
you woulde inveigle me to shake handes with chastitie".

165. *Witches*: note that these form a perpetual subject of allusion with
the Duke and his brother. Cf. I. I. 344; II. 5. 66; III. I. 92. Later
it is on wolves that the Duke's mind runs, until he ends by believing
himself one.

173. *That Gallery*: does this mean that the Duke is meant to be visible
to the audience while crossing the upper stage, before he actually
appears in the Duchess's room about 69?

174. *I would this terrible thing would come againe.* One almost wishes
that Webster had spared his Antonio at all events this bluster of
courage after the event, this *esprit d'escalier.*

186–8. Cf. *W.D.* IV. 2. 141.

201 ff. There is a certain lack of invention in Webster's repetition of
this expedient of distracting suspicion by a pretence of theft, exactly
as in II. 2 above.

203–9. *My brother stood engag'd...protested Against*: *i.e.* the Duke had
become security for money borrowed (ta'ne up) by the Duchess
from Jews in Naples. Antonio, by failing to make some payment
that had fallen due, had "let the bonds be forfeyt". Accordingly the
Jews "protested", *i.e.* made a written declaration that the bills backed
by the Duke had not been met, as a preliminary to legal action for
recovery of the debt. Cf. Massinger, *City Madam*, I. 3:

> I must and will have my money,
> Or I'll protest you first and, that done, have
> The statute made for bankrupts served upon you.

214. *Runnes upon engenous wheeles.* "To run on wheels" is "to move
swiftly or uninterruptedly". Cf. Breton, *Pasquil's Passe (Wks.*
(Grosart), I. 8/2): "A madding witte that runnes on wheeles". It
is because of this *rapidity* that "short sillables, Must stand for periods".

Engenous seems to supplement the idea of swiftness with that of
intricacy, as of "wheels within wheels". Dyce quotes Dekker, *Whore
of Babylon* (1607), sig. C 2.

> For that one act gives, like an enginous wheel,
> Motion to all.

217. *Magnanima Mensogna*: from Tasso, *Gerus. Lib.* II. 22. An image
of the Virgin, seized by the infidel tyrant of Jerusalem and placed

in the temple of Mahomet, mysteriously vanishes. In revenge the tyrant begins a wholesale persecution of the Christians; the *magnanima menzogna* is the pious fraud of a Christian maiden called Sofronia, who, to save her fellows, falsely takes the blame upon herself. Tasso's phrase was, of course, based in its turn on the famous *splendide mendax* applied by Horace (*Odes*, III. 11. 35) to Hypermnestra, who alone of the fifty daughters of Danaus broke her word to her father and saved her husband Lynceus, instead of slaying him on their marriage-night.

For Tasso, see also Hist. Introd. p. 16.

224. *Quietus*: see on I. 1. 532. The word must carry for the Duchess and her husband (and for the audience) a poignant association with that earlier, happier scene where she had signed his *Quietus* on Antonio's lips. And in the lines that follow, playing though she is for the life and honour of both, she cannot resist playing also with such double-edged hints at their secret love as—"that cur'de you Without helpe of a Doctor"—"I would have this man be an example to you all, So shall you hold my favour"—"h'as done that you would not thinke of". And with the same ambiguity Antonio answers "I am all yours".

227. *let him*: "let him go". The phrase is ambiguous; and might mean the exact opposite—"stop him": as in *Haml.* 1. 4. 85: "I'll make a ghost of him that lets me". In *Winter's Tale*, 1. 2. 40–2, there is the same doubt:

> I'll give him my commission
> To let him there a month behind the gest (time)
> Prefix'd for's parting.

Schmidt (*Lexicon*) and *N.E.D.* explain this—"so as to let him remain"; Malone—"to keep himself" ("him" for "himself"). Still the latter is much less plausible; and here, since the Duchess "intends to be rid of him", "let" probably means "let go", cf. 230. On the stage a gesture would make all clear. Cf. "Beaum. & Fl.", *Spanish Curate*, v. 2:

> Good sir, intend this business
> And let (*i.e.* let alone) this bawling fool.

Besides there is probably a play on "pray let him be an example".

249–51. Cf. Suetonius, *Vespasian*, (16) where that emperor is described as adopting this policy with his officials—"so that the common talk was he used them as sponges, letting them soak when they were dry and squeezing them out again when they were wet". The idea reappears in *Hamlet*, IV. 2. 16–23.

254. *abide to see a Pigges head gaping*. Dyce quotes *Merch. of Ven.* IV. 1. 54: Why he cannot abide a gaping pig.

(Though there the cause is hysteria, not Judaism.)

256. *I would you had bin his Officer*: *i.e.* you would have found it more profitable than being his mistress. Cf. Bacon. *Apophthegms* (1624), 10

(*Wks.* ed. Spedding VII. 126): "Bishop Latimer said, in a sermon at court; *That he heard great speech that the King was poor and many ways were propounded to make him rich: For his part he had thought of one way, which was, that they should help the King to some good office, for all his officers were rich*".

259. *blacke wooll*: H.D.S. explains the colour by a quotation from certain *Depositions from York Castle* in *The Denham Tracts* (ed. Hardy for the Folk-Lore Society, 1892), II. 294; in which a witness mentions how he went to a wise woman for ear-ache and "shee told him that blacke wool was good for itt". See *N.Q.* II. XI. 118, 247.

266. *gold Chaine*: the steward's regular badge. Cf. *Twelfth Night*, II. 3. 129 (to Malvolio): "Go, Sir, rub your chain with crumbs" (Vaughan). Allen suggests that *fly* in the previous line is indicative; but it is clearly imperative, as a malediction.

277. *a sort of flattring rogues*: *i.e.* a set, company of them. Cf. Jonson, *Ev. Man in his H.*, I. 4: "I was requested to supper, last night, by a sort of gallants". It is not necessarily contemptuous, as has been suggested: cf. the compassionate cry of one of the judges of Babington's Conspiracy: "O Ballard, Ballard, what hast thou done! A sort of brave youths, otherwise endued with good gifts, by thy inducements hast thou brought to their utter destruction and confusion".

279–80. *I.e.* the flatterers pretend that the princes have not vices, and the princes that the flatterers are not lying.

283. *Pluto the god of riches.* This fable occurs, as Vaughan points out, in Bacon's "Of Riches" (1625 ed.). Pluto should, of course, more strictly be Plutus. In origin Πλούτων is indeed merely a by-form of Πλοῦτος, Wealth; and this name was transferred to Hades, the god of the underworld, by a propitiatory euphemism, just as the name of the Black Sea was changed from Ἄξεινος (friendless) to Εὔξεινος (friendly). The link of association may have been that wealth came from underground (cf. Plato, *Crat.* 403 A; Cicero, *De Nat. Deor.* II. 66). Ultimately, however, the two deities became quite distinct, though we still find Plutus occasionally called Pluto—see Aristophanes, *Plutus*, 727 and Pearson's note on Sophocles, *Fragm.* 273; and cf. *Jul. Caes.* IV. 3. 101, *Troil. and Cress.* III. 3. 198 (where *Pluto* is wrongly emended to *Plutus* in some editions).

287. *by scuttles*: with a quick, hurried run.

292–3. Cf. Aristotle's ideal μεγαλόψυχος or "magnanimous man", who values himself neither too much nor yet too little (*Ethics*, IV. 3).

294. From Jonson's Dedication of his *Masque of Queens* (1609) to Prince Henry: "both your virtue and form did deserve your fortune". The passage is more extensively borrowed from in *Mon. Col.* 23–30. (C.)

295. From *Arcadia*, I. (*Wks.* I. 32): "A wit which delighted more to judge it selfe, then to showe it selfe." (C.)

297. Cf. *Mon. Col.* 78–9.

300–1. From *Arcadia*, I. (*Wks.* I. 15): "I am no herald to enquire of mens pedigrees, it sufficeth me if I know their vertues". (C.)

307. *the Bermoothes*: the Bermudas, famous for storms ("still-vexed"). Special interest in them had been excited by the wreck there in 1609 of Sir George Somers, to accounts of which *The Tempest* is indebted (see the edition of that play in the new *Cambridge Shakespeare*). Cf. the fine lines of Fulke Greville's *Caelica*, LIX:

> Whoever sailes neere to Bermuda coast
> Goes hard aboord the monarchie of Feare,
> Where all desires but life's desire are lost,
> For wealth and fame put off their glories there.

See, too, *A.Q.L.* v. 1. 350 ff.

312–4. The idea recurs in *Arcadia*, I: "It can never be said that evil happeneth to him who falls accompanied with vertue".

325. *Seminary*: seed-plot, nursing-ground.

341. *Heralds...coates, to sell.* The sale of honours, then as now, was a perpetual subject of bitter allusion. The climax was reached when in 1616 Ralph Brooke, York Herald, tricked Segar, Garter King, into granting a coat of arms to Gregory Brandon, the London hangman. Cf. Jonson's supposed gibe at Shakespeare's new-bought coat with its motto *Non sanz droict*, when in *Ev. Man out of his Humour* Puntarvolo suggests for Sogliardo's "boar without a head, rampant" the legend "Not without mustard". (See *Sh.'s Eng.* II. 74–90.)

345. Cf. *Haml.* III. 2. 78: "I will wear him in my heart's core". (Dyce.)

353–4. *faigne a Pilgrimage To our Lady of Loretto.* In Belleforest-Painter this suggestion comes from the Duchess's woman. Why should Bosola make it here, thus furthering his victim's escape for the time being? Perhaps the best answer is to be found in the parallel situation in *W.D.*, where (IV. 1) Florence himself engineers Vittoria's flight with Brachiano and, when they escape to Padua, explains his motive (IV. 3. 55 ff.):

> How fortunate are my wishes! Why! 'twas this
> I onely laboured...Thy fame, fond Duke,
> I first have poison'd.

Similarly it would seem here that Bosola intends the Duchess to discredit herself with the world and her own subjects: the only alternative is to suppose that he really wants her to escape. That I can hardly believe, though it is certainly clear that he has at times a good deal of feeling for his victim.

354. *Loretto*: fifteen miles S.E. of Ancona. Its chief relic is the Holy House, supposed to be that of Mary at Nazareth. When threatened by the Turks in Palestine, this was carried through the air by angels to Tersatto in Dalmatia (A.D. 1291). Three years later it flew across the Adriatic to a wood (*lauretum—Loreto?*) near Recanati; and thence in 1295 to the hill where it has since remained. It contains a black image of Virgin and Child, attributed to St Luke; and is still visited by tens of thousands of pilgrims every year. (See *Encycl. Brit.* "Loreto".)

362. *Leuca*: see on II. I. 64 above.

363–4. *Spaw In Germany*: Spa in Belgium, famous for its waters (the inhabitants of the Low Countries being included by the Elizabethans under the name "Dutch" or "Germans"). It seems to have escaped the lynx-eyes of both C. and H.D.S. that this combination of places was probably suggested to Webster by a passage in Montaigne II. 15: "Those of Marca d'Ancona, in Italy, make their vowes, and goe on pilgrimage, rather unto James in Galicia, and those of Galicia rather unto our Lady of Loreto. In the country of Liege they make more account of the Bathes of Luca; and they of Tuscany esteeme the Baths of Spaw more than their owne".

371. *Polititian...quilted anvell.* Cf. Chapman, *Byron's Tragedy* (pub. 1608), I. 2. 53–4:   great affairs will not be forged
But upon anvils that are lined with wool.

373. Cf. *Char.* "A Jesuite", 18–9.

III. 3.

Outer stage.

s.d. Webster may conceivably have derived the name Malateste or Mallateste, though nothing more, from Malatesta Baglioni, one of a noble family of Perugia, who was a famous *condottiere* of this time and insisted on surrendering Florence to the Imperialists in 1530. But the name was in any case well-known as that of the ruling family of Rimini, to which Francesca's Paolo belonged.

2. *The Emperour*: Charles V.

2–6. The Cardinal, before entering the Sacred College, had been Marquis of Gerace and a tried soldier in his youth. (See Hist. Introd. p. 7.)

5. *the Marquis of Pescara*: Ferdinando Francesco d'Avalos (1489–1525), was in history the brother of the Duke Ferdinand's wife, Ippolita d'Avalos. He was born at Naples, of Spanish origin, and became the husband of the famous Vittoria Colonna. Webster makes him old. In reality he died, worn out and disappointed though only thirty-six, in the very year of his brilliant victory over Francis I at Pavia.

6. *Lanoy* (*c.* 1487–1527). Charles de Lannoy, Viceroy of Naples, was born at Valenciennes and became a favourite of Charles V. To him alone would Francis I give up his sword at Pavia.

10. *plot*: plan.

18. *gun-powder, in's hollow tooth*: doubtless because of the anodyne effect of the nitre in it. Cf. Pliny XXXI. 10 (of nitre): "A collution made thereof, sodden in wine with pepper, easeth the tooth-ache". Cf. *Char.* "A Roaring Boy", 18–21.

22. *sent*: *i.e.* the smell of garlic.

23. *service*: military operations.

24. *City Chronicle*. Sampson suggests that this means Stowe's *Annales* (1592—new edit. 1605) or Grafton's *Chronicle at Large* (1568—new edit. 1611). But "all the *late* service" suggests something much more up-to-date in the way of news, some current periodical rather than a whole history. And it seems to me more likely that the City Chronicle compiled by the official City Chronologer (an office held by Middleton, Jonson, and Quarles) is here intended. Sampson objects that the City Records were not public enough. But we can hardly imagine that distinguished literary men were salaried by the City to compile some dry summary of events only to be locked away in a drawer. By the terms of Middleton's appointment he is forbidden to *print* anything except with the permission of the Court of Aldermen; presumably, therefore, such records were of a sufficient topical interest for them to be worth printing. This impression is borne out by the numerous extra payments made to Middleton, and by Oldys's story of two MSS. of his sold by auction about 1735 and since lost: (1) *Annales*, dealing with strictly civic events. (2) *Middleton's Farrago*—social, political, and miscellaneous. The latter might well mention military events on the Continent. The most serious difficulty is the uncertainty whether the office of Chronologer existed before Middleton's appointment in 1620: it came to an end in 1669.

25–6. *Painters...Battailes in modell*: *model* was the regular word for "plan", of a house or the like; cf. 2 *Hen. IV*, i. 3. 41–2: "When we mean to build We first survey the plot, then draw the model". With the reading *Pewterers* (see Text. Note) *model* might be explained as referring to leaden soldiers. Cf. Jonson, *The Devil is an Ass*, III. 1:

> Get him the posture-book, and's leaden men
> To set upon a table, 'gainst his mistress
> Chance to come by, that he may draw her in
> And shew her Finsbury battles.

27. *fight by the booke*: Sampson explains *the booke* as "Vincentio Saviolo his Practise" (1595), a work in two parts: (1) On the use of the rapier and dagger; (2) On honour and honourable quarrels. It is the source of Orlando's wrestling-match and Touchstone's disquisition on Lies; but I doubt if it is meant here. *By the booke* simply means with all the preciseness of a book, whether in a good sense or a bad. Cf. *Rom. and Jul.* i. 5. 114: "You kiss by the book"; and a letter of Donne's quoted in E. Simpson's *Study of the Prose Works of J. Donne* (p. 295): "To know how to live by the booke is a pedantery" (*i.e.* a merely *theoretical* knowledge of life, as here of fighting). Cf. too the similar phrase *without booke, e.g.* in *W.D.* v. 3. 22 (see note), where there can be no question of any particular book.

32. *taffita*: "a plain-wove glossy silk", *N.E.D.*

38. *pot-gun*: *lit.* "pop-gun", thence "one who is charged with wind", "a braggart". Cf. Congreve, *Old Bachelor*, III. 3 (of a *miles gloriosus*): "that sign of a man there, that pot-gun charged with wind".

41–2. He is a mere ornamental appendage of the Court on its progress from place to place: *guarded*, (1) trimmed, (2) protected. Cf. *F.M.I.* v. 3. 319.

46. *Foxes*: an allusion to the jackals which Samson tied tail to tail (cf. *heads...devided*) to fire the corn of the Philistines. (*Judges* xv. 4.) Cf. *Char.* "Petifogger", 1.

50 ff. For this description of pedantry, cf. Montaigne's description (1. 38) of the scholar who ruins his life "to teach posteritie the measure of Plautus verses and the true orthography of a Latine word" (copied, as C. points out, by Marston, *Fawn*, IV. 1. 218–28; and Donne, *Progr. of the Soul*, 281–9). But in its concentration on *mythology* in particular, Webster's passage recalls rather the account of Tiberius in Suetonius (ch. 70): "Maxime tamen curavit notitiam historiae fabularis usque ad ineptias atque derisum"—asking the learned absurd questions about the name of Hecuba's mother, what Achilles was called when disguised as a girl, and what song the Sirens sang.

61. *oppression*: stress of emotion.

63. *He lifts up's nose.* Cf. Massinger, *Roman Actor*, IV. 1 (of an informer):

> Here he comes
> His nose held up; he hath something in the wind.
> (T. S. Eliot.)

63–4. *Por-pisse...storme*: *Por-pisse—porcus, piscis—*porpoise (cf. Germ. *Meerschwein*). For its boding of storms cf. Dryden, *All for Love*, IV. 1: "That porc'pisce bodes ill-weather" (where Saintsbury in the *Mermaid* ed. gives the explanation "porcupine"!). Similarly in *Volpone*, II. 1, three porpoises appear "above the bridge"; and one at London Bridge ("always the messenger of tempests") in *Eastward Ho!* III. 3. Cf. Brand, *Pop. Antiq.* p. 711.

70–1. *deformed silence...charmes.* Cf. *Char.* "Usurer" 17–9.

75–6. *like leaprosie—The whiter, the fowler*: from Chapman, *Seven Penitential Psalms*, "A Great Man":

> th' embroidery
> Wrought on his state, is like a leprosy,
> The whiter, still the fouler. (C.)

82–3. The only mention of the Duchess's son by her first marriage, whose existence is rather hard to reconcile with the Duke's hope to inherit a mass of treasure by his sister's death. See Hist. Introd. p. 8.

III. 4.

Whole stage: doubtless the pilgrims on the outer stage watched the ceremony going on in the inner, which would represent the shrine.

This scene appears to be described in a contemporary Italian account, the *Anglopotrida* of Orazio Busino (Feb. 7th 1618—quoted by Stoll, p. 29): "Prendono giuoco gli Inglesi della nostra religione come di cosa detestabile, et superstitiosa, nè mai rappresentano qualsivoglia attione pubblica, sia pura Tragisatiricomica, che non inserischino dentro vitii, et scelleragini di qualche religioso catolico, facendone risate, et molti scherni, con lor gusto, et ramarico de' buoni; fu appunto veduto dai nostri, in una Commedia introdur' un frate franciscano, astuto, et repieno di varie impietà, così d' avaritia come di libidine: et il tutto poi riuscì in una Tragedia, facendoli mozzar la vista in scena. Un' altra volta rappresentarono la grandezza d' un cardinale, con li habiti formali, et proprii molto[1] belli, et ricchi, con la sua Corte, facendo in scena erger un Altare, dove finse di far oratione, ordinando una processione: et poi lo ridussero in pubblico con una Meretrice in seno. Dimostrò di dar il Velleno ad una sua sorella,[2] per interesse d' honore: et d' andar in oltre alla guerra, con depponer prima l' abito cardinalitio sopra l' altare col mezzo de' suoi Cappellani, con gravità, et finalmente si fece cingere la spada, metter la serpa (sciarpa, scarf), con tanto garbo, che niente più: et tutto ciò fanno in sprezzo delle grandezze ecclesiastice vilipese, et odiate a morte in questo Regno.

Di Londra a' 7 feb^aio 1618".

In quite another way also this scene, though not particularly striking in itself, gains a certain extraneous interest when we find it chosen to provide the opening of Mr Waley's charming transposition of *The Duchess of Malfi* into the form of a Nō play. His object was to help the readers of Nō plays; but I do not see why the readers of *The Duchess of Malfi* should not also have the benefit; and by Mr Waley's kindness I am enabled to quote his adaptation here.

"The persons need not be more than two—the Pilgrim, who will act the part of *waki*, and the Duchess, who will be *shite* or Protagonist. The chorus takes no part in the action, but speaks for the *shite* while she is miming the more engrossing parts of her rôle.

The Pilgrim comes on to the stage and first pronounces, in his *Jidai* or preliminary couplet, some Buddhist aphorism appropriate to the subject of the play. He then names himself to the audience thus (in prose):

'I am a pilgrim from Rome. I have visited all the other shrines of Italy, but have never been to Loretto. I will journey once to the shrine of Loretto.'

---

[1] *molti* as quoted by Stoll and Chambers (III. 511).

[2] This seems a confusion of the deaths of Julia and the Duchess.

Then follows (in verse) the *Song of Travel* in which the Pilgrim describes the scenes through which he passes on his way to the shrine. While he is kneeling at the shrine, *Shite* (the Protagonist) comes on to the stage. She is a young woman dressed, 'contrary to the Italian fashion', in a loose-bodied gown. She carries in her hand an unripe apricot. She calls to the Pilgrim and engages him in conversation. He asks her if it were not at this shrine that the Duchess of Malfi took refuge. The young woman answers with a kind of eager exaltation, her words gradually rising from prose to poetry. She tells the story of the Duchess's flight, adding certain intimate touches which force the priest to ask abruptly, 'Who is it that is speaking to me?'

And the girl shuddering (for it is hateful to a ghost to name itself) answers: '*Hazukashi ya!* I am the soul of the Duke Ferdinand's sister, she that was once called Duchess of Malfi. Love still ties my soul to the earth. *Toburai tabi-tamaye!* Pray for me, oh, pray for my release!'

Here closes the first part of the play. In the second the young ghost, her memory quickened by the Pilgrim's prayers (and this is part of the medicine of salvation), endures again the memory of her final hours. She mimes the action of kissing the hand (*vide* Act IV. Scene 1), finds it very cold:

> I fear you are not well after your travel.
> Oh! horrible!
> What witchcraft doth he practise, that he hath left
> A dead man's hand here?

And each successive scene of the torture is so vividly mimed that though it exists only in the Protagonist's brain, it is as real to the audience as if the figure of dead Antonio lay propped upon the stage, or as if the madmen were actually leaping and screaming before them.

Finally she acts the scene of her own execution:

> Heaven-gates are not so highly arched
> As princes' palaces; they that enter there
> Must go upon their knees. (*She kneels.*)
> Come, violent death,
> Serve for mandragora to make me sleep!
> Go tell my brothers, when I am laid out,
> They then may feed in quiet.
>   (*She sinks her head and folds her hands.*)

The chorus, taking up the word 'quiet', chant a phrase from the Hokkekyō: *Sangai Mu-an*, 'In the Three Worlds there is no quietness or rest'.

But the Pilgrim's prayers have been answered. Her soul has broken its bonds: is free to depart. The ghost recedes, grows dimmer and dimmer, till at last

> *use-ni-keri*
> *use-ni-keri*

it vanishes from sight." (From *The Nō Plays of Japan*. By Arthur Waley. 1921.)

9 ff. The authorship of this Ditty which Webster disclaims (as well he might), is unknown.

11–2. *flie-thee, nigh-thee*: note this use of hyphen (as again in the next stanza) to throw the stress on the syllable before it. Cf. II. 5. 68.

31. *determine of*: "This usage of the word, 'limiting the freedom of' a person, is apparently not recorded" (Sampson, followed by Allen). But why should it not mean simply "make decisions about", "adjudicate upon"? Thus H.D.S. quotes Massinger, *Renegado*, IV. 2:

> I claim the law and sue for
> A speedy trial; if I fail, you may
> Determine of me as you please.

45 ff. Cf. Montaigne II. 31: "The mischiefe is that after you are once falne into the pits it is no matter who thrusts you in, you never cease till you come to the bottome. The fall presseth, hasteneth, mooveth, and furthereth it selfe". (C.)

III. 5.

Outer stage.

1. *Banish'd Ancona!* A weaker echo of the thunder-crash which opens *The White Devil*, I. I. I.

8. *buntings*: a bird akin to the lark, but without its song. For the idea cf. *Timon* (first printed, as far as we know, in the First Folio of 1623), III. 6. 32:

> *Sec. Lord.* The swallow follows not summer more willingly than we your lordship.
> *Tim. (aside).* Nor more willingly leaves winter; such summer birds are men.

11–3. Cf. *Timon*, III. 3. 11:

> His friends, like physicians,
> Thrice give him over.

On which commentators quote this passage of Webster to support the reading *like physicians Thrive*. (Dyce.)

21–4. *Pearles...teares*: this interpretation of the dream is oneiro-critically quite correct (cf. Smedley, *Occult Sciences* (1855), p. 249). A writer in *N.Q.* 8. XI. 146, cites a story to the effect that Marie de' Medici dreamed of pearls before the assassination of her husband Henri IV, and was told it betokened tears. (Not that she appears in the upshot to have shed many: for she was not, in the words of le président Hénault, "assez surprise ni assez affligée de la mort funeste d'un de nos plus grands rois".)

25–6. *Birds...wilde benefit of Nature.* Cf. *Arcadia*, IV. (*Wks.* II. 119): "to have for foode the wilde benefites of nature". (H.D.S.) Repeated in *A.Q.L.* IV. I. 81–2. Cf. *Macbeth*, IV. 2. 31, where little Macduff says he will live, now that he is fatherless, "As birds do, mother".

38. *equivocation*: using words in double senses to deceive. It became a byword owing to the use of it by Henry Garnet, superior of the Jesuits in England, during his trial for complicity in the Gunpowder Plot. Cf. *Macbeth*, II. 3. 10 (a supposed allusion to Garnet).

44. *have his heart*: for this particular "equivocation" cf. Whitelaw's rendering of the double meaning in Sophocles, *Electra*, 1451, where Electra says to Aegisthus after Orestes and Pylades have lulled Clytemnestra:

> They have found their way to their hostess' heart.
> (φίλης γὰρ προξένου κατήνυσαν.)

53–5. *league...politick Kings*: was this suggested to Webster by the infamous treaty of 1501 between Ferdinand the Catholic and Louis XII, by which the Spaniard sold his ally Federico of Naples (Antonio's master) to the invading French, in return for a share of the spoils? As the Spanish troops were unsuspectingly allowed to occupy the strong points of the Neapolitan Kingdom, Ferdinand easily made himself "of strength and powre To be the after-ruine" of the unfortunate Federico.

58. *this*: the letter.

66. *Adamant*: loadstone. See on *W.D.* I. 2. 163.

70. *flye towards Millaine*: for Webster's departure here from the original story, see Hist. Introd. p. 10.

72. *bottom*: "hold" and so "ship". Cf. *Merch. of Ven.* I. 1. 42.

75–8. Cf. Donne, *Anatomy of the World, A Funeral Elegy*, 37–46:

> But must wee say she's dead? may't not be said
> That as a sundred clocke is peecemeale laid,
> Not to be lost, but by the maker's hand
> Repollish'd, without errour then to stand...?

Similarly *Mon. Col.* 241–4.

81 ff. *Thou art happy...not understanding*. Cf. Sophocles, *Ajax*, 552–4:

> καίτοι σε καὶ νῦν τοῦτό γε ζηλοῦν ἔχω,
> ὁθούνεκ' οὐδὲν τῶνδ' ἐπαισθάνει κακῶν.
> ἐν τῷ φρονεῖν γὰρ μηδὲν ἥδιστος βίος.   (Vaughan.)

82–4. *wit...sorrow*. Cf. *Ecclesiastes* i. 18: "For in much wisdom is much grief: and he that increaseth knowledge, increaseth sorrow".

84–5. From *Arcadia*, II. (*Wks.* I. 233): "she sought all meanes...to send her soule, at least, to be married in the eternall church with him". (C.) Cf. H. King, "The Departure":

> 'Tis onely the Triumphant Church where we
> Shall in unsever'd Neighbourhood agree.

The *eternall Church* is the congregation of the saved in Heaven.

89. *Man (like to Cassia)*...: see on *W.D.* I. 1. 47–8.

90–1. *slave-borne Russian...tyranny*: from Sidney, *Astrophel and Stella*, II:

> And now like slave-borne Muscovite
> I call it praise to suffer tyrannie.

Cf. *F.M.I.* v. 3. 74: *Selimus*, 479. We have to remember that Ivan the Terrible had died as recently as 1584. Accounts of Sir Jerome Bowes's embassy in 1583 give a vivid impression of the contrast felt between the two nations. For Sir Jerome's benefit Ivan bade one of his courtiers leap out of a window, so that he was killed: to which the ambassador replied with some contempt that "his mistress did set more store by, and make better use of, the necks of her subjects". He also refused, it is said, to doff his cap before the Czar, though the French Ambassador had had his hat nailed to his head for similar boldness. (See "Sir J. Bowes" in *D.N.B.*) On another occasion Ivan is related to have addressed one of his boyars—"God save thee, my dear Boris, thou deservest a proof of my favour"; and so saying he struck the man's ear off. The boyar returned thanks for this graciousness and wished him a long reign. (Bell's *Hist. of Russia*, 1. 265.)

92. *Heaven...heavy*: doubtless intentional word-play.

93–5. *top...scourge-sticke*: from *Arcadia*, ii. (*Wks.* i. 227—one of the few occasions when Webster borrows from Sidney's *verse*):

> Griefe onely makes his wretched state to see
> (Even like a toppe which nought but whipping moves)
> This man, this talking beast, this walking tree...
> But still our dazeled eyes their way do misse,
> While that we do at his sweete scourge repine,
> The kindly way to beate us to our blisse. (Not in C.)

95. *scourge-sticke*: whip for the top.

97–8. Cf. Donne, *Anat. of the World, First Anniversary*, 155–7:

> Wee seeme ambitious, Gods whole worke t' undoe;
> Of nothing hee made us, and we strive too,
> To bring our selves to nothing backe. (C.)

104. *an holy Anchorite*: we may be reminded here that it was as a holy Anchorite in a close cell that Ferdinand bade the Duchess keep her lover (iii. 2. 119).

108. *Laurell...withered*: perhaps an echo of Cleopatra's parting cry (*Ant. and Cleop.* iv. 13. 64):

> O, wither'd is the garland of the war.

It must be remembered, however, that the withering of the naturally evergreen bay was an evil omen. Cf. *Rich. II*, ii. 4. 7–8:

> 'Tis thought the king is dead: we will not stay.
> The bay-trees in our country are all wither'd.

So Evelyn, *Sylva*, ii. 5: "In the year 1629 at Padua, preceding a great pestilence, almost all the Bay-trees about that famous University grew sick and died".

112. *Fortunes wheele...Princes*. Cf. Boethius ii. Prose 1. 2; Metre 1 (Vaughan).

114. *adventure*: quarry. H.D.S. quotes Marmion, *Holland's Leaguer*, I. 5:

> I have a bird i'th' wind, I'll fly thee on him:
> He shall be thy adventure, thy first quarry.

122. *flye in peeces.* Cf. *D.L.* III. 3. 297; and Donne, *Of the Progress of the Soul*, 181 (of a soul passing from the body at death):

> Thinke that a rustie Peece, discharg'd, is flowne
> In peeces.

130–2. From *Arcadia*, III. (*Wks.* I. 488): "with the same pittie as folkes keepe foule, when they are not fatte inough for their eating". (C.)

140. *base, low-fellow.* Bosola lightly sheds his democratic sentiments of a few pages before.

142. *counterfeit face*: Bosola is masked.

153. *high state of floods.* Cf. *2 Hen. IV*, V. 2. 132:

> Where it shall mingle with the state of floods. (Dyce.)

As R. P. Cowl points out, this parallel in Webster makes even more improbable Hanmer's emendation of the Shakespeare passage to *floods of state.*

169. Cf. *W.D.* IV. 1. 26–7. The meaning is apparently—"Misery and greatness go together".

IV. 1.

If the wax-figures are revealed in the "study", this scene must begin on the outer stage, the curtains of the study being closed again, to permit the removal of the wax-works, after l. 133. But it is hard to be sure.

It is generally assumed that the supposed scene is again Amalfi. Certainly Bosola said in the last scene that the Duchess was being carried "to your pallace". And yet four days after her murder here, we find her grave to be in Milan (V. 3). We can best reconcile the discrepancy by supposing that Bosola was lying and the Duchess was really cast into some castle of the Duke's near Milan, where the present Act would then take place. But the real answer is, I think, that neither Webster nor his audience cared for such precision: for them it was merely "Somewhere in Prison".

4–6. From *Arcadia*, II. (*Wks.* I. 332): "But *Erona* sadde indeede, yet like one rather used, than new fallen to sadnesse...seemed rather to welcome then to shunne that ende of miserie". (C.)

6–7. From *Arcadia*, I. (*Wks.* I. 16): "behaviour so noble, as gave a majestie to adversitie". Elsewhere Sidney says of Erona that one could "perceive the shape of loveliness more perfectly in woe than in joyfulness". (C.)

15. *Like English Mastiffes...tying.* Cf. *Arcadia*, 1. (*Wks.* 1. 25): "Leave women's minds, the most untamed that way of any; see whether any cage can please a bird? or whether a dogge grow not fiercer with tying". (C.)

23–4. Cf. *W.D.* 111. 2. 198–9.

35 ff. This scene with the dead hand and the mock corpses recalls, as C. points out, the pretended executions of Philoclea and Pamela in the sight of those dearest to them in *Arcadia*, 111.—with the difference however that Sidney's attempts to be terrifying are painfully ineffective.

40. *Cubbs*: the first touch of the Duke's future lycanthropia? His mind runs again more openly on wolves at the end of the next scene.

42–4. Almost repeated in *D.L.* 1v. 2. 278–80.

50. *too much i'th' light*: too publicly conspicuous. Cf. *D.L.* 1. 2. 52; in *Hamlet*, 1. 2. 67: "I am too much i'the sun" the metaphor seems different—"too much turned out of doors".

68–71. Cf. David when his son was dead (2 *Sam.* xii. 22–3).

74–6. *picture...dung-hill*: from Chapman, *Seven Penitential Psalms*, "A Fragment":

> like prick'd pictures charm'd,
> And hid in dung hills. (C.)

This familiar form of sympathetic magic is too common from N. America to Australia, from ancient Egypt to the Scotland of the last century even, to need much illustration. (See Frazer, *Golden Bough*, 1. 55–70.)

The point of the dunghill was doubtless that its heat slowly melted the figure. Jonson in a Note on his *Masque of Queens* (1609: copied by Webster elsewhere) mentions "a relation of a French Ambassador's, out of England, of certain pictures of wax, found in a dunghill near Islington, of our late queen's: which rumour I myself (being then very young) can yet remember to have been current". Similarly in the room of the wife of the Maréchal d'Ancre there was said to have been found a wax image of the young Louis XIII, with one leg melted away (1617).

79. *bind...truncke*: the idea comes originally from Virgil, *Aeneid*, viii. 485–8, where this form of torture is ascribed to the Etruscan Mezentius. Cf. Marston, *Fawn*, 1. 2. 203 ff.: "O Mezentius, a tyranny equal if not above thy torturing: thou didst bind the living and dead bodies together, and forced them so to pine and rot...".

84. *Portia*. Cf. Plutarch (North's transl.), *Brutus*, ch. 53: "As for Porcia, Brutus's wife, Nicolaus the Philosopher and Valerius Maximus do write, that she determining to kill herself (her parents and friends carefully looking to her to keep her from it), took hot burning coals and cast them into her mouth, and kept her mouth so close that she choked herself" (after her husband's fall at Philippi. Cf. *Jul. Caes.* 1v. 3. 154).

90. *starve my selfe*: for a discussion of the legitimacy of this particular form of self-murder, with the same plea that fasting is legitimate, see Donne, *Biathanatos*, II. 6. 5.

99–106. From *Arcadia*, II. (*Wks.* I. 333): "But she (as if he had spoken of a small matter, when he mencioned her life, to which she had not leisure to attend) desired him if he loved her, to shew it, in finding some way to save *Antiphilus*. For her, she found the world but a wearisom stage unto her, where she played a part against her will: and therefore besought him, not to cast his love in so unfruitfull a place, as could not love it selfe". (C.)

109. *Ser.* Sampson suggests that this servant is perhaps *Cariola*. But in that case why should she not be called by her real name? It is simpler and better to suppose that the Duchess suddenly turns in her agony on some menial assistant of Bosola's. In any case Webster's main concern here was, clearly, to work in the retort he had admired in *Arcadia*, III. (*Wks.* I. 485): "and he with an angry voice asked, Who was there? A poore Gentlewoman (answered the partie) that wish long life unto you. And I soone death to you (said he) for the horrible curse you have given me". (C.)
It is imitated by Shirley (*Love's Cruelty*, III. 4):

> *Bel.* Do I live still?
> *Ser.* And shall, I hope, long.
> *Bel.* Thou'rt most uncharitable.

120. *the Starres shine still.* In this climax Bosola's cynicism rises to the sublime, as in four monosyllables he expresses the insignificance of human agony before the impassive Universe.

122. *make lanes...families*: from Chapman, *Seven Penitential Psalms*, "A Fragment": "Wars that make lanes thro whole posterities". Cf. *Bussy d'Ambois*, III. 2. 469 ("a murthering piece, making lanes in armies") where the cannon-metaphor is clearer. There is a vivid passage in Rider Haggard's *Jess*, where a maxim is described as cutting lanes in an attacking mass like those in Kentish hop-gardens seen from the train.

135. Wax images of the dead were much more familiar to Webster's audience than to us. A year or two before this play was acted, the citizens had watched a wax effigy of the dead Prince Henry borne through the London streets. "On the evening of that Sunday (Dec. 6th 1612) was brought a representation of the Prince, made at short notice, though extremely resembling him, and apparelled with clothes ...in short everything he wore at the time of his creation. This figure was laid on its back on the coffin, and fast bound to it; the head being supported by two cushions, just as it was to be drawn along the streets in the funeral chariot with eight black horses" (Birch, *Life of Prince Henry*, 1760, p. 362). The figure subsequently took its place among the other wax-works in Westminster Abbey.

Long search has failed to throw any light on Vincentio Lauriola.

The nearest approach to the name that I can find is the Cardinal Vincentio Laureo mentioned as having letters from Mary Queen of Scots just before her execution, in de Thou's *History* (1626 edit.), LXXXVI. 167 b (an account of Vittoria Accoramboni which Webster might have read, occurs in the same work, LXXXII. 42–3). But this is very remote indeed. Vincentio Saviolo who wrote a book on duelling well-known to the Elizabethans (1595; see on III. 3. 27) might just conceivably have suggested this name, *if* it is an invented one.

155. *full o'th'moone*: when mad-men were supposed maddest. Cf. Donne, *Satyres*, "Upon Mr Thomas Coryat's Crudities":

> When wilt thou be at full, great Lunatique?

162. *my intelligence*: my acting as intelligencer or spy in her court.

IV. 2.

Whole stage. The Duchess may have sat in the inner stage, as in her cell. But she appears to be strangled on the outer stage since Bosola bears off her body at the end, though this point cannot be pressed.

2. *consort*: company.

15–6. *Robin...cages*. Cf. Tofte's Ariosto (1608), *Sat*. III:

> The cage is to the Nightingale a hell,
> The Thrush and Black-bird both do love it well;
> The Robin red-brest rob'd of libertie,
> Growes sad and dies with inward melancholy. (Sampson.)

19. *mad-man...eyes open*: an idea perhaps suggested by some kinds of somnambulism where the sleeper's eyes remain open.

22–3. Cf. Tennyson, *Maud*:

> Ah Christ, that it were possible
> For one short hour to see
> The souls we loved, that they might tell us
> What and where they be!

29–30. For these famous lines, cf. *Mon. Col.* 162–3; and Marston, *Malcontent*, III. 1. 162–3:

> The galley-slave, that all the toilsome day
> Tugs at his oar against the stubborn wave.

There is a curious resemblance in a fine passage of D'Annunzio's *Paolo e Francesca*:

> Paolo.   Come debbo io morire?
> Francesca. Come lo schiavo al remo
>   nella galea che ha nome Disperata,
>   così dovete voi morire.

33–4. So in *Arcadia*, I. Pyrocles, entranced at the sight of Philoclea, stands "like a well wrought image, with some life in shew, but none in practise".

35–6. See on v. 3. 10 ff.

37. *Fortune...eie-sight.* The Duchess spoke only too truly when she offered herself to Antonio as his blind Fortune (I. I. 565–7): now the bandage has fallen.

45–6. Cf. Donne, *Of the Progress of the Soul*, 477–9:

> When no Physitian of redresse can speake,
> A joyfull casuall violence may breake,
> The dangerous Apostem in thy breast. (C.)

But the idea of such accidental cures is an old one.

46. *impost-hume*: ulcer.

49 ff. The modern reader has to remember in the scene that follows that to the audiences of the Globe madness was primarily funny. (Cf. the Bedlam-scenes of *Northward Ho!* IV. 3–4: Dekker, *Honest Whore*, Pt. I. v. 2.) Even the marriage-festival of the Princess Elizabeth was cheered with a masque of lunatics. It was therefore a refinement on this convention, far more novel to the Elizabethans than to us, when, as in *Hamlet* and *The White Devil* and here, what had been a mere matter of horseplay was used to deepen tragic pity and terror.

49. *secular Priest*: the "secular" clergy were those who lived in the world as contrasted with the monastic orders.

53. *day of doome.* Thus the astrologer Stoeffler predicted, owing to a conjunction of three planets in Pisces, a universal deluge for February 1524—a month, as it turned out, of unusual drought. A certain notable of Toulouse was, according to Voltaire, so convinced as to build himself an Ark, like the carpenter in Chaucer's *Miller's Tale*.

54–5. Webster, though born free of the Merchant Taylors, does not spare the trade. For jests on the English craze for new-fangled fashions, cf. *Merch. of Ven.* I. 2. 76 ff.; *F.M.I.* IV. 2. 125 ff. So Fynes Moryson: "No people in the world is so curious of new fangles as they of England be". Coryat in his *Crudities* describes the Italians as depicting the Englishman naked with a pair of shears "making his fashion of attire according to the vaine invention of his braine-sicke head". Cf. Lyly, *Euphues*, p. 437: and the lines on this subject in A. Borde's *Introduction of Knowledge*, beneath a print of a similar naked Englishman (*temp.* Henry VIII):

> I am an Englishman and naked I stand here,
> Musing in my mind what raiment I shall wear:
> For now I will wear this and now I will wear that
> And now I will wear what? I cannot tell what.

Similarly Harrison, in his *Description of England*, II. 7 (in Holinshed), indulges in a long lament on the same subject, rising to the climax: "except it were a dog in a doublet, you shall not see anie so disguised as my countrymen of England".

58. *"how do you"*: I know no other instance of this plural without the "s" which is normally added, as in G. Harvey, *Letterbook*

(Camden), 90: "To requite your gallonde of godbwyes, I regive you a pottle of howedyes".

59. *knave in graine*: (1) in dye, *i.e.* fast-dyed, incorrigible; (2) in the grain-trade. Cf. "Beaum. & Fl.", *Maid in the Mill*, v. 2: "a miller, a thief in grain, for he steals corn".

Cf., for the idea, the farmer in *Macbeth*, II. 3, who "hang'd himself on th' expectation of plenty".

60. *transportation*: export. By 1 Jac. I, c. 25 (1603–4), grain is allowed to be exported, when wheat costs not more than 26s. 8d. per qr., rye not more than 15s., barley not more than 14s.; with the proviso that the king can prohibit export either from the realm as a whole, or from the ports of any particular county. This regulation is modelled on previous enactments of the same nature, of which the first is a statute of Henry VI (1436). The average prices given by Rogers, *Hist. of Agric. and Prices in Engl.* vol. v, do not in fact ever fall below the legal limit which would have permitted export, between 1603 and 1619–20. But it is interesting to note that on Jan. 18th 1613 there was issued a special proclamation against the transportation of corn and grain on account of its high price and an apprehended scarcity (*Cal. State Papers, Dom.* (1611–8), p. 168). On Nov. 28th 1614, however, the Earl of Suffolk writes to the Customs Officers at London that the Eastland Merchants are to be allowed to re-transport their corn without export-duties, in case of its not finding sale in England (*ibid.* p. 261). The first date fits in quite well with the date assigned to the play.

61. *Broaker*: pawnbroker.

70. *b[e]ll*: bellow.

71. *yerk-some*: irksome.

72. *corasiv'd*: corroded. The *a* is due to confusion between *corrōdere*, to corrode, and *corrādere*, to scrape. Writers of the time sometimes try to distinguish the two, *e.g.* T. Adams, *Exp. 2 Peter*, II. 9 (1633): "They are our corrosives, corrasives, used only to pare off our excrements".

77 ff. 1. *Mad-man*, 2. *Mad.*, etc. I have sought to introduce a little method into this madness, by trying to identify their professions on the basis of the Servant's description above and their own remarks.

78. *perspective*: not here "magic-glass" (Sampson), but "telescope". Cf. Brereton, *Trav.* (1634–5: pub. 1844), 60: "perspectives which shew the new-found motion of the stars about Jupiter".

79–80. *pillow...stuff't...Porcupines*. Cf. *W.D.* 1. 2. 77–8; H. King, "Elegy occasioned by sickness": "His Pillow quilted with a Porcupine".

81. *glasse-house*: glass-factory. See on *W.D.* 1. 2. 134.

88–9. *sore throates*: *i.e.* with perpetual preaching.

92–3. *wood-cockes head, with the Braines pickt out*: the woodcock being a proverbially stupid fowl.

93. *ancient*: ironically—another jest at the mushroom nobility and gentry of the day.

94. *Greeke is turn'd Turke*: *i.e.* the Greek text of the Bible has been enlisted in the service of infidelity. The priest is satirized as a Puritan and so disapproves of all other translations except the Genevan; and he is here perhaps thinking of the Douay version of 1609–10 and the recent Authorized Version (1611). "To turn Turk" means ordinarily "to turn Moslem"—and so "become infidel"; and W. J. Craig's explanation "turn cruel" lacks either authority or meaning in this context.

95. *the Helvetian translation.* This is certainly not Coverdale's Bible of 1535 (Vaughan), but the Genevan or "Breeches" Bible of 1560. The whole point of this passage has been missed through commentators failing to see that it is a satire on Puritans.

The Genevan Bible, the work of a band of Puritan exiles, including Coverdale and Knox, had marginal notes of such a Calvinistic and anti-monarchist tendency that its printing was prohibited in England till Archbishop Parker's death in 1576. For instance, it observed on 2 *Chron.* xv. 16, that Asa after deposing his mother ought also to have put her to death; on *Rev.* ix. 3, it remarks: "Locustes are false teachers, heretikes, and worldlie suttil Prelates, with Monkes, Freres, Cardinals, Patriarches, Archbishops, Bishops, Doctors, Baschelers, and masters which forsake Christ to maintaine false doctrine". The 1569 edition also contained Calvin's Catechism; and shows a characteristic Puritan trait in recommending to parents a list of names for their offspring which includes such portents as Artashaste, Kerentrappuch, Mahazioth, Retrabeam, Tanhumeth, and Vopsi.

Accordingly it is little wonder that James I said at the Hampton Court Conference that "he thought the Geneva translation was the worst, and many of the notes very partial, untrue, seditious, and savouring too much of dangerous and traitorous conceits"; or that Laud should have tried to suppress it (one of the charges brought against him at his trial in 1637).

The Genevan version was, on the other hand, exceedingly popular (it was the first to introduce Roman type and the verse division of chapters) and went through some two hundred editions. The last Quarto of it was printed in England in 1615, the last Folio in 1616; but even then copies continued to flow in from Holland up to the middle of the century. (See Dore, *Old Bibles*, 1888.)

96. *lay the law*: expound it.

98. *drinkes but to satisfie nature*: for this suggestion of clerical tipsiness cf. *W.D.* v. 3. 121–2.

99. *If I had my glasse here*: it is suggested that this is some crystal or divining glass. But the sense remains obscure. Perhaps some kind of "perspective" glass is meant which produced an indecent illusion when looked through.

101. *rope-maker*: *i.e.* confederate of the hangman. Nash constantly gibes at Gabriel Harvey for being the son of one. Cf. *Char.*"Sexton", 16.

102. *snufling knave*: with allusion to the notorious nasal whine of the Puritans.

102–3. *shewes the tombes...placket*: *i.e.* he is a sort of Tartuffe, pointing with a *memento mori* at the tokens of mortality, while attempting seduction.

107. *paired the divells nayles.* Vaughan quotes *Twelfth Night*, IV. 2. 140 ff., where the Vice calls to the Devil to pare his nails. Malone explains that this is an insult to that personage, because he likes to keep his nails long. For nail-parings in popular superstition, cf. Frazer, *Golden Bough*, IX. 57–8.

109. *possets*: made of hot *milk*, curdled with ale or wine, to which sugar and spice were added.

111. *Colledge...caps.* Cf. *Char.* "A Quacksalver", 10: "All the learned doctors may cast their Caps at him". But what is the meaning? *N.E.D.* renders the phrase as "show indifference to, give up for lost". But this makes no sense here; the idea seems rather—"they may do their utmost against me, but it will be in vain". So in Dekker's *Dead Term* (Grosart, p. 82) we have—"if he went away with it cleare (*i.e.* brought off his trick), all the fresh men in Cambridge should throw up their cappes at him, and not mend the devise". From this the transition is not difficult to the meaning: "to give up a person or a thing in despair, since doing one's utmost is in vain"; thus Chamberlain writes to Carleton on July 5th 1617 that Lord Hay is vainly trying to appease the Earl of Northumberland whose daughter he is marrying: "But he (Hay) may cast his cap at that, seeing him (the Earl) so incensed". Equally decisive is *Timon*, III. 4. 103–4: "our masters may throw their caps at their money; these debts may well be called desperate ones". Mr Hayward points out a similar usage of this gesture of despair in La Fontaine, *Fables*, II. 18:

> L'affaire est consultée: et tous les avocats
> Après avoir tourné le cas
> En cent et cent mille manières
> Y jettent leur bonnet, se confessent vaincus.

112. *Soape-boyler costive*: a peculiarly difficult feat, soap being used for suppositories.

123. *salvatory*: ointment-box.

124. *greene mummey*: for mummey see on *W.D.* I. I. 16. *greene*: undried (of any kind of flesh, *e.g.* "greene beefe").

124. *cruded milke*: curdled. Cf. Donne, *Of the Progress of the Soul*, 165–6:

> This curded milke, this poor unlittered whelpe,
> My body. (C.)

Only Krusius however has noted the echo of *Job* x. 9–10:

> Remember, I beseech thee, that thou hast made me as the clay;
> And wilt thou bring me into dust again?
> Hast thou not poured me out as *milk*,
> And *curdled* me like cheese?

Here again the Bishops' Bible is even nearer than the A.V. to Webster, reading:

> Hast thou not poured me as it were milke, and turned me to cruddes like cheese?

125. *puffe-paste*: a light and flimsy sort of pastry. Applied to flimsy, worthless persons. Cf. "Beaum. & Fl.", *Wit at Several Weapons*, *Dram. Personae*: "Pompey Doodle, a Clown, Sir Gregory's Man, a piece of puff-paste".

127–8. *Larke in a cage.* Cf. *W.D.* iv. 2. 67.

135. *merry milkemaydes.* Cf. *Char.* "A fayre and happy Milke-mayd".

135–6. *mouse...cats eare.* The earliest instance of the phrase given by *N.E.D.* is in Lydgate, *Minor Poems* (Percy Society, p. 167), "The Order of Fools":

> An hardy mowse, that is bold to breede
> In cattis eeris, that breede shall never the (*i.e.* thrive).

Cf. Lyly, *Gallathea*, iv. 1. 45–6.

138. *unquiet bed-fellow*: a poignant echo to our ears of the playful mirth of iii. 2. 17.

141–2. Cf. *W.D.* v. 1. 38–9 and note.

153 ff. This change to sepulchral-figures recumbent on their elbows makes its appearance in the sixteenth century—perhaps owing to the Renaissance influence of Etruscan tombs with their effigies lying as at table.

173. *Bell-man.* The bellman's bell, like the passing-bell in churches, was probably meant in origin to drive away the evil spirits that lie in wait for the departing soul; later, to invite also the prayers of the faithful. According to Douce (quoted in Brand, *Pop. Antiq.* p. 428) down to the middle of the eighteenth century a bellman of the dead used to walk the streets of Paris in a dress ornamented with death's-heads, bones, and tears, crying out: "Awake, you that sleep, and pray to God for the dead".

There is however both here and in the parallel passage in *Macbeth*, ii. 2. 4 ("It was the owl, the fatal bellman, Which gives the stern'st good-night"), a possible allusion to a recently established London custom. Mr Robert Dowe, a Merchant Taylor like Webster himself, who died just before this, in 1612, had in 1605 (the probable date of *Macbeth* is 1606) given an endowment of £50 (26s. 8d. *per annum* for ever) to the parish of St Sepulchre's, to pay the clerk of that church for tolling the church-bell and going himself as bellman to exhort condemned criminals in the neighbouring Newgate on the night before their execution. He was to stand before their cell-window at midnight and give "12 solemn towles by double strokes" on a hand-bell provided by Mr Dowe's munificence. He was then to exhort them as follows:

> "You Prisoners that are within
> Who for your Wickedness and Sin,

after many Mercies shew'd you, are now appointed to be Executed to Death to-morrow in the Forenoon, give ear and understand that to-morrow morning the greatest Bell of St Sepulchre's Parish shall toll for you from six till ten in order and manner of a Passing Bell, which used to be toll'd for those who lie at the point of Death, to the end, that all godly People, hearing that Bell, and knowing it is for you going to your Deaths, may be stirr'd up to hearty prayer to God to bestow his Grace and Mercy on you whilst you yet live, etc." Not content with these consolations Mr Dowe ordained that the bellman should again exhort his victims in the early morning and deliver from the wall of St Sepulchre's churchyard another "pious and aweful admonition" to them in the cart on their way to Tyburn.

The Beadle of the Merchant Taylors' Hall was also paid from this endowment to see that the bellman did his business properly. So that the ceremony must have been doubly familiar to Webster; and his audience at this point must certainly have been reminded of the last nights of the condemned in Newgate. (See Wheatley, *London Past and Present*, III. 229–30; J. W. Hales in *Athenaeum* for Sept. 13th 1902; Munday's *Stowe* (1618), p. 25; Hutton's *New View of London* (1708), p. 707.)

181. *whistler.* Cf. Spenser, *F.Q.* II. 12. 36: "The Whistler shrill, that whoso hears doth die" (Dyce). This name is sometimes applied to the wigeon, the ring-ouzel, and the golden-eye (*Clangula glaucion*). But the superstition is attached rather to the cry of the so-called "Seven Whistlers", voices heard flying overhead in the darkness of the night. This cry was always regarded as an evil omen; and it is said that Leicestershire colliers would not go underground on a day when the Whistlers were heard. Sometimes the voices were supposed to be the wandering souls of Jews who took part in the Crucifixion; sometimes they were imagined as the hounds of a ghostly hunt and, near Sheffield for instance, called the Gabriel hounds, in Devonshire the Wish hounds. Cf. Wordsworth:

> The poor old man is greater than he seems.
> He the seven birds hath seen that never part,
> Seen the seven whistlers on their nightly rounds
> And counted them: and oftentimes will start,
> For overhead are sweeping Gabriel's hounds.
> (*Miscell. Sonnets*, XXIX; i. 457 in Nowell Smith's edit.)

What bird is the source of the cry and the legend, remains disputed; it has been identified as the golden plover, the curlew, or the migrant bean-goose. Mr H. W. Richmond, however, has pointed out to me yet another candidate, the whimbrel, a small relation of the curlew, which has the habit of whistling *seven times*. Cf. Yarrell's *British Birds* (1884), III. 510: "Whimbrels are often spoken of in the South and West as 'the seven Whistlers', the rippling whistle being repeated seven times". This certainly provides an explanation of the number—if indeed the mystic "seven" needs one. (See Swainson, *Folk-lore of British Birds*, pp. 180, 200; *N.Q.* 4. VIII. 134, 268.)

185. *competent*: sufficient.

190. *mist of error*: the essence of the greatest tragedy, the ἁμαρτία or Tragic Error of Aristotle's *Poetics*. Cf. the dying words of Flamineo and of Bosola (*W.D.* v. 6. 260; *D.M.* v. 5. 118).

192. *haire, with powders sweete*: a pathetic echo of the Duchess' laughing prediction (III. 2. 68).

201. *Remoove that noyse*: it has been suggested that this refers to the musicians (if there are any) to whose accompaniment the dirge is sung, if sung it is. "Noise" was indeed a regular word for a band of musicians; cf. Jonson, *Tale of a Tub*, I. 2: "Press all noises of Finsbury". But here only a commentator would apply the word to anything but the screams of Cariola, who is obviously meant.

213. *cathar*: "catarrh"—used to mean not only "a cold in the head" but, as here, "cerebral haemorrhage", which was once (wrongly) supposed regularly to accompany apoplexy.

215. *Doth not death fright you?* Cf. *W.D.* v. 6. 223.

217. *such excellent company*: the same consolation as Socrates gives himself, when he faces death and his judges in Plato, *Apology*, XXXII.

222 ff. Cf. Donne, *Fifty Sermons* (1649 ed.), p. 235: "This whisperer wounds thee, and with a stilletta of gold, he strangles thee with scarfes of silk, he smothers thee with the down of phoenixes, he stifles thee with a perfume of Ambar". (Cf. *whispering* in 229; was Donne thinking of this passage?)

227–8. *hinges...both wayes*: the meaning is apparently that Death can open the door out of life from his side, or man can open it from his: our exit may be by act of God or of man. This is unsatisfactory: but I see no alternative.

228–9. *any way...whispering*. Cf. *Rich. II*, IV. 1. 315 (the deposition-scene): "Whither you will, so I were from your sights".

235. *Dispose my breath, how please you*: irony to the end? Cf. Socrates' jesting answer to Crito's question how they should bury him (*Phaedo*, 115 c): "As it pleases you, if you can catch me".

239–41. *heaven gates are not so highly arch'd...knees*. Cf. *Cymbeline*, III. 3. 2 (Dyce):

> Boys, this gate
> Instructs you how to adore the Heavens; and bows you
> To a morning's holy office; the gates of monarchs
> Are arch'd so high, that giants may jet through
> And keep their impious turbans on, without
> Good morrow to the sun.

It seems to me possible that this passage in its turn was suggested by the legend of Mahomet's first miracle (cf. *impious turbans*) in Mandeville XVI, where we are told how the Prophet was a humble camel-driver in his youth. "And at the desertes of Arabye he wente in to a chapell where a Eremyte duelte, And whan he entred in to the chapell that was but a lytill and a low thing and had but a lytil dore and a low, than the entree began to wexe so gret and so large and so high as though it had ben of a gret mynstre or the gate of a paleys."

241–2. *death, Serve for Mandragora.* Cf. Donne, *Anat. of the World, A Funeral Elegy,* 79–80:

> And the worlds busie noyse to overcome,
> Tooke so much death, as serv'd for *opium.* (C.)

259. *your wedding Ring.* Cf. Painter (p. 37): "and instead of a Carcanet placed a rope about her neck" (Stoll).

266. *This two yeeres. This* for *these* (of which it is an old variant-form found from the twelfth to the seventeenth century) is, naturally, commoner with plurals which, as here, may be thought of as a single whole; cf. "within this three hours" (*Rom. and Jul.*); "by this means"; and even "against this fearful odds" (Southey).

266. *When!*: exclamation of impatience.

267. *quicke with child.* Cf. the similar plea of Joan of Arc in I *Hen. VI,* v. 4 (based on a calumny of Holinshed's).

272. Here Bosola, if the children have been strangled off the stage (see Text. Note on 246–7), must "discover" their bodies by drawing back the curtain of the inner stage.

275. *young Wolffes.* Note that the Duke's mind, as though to lead up to his lycanthropic mania, is already running on wolves, cf. IV. I. 40; 332 below.

279–80. Craig points out a parallel in Nash, *Unfortunate Traveller* (ed. Brett-Smith), 115: "water powred forth sinkes downe quietly into the earth, but bloud spilt on the ground sprinkles up to the firmament".

281. *dazell*: the intransitive sense as here (= "are dazzled") is the original one.

This well-known line needs no comment; but, as a curiosity, it is perhaps worth preserving William Archer's contemptuous dismissal of it: "It is not difficult to hit upon sayings which shall pass for highly dramatic simply because they are unforeseen and unlikely".

282–3. The just fame of the preceding line has overshadowed the quieter beauty of these two that follow.

304. *infinite masse of Treasure.* See on III. 3. 82–3.

308–9. *good Actor...villaines part.* We have to remember that these lines were originally spoken by Burbage, the most famous of all Elizabethan actors.

310. Cf. *W.Ho!* I. I (p. 71).

332. *The Wolfe...*: see on *W.D.* v. 4. 97.

347. *Like two chain'd bullets.* Cf. Heywood, *Challenge for Beauty*, ii. (*Wks.* v. 26):

> My friend and I
> Like two chaine-bullets, side by side, will fly
> Thorow the jawes of death. (Dyce.)

Similarly Chapman, *Rev. of Bussy*, v. 1. 7 (of divine justice):

> who in th' act itself
> Includes th' infliction, which like chained shot
> Batter together still.

349. *take...in a blood*: goes by families. *Take* = "take effect", as we speak of vaccination "taking".

352–3. Cf. *K. John*, iv. 2. 242, where John cries to his tool Hubert on the news of Arthur's murder:

> Out of my sight, and never see me more. (Dyce.)

360. *hunt the Badger, by Owle-light.* Cf. Topsell, *Four-Footed Beasts*: "These Badgers are very sleepy, especially in the daytime, and stir not abroad but in the night, for which cause they are called *Lucifugae*; that is *avoiders of the light*". Turberville says in his *Noble Art of Venerie* (1611 ed., ch. 69): "He that would hunt the Badgerd, must seeke the earths and burrows where they lie, and in a faire mooneshine night" (the whole passage is well worth reading).
Owle-light: dusk.

362. *my painted honour*: generally taken to mean his disguise (Sampson, Allen). But what *honour* there is in being disguised as an old bell-man, I cannot imagine. Surely *painted* here means, as so often in Webster, "deceptive"; and *honour* refers to his advancement in the world. He had received the provisorship of the Duchess's horse; he had hoped to be rewarded with further promotion. And he now sees that all his hopes are vain. Cf. iii. 2. 321: "wealth and painted honors".

367. *She stirres.* Dyce compares *Othello*, v. 2. 115, where Desdemona revives in the same way. Had the commentators on that scene remembered this passage, they might have saved all those medical disquisitions, which fill pages of Furness's *Variorum* edition, on the question whether a person once suffocated can first revive and then die, or whether we must suppose Othello to have used his dagger also. Whether or no it is actually possible to revive and then expire after suffocation, matters little; Webster's words prove decisively that to Elizabethans it *seemed* possible; and that is all we need to know.

373. *pitty would destroy pitty*: i.e. calling for help to save her life would only seal her death, by bringing back Ferdinand.

380. *attonement*: reconciliation (at-one-ment).

381. *Mercy!*: "she is probably acknowledging the mercy of God" (Allen). This is an edifying conception; but it seems to me much more likely to be a last half-conscious appeal to her murderers to spare her.

382. *the cords of life broake.* Cf. *Eccles.* xii. 6: "Or ever the silver cord be loosed, or the golden bowl be broken" (Krusius); (the met. is of a golden lamp hung from the ceiling by a silver cord: the cord gives way and the lamp is smashed in sudden darkness). Here the Bishops' Bible is quite unlike—"Or ever the sylver lase be taken away, and or the golden wel be broken".

389. *manly sorrow:* of course, ironic.

390–1. Cf. iv. 1. 166.

391–2. *below The degree of feare:* i.e. past fearing for, as being utterly desperate. Cf. *Arcadia*, ii. (*Wks.* i. 208): "our state is soncke below the degree of feare". (C.)

V. I.

Outer stage.

6. *hold...in Cheit:* i.e. "subject to escheat"; "escheat" (*lit.* chance, accident) signifies the reversion of land held "in fee" to the lord of the fee, on the death of the tenant intestate and without heirs, or when he had committed treason or other felony. Doubtless Antonio was held to have committed a felony.

20. *St. Bennet:* St Benedict.

51–2. From Montaigne i. 29 (which probably suggested the whole episode); there it is related how Epaminondas, having refused the freedom of a youth in prison to his friend Pelopidas, yet granted it to the youth's mistress, "saying it was a gratification due unto a Courtizan, and not to a Captaine". (C.)

67. *noble old fellow:* Pescara (who was actually only thirty-six at his death in 1525).

77. *fraight:* fraught.

81. *fall once...ever falling:* from Montaigne i. 32: "there is no man so base minded that loveth not rather to fall once than ever to remaine in feare of falling". (C.)

V. 2.

Whole stage: it seems impossible that Ferdinand should appear literally in the "gallery" or upper stage (cf. l. 3); for he could not there be seen throwing himself on the ground to catch his own shadow.

7. *Licanthropia:* the mania of one who believes himself a were-wolf. Webster's source is Goulart's *Histoires Admirables* (1600), translated by Grimeston (1607), pp. 386–7 (the section containing the story of the *D.M.* ends on p. 368): "For there be *Licanthropes* in whom the melancholike humor doth so rule, as they imagine themselves to be transformed into Wolves...and all night doe nothing but runne into Church-yardes, and about graves...one of these melancholike *Licanthropes*...carried then upon his shoulders the whole thigh and the legge of a dead man....A Countri-man neere

unto Pavia, in the yeare 1541...did constantlye affirme that he was a Wolfe, and that there was no other difference, but that Wolves were commonlie hayrie without, and hee was betwixt the skinne and the flesh. Some (too barbarous and cruell Wolves in effect) desiring to trie the truth thereof, gave him manie wounds upon the armes and legges"—(as the result of which the man died).

So Bishop Hall saw a man executed at Limburgh, "who confessed on the wheel (where indeed most of us would have confessed anything) to have devoured two and forty children in that form"; and Peucer (1525–1602) states that the sorcerers of Livonia, whom the devil changed annually into wolves, were only to be identified by their having wolf's hair under their skins.

The disease is, however, despite these fables, a real one. Morel (*Études Cliniques*, 1852, II. 58) describes a patient who was so convinced he was a wolf, that he demanded raw meat and rejected it as not rotten enough. "See this mouth," he exclaimed, separating his lips with his fingers, "it is the mouth of a wolf; these are the teeth of a wolf; I have cloven feet; see the long hairs which cover my body; let me run into the woods and you shall shoot me." (See Hack Tuke, *Dict. of Psycholog. Medicine*, 1892, II. 754.)

A Lycanthropic Madman appears also in the "Masque of Melancholy" in Ford's *Lover's Melancholy* (III. 3), crying: "Bow-wow! wow-wow! the moon's eclipsed; I'll to the church-yard and sup, etc."

26. *Parac[el]sus* (c. 1490–1541) was the Swiss-born son of a German physician. It is hard to separate clearly the scientist in him from the quack; or the bold advocate of a return to nature and the use of one's own eyes in medicine in place of the formulas of Galen and Avicenna, whose volumes he burnt as lecturer at Bâle, from the mystery-monger who kept a familiar spirit in his sword-hilt and captured the imagination of posterity with his fantastic dreams.

31. *Eagles...alone.* From *Arcadia*, I. (*Wks.* I. 56): "Eagles we see fly alone, and they are but sheepe which alwaies heard together". (H.D.S.) Cf. Sir Philip Francis on the hated Pitt, whom he yet admired for his splendid isolation: "The lion walks alone. The jackals herd together".

49. *sheepe-biter*: "a dog that worries sheep" thence "a sheep-stealer"; and so "any sneaking thief". Cf. *W.Ho!* IV. I. (p. 133): "Master Justiniano here hath layed lurking, like a sheep-biter".

Sampson suggests that Ferdinand's idea of himself as a wolf is still influencing him; but this is not very convincing.

51–2. Cf. *Othello*, v. 2. 302–3 (Dyce), where Iago says:

Demand me nothing: what you know, you know:
From this time forth I never will speak word.

56–7. *beard saw'd off...eye-browes Fil'd*: perhaps the doctor is meant to add point to this remark by standing with a stiff, statuesque dignity which suggests to Ferdinand the idea of improving his appearance

with file and saw, as if he really were a graven image. Stoll quotes
Lear, III. 6. 84, where the mad King says to Edgar: "Only I do
not like the fashion of your garments: you will say they are Persian
attire: but let them be changed". Still the resemblance is not very
striking.

57. *more civill*: (1) "more decent"; (2) with allusion, I think, to the
lack of civility in the doctor's hectoring attitude, "more polite".

69. *put off your gowne?* The Q. of 1708 has the stage-direction, doubtless
traditional, "puts off his four cloaks, one after another". Dyce mentions that the Grave-digger in *Hamlet* used as late as 1830 to go
through a similar piece of buffoonery.

76. *Cullice*: strengthening broth, made partly by *bruising* the flesh and
bones of a fowl or the like. See on *W.D.* v. 4. 23–4.

76. *An[a]tomies*: skeletons.

77. *Barber-Chyrurgeons hall*. The Barber Surgeons were granted a
charter as a Company by Henry VIII in 1541—a scene represented
in a famous picture, partly by Holbein, which Pepys once thought
of buying. Their Hall was in Monkswell St; and they were granted
the bodies of four executed felons a year.

80. *tongue, and belly*: the tongue and the entrails being often among
the parts left for the gods in ancient sacrifices.

89 ff. It is noticeable that even when the Cardinal lies about his family,
it is the curse of avarice that runs in his mind; and indeed it is possible
that we are meant to believe in the vision of the old woman (to which
the Cardinal appeals as if a matter of common knowledge) as an
actual superstition of the house of Aragon (like the white bird of the
Oxenhams) and a superstition symbolic of the family avarice. So that
we may suppose the Cardinal to be lying only in the assertion that
his brother had actually seen it.

109. *th'ingagement*: the employment of Bosola.

112. *oft-di'd garment*. Cf. Donne, *Anat. of the World, First Anniversary*, 355–6:

summer's robe growes
Duskie, and like an oft dyed garment showes. (C.)

121–2. Cf. *Arcadia* I. (*Wks*. I. 60): "too much thinking doth consume
the spirits: & oft it falles out, that while one thinkes too much of his
doing, he leaves to doe the effect of his thinking". (H.D.S.)

136–7. *religion But a Schoole-name*: it seems strange that this intellectual
boldness should be attributed to the mild and superstitious Antonio.

168. One of Webster's beloved equivocations.

170. *kissing comfits*: sweetmeats to scent the breath.

173. *arme*: embrace.

174–5. *Compare...miracle*: from *Arcadia*, v. (*Wks*. II. 186): "Let
her beawtie be compared to my yeares, and such effectes will be found
no miracles". (Not in C.)

183–4. With a *double entendre*. From *Arcadia*, I. (*Wks*. I. 106): "doing all things with so pretie grace, that it seemed ignorance could not make him do amisse, because he had a hart to do well". (C.) Cf. *Char.* "Milke-mayd", 21–3.

219–20. *mice...falling houses.* Cf. Pliny VIII. 28 (H.D.S.): "When an house is readie to tumble downe, the mice goe out of it before; and first of all the spiders with their webs fall down". So Lupton, *A Thousand Notable Things,* II. 87: "It is found by observation that Rats and Dormice will forsake old and ruinous houses, three months before they fall".

228–9. *feather-beds...blockes*: from *Arcadia,* III. (*Wks.* I. 419): "she was like them that could not sleepe, when they were softly layed".

237–8. Cf. Chapman, *Gentleman Usher,* III. 2. 372–3:

> For he that cannot turn and wind a woman
> Like silk about his finger is no man.

238–9. S.D. She hides him in "the study" and draws the curtain.

244. *lingring consumption.* Cf. "Overbury's" "A Very Woman": "She is Solomon's cruell creature and a man's Walking-consumption".

249. *Secretary*: confidant, repository of secrets (the original sense of the word).

260–1. Cf. I *Hen. IV,* II. 3. 114:

> for secrecy
> No lady closer; for I well believe
> Thou wilt not utter what thou dost not know. (Dyce.)

277. *triall of my constancy.* Cf. Brutus and Portia in *Jul. Caes.* II. 1 (Sampson), esp. l. 299:

> I have made strong proof of my constancy.

283. *breasts hoop'd with adamant*: a phrase ultimately derived from the famous Horatian—

> Illi robur et aes triplex
> Circa pectus erat. (*Odes,* I. 3. 9.)

Cf. Chapman, *Bussy d'Ambois,* III. 2. 224; Marston, *Antonio's Revenge,* IV. 1. 66.

294 ff. From Julia's agitation as she realizes that she has put the Cardinal's vital secret in Bosola's hands, it is clear that, however wanton, she still cares for her old lover.

295. *how setles this?* It seems to be a metaphor of a turbid liquid subsiding and clearing (Sampson). Less probably it might mean: "Is this sinking down into the secrecy of your heart?"

314–5. *weakenesse...done*: from *Arcadia,* I. (*Wks.* I. 24): "But since it is weakenes too much to remember what should have beene done". (H.D.S.)

315–6. Cf. *W.D.* v. 6. 248–9.

328–9. *marble colours...rotten purposes*: i.e. like one painting rotten wood to resemble marble. Cf. *Arcadia,* II. (*Wks.* I. 260): "Shall I labour to lay marble coulours over my ruinous thoughts?" (H.D.S.)

330–2. *great Treasons...Actors in't*: from Chapman, *Seven Penitential Psalms*, "A Great Man":

> Plots treason and lies hid in th' actor's grave. (C.)

345. *the common B[ie]re, for Church-yards*. Cf. Swinburne's humorous self-criticism in one of his letters (ed. Hake and Rickett, p. 89): "If I write any more necrological eulogies on deceased poets, I shall be taken for an undertaker's laureate, or the forehorse of a funeral cart hired out to trot in trappings on all such occasions as regularly as Mr Mould and his Merry Men and shall feel like Bosola in the *Duchess of Malfi*".

371. *Beares up in blood*: keeps his courage. It does *not* mean "keeps on in his bloody course of action". *In blood* is a technical hunting-term of a stag in full mettle (as contrasted with "out of blood"). Cf. *Love's Lab. Lost*, iv. 2. 4; 1 *Hen. VI*, iv. 2. 48 ("If we be English deer, be then in blood"); *Coriolanus*, i. 1. 165; *Sejanus*, ii. 2.

372. *Securitie*: confidence that one is secure.

376. *biters*: deceivers.

379–80. *weakest Arme...Justice*: from *Arcadia*, iii. (*Wks.* i. 422): "Think not lightly of never so weake an arme, which strikes with the sword of justice"; cf. *Char.* "Commander", 27–8.

V. 3.

Outer stage.

[*Milan.*] This is a good example of the inappropriateness of the geographical pedantries too common in modern editions of Elizabethans. There is here no conceivable reason why the Duchess should be buried at Milan, where none the less the scene is certainly laid in so far as it is laid anywhere definite. But that is the whole point; for an Elizabethan audience the scene here was not some precise spot on the map, but somewhere near both to the Cardinal's dwelling and to the Duchess's grave.

10–3. *I doe love...History*. From Montaigne iii. 9: "And yet I cannot so often survay the vast toombe of that Citie (Rome), so great, so populous, and so puissant, but I as often admire and reverence the same.... 'for which way soever we walke, we set our foote upon some History'". (A rendering of Cicero's "quacunque enim ingredimur, in aliquam historiam vestigium ponimus".) (C.) There is a not dissimilar passage in Marston, *Sophonisba*, iv. 1. 144 ff.

In a work called *Really and Truly* by "C.F." (Robert Ross) (1915), p. 8, there is the following foot-note which not all readers I hope, will find irrelevant: "In some trenches near Ypres, there was quartered a sulky young Scotchman of my acquaintance. For many weeks he had not exchanged a word with any of his brother officers beyond what the exigencies of the trenches demanded. One early morning moved by the silhouette of the battered city against the coming dawn, he murmured half aloud to himself Antonio's lines in the *Duchess of Malfi* (v. iii):

> I do love, etc.

A young Englishman near him immediately took up the quotation with the end of the speech—

> Churches and cities, which have diseases like to men,
> Must have like death that we have.

They became great friends. A common interest in literature achieved that which the terrible realities of warfare had failed to bring about".

So romantic a feeling for old ruins strikes us as belonging more to the age of Scott than of Shakespeare: it is all the more curious to find the same mood in an almost contemporary French poem, Saint-Amant's "La Solitude" (*c.* 1619):

> Que j'aime à voir la décadence
> De ces vieux châteaux ruinés,
> Contre qui les ans mutinés
> Ont déployé leur insolence.

Webster need not however fear the comparison; Saint-Amant, expressing himself at much greater length, fails to keep up this level and produces far less effect; indeed we may say here of Webster, as Johnson of Gray in the not dissimilar mood of the *Elegy*, "Had he written often thus, it had been vain to blame, and useless to praise him".

21. *Eccho.* An interesting study might be written on Echo-scenes (in which Echo catches up and twists the ends of a speaker's sentences) from Euripides to Thomas Hardy. It is a device which has produced much frigidity of conceit, some humour, and very rarely, as here, a shimmering, unearthly beauty. The earliest example known to me occurs in some charming fragments of Euripides' lost *Andromeda*, where the heroine waits chained and weeping by the sea-cliff for the coming of dawn and with it the devouring monster of the deep, while Echo in the caverns of the rocks answers lament for lament. It was a famous scene, famously parodied by Aristophanes (*Thesmophori-azusae*, 1056–97). The subsequent popularity of the device may be seen from the list which follows and does not pretend to be exhaustive: Callimachus, *Epigr.* 30; Ovid, *Metam.* iii. 380–92 (a typical piece of his charming un-Roman grace—"Dixerat 'ecquis adest?' et 'adest' responderat Echo"); Martial ii. 86. 3: Gauradas (in *Appendix Planud.* of *Palat. Anthol.* 152); Politian, *Miscell.* xxii; Erasmus, *Colloquia*, "Echo"; Gascoigne's Masque at Kenilworth, 1575 (the Queen was met, coming from hunting, by a wild man "all in ivie", who held a dialogue with Echo); R. Wilson, *Cobler's Prophesie*, sig. C 2 (H.D.S.); *Arcadia*, ii. (*Wks.* i. 352–3); Lodge, *Wounds of Civil War*, iii; Heywood, *Love's Mistress*, i. 1; Dekker, *Old For-tunatus*, i. 1; Jonson, *Cynthia's Revels*, i. 1; *Return from Parnassus*,

II. 2; *The Hog hath lost his pearl* (Hazlitt's *Dodsley* (1874), XI. 477); *A.Q.L.* v. 1. 391 ff.; Herbert, *Poems*, "Heaven"; Butler, *Hudibras*, I. 3. 189; Poe, "The Raven"; T. Hardy, *Human Shows; Far Phantasies*, p. 201. It may be added that Addison discusses the form in connection with "false wit" in *The Spectator*, No. 59.

Many of these passages are poor enough. The most ingenious and amusing is Erasmus (whose Echo shows, incidentally, a fine disregard of false quantities). A few of the remarks and answers may be quoted in illustration: "Quid superest remedii, ubi quem adstrinxerit iam nodus insolubilis (of marriage)? *Echo.* Bilis!... Quid captant plerique qui ambiunt sacerdotium? *Echo.* Otium!... Praeterea nihil habet sacerdos? *Echo.* κέρδος .... Decem iam annos trivi in Cicerone. *Echo.* Ὄνε.... Non me delectant sermones dissyllabi. *Echo.* Abi!"

Disraeli in his *Curiosities of Lit.* (1881 ed. II. 236) quotes a peculiar poem from the end of a comedy by F. Cole acted at Trinity College, Cambridge, in 1641, in which Echo even becomes political—

"Now, Eccho, on what's religion grounded?"
                      "Round-head."
"Whose its professors most considerable?"
                      "Rabble."
"How do these prove themselves to be godly?"
                      "Oddly."

Echo-scenes form an interesting literary by-way, though it has proved a blind alley for most who have followed it. And the present scene is one more example of Webster's power of remoulding the commonplace and making beautiful what most of his contemporaries made banal.

22. *the Eccho hath caught you*: an effective phrase—as if Echo, the voice of Fate, were here Fate itself seizing hold of its victim.

55. *mark'd*: heeded. These three lines, though themselves little heeded by past criticism, are as lovely as any in the play.

62. *I will not henceforth save my selfe by halves*: Antonio's character has strengthened with despair.

66. *his*: the Cardinal's.

69. *How ever*: "however things happen", "in any case"—a common use.

V. 4.

Whole stage.

31. *I would pray now*: this recalls the remorse of the guilty Claudius in *Haml.* III. 3 (cf. too 48–9 below—"Could I take him At his prayers").

45. *blacke deedes...cur'de with death*: again an adaptation of the Senecan:
            Per scelera semper sceleribus tutum est iter.
See on *W.D.* II. 1. 315.

48–9. *Could I take him At his prayers*, etc. Doubtless Bosola imagines himself to be meant here by *him*; *i.e.* he mistakes Antonio for some cut-throat who hopes to get a pardon from the Cardinal in return for murdering the inconvenient Bosola. Hence Bosola's instant stab in reply. In the state of nervous tension which he has now reached, it is quite plausible.

52. *suit*: probably "petition"; cf. *to pray* in the previous line. It might however mean "quarrel".

57. *To appeare my selfe*: Sampson and Allen explain this—"to appear in my true light as a most wretched thing". Or does it mean: "Now at last with death the need for hiding and secrecy is over—I can at all events die openly, if I could not live, as Antonio Bologna"?

Was there also running in Webster's mind the famous tag of Seneca's *Thyestes* (401–3)?—

> Illi mors gravis incubat
> Qui notus nimis omnibus,
> *Ignotus moritur sibi.*

The general sense is different: but Webster's idea of self-realization in death *may* have been partly suggested by this opposed self-ignorance in Seneca.

63. *Starres tennys-balls.* Cf. *Arcadia*, II. (*Wks.* I. 330): "he quickly made his kingdome a Tenniscourt, where his subjects should be the balles"; and, again, *Arcadia*, v. (*Wks.* II. 177): "(mankind) are but like tenisbals, tossed by the racket of the hyer powers" (part of a sentence copied also below in v. 5. 125 ff.). (H.D.S.) The earliest expression of the idea known to me is Plautus, *Captivi*, Prol. 22:

> di nos quasi pilas homines habent.

This is quoted, of the vicissitudes of ambition, by Carleton writing to Sir T. Edmondes, July 17th 1610 (Birch) and was doubtless one of the familiar tags of an educated man of the time. Cf. also Montaigne III. 9.

65 ff. Notice that of the two lovers, the Duchess and Antonio, each dies with the voice of Bosola whispering, like an evil angel turned pitiful at last, tidings of the other's fate. Cf. IV. 2. 377.

73. *in sadnes*: in serious truth, really (with the old sense of "sad" = "earnest"). But it is likely, I think, that *sad* in the previous line should be *glad*. This is slightly supported by *F.M.I.* IV. 2. 353:

> do not entertain't
> With too quick an apprehension of joy,
> For that may hurt thee, I have heard some dye of't.

81. *processe*: story, account. Cf. *Haml.* I. 5. 37: "a forged process of my death".

84. *flie the Courts of Princes*. Cf. Vittoria's last words, *W.D.* v. 6. 261.

88. *I doe not aske thee that*: (sadly ironic)—*aske* = "require", "ask for", not "inquire". "There is no need for reconciliation now."

93. *misprision*: "mistake". There are two distinct words of this form (similarly with the verb "to misprize"): (1) "mistake", from Lat.

minus, prehendere, Fr. *méprendre,* "to get hold of wrongly". (2) "Contempt", from Lat. *minus, pretiare,* Fr. *mépriser,* "to value little".

94 ff. The invincible individualism of the Renaissance. Cf. *W.D.* v. 6. 256 ff.

v. 5.

Inner stage, representing the Cardinal's Study: Malateste and his companions appear on the upper stage at 25 (cf. 31, "goe *downe* to him").

Cardinall (with a Booke): Stoll has pointed out that these appearances book in hand are a common feature of Revenge Tragedy. Cf. Marston, *Antonio's Revenge,* ii. 2; *Second Maiden's Tragedy* (Hazlitt's Dodsley (1874), x. 450); Hieronimo in *Spanish Trag.* after the scene with the Painter.

4. *Lay him by.* There is something very fine in the intense hopelessness of this. The final moment is approaching when the Cardinal will himself be "layd by and never thought of".

27. *My Dukedome, for rescew!* Cf. *Rich. III,* v. 4. 7 (Sampson): "A horse! a horse! my kingdom for a horse!" The resemblance is clearer at 64: "give me a fresh horse".

56–8. *thy Greatnes...drive thee*: from *Arcadia,* ii. (*Wks.* i. 332): "Antiphilus that had no greatnesse but outwarde, that taken away, was readie to fall faster then calamitie could thrust him". (H.D.S.)

66. *I give you the honour of Armes*: "martial salute" (Sampson, Allen). But surely even the Duke is not so mad as to cry "Yield" in one breath, "I salute you" in the next. He means "I will grant you quarter and a fair surrender with the honours of war".

71. *There flies your ransome*: because, being killed, he cannot be held to ransome.

74. *Sorrow...sin.* Cf. *W.D.* v. 4. 18–9.

84. *wet hay...broken-winded.* Cf. G. Markham, *Masterpiece Revived* (1688 ed.), p. 72: "The best diet for a horse in this case (broken-winded) is Grass in Summer, and Hay sprinkled with water in Winter".

86. *vault credit*: "do incredible things" (Sampson, Allen). But surely it means "disregard probability, overleap rational expectation and aspire to ('affect') high pleasures in another world". "High pleasures" hereafter were not a *probable* prospect, under any scheme of Divine Justice, for the soul of Duke Ferdinand.

89. *neere the bottom.* Cf. *W.D.* v. 6. 254.

92. Cf. the lines attributed to Charles I in Perinchief's life of him (Disraeli, *Curiosities of Lit.* (1881 ed.), ii. 334):

> With my own power my majesty they wound;
> In the king's name, the king himself uncrowned;
> So doth the dust destroy the diamond.

94. *soule...teeth*: from Montaigne ii. 35: "the soule must be held fast with one's teeth". (C.)

95. Cf. *W.D.* v. 6. 295.

108. *Neglected*: Bosola's rankling grievance dies only with Bosola himself. It is the first note he strikes, and almost the last.

112–3. *let me Be layd by, and never thought of*: a wish not without historical counterparts at this time. We may recall Marston's chosen epitaph "*Oblivioni sacrum*"; and Lord Chancellor Egerton, three years after this, "gave order in his will to have no solemn funeral, no monument, but to be buried in oblivion, alleging the precedents of Seneca, Warham, Archbishop of Canterbury and Chancellor, and Budeus, the learned Frenchman, who all took the like course". (Chamberlain to Carleton, March 29th 1617.)

116. *thing of blood*. Cf. *Coriol.* II. 2. 114:

> He was a thing of blood, whose every motion
> Was tim'd with dying cries.

118. *In a mist*. Cf. *W.D.* v. 6. 260. Both of Webster's villains die with darkened eyes at last.

125–6. *shadow...live*: from *Arcadia*, v. (*Wks.* II. 177): "In such a shadowe, or rather pit of darkenes, the *wormish* mankinde lives, that neither they knowe how to foresee, nor what to feare: and are but like tenisbals, tossed by the racket of the hyer powers". (H.D.S.)

132. It is worth noting that both Webster's tragedies close with the reconciling figure of a child. This "yong hopefull gentleman", however, was destined to get his author into trouble with neo-classic criticism, as an awful example of the violation of the Unity of Time. Thus C. Gildon in *The Laws of Poetry* (1721) states that an infant grows to manhood in the course of the play: and Malone most unreasonably thought that Ben Jonson was alluding to *The Duchess of Malfi* in the prologue to *Ev. Man in his H.* (printed 1616):

> To make a child new-swaddled to proceed
> Man, and then shoot up in one beard and weed
> Past three score years. (See Malone's note on *Timon*, III. 3.)

There is no reason to imagine Antonio's son as more than a child. The historical Antonio's eldest son must have been about seven or eight when his father was murdered. But Webster seems to forget that the Duchess's heir was her son by her first husband, whom he mentions at III. 3. 82.

146. Cf. the last words of the prose Epilogue to *W.D.*

TEXTUAL NOTES

THE DUCHESS OF MALFI

For details of editions, see Bibliography. In the notes that follow

A = the Quarto of 1623. (Brit. Mus. 644 f. 72.)
A₁ = Dyce's copy at S. Kensington. (No. 10,494.)
B = the Quarto of 1640.
C = the Quarto of 1678.
D = the Quarto of 1708 (only of occasional interest).
Qq = the consensus of ABC.
(For the Quarto of 1664, a simple rebinding of B, see Bibliography.)

Here, as in *The White Devil*, it is easily seen that of BCD each was printed from its immediate predecessor[1]. And as with *The White Devil*, it will be seen that there are certain differences between various copies of the first Quarto. These however are of minor importance; the four differences which Dyce notes all occur in sig. G (III. 2. 127–III. 3. 40) and two are obvious errors of A corrected by A₁. Which makes it clear that, unlike Dyce and Sampson, we should follow A₁ in the two doubtful cases also (see on III. 2. 239, III. 3. 25). With A₁ agrees the Harvard copy mentioned by Sampson, with A the Forster copy at S. Kensington (No. 9333). The Second Quarto was printed from a copy resembling A₁.

The basis of the present text is then a rotograph reproduction of A, corrected by A₁ in sig. G, and supplemented by the conjectures of BCD.

THE ACTORS' NAMES

This list (apart from the bracketed additions) is that found in A. C and D give the various parts to later casts of actors—Ferdinand to Harris and Verbruggen; Antonio to Smith and Booth; the Cardinal to Young and Keen; Bosola to Betterton and Mills; and the Duchess to Mrs Betterton and Mrs Porter.

It seems possible that the bracket against Pallant's name should really cover only The Doctor and Cariola.

The Dedication and Verses are omitted by BC.

I. I.

Actus Primus, Scena Prima. Italic here in A, though subsequent headings are roman. Throughout, the Qq print at the head of each scene all the persons who appear in it: that practice is here recorded once for all. It is probably due to the first edition having been set up from a prompt-copy.

7. *the*[*ir*]] *there* AB (a mere variant spelling).

8–11. The punctuation of this awkward passage (see Commentary) is exactly as in A, except that I have added the comma after *Sicophants* (as in BCD) and the dash.

---

[1] Cf. for instance III. 2. 320: BC omit the line, D invents a stop-gap—*to prefer true Merit | To wealth* etc.: again v. 2. 25 is omitted by BCD. See footnote on p. 273 of vol. I.

32 ff. All prose speeches in the play are printed in A with initial capitals, as if verse—a good example of Elizabethan dramatists' indifference about the published form of their work, especially when we consider that Webster had taken sufficient interest in the publishing to write a dedication.

54. *an*[*d*] BC: *an* A.

58. *di*[*e*]*d* BC: *did* A.

59. *p*[*ar*]*don* BC: *pleadon* A.

*60. *dogges,* ᴧ *when* BC Dyce: *dogges and when* A. Probably *and* is a mere slip (cf. on III. 2. 273); though it is possible that a word has dropped out, e.g. *horses.* Cf. Massinger, *Bashful Lover,* v. 1:

> Few masters think of their servants, who, grown old,
> Are turn'd off, like lame hounds and hunting horses,
> To starve on commons.

Reward however in its technical sense (see Commentary) only suits hawks and dogs.

67. [*like*] BC: *likes* A.

73. *Foux* A: *Foyx* B: *Fox* C: *Foix* D.

83. Here follows in Qq Scena II with the usual initial list of the characters destined to appear in the course of it.

The only real uncertainty is about the point where Julia enters—is it here, with her husband (as Sampson) or afterwards, with her lover the Cardinal (as Dyce, whom I follow)?

91. *Antoni*[*o*] C: *Antonia* AB.

117–8. *How...Gennit?*] Sampson suggests giving to Ferd. But the gibe in *reeles from the tilt* is a somewhat audacious insult to apply to the Duke's own horse: whereas it is natural enough that Castruchio should want to lead the subject away from his wife under the circumstances; and that he should be taunted as no very gallant rider.

126. *laugh when*] *not laugh but when* D: *laugh but when* Dyce. But if stress enough is laid on *I*, the sense is clear enough without alteration.

162. *Flatter*[*er*]*s* C: *Flatters* AB.

173. *Twins?* A: *Twins.* BC. But the omission of question-marks is so frequent, that this may as easily be a slip in BC as an intentional change. It is certainly a needless one.

185. [*shrewd*] BC: *shewed* A.

192. *you*[*r*] BC: *you* A.

*196–8. A difficult sentence (see Commentary): it would be eased, if *Then* could be changed to *And* (*And* might have got corrupted to *Then* (= than) owing to the expectation of *than* to follow, created by *lesse* in the preceding line). The meaning would then be such as M. Camille Cé seems to imply in his rendering: "et l'on souhaite, émerveillé, qu'elle considère que discourir n'est point tant une vanité, et point tant une pénitence pour vous de l'ouïr." But this is not satisfactory enough, I think, to justify altering the text. The confusion may have arisen through alternative versions in Webster's own text: there is a not altogether dissimilar corruption in *D.L.* v. 1. 10–1: *more terrible...As* (for *than*), perhaps due to the same cause.

200. *able raise* AB: *able to raise* C (perhaps rightly: I can find no parallel for the omission of *to*).

223. *entreat for*] ? *entreat for him.*

228–9. *Wee* [*are*] *now upon parting* D Dyce Sampson: ABC omit [*are*]. Sampson alternatively suggests changing the colon after *parting* to a comma, so that *Wee* becomes subject of *do commend.*

230. *League[r]* BC: *Leagues* A.

232. *[Duch.]* Sampson: *Ferd.* Qq Dyce. But it is patent from Ferdinand's previous speech and from l. 139, that he knows already whither Silvio is going.

234. Needlessly broken by Sampson into two lines. Scan:

Bring the | Carroch|es; we'll bring | you down | to the Hav|en.

245. Sampson is perhaps right in moving *abide you* to begin 246.

288. *[to]* D adds.

300. *[o'er]] ore* BCD: *are* A.

312. *Proviso[r]-ship* BC: *Provisors-ship* A.

*317. After this Sampson marks Scene II, though Ferdinand clearly remains on the stage. His reason is that Cariola has told Antonio (at 215) to meet the Duchess *in the gallery*. But who supposes that an Elizabethan audience cared for so nice a point? In play after play the scene changes imperceptibly —as, for instance, in *A.V.* II. 3 from Appius' ante-chamber to his closet. Dryden, indeed, in his *Essay of Dramatic Poesy* complains that the French stage does the same thing. Cf. Chapman, *Bussy* III. 2. 321 (Parrott's note, which refers also to *Eng. Studien* XXXIV. 1). It is clear that the present passage was played without any semblance of a break: and it is misleading to insert one.

325. *luxurious] uxorious* Thayer. But what is wrong with *luxurious* (= "lustful")? And how can a woman be *uxorious*, when the word means "overfond of one's *wife*"?

*340. *You live in a ranke pasture here, i'th Court—]* A has a comma after *Court*, which Dyce and Sampson respectively strengthen to semi-colon (so D) and full stop. It is rather tempting however to leave the comma after *Court* and place a dash or semi-colon after *pasture*, so that *here, i'th Court* adds a little more point to the following line.

353. *E[a]ves] Eves* Qq (at first a mere variant spelling): Dyce however retains it in his modernized text, as though he thought of it as the plural of *eve* (evening). No doubt there is some shade of association with this word, *night* coming so close after; but *eaves* is certainly the primary sense intended.

358. *Such weddings,]* the comma may be meant to mark an impressive pause in saying the line. But the punctuation of A is too unreliable for us to be sure that it is not a mere slip here.

372. *to give* A Sampson: *give* BC Dyce.

375. *woemen like] woemen, like* A.

412. *[these] triumphs* Dyce Vaughan: *this triumphs* AB: *this triumph* C Sampson. But *this* would be slightly less likely to be repeated with *large expence*, had it already occurred with *triumph*; and it is easier to imagine *these* getting shortened to *this* than *triumph* lengthened to *triumphs*; lastly, *this* as an actual by-form of *these* occurs from the twelfth to the seventeenth century (the last instance in *N.E.D.* is dated 1622).

416-7. One line in Qq.

420. *The]* ends 419 in Qq.

432. *distr[a]ction* C: *distruction* AB.

435. *yo[u]* BC: *yon* A.

437. *that first good deed began* A: *that good deed that first began* BC (a needless attempt to emend).

445. *Win[i]frid* Dyce Vaughan: *Winfrid* Qq Sampson. But there is no point in the Devon saint, and some appropriateness in the Welsh virgin (see

Commentary): it is also of some slight weight that Winifrid recurs as the name of the waiting-woman in *D.L.*

446. *strange* Qq: *stranger* Dyce, Sampson (in note), Vaughan. But the correction is needless; it eases the metre with the Qq arrangement of the lines (see next note); but metrical harshness is too common in Webster to justify alteration, and can here be more simply remedied. Antonio is merely echoing the *strange will* of the Duchess's last speech. Cf. *A.V.* iii. 2. 9–10.

447. *If...you*] ends 446 in Qq: Brereton corrects. It is not essential, but, I think, an easy improvement.

486. *visitan[t]s*] *visitans* AB.

508. *wo[o]* C: *woe* AB (ambiguous spelling).

548. *[de]* Sampson added. But it would, of course, be quite possible for Webster whose knowledge is often rather uncertain (though not, as a rule, on *legal* matters) to get the phrase slightly inaccurate.

II. I.

1. *taken—for*] The dash represents a comma in A, which may be accidental, but makes quite an effectively sardonic pause before naming Castruchio's absurd ambition.

25. *These...*] No gap in Qq. Some word like *dimples* is probably missing, though no doubt Bosola insolently points with his finger as well.

*32. *[I]*] *you* Qq edd. But how could the Old Lady conceivably be supposed to call it anything so uncomplimentary to herself? And she had asked Bosola what *he* called it. *I call* might easily have been changed to *you call* through confusion with the line above, owing to the words *you call* coming immediately over *[I] call*. *No, no, but call it* would also be possible.

32. *[it]* C: AB omit, perhaps because the similarity of *call* and *carr-* caused the compositor's eye to jump the gap in the MS.

37 ff. Printed, like all the prose in the play, as verse in Qq. A kind of metre *can* be made of it, as Sampson points out, with lines ending in *witchcraft* | *spawne* | *ordures* | *eate* | *feete* | *fasting* | *youth* | *Physition* | *Spring* | *fall* | *loath*. But this seems very unlikely: and it is more appropriate that *Observe my meditation now* should be followed by a change from prose to metre, as elsewhere in the plays by a change from one metre to another.

39. *children['s] ordures*] *children ordures* A: *children's ordure* BC Dyce Sampson. The plural *ordures*, though commoner in older English, is also found later still, *e.g.* in Dryden.

63–5. Edd. except Sampson print as prose.

89. *of [f]ashion* BC: *off shashion* A.

107. *goe* A: *to goe* BC. A is slightly supported by the parallel passage from Montaigne (see Commentary).

117. *pils* Qq: *peel* D. See Commentary.

118. *so troubled*] begins 119 in Qq: Brereton corrects.

121–2. Brereton makes lines end with *say* | *fore* (neat, but not indispensable).

121. *Courtie[r]s* BC: *Courties* A.

126. *[Duch.]* D adds.

134. *M[e]thought* D: *My thought* Qq.

160. *a bettring* A Sampson: *bettring* BC Dyce Vaughan. But it is far more likely that B dropped *a* by inadvertence than that A interpolated it. So at 178 below BC (quite clearly by mistake) omit *most*.

II. 2.

*1–3. Dyce makes the Old Lady enter only after *breeding*, where he puts a full stop. Then Bosola turns on her, as here, with the question *Now?* AB print these three lines as if all addressed directly to the Old Lady; with only a comma after *breeding* (C has a colon). It is possible that Bosola *might* thus try to spring her, by a direct question, into a sudden admission of the truth (she is, apparently, serving as the Duchess's midwife). But the first two lines read much more like a soliloquy; and Bosola's subsequent remarks to the Old Lady are not at all direct, only a series of innuendoes. (Cf. however 35 for *now* tagged on to the end of a question of Bosola's, as here, if we follow the reading of AB.)

11. *woemen?*] The Elizabethan *?* should perhaps here, as so often, be changed to *!* (with *still* = "always").

13. *bear[s]* C: *beare* AB.

18. *Dan[a]es*] *Danes* AB: *Dames* C: *Danae's* D.

37–8, 43–7. Dyce Sampson print as prose: Qq as here.

38. *A Switzer*] ends 37 in Qq.

50. *office[r]s* BC: *offices* A.

77. *look[s]* BC: *looke* A.

87–9. *Enter Car. with a Child*] supplied by D.

II. 3.

Enter...lanthorn] This and the next stage-direction are from D.

10. *[who's]* C: *whose* AB.

38. *it*] *I* Sampson (perhaps by oversight). Qq have a comma after *you*, here removed as slightly misleading; (the right sense being, of course, "and if it doe offend you *that* I doe so").

54. *[Bos]*] as two successive speeches are marked *Ant.*, a remark of Bosola's seems to have dropped out, especially since the sense is very obscure as the text stands. See Commentary.

56–9. In Qq three lines ending with *No, sir* | *to't* | *count.*

61. *wrought* AB: *wrote* CD Dyce Vaughan. See Commentary.

62–3. One line in Qq. Sampson alters 62–4 to end with *(sir)* | *safe* | *lying-in.*

67. *[quit]* C: *quite* AB.

79. *eight* Qq: *eighth* Dyce Sampson. But *eight* for *eighth* is quite common in the English of the time.

80. *Cæte[r]a*] *Cæteta* A.

84. *[cas'de-up]*] *caside-up* A. Cf. III. 2. 162.

92. *ne['e]r*] *nea'r* A (probably a misprint for *nev'r*), though *neare* is a sixteenth-century variant spelling.

II. 4.

15. *Lord?*] *Lord!* Dyce: but since the Cardinal answers her, it may be left as a question.

16–7. One line in Qq.

18. *turning[s]* C: *turning* AB.

20. *woemen,* Dyce: *woemen;* Qq: *woemen:* Sampson. But if *generally for woemen* were a separate answer by itself to Julia's question (as Qq and Sampson imply), we should expect *in woemen*, not *for*. *For* must mean "As for" and lead up to the sentence that follows.

35. *me make* A: *make me* BCD Dyce Sampson.
62. [*You*]] *Your* A.
88. *seeth'*[*t*] Dyce: *seeth's* AB: *seeth'd* C.
92. *That*] ends 91 in Qq.

II. 5.

4. *pro*[*deg*]*y*] *progedy* AB.
20. *here'it*] Dyce, Sampson wrongly shorten to *here't*: see Commentary.
41. *mother*[*'s*] BC: *mother* A.
50. *Thus*] a line by itself in A.
*53. *somewhat, quickly* Qq Sampson: *somewhat quickly* Dyce (with absurd bathos).
58. [*o'*] C adds.
63. *shall* A: *can* BC.
65. *which carries you*] begins 66 in Qq.
73. *Yes* Qq: *Yes, but* Dyce: ? *Yet* Sampson: *Yes, yet* Brereton. This last is the easiest: but not absolutely essential, if we imagine the Cardinal answering with stress on the pronoun: "Yes!—*I* can be angry..."
74. *rupture*] ? *rapture* Dyce.
92. *to boile*] *to-boile* Dyce. We may cf. Chaucer, *Troylus* III. 348 "to-melt" (intrans.). But for the insertion of *to* where the syntax does not need it, cf. *A.V.* I. 3. 17; II. 3. 93. In the light of which the text had better stand.

III. 1.

46. ∧ *be-speake*] *be be-speake* A.
64. [*were*] C: *where* AB.
69. Dyce makes Bosola enter here: Sampson, more simply, at 42.
91. *lenative*] *lenitive* Dyce. But see Commentary.
109. *thinke then, pray?*] *thinke then? pray?* A. It is quite possible to retain this, supposing Ferdinand to add *pray?* (= pray do tell me) as a separate and crowning sneer.
111. *Are*] ends 110 in Qq and edd. before Sampson.
111. *Chronicle*] ? *Chronicler* Sampson. But cf. *Char.* "An intruder", 12–3.

III. 2.

6. *Noblemen* Dyce: *Noble men* Qq: *noble men* Sampson. But the capital letter, if nothing else, proves Dyce right.
20. *I pray thee* ABC Sampson: *I* (= *Ay*), *prithee* D: *Ay, pray thee* Dyce.
32. [*f*]*light* Dyce: *slight* Qq, which might be defended as meaning "contemptuous refusal". But her flight is too essential a part of the story.
33. *Siri*[*n*]*x*] *Siriux* Qq.
34. *Anaxar*[*e*]*te*] *Anaxarate* Qq.
69. *I entred you* A: *I entred* BC: *it entred* D: ? *you entred* Sampson (quite needless).
69–71. [*Enter...unseen*] D adds.
71. *brothers*] ? *brother* Sampson (because of *His* in next line). But the change is not really necessary: and cf. 75.
77. *'Tis welcome*] ends 76 in Qq.
82. *ecclipze* A: *clip* BC (this has a certain extra force of double meaning (*clip* = embrace); and *to clipse* or *clips* is an old variant of *ecclipse*). But A is probably right.
91. [*us*] D adds.

101. *could change*] begins 102 in Qq.

104. con[*fe*]*deracy* C: *considdracy* AB.

106. *the*[*e*] D: *the* Qq (originally a mere matter of spelling).

112. *damp*[*n*]*e*] *dampe* A. (*N.E.D.* recognizes an old variant *damp* but not later than the fourteenth century.)

123. *use*] *use*, Qq.

157. [*shooke*] A₁BC Dyce Sampson: *shooked* A (as if a confusion between "shook" and "shaked"). A₁ is here (sig. G) the better text: cf. on 239 and 273.

165. *Enter...Pistoll*] after *apparition* in Qq.

180. *seem'd*] begins 181 in Qq.

183. *and*] begins 184 in Qq.

191. *unjust*] ? *that unjust* Sampson.

205. *forfeyt*] ? *forfeyted* Sampson.

206. [*aside*] Dyce: Sampson omits. But it is unthinkable that it should be said aloud to the Duchess—unless Bosola is merely referring to Antonio's supposed fraud. And it soon becomes clear that he does not believe Antonio dishonest at all.

213. *Jew*[*e*]*lls*] *Jewlls* A.

236. *service,...see:* Qq: *service!...see,* Dyce Sampson. The change does not seem essential, though quite likely.

*239. [*As*] *loth* A₁BC: *A-loth* A Dyce Sampson. "A-loth" is not in *N.E.D.*; though "a-loathe" (verb) and "a-loathing" are found in the thirteenth to fourteenth centuries. But A₁ is, in any case, here a better text. Cf. on 157 and 273.

254 ff. Qq print as verse, like the rest of the prose in the play, with arbitrary and impossible line-divisions—*gaping | Jew | sake | money | came | hearing | a woman | full | goe | him | Chaine.* Brereton would arrange as verse, dividing—*abide | grace | Officer | money | came | hearing | hermophrodite | prowd | goe | Buttrey | us.* But this is not satisfactory: and it is hard to see why the confusion arose, if the lines were written as Brereton suggests, in the original. Though, of course, there is always the faint possibility that such a passage may be a later addition written in the margin and so disordered.

259. *and (to those*] *and to (those* A.

273. *first-borne* ∧ A₁: *first-borne and* A.

287. [*On*] BC: *One* A.

307–9. Two lines in Qq, divided after *Polittsians* .

314. *Considering thy fall*] ends 313 in Qq.

320. BC omit. D, as often, patches by reading *prefer true Merit | To Wealth etc.*

325. *peace,* AB Sampson: *peace:* C: *peace.* Dyce.

326. *but:* A Sampson: *but* BC Dyce.

350. *Wh*[*i*]*ther*] *Whether* AB (variant-form, but ambiguous): similarly several times elsewhere.

361–3. In Qq lines end with *opinion | bathes | Spaw:* in Dyce as here: in Sampson there are only two lines ending *progresse | Spaw.*

III. 3.

18–9. One line in Qq. Dyce Sampson print as prose.

25. *keepe*[*s*] BC: *keepe* A.

*25. [*Painters*] A₁BC: *Pewterers* A edd. In sig. G A₁ is superior (cf. on

III. 2. 157, 273): otherwise *Pewterers* might have seemed preferable (see Commentary). Possibly Webster wrote that first, then altered it for greater clearness. For *Pewterers* is slightly mystifying.

50–7. Dyce Sampson print as prose: I have left the Qq as unchanged as possible, though the metre is very dubious.

52. *Was in*] ends 51 in Qq.

55. *The*] ends 54 in Qq.

55–7. Two lines in Qq, the first ending with *this*.

61–4. Dyce Sampson print as prose: 61 will just scan:

That Card|inall hath made | more bad fac|es with | his oppress|ion.

Good verse it is not: but there are plenty as bad in Webster.

63–4. One line in Qq.

70–1. One line in Qq: as prose in Dyce: as here in Sampson.

74. *beauty*] begins 75 in Qq.

88. *li[f]e* BC: *like* A (owing to *like* following).

III. 4.

8–9. S.D. 2. [*of*] BC: A omits.

11. Marginal note occurs only in A.

III. 5.

S.D. [*Enter*]...*Servants.* Qq, giving, as usual, the names of all the characters who appear in the course of the scene, add here *Bosola, Souldiers, with Vizards*; as *with Vizards* has some stage-interest, I have restored it to the text, whence previous editors had omitted it altogether, at 110.

31. *Ferdinand...your brother*] the dots represent a semi-colon in A. Which may be a slip, but may on the other hand represent an intentional pause. For there is indeed a distance between Ferdinand and brotherliness. Similarly at 69 below.

36–7. S.D. *A Letter*] begins 37 in Qq as if part of the Duchess's words: which it just conceivably might be, instead of a stage-direction. But the latter is much more likely.

37–8. One line in Qq.

74. *farewell: Since we must part,*] (A has no stop after *part*, Sampson, a comma): *farewell, since we must part:* Dyce Vaughan. It is exaggerated to say, with Sampson, that this destroys the whole point. But the capital of *Since* is strongly against it (cf. v. 2. 98).

95. *Go right*] ends 94 in Qq.

112. *Princes*] ? *poises* Daniel (*i.e.* "weights"!).

117. *whether*] begins 118 in Qq.

121. *ore-char[g]'d*] BC: *ore-char'd* A.

126–7. In Dyce Sampson three lines ending with *heard | ore | againe*. But there is no real objection to the Alexandrine *All...againe*.

129. *Pitie!*] begins 130 in Qq.

165–6. *stretched...wretch[e]d* D: *stretched...wretch'd* AB: *stretch'd... wretch'd* C Dyce.

IV. 1.

*10. *foure* Qq Dyce Sampson: *for* Collier Hazlitt Vaughan. Had they remembered *W.D.* v. 6. 36, *D.L.* II. 2. 5, v. 4. 175, this conjecture would hardly have been made. Cf. too *Hamlet* II. 2. 160, *Lear* I. 2. 175, *W. Tale* V. 2. 155.

17. *she's*] ? *that she's* or *she is* Sampson.

41. *Whom!*] *Whom?* Qq edd. But the Duchess is surely indignant, not puzzled.

92. *the Bee*] begins 93 in Qq Sampson: Dyce corrects.

106. *it*[*self*] D: *it* Qq.

108. Dyce Sampson make the Servant enter here: and Sampson makes him go out again at 111. But this Servant may be one of those who brought in lights at 64; and his exit may perhaps be left till 133.

112. *No*] begins 113 in Dyce.

131–2. One line in Qq.

IV. 2.

39. *How now,*] ends 38 in Qq edd. Brereton corrects.

55. *fashion* A Sampson: *fashions* BC Dyce.

*64. [*Enter Madmen*] D adds this (in the form *Enter Madman*) and places it *before* the Servant's descriptive speech. Dyce and Sampson insert it here: and this is strongly supported by 63, *let them loose when you please*; besides, Webster was practical dramatist enough to know that no audience would lend their ears to his description, if their eyes were distracted by the lunatics themselves.

70. *b*[*e*]*ll* BC: *bill* A.

82. *womens* A: *mens* BC (but cf., if proof were needed, II. 2. 9).

112–3. s.d. (*like an old man*) Qq: *like an Old Bell-man* D.

119–22. The lines should perhaps end with *since* | *insensible* | *sure* | *I?* (119–20 thus becoming verse).

124. *cruded* A: *curded* BC.

158. *Their*] ends 157 in Qq.

179. [*Rings his bell*] D adds.

209–10. [*Cariola...off*] D adds.

*246–7. [*Re-enter...Cariola.*]] *Enter Cariola.* D Sampson: *Cariola and Children are brought in by the Executioners; who presently strangle the Children.* Dyce. But there is no necessity for inflicting the strangling of the children on the eyes of the audience; the distinction between *Fetch her* (Cariola) and *Some other strangle the children* gives some slight reason for supposing them to be strangled "off". Further Dyce is driven by his view to change *this* to *these* in 270. No doubt an Elizabethan audience would have seen little objection to the murder of the children *coram populo*. Only the evidence in this case seems slightly to favour their being killed out of sight and their dead bodies revealed at 272, perhaps by drawing a curtain.

270. *this*] *these* Dyce (see last note).

305. *And that was the mayne cause;* A Sampson: *And what...cause;* B: *And what...cause?* CD Dyce.
Marriage—] *Marriage,* Qq (which makes *That* in the next line seem = *Which*).

321. *sentence* A: *service* BCD.

321. *yours—*] I have put a dash, since A has no stop. But the omission of one may, of course, easily be accidental, and a full-stop the right punctuation.

347. *two chain'd bullets*] *two-chain'd bullets* A. Perhaps for *two chain'd-bullets* (so BC): cf. the Heywood passage quoted in Commentary.

375. *mer*[*c*]*y* BC: *merry* A.

391–7. In Qq lines end with *suncke* | *were* | *living?* | *sight* | *sword* | *hence.* Sampson suggests ending with *below* | *fountaines* | *up* | *soule* | *father.*

403. [*with the body*] D adds.

V. 2.

25. Omitted by BC: D omits the whole sentence—*If...dream'd of.*

37. [*Throws...ground*] D adds.

51–2. Dyce as prose.

53. (*my Lord?*)] begins 54 in Qq.

56. *browes*] begins 57 in Qq.

68. *To feare me*] ends 67 in Qq: Dyce prints the speech as prose.
Here D adds s.d. *puts off his four Cloaks one after another.* See Commentary.

74. *him*—] the dash represents a comma in AB, which may however be a printer's error.

76. *An[a]tomies* BC: *Anotomies* A.

78. [*Throws...him*] D adds.

105–6. [*Exeunt...Bosola*] D adds.

116. *on[e]* BC: *on* A.

118. [*I'll*]] *I'll'd, I'ld* (=*I'd*) Qq Sampson: *I'd* Dyce.

145. [*bought*] Dyce: *brought* Qq.

157. *How now?*] Brereton moves to begin 158.

175–6. One line in Qq.

183. *Why, ignorance*] Sampson moves to end 182. But scan, with a stress on *you*: "Why, ign|orance in court|ship can|not make *you* | do amisse." This is harsh: but so Webster's metre often is. And it makes better sense.

206. BCD omit.

212–3. One line in Qq.

*246. *quit off* AB Sampson: *quit off her* CD: *quit of her* Dyce. *Quit[e] off* is, I think, probably the right reading: in eighteenth-century English one finds such phrases as "His illness being now quite off"; "His fever seemed quite off". And for "off" in this special sense *N.E.D.* also quotes Steele, *Tatler,* 223: "A Youth married under Fourteen Years may be off if he pleases when he comes to that age". *Quit off* can however be supported by the analogy of "rid off" (*v. N.E.D.*). Cf. *C.C.* II. 4. 39; I. 1. 499 above.

247. *What ailes you?*] Sampson moves to end 246.

252–4. Brereton alters to end with *love* | *of it?* | *when you.*

271–3. Qq punctuate: *Very well, why imagine...?*

295. *bosome*] begins 296 in Qq.

299. *No?*] begins 300 in Qq.

315. *I go*] begins 316 in Qq.

326–7. One line in Qq.

345. *B[ie]re*] *Beare* A (a recognized form, but ambiguous to the modern reader).

353–4. One line in Qq.

358. *rod[e]* BC: *rod* A (a common variant form).

364. *Exit*] a line earlier in Qq.

381. D adds the direction *Starts.*

V. 3.

32. *wi[f]es*] *wives* Qq Sampson (a common variant: but clearly Antonio and the Echo must agree, and we must have the same form in this line and the next).

34. *let's* D: *let's us* Qq: *let us* Dyce.

*42. *pass[ag]es* D Dyce Sampson: *passes* Qq Brereton. H.D.S. compares *Meas. for Meas.* v. 1. 370:

> When I perceive your Grace, like power divine,
> Hath look'd upon my passes.

(But there may it not = "trespasses"?)
Cf. however *D.L.* IV. 2. 17–8:

> expect to what a violent issue
> These passages will come.

This seems almost decisive.

Brereton, to ease the metre, moves *Of* from 43 to end this line.

45. *[Eccho]* Qq omit.

*69. *[Ant.]* Qq Dyce Sampson omit. The speech however begins on a fresh line (exactly as in text), as if there were a fresh speaker; and the stoic words about suffering come better from Antonio than as a preachment to him from Delio. Cf. too Antonio's previous speech.

v. 4.

2. *recover'd*] *? recoveréd* Sampson.
13. *ou[r]* BC: *out* A.
38. *quie[t]* BC: *quiein* A.
40–2. Dyce Sampson print as prose.
41. *So—it*] Qq have no stop: Dyce semi-colon: Sampson colon.
49. *At his prayers*] ends 48 in Qq Dyce Sampson: Brereton corrects.
72. *sad*] *? glad* Brereton: see Commentary.
84. Should perhaps end with *Sonne*.

v. 5.

4. *Lay him by:*] Daniel suggests that this may be a stage-direction. (As if a stage-direction would call a book *him*!)
7–8. One line in Qq: Dyce Sampson make 7 end with *come*.
14–5. One line according to Brereton.
20–1. One line in Qq Dyce Sampson. Brereton corrects.
25–6. *[Enter...above]* D adds, (except for *Grisolan* supplied by Dyce).
35. *serve;...honour!*] *serve;...honour.* AB: *serve...honour.* C Dyce Sampson (quite possibly rightly).
38. *[let]'s* BC: *lets's* A.
45–8. In Qq three lines, ending with *doore | rescew | life*: in Dyce Sampson four, ending with *first | doore | rescew | life*.
*69. *The divell?* Qq D: Dyce Sampson change *?* to *!*. But Ferdinand need not be merely swearing; he may think in his mania that he *is* brother to the devil; the next line, however, slightly supports Dyce, by its fresh mention of *my brother*.
88–9. One line in Qq.
*104. *[t]his* D Dyce Sampson: *his* Qq.
117–20. Sampson queries re-arranging in three lines, ending with *mist | as I | gone*. But the short lines suit the dying Bosola's shortness of breath.
122. *yeildes* Qq: *yield* Dyce. But the old Northern plural is sometimes found in places where rhyme proves it right, as in Shakespeare, *Sonnets*, XLI:

> Those pretty wrongs that liberty commits. . .
> Thy beauty and thy years full well befits.

THE DEVIL'S LAW-CASE

THE DEVIL'S LAW-CASE

DATE

THE title-page bears the date 1623. Further, it states that
the play was acted by the Queen's Majesty's Servants. Now
Queen Anne died on March 2nd 1619; but the London
Company which had enjoyed her patronage, though by rights
called thereafter simply "the Red Bull Players", did also naturally
enough cling to their old royal title, as "the late Queen Anne's
Servants"; and it was only in the summer of 1622 that this
company finally came to an end, seven of its survivors being
licensed to train children, as a new body called the Children,
or the Players, of the Revels (J. T. Murray, *English Dramatic
Companies*, I. 197, 205; II. 194). This licence was ready on
July 25th 1622: and *The Devil's Law-Case* must accordingly
have been performed before that date at latest.

On the other hand Dyce in his edition and Sykes in *N.Q.* 11.
VII. 106 have pointed out that I. 2. 193 ff. and II. 1. 164 ff.
of our play (see Commentary) both seem borrowed from Jonson's
The Devil is an Ass (II. 1)—which was acted in 1616, though
not printed until 1631. These imitative passages do not look
like later insertions; so that the whole play is probably later
than 1616.

Fleay, indeed, adding Romelio's age (38) to the year of his
birth (1572—supposing, that is, that his mother's intrigue occurred after March 1571), throws the play back to 1610. But
we cannot thus lightheartedly identify the date of the action
with the date of composition, in the face of all other evidence.

Dyce, on the contrary, suggested 1623, seeing in IV. 2. 11–3
an allusion to the Massacre of Amboyna in the East Indies,
in February 1623 (1622 on the old reckoning, when the year
began in March). But this is impossible, for the news only
reached England in May 1624, when the play was already in
print.

There is, then, no ground for going outside the limits 1616–22
in the company of Fleay or Dyce. But attempts to narrow them
still further have been for the most part inconclusive.

Thus Stoll (p. 31), who dates the play between the end of 1620 and the middle of 1622, has given a different explanation of Dyce's East Indian passage in IV. 2. 11–3:

How? goe to the East Indies! and so many Hollanders gone to fetch sauce for their pickeld Herrings! some have bene pepperd there *too lately*.

He pointed out that in August 1619 (he should as a matter of fact have said on Oct. 1st) four English ships lading pepper on the Sumatra coast were overpowered by the Dutch. For the news of this to reach England Stoll allowed from nine to fifteen months and attributed the play to some time after the end of 1620. He failed to discover that this news did in fact arrive in eight and a half months, on May 19th 1620 (*Cal. State Papers, Colon., E. Indies*, 1617–21, pp. 315, 321).

But, even with this correction, one cannot share all Stoll's confidence. For to begin with, the whole passage is just the sort of topical allusion that might be inserted at any revival of an old play; secondly, hostilities were incessant in the East Indies between English and Dutch from the beginning of 1617 to the end of 1620; and even after their cessation ill-feeling continued, as can be seen from such an entry as this in the Stationers' Register under June 24th 1622—"*Newes out of Holland*,...Contayning, *a true Copie o a Dut*[c]*h treatise* there published, *of the grosse abuses of their Maiours to the English, in the East Indies*". We can only say that this passage, and very possibly the whole play, is subsequent to April 1618 when the news of the first fighting reached England (*Cal. State Papers, E. Indies*, 1617–21, p. 154); while further admitting that the battle of October 1st 1619, as one of the most important incidents in the struggle, may quite well be the subject of this particular reference.

Another attempt to use internal evidence has been made in a long-forgotten note by "Benj. Easy" (*N.Q.* 3. IV. 225), who sees a resemblance between *D.L.* II. 3. 59 ff. (see note) and a passage in Sir R. Hawkins's *Observations in his Voyage into the South Sea* (Hakluyt Soc. edition, pp. 8–10). The parallel is better than such things often are; but as the book was only published shortly after Hawkins's death in April 1622, this brings us uncomfortably close to our other limit—the winding-up of the Queen's Majesty's Servants early in the following summer. The passage in the play may be a coincidence, or an insertion made before the publication of 1623.

Once more it has been suggested (cf. Stoll, p. 155; R. Brooke, p. 251) that Webster's plot *may* be indebted to *The Spanish Curate* (written March–October 1622) or to its source *Gerardo the Unfortunate Spaniard* (registered March 11th 1622), though more probably to *Lust's Dominion* (*c.* 1600). But here, clearly, all is too uncertain.

Baron A. F. Bourgeois (*N.Q.* 11. x. 41) goes even further afield and sees allusions in v. 4 to the firmness before execution of Sir Walter Raleigh in Nov. 1618 and in III. 1 to the Mompesson scandal[1]; and also, more generally, to the Lake-Roos trial of Jan. 1618–Feb. 1619. His limits are accordingly Feb. 1619–summer of 1620.

The daughter of Sir Thomas Lake had married Lord Roos, grandson of the Earl of Exeter. There was a family quarrel about property and Lady Lake accused Lord Roos of incest with his step-grandmother, the young Countess of Exeter. She maintained that the Countess had even read and signed a confession of her own guilt in a room at Wimbledon, as could be witnessed by Lady Lake's maid, Sarah Swarton, who had been hidden behind the arras. The bottom fell out of this pleasant tale, however, when James I, with one of his flashes of Sancho Panzan shrewdness, insisted on seeing the room and discovered that the said arras did not reach to within two feet of the floor, so that nothing but an ostrich could have hidden behind it. There is not here, I think, much resemblance of detail; and Webster was doubtless quite capable of drawing a hussy of a waiting-woman without the inspiration of Mistress Sarah Swarton. But undoubtedly this case was one of the causes of that wave of exasperation against domineering women which partly occasioned the play. It was not however an isolated example. No less notorious was the absurd warfare of Chief Justice Coke and his lady, who persecuted him with a tenacity that contributed to the gaiety of England for years, beginning in 1617 when they quarrelled about their daughter's marriage (see on *A.Q.L.* v. 1. 229–30, where there is a clear allusion). This will

---

[1] In what exactly this allusion consists he does not explain nor is it easy to see. Nor again does a reference to an event of 1621 square with his view that the play was finished in 1620.

not help to narrow our limits by itself. But I have found among Chamberlain's letters to Carleton what *may* even be a direct allusion to our play. The letter dates from Feb. 12th 1619–20, and relates that "our Pulpits ring continually of the insolence and impudence of Women; and to help forward, the Players have likewise taken them to task, and so to the Ballads and Ballad-Singers". Now it may be remembered that in IV. 1. 33–4 (see Commentary), Ariosto exclaims:

> Oh women, as the Ballet[1] lives to tell you,
> What will you shortly come to?

This piece of evidence seems to me to point very strongly to 1620, or possibly the later part of 1619.

Two other considerations seem to me rather to support this. The very cryptic allusion to the smuggling of gold oversea (II. 1. 213: see Commentary) may refer to the trial before the Star Chamber, in the summer and autumn of 1619, of certain foreign merchants, who were accused of conveying £7,000,000 out of the country and sentenced to enormous fines totalling £140,000. We have to remember, however, that the offence was not uncommon: cf. *W.D.* v. 3. 83.

Secondly, Howes relates that there was a great frost, during which the Thames froze over, in 1621–2. Now Winifrid in IV. 2. 443 (see Commentary), trying to prove her age to be as great as possible, claims that she can remember two great frosts. There had been frosts of outstanding severity in 1607–8 and in 1564. Clearly Winifrid wants to imply that she is old enough to remember that of 1564; and the audience were meant to make the rough calculation for themselves; but for this purpose, *after* the winter of 1621–2 Winifrid would have had to say "*three* great frosts".[2] So that the play is probably earlier than December 1621.

In fine the most probable year of performance seems to me 1620[3]; next to that, 1619; next to that, 1621.

[1] This same ballad is alluded to in May's *The Heir*, v. which does definitely belong to 1620.

[2] It is true that the *supposed* date of the action appears from IV. 2. 375, 438 to be 1610: but in a topical allusion an Elizabethan dramatist would certainly ignore that consideration.

[3] See also on IV. 2. 637.

SOURCES

There is no source known for the plot as a whole; and it is perhaps Webster's own invention.

Parallels, however, to certain episodes in it are to be found elsewhere. Thus the peripeteia by which Romelio, stabbing Contarino to kill him, accidentally performs the operation that saves his life, was probably found by Webster, as Langbaine suggested, in Goulart's *Histoires Admirables* (Paris 1600: Rouen 1606), translated into English by E. Grimeston (1607), p. 289—"An Extraordinarie Cure":

> A certaine Italian having had a quarrell with another, fell so grievously sicke, as they did not hope for life of him. His enemie hearing thereof, came to his lodging, and inquires of his servant, where his master was. The servant answered him, he is at the point of death, and will not escape this day. The other grumbling to himselfe, replied, he shall die by my handes: whereupon he enters into the sicke man's chamber, gives him certaine stabbes with his dagger, and then flies. They binde up the poore sicke mans wounds, who by the meanes of so great a losse of blood, recovered his health. So he recovered his health and life, by his meanes who sought his death. R. Solenander, *lib. 5 of his Counsels. 15. Cons. 9. sect.*

A similar story, as Langbaine also remarks, is told in Valerius Maximus (I. 8) of Jason, tyrant of Pherae. It is indeed the sort of story, with its neatly topsy-turvy issue, that once invented was bound to go on being retold. (Cf. Montaigne, I. 31; and see on III. 2. 170–2.)

Secondly, the part of Romelio is clearly influenced by Marlowe's *Jew of Malta*.[1] Indeed the Neapolitan merchant almost publicly owns how much he has borrowed from the Jew when, disguised as a Jewish physician, he says (*D. L.* III. 2. 1 ff.):

> Excellently well habited!—why me thinks
> That I could play with mine owne shaddow now,
> And be a rare Italienated Jew;
> To have as many severall change of faces
> As I have seene carv'd upon on[e] Cherrystone;
> To wind about a man like rotten Ivie,
> Eate into him like Quicksilver, poyson a friend
> With pulling but a loose hair from's beard, or give a drench,

---

[1] Well pointed out in O. Schröder, *Marlowe und Webster*, pp. 8–11.

He should linger of't nine yeares, and nere complaine,
But in the Spring and Fall, and so the cause
Imputed to the disease naturall; for sleight villanies,
As to coyne money, corrupt Ladies Honours,
Betray a towne to'th Turke, or make a Bonefire
A' th Christian Navy, I could settle [to]'t,
As if I had eate a Politician,
And disgested him to nothing but pure blood.

We remember how Barabas too had said (*J. of M.* II. 3. 184):

Being young, I studied *physic,* and began
To practise first upon the Italian.

And there is no need to labour in further detail how both merchants boast poetically of their vast wealth and their scorn of mere silver; how Romelio promises his sister, as Barabas his daughter, to two rival suitors, whose friendship is thereby ended in a duel fatal (though only apparently so in Webster) to both alike; how Romelio plans to put out of the way the two surgeons who know his guilt, as Barabas the two friars; or how both villains mock religion and friardom, and show, when brought to bay, a courage that redeems their avarice from mere meanness.[1] It is very interesting, however, to notice how this Marlowesque-Machiavellian type recurs through Webster's work, to some extent in the Duke of Florence (who is called a "Machiavillian") and the Cardinal of Aragon; more clearly perhaps, as Stoll suggests, in the lost *Guise,* and in the present play; and once more in the major and minor villains of *Appius and Virginia.*

But the chief episode in *The Devil's Law-Case* that appears to be derivative is Leonora's attempt to injure her son, even at the cost of her own honour, by accusing him of bastardy. It will be noticed that this motive recurs again later in *The Fair Maid of the Inn,* now attributed in part also to Webster. It is found likewise in the old play *Lust's Dominion* (c. 1600: publ. 1657); and there is a much vaguer resemblance in *The Spanish Curate* (licensed Oct. 1622).

In *The Devil's Law-Case* a woman, to revenge the murder of her lover by her son, tries to dishonour and disinherit him by asserting him to be the bastard offspring of her own adultery: the case is pleaded in court by a knavish advocate. In *Lust's*

---

[1] Cf. even the clumsy device of Leonora's paper (v. 5. 62–4) with Abigail's (*J. of M.* III. 6. 28).

Dominion a woman takes exactly the same course, in order to revenge injuries done to her lover by her son; she makes public avowals of her shame, but there is no court-scene. In *The Fair Maid of the Inn* a woman, to save her son from a dangerous family-feud, asserts that he is, not indeed a bastard, but supposititious—the child of her falconer, foisted by her on a husband impatient for offspring: she makes her confession before the Duke, who gives sentence as a judge, but there is no advocate. Lastly, in *The Spanish Curate* a man tries to disinherit his younger brother by acknowledging as his rightful heir a child who is really his, though illegitimate: his case, like Leonora's, is pleaded in court and by a knavish advocate.

It will be seen then that the closest resemblance lies between *The Devil's Law-Case* and *Lust's Dominion*, remotely unlike as that grotesque play is in every other respect. In *The Fair Maid of the Inn*, on the other hand, the mother's motives are good, and the son is said to be supposititious, not a bastard. While the main resemblance of *The Spanish Curate* lies simply in the court-scene; and there is no real reason to believe that it influenced *The Devil's Law-Case* at all; indeed it is probably later in date.

Now the tale of the mother who falsely disowns her own son and is convicted by a wise judge of her falsehood is found elsewhere, as Stoll has pointed out—in Laurentius Venetus, *alias* Justinianus Venetus, *alias* Bernardo Giustiniani (*De Origine Urbis Gestisque Venetorum*, 1492—v. 1. p. 51 in the edition of 1725); in Joannes Magnus, Bishop of Upsala (*De omnibus Gothorum Sueonumque Regibus*, Rome, 1554—IX. 29. 333–4) who copies Giustiniani *verbatim*; and, in a fuller form, in the *Sainte Cour* of Nicholas Caussin (Paris, 1624: p. 285 in Sir Thomas Hawkins's translation, 1650 ed.), who gives as his source both the two previous authorities and a manuscript of Père Sirmond, a fellow-Jesuit and friend. This story of Caussin's was in its turn transcribed by Wanley in his *Wonders of this Little World* (1678): and Langbaine pointed out a few years later the resemblance between Wanley and *The Fair Maid of the Inn*.

Now there are certain differences between the story of Giustiniani-Magnus and that of Caussin-Wanley; to which of these versions is Webster more likely to be indebted? By the first we are told that in the reign of Theodoric a widow had promised her hand in second marriage to her lover, promising also to turn out of the house her son by her first husband. The son complained to Theodoric. The woman then pleaded that he was really a suppositious child. "Very well", said the King, "your supposed son is younger and handsomer than your proposed husband. Marry him instead". The woman tried by every sort of excuse to evade this command; but the king, with growing suspicion, threatened punishment unless she obeyed. Then she broke down and confessed.

In Caussin, on the other hand, the widow's son has been lost since childhood: he comes to Rome, finds her in her lover's absence, and is gladly acknowledged. The lover returns, and from jealousy or avarice (at the idea of having to support the youth), refuses marriage unless the newcomer is dismissed. The widow yields; the son appeals to Theodoric. His mother replies that he is an impostor; and the rest of the story is the same, though slightly more circumstantial (both versions are quoted by Stoll, pp. 156–9).

Now of these versions the first, that of Giustiniani-Magnus, where the mother goes out of her way to deny the legitimacy of a son who had been brought up by her and never had the slightest doubt cast on his paternity before, is clearly nearer to *The Devil's Law-Case* and *The Fair Maid of the Inn*. But, as Stoll argues, this is the sort of popular story which gets into the air in a way that makes its transmission very hard to trace. He suggests, however, that Magnus, or some other collection of tales, gave rise to *Lust's Dominion*, *Lust's Dominion* to *The Devil's Law-Case*; but that *The Fair Maid of the Inn* (which he, of course, attributes to Fletcher), with its inclusion of the wise judgment, was based on Caussin whose *Cour Sainte* had just appeared in Paris (1624)—too late to influence *The Devil's Law-Case*. There is however no real reason for this beyond the coincidence of date; and if *The Fair Maid of the Inn* is in part Webster's, it seems more likely that it had the same source as *The Devil's Law-Case*. And that common source would, of course, be some form of the complete tale, such as Magnus, not *Lust's Dominion*, which omits the essential point; for, curiously enough, *The Fair Maid of the Inn* is the only one of the three plays apparently based on this legend which shows any knowledge of the central incident of the story—the clever judgment of Theodoric, which, like Solomon's, automatically compels the guilty to disclose her guilt.

In any case the answer must remain inconclusive and unimportant. We cannot say from what particular tree in the forest Webster picked his chestnut; it is enough to have found the forest.

THE PLAY

I sing not, siren-like, to tempt,
For I am harsh.   DONNE.

Between *The Duchess of Malfi* and *The Devil's Law-Case*
lies a gulf. Half a dozen years separate the tragedy from the
comedy: for our knowledge of the dramatist they are silent.
And now it is in a changed mood that we find him here—resigned
to live, and to take life as the bitter comedy it may become to
the head, when the heart has begun to harden and not to care.
And yet his is a mind, as Rupert Brooke has said, that shows
less well in such a bleak and bitter daylight than in the darkness
of nights of storm. We see more clearly the inequalities and the
defects in this erratic, spasmodic imagination; the cloudy moonlit
glories of his poetry have almost disappeared; and what seemed
in the gloom a Teneriffe, shows now in this grey atmosphere
as a scarred and rugged height far less lofty than before. Gone
for ever is the author of *White Devil* and *Duchess of Malfi*,
the man who seemed to cry in the words of Beddoes:

> I'll go brood
> And strain my burning and distracted soul
> Against the naked spirit of the world
> Till some portent's begotten.

First, however, the plot had better be retold. For Webster's
motivation has become so extraordinary and he has troubled so
little to make clear for the reader of his written word what the
action may have explained well enough on the stage, that the
pleasure of a first reading may easily be lost in bewilderment.
Pleasure there is; but life is short, and human patience; not many
will read this play a second time.

The scene is Naples. A nobleman, Contarino, loves and is
loved by Jolenta, the sister of the merchant Romelio, a purse-
proud, unscrupulous man with an ambition nothing can satisfy
and an audacity nothing can disconcert. This Romelio has made
up his mind that his sister shall marry not Contarino, who is a
spendthrift, but Contarino's friend Ercole. Contarino's discovery of this scheme breaks the friendship of the two young
nobles and a duel follows in which both are wounded, seemingly

to death. In his will Contarino had left all to Jolenta; and now Romelio, furious with him for killing Ercole and determined also that he shall not live to alter his will, visits the wounded man in bed, disguised as a Jew physician, and there stabs him. By a strange accident, however, Romelio's stiletto happens to perform that very operation which, owing to its danger, Contarino's surgeons had not dared to undertake; so Contarino recovers, but conceals his recovery; and Ercole, as it happens, likewise survives unknown. Meanwhile Romelio goes home and calmly tells his mother Leonora that he has made all sure by murdering Contarino in his bed. Now Leonora had herself fallen secretly in love with Contarino, partly through a misunderstanding, when he came to court her daughter: she is shattered by Romelio's avowal and henceforth her only thought is vengeance on her son for killing the man she loved. Hence "the Devil's Law-Case". She forms the plan of accusing herself of adultery and Romelio of bastardy: he will thus be stripped both of wealth and honour at one blow. The court-scene, as in *The White Devil*, is the most brilliant episode in the play. With the aid of her completely shameless waiting-woman Leonora makes a strong case: but again chance intervenes. She avers that her lover, Romelio's true father, had been a youth named Crispiano. Since then forty years have passed: and Leonora has consequently failed to recognize that the presiding judge is, as he now reveals, Crispiano himself. He easily disproves Leonora's story by an *alibi*; her case collapses, and Romelio seems saved. But at this moment Ercole rises dramatically in the body of the court and denounces Romelio as the murderer of Contarino. This he had accidentally learnt from Leonora, but since he has no proof of it, a trial by combat is appointed. The disguised Contarino, also present as a spectator in the court, now offers himself as second to Ercole, who does not recognize him. Had Contarino at this point revealed himself, Romelio could have been convicted of the attempted murder and Ercole saved from risking his life: but it is apparently part of Contarino's aristocratic code of honour to settle everything he can in the duelling-field. Accordingly the combat between principals and seconds takes place on the stage, doubtless to the great delight of the groundlings, for whose benefit a stage-direction enjoins that the fighting be "continued to a good length". Finally, however, the conflict is interrupted by the appearance of Leonora and her confessor, who are able to reveal that Contarino has never been murdered at all. So the comedy ends, with three marriages, apparently,—between Romelio and a nun he has seduced, between Ercole and Jolenta, and between Leonora (who is at least nearly sixty[1]) and Contarino. This last is an astonishing *dénouement*; but no doubt seems possible that such was the author's purpose.

The play is not, until it goes to pieces in the last act (which contains many other absurdities of detail), more improbable than most Elizabethan drama: but it is certainly unusual in the obscurity which wraps at moments the thoughts and motives of the characters. This weakness of motivation is indeed the besetting weakness of the later Webster. And yet, well acted, the first four acts might, I think, seem not unworthy of their author. For there are superb scenes—above all, the first duel and the trial; there are ever and again those "bitter flashes" that light up the dimmer stretches of the dialogue; and there are moments when poetry still breaks from an imagination fast drying up into cynicism and prose, as a round and fiery sun peers at instants through the fog-banks of a desolate winter afternoon. Gone are the lips of Vittoria with their tremendous vision of the Judgment Day—

> I prethee yet remember,
> Millions are now in graves, which at last day
> Like Mandrakes shall rise shreeking:

and yet from the glib tongue of a vile and pettifogging lawyer there breaks suddenly an echo of her eloquence—

> And you shall goe unto a peacefull grave,
> Discharg'd of such a guilt, as would have layne
> Howling for ever at your wounded heart,
> And rose with you to Judgement.

It is no longer the young Duchess of Malfi, but a middle-class and middle-aged widow, whose head seems to "fly in pieces" in her agony as she wails for the lover she has lost:

> Is he gone then?
> There is no plague i'th world can be compared

---

[1] This might however seem less strange to an Elizabethan audience remembering the tenderness of the great Queen for Essex in her old age. Cf. Leonora's own allusion to their relations in III. 3. 304 ff.

To impossible desire, for they are plagued
In the desire it selfe: never, oh never
Shall I behold him living, in whose life
I lived farre sweetlier then in mine owne...
               Oh I shall runne mad,
For as we love our youngest children best:
So the last fruit of our affection,
Where ever we bestow it, is most strong,
Most violent, most unresistable,
Since tis indeed our latest Harvest-home,
Last merryment fore Winter.

And, once more, it is not the white-haired Cornelia, but a cheating money-lender who suddenly breaks into such another dirge as called in *The White Devil* for the robin red-breast and the wren:

All the Flowers of the Spring,
Meet to perfume our burying:
These have but their growing prime,
And man does flourish but his time.
Survey our progresse from our birth,
We are set, we grow, we turne to earth.
Courts adieu, and all delights,
All bewitching appetites;
Sweetest Breath, and clearest eye,
Like perfumes goe out and dye;
And consequently this is done,
As shadowes wait upon the Sunne.

Such poetry on such lips! Moonlight shining on a dunghill! So moonlight does: and remains moonlight still. After all, feeling does not go by rank; and a merchant's widow on the edge of old age and loneliness, may suffer agonies as deep as Duchesses in dungeons. But such words in the mouths of attorneys! What then? Even Dukes in the real world, for that matter, do not speak in verse. And the way to enjoy the Elizabethans is to be thankful for their poetry wherever we find it, whether it be on the lips of usurers or queens.

And yet there is something more in the play than fragments of poetry. Despite all its faults, I have again and again been struck by its cleverness and vividness; above all, in that most brilliant trial-scene. (And there must be something real in any literary pleasure which can survive even editing.) But of course —I had forgotten—the trial is highly shocking; descends, in fact, almost to the level of a modern divorce-case. Well, let those who find it so, pass by, in silence. Elizabethan criticism in general has resounded too long with the outraged shrieks of moralizing critics, small souls that have become, in Romelio's superb phrase,

Too full of choler with living honest.

The play indeed is fuller of choler than of honesty. What a strange cynical personality it seems to reveal! Had Webster lost faith at last, like his Ferdinand, in virtue save as a mere name? Or had he gained the absolute imperviousness of the pure artist to all instincts of mere moral approval or indignation? One virtue alone remains outstanding, like a great rock in the bitter sea of his indifference; one commandment, Webster's first and last, still keeps its force—"Thou shalt not be afraid".

Capuchin.　　　　　　　I would make you
　　A good Christian.
Romelio.　　　　　　　Withall, let me continue
　　An honest man, which I am very certaine,
　　A coward can never be;...for, I pray, what is death?
　　The safest Trench i'th world to keepe man free
　　From Fortunes Gunshot; to be afraid of that,
　　Would prove me weaker then a teeming woman,
　　That does indure a thousand times more paine
　　In bearing of a child.

Romelio's "honesty" remains indeed a curious quality by common standards: but it is little that his creator seems to care. For Webster appears in his later work to think less and less of his figures as individuals, more and more to sacrifice their characters and our respect for them to mere *coups de théâtre*. These strange creatures—need we review them one by one? Thinking of *The Devil's Law-Case*, which of its people do we remember outside and apart from their situations? Romelio. Partly because through the eye-holes of his mask we seem to catch ever and again the glint of Webster's own eyes—"fir'd with scorn and laughter". Antonio doubted of marriage: but what a mockery is here in this loveless union, forced upon Jolenta while her brother and her mother sneer to her very face at the reluctance of the girl they are selling!

Leonora. Great persons doe not ever come together—
Romelio. With revelling faces, nor is it necessary
　　They should...
Leon. And truely I have heard say,

> To be a little strange to one another,
> Will keepe your longing fresh.
>
> *Rom.*   I, and make you beget
> More children when y'are maried: some Doctors
> Are of that opinion. You see my Lord, we are merry...

The acid, savage contrast that follows, between this *bourgeois*
mentality and the courtesy of an Ercole, takes us far from the
days when, as second-string to the good honest Dekker, Webster
had played "Westward Ho!" to tickle the ears of the worthy
citizens of London with the contrast between middle-class virtue
and wicked lords. At some point since then he had become
impressed with the difference breeding makes.[1] That conviction
had appeared already in *The Duchess of Malfi*, in the contrast
between the deaths of the noble heroine and her screaming
maid; and so here we miss one of the essential things in the
play, if we do not mark the difference between the way men
deal in the house of the money-lender and on the duelling-field
of the *noblesse*, in that scene between Ercole and Contarino
which deserves to the full Lamb's praise of its perfect gentleness
and gentlemanliness:

> *Contarino.*   Signior, I must tell you,
> To draw the picture of unkindnesse truely,
> Is to expresse two that have dearly loved,
> And falne at variance; tis a wonder to me,
> Knowing my interest in the fayre *Jolenta*,
> That you should love her.
>
> *Ercole.*   Compare her beauty and my youth together,
> And you will find the faire effects of love
> No myracle at all.

And yet these two fine gentlemen (how like life!) hold our
interest only while they are fighting or making love; and we
find our minds being irresistibly drawn back once more to that
curious, repellent, inscrutable Romelio, who has brains enough
for two of them, and who is wrought far more in the image of
his maker, so that he shows even Webster's taste for the macabre,
with a mind that dwells curiously on the winding-sheet as the
one garment "never out of fashion", or flashes, for its crowning
curse on woman, into the cry—

> Hard-hearted creatures, good for nothing else,
> But to winde dead bodies.

[1] See also footnote to vol. III. p. 128.

Romelio indeed is more real and more alive than Ercole and Contarino could ever be: him above all we remember, him and that incomparable, unutterable "baggage" of a serving-woman, Winifrid, the naked, the unashamed, the too too human. It is this sour sharpness of its characters and situations that leaves *The Devil's Law-Case*, if not a good play, at least no insipid one.

This has been no logical, ordered criticism, marching on from point to point; it has been as disordered as the play. Yet enough has been said, it may be, to arouse some reader's interest to start for himself the strange fowl that brood on this strange nest. Harsh cries he will find in answer and evil droppings: but now and again some swift swoop of angry beak and whirring wing, or some momentary glint of coloured plumage in the sun will repay the few who penetrate the thickets of this almost forgotten play.

THE DEUILS LAW-CASE

The Deuils Law-cafe.

OR,

When Women goe to Law, the
Deuill is full of Bufineffe.

A new Tragecomædy.

The true and perfeft Copie from the Originall.

As it was approouedly well Acted
by her Maiefties Seruants.

Written by IOHN WEBSTER.

Non quam diu, fed quam bene.

[Printer's Device]

LONDON,
Printed by *A. M.* for *Iohn Grifmand,* and are
to be fold at his Shop in Pauls Alley at the
Signe of the Gunne. 1623.

The Scæne, NAPLES.

The Actors Names.

ROMELIO, a Merchant.

CONTARINO, a Nobleman.

CRISPIANO, a Civill-Lawer.

ERCOLE, a Knight of Malta.

ARIOSTO, an Advocate.

PROSPERO.

JULIO, [son to *Crispiano*.]

A Capouchin.

C[O]NTILUPO.

SANITONELLA.

[BAPTISTA.]

LEONORA, [mother of *Romelio* and *Jolenta*.]

JOLENTA, [her daughter.]

[WINIFRID,] a wayting Woma[n].

[ANGIOLELLA.]

[*Two Surgeons, Judges, Lawyers, Bellmen, Register, Marshal, Herald, and Servants.*]

TO THE RIGHT
WORTHIE, AND
All-accomplisht Gentleman,
Sir THOMAS FINCH, Knight
BARONET.

SIR, let it not appeare strange, that I doe aspire to your Patronage. Things that taste of any goodnesse, love to bee shelter'd neere Goodnesse: Nor do I flatter in this (which I hate) onely touch at the originall Copy of your vertues. Some of my other Works, as *The white Devill, The Dutchesse of Malfi, Guise*, and others, you have formerly seene; I present this humbly to kisse your hands, and to find your allowance. Nor doe I much doubt it, knowing the greatest of the *Cæsars*, have cheerefully entertain'd lesse Poems then this: and had I thought it unworthy, I had not enquired after so worthy a Patronage. Your 10 selfe I understand, to bee all curtesie. I doubt not therefore of your acceptance, but resolve, that my election is happie. For which favour done mee, I shall ever rest

Your Worships humbly devoted,

JOHN WEBSTER.

TO THE JUDITIOUS
READER.

I *Hold it, in these kind of Poems with that of* Horace; Sapientia
prima, stultitia caruisse; *to bee free from those vices, which
proceed from ignorance; of which I take it, this Play will
ingeniously acquit it selfe. I doe chiefly therefore expose it to the*
Judicious: Locus est, [et] pluribus Umbris, *others have leave to
sit downe, and reade it, who come unbidden. But to these, should a
man present them with the most excellent Musicke, it would delight
them no more, then* Auriculas Citheræ collecta sorde dolentes.
I will not further insist upon the approovement of it, for I am so farre
10 *from praising my selfe, that I have not given way to divers of my
Friends, whose unbeg'd Commendatory Verses offered themselves
to doe me service in the Front of this Poeme. A great part of the
grace of this (I confesse) lay in Action; yet can no Action ever be
gracious, where the decency of the Language, and Ingenious structure
of the Scæne, arrive not to make up a perfect Harmony. What I
have fayl'd of this, You that have approoved my other Workes,
(when you have read this) taxe me of. For the rest,* Non ego
Ventosæ Plebis Suffragia venor.

The Devil's Law-Case.

OR,

When Women goe to Law, the Deuill
is full of Businesse.

[ACTUS PRIMUS, SCENA PRIMA.]

[Naples.   Leonora's House.]

Enter Romelio, and Prospero.

PROSPERO.

YOu have shewen a world of wealth; I did not thinke
There had bene a Merchant liv'd in Italy
Of halfe your substance.
ROM. Ile give the King of Spaine
Ten thousand Duckets yearely, and discharge
My yearely Custome. The Hollanders scarse trade
More generally then I: my Factors' wives
Weare Shaperoones of Velvet, and my Scriveners
Meerely through my imployment, grow so rich,
They build their Palaces and Belvidears   10
With musicall Water-workes: Never in my life
Had I a losse at Sea. They call me on th'Exchange,
The Fortunate Young Man, and make great suite
To venture with me: Shall I tell you Sir,
Of a strange confidence in my way of Trading?
I reckon it as certaine as the gaine
In erecting a Lotterie.
PROS. I pray Sir, what doe you thinke
Of Signiour *Baptist[a]'s* estate?
ROM. A meere Begger: 20
Hee's worth some fiftie thousand Duckets.
PROS. Is not that well?
ROM. How, well? for a man to be melted to snow-water,
With toyling in the world from three and twentie,
Till threescore, for poore fiftie thousand Duckets!

PROS. To your estate 'tis little I confesse:
You have the Spring-tide of Gold.
    ROM. Faith, and for Silver,
Should I not send it packing to th'East Indies,
30 We should have a glut on't.   *Enter Servant.*
    SER. Here's the great Lord *Contarino.*
    PRO. Oh, I know
His busines, he's a suitor to your sister.
    ROM. Yes Sir, but to you,
As my most trusted friend, I utter it—
I will breake the alliance.
    PROS. You are ill advised then;
There lives not a compleater Gentleman
In Italy, nor of a more ancient house.
40   ROM. What tell you me of Gentrie?—'tis nought else
But a superstitious relique of time past:
And sift it to the true worth, it is nothing
But ancient riches: and in him you know
They are pittifully in the wane; he makes his colour
Of visiting us so often, to sell land,
And thinkes if he can gaine my sisters love,
To recover the treble value.
    PROS. Sure he loves her
Intirely, and she deserves it.
50   ROM. Faith, though shee were
Crookt-shoulderd, having such a portion,
Shee would have noble Suitors; but truth is,
I would wish my noble Venturer take heed—
It may be whiles he hopes to catch a Gilthead,
He may draw up a Gudgeon.   *Enter Contarino.*
    PROS. Hee's come: Sir, I will leave you.
               [*Exeunt Prospero & Servant.*]
    CON. I sent you the Evidence of the peece of land
I motioned to you for the Sale. ROM. Yes.
    CON. Has your Counsell perus'd it?
60   ROM. Not yet my Lord: Doe you
Intend to travell? CON. No. ROM. Oh then you loose
That which makes man most absolute.
    CON. Yet I have heard
Of divers, that in passing of the Alpes,

Have but exchang'd their vertues at deare rate
For other vices.
    Rom. Oh my Lord, lye not idle;
The chiefest action for a man of great spirit,
Is never to be out of action: we should thinke
The soule was never put into the body,   70
Which has so many rare and curious pieces
Of Mathematicall motion, to stand still.
Vertue is ever sowing of her seedes:
In the Trenches for the Souldier; in the wakefull study
For the Scholler; in the furrowes of the sea
For men of our Profession—of all which
Arise and spring up Honor. Come, I know
You have some noble great Designe in hand,
That you levy so much money.
    Cont. Sir, Ile tell you,   80
The greatest part of it I meane to imploy
In payment of my Debts, and the remainder
Is like to bring me into greater bonds,
As I ayme it.
    Rom. How Sir?
    Cont. I intend it
For the charge of my Wedding.
    Rom. Are you to be married, my Lord?
    Cont. Yes Sir; and I must now intreat your pardon,
That I have concealed from you a businesse,   90
Wherein you had at first been call'd to Counsell,
But that I thought it a lesse fault in Friendship,
To ingage my selfe thus farre without your knowledge,
Then to doe it against your will: another reason
Was, that I would not publish to the world,
Nor have it whispered, scarce, what wealthy Voyage
I went about, till I had got the Myne
In mine owne possession.
    Rom. You are darke to me yet.
    Cont. Ile now remove the cloud. Sir, your sister and I   100
Are vowed each others, and there onely wants
Her worthy mothers, and your faire consents
To stile it marriage: this is a way,
Not onely to make a friendship, but confirme it

For our posterities. How doe you looke upon't?

ROM. Beleeve me Sir, as on the principall Colume
To advance our House: why you bring honour with you,
Which is the soule of Wealth. I shall be proud
To live to see my little Nephewes ride
110 O'th upper hand of their Uncles; and the Daughters
Be ranckt by Heraulds at Solemnities
Before the Mother: all this deriv'd
From your Nobilitie. Doe not blame me sir,
If I be taken with't exceedingly:
For this same honour with us Citizens,
Is a thing we are mainely fond of, especially
When it comes without money, which is very seldome—
But as you doe perceive my present temper,
Be sure I am yours—*[aside]* fierd with scorne and laughter,
120 At your over confident purpose—and no doubt,
My mother will be of your mind.

CONT. Tis my hope sir.　　　*Exit Romelio.*
I doe observe how this *Romelio*,
Has very worthy parts, were they not blasted
By insolent vaine-glory: there rests now
The mothers approbation to the match—
Who is a woman of that State and bearing,
Tho shee be Citie-borne, both in her language,
Her Garments, and her Table, shee excels
130 Our Ladies of the Court: shee goes not gawdy,
Yet have I seene her weare one Diamond,
Would have bought twenty gay ones out of their clothes,
And some of them, without the greater grace,
Out of their honesties.
Shee comes, I will trie　　　*Enter Leonora.*
How she stands affected to me, without relating
My Contract with her Daughter.

LEON. Sir, you are nobly welcome—and presume
You are in a place that's wholly dedicated
140 To your service.

CON. I am ever bound to you
For many speciall favours.

LEON. Sir, your fame
Renders you most worthy of it.

CONT. It could never have got
A sweeter ayre to fly in, then your breath.
    LEON. You have bin strange a long time, you are weary
Of our unseasonable time of feeding:
Indeed th'Exchange Bell makes us dine so late;
I thinke the Ladies of the Court from us   150
Learne to lye so long a-bed.
    CONT. They have a kind of Exchange among them too,
Marry, unlesse it be to heare of newes, I take it,
Theirs is like the New Burse, thinly furnisht
With Tyers and new Fashions. I have a suite to you.
    LEON. I would not have you value it the lesse,
If I say, Tis granted already.
    CONT. You are all Bounty,
Tis to bestow your Picture on me.
    LEON. Oh sir,   160
Shaddowes, are coveted in Summer, and with me,
Tis Fall o'th Leafe.
    CONT. You enjoy the best of Time;
This latter Spring of yours, shewes in my eye,
More fruitfull and more temperate withall,
Then that whose date is onely limitted
By the musicke of the Cuckow.
    LEON. Indeed Sir, I dare tell you,
My Looking-glasse is a true one, and as yet
It does not terrifie me. Must you have my Picture?   170
    CONT. So please you Lady, and I shall preserve it
As a most choyce Object.
    LEON. You will enjoyne me to a strange punishment:
With what a compeld face a woman sits
While shee is drawing! I have noted divers,
Either to faine smiles, or sucke in the lippes,
To have a little mouth; ruffle the cheekes,
To have the dimple seene, and so disorder
The face with affectation, at next sitting
It has not been the same; I have knowne others   180
Have lost the intire fashion of their face,
In halfe an houres sitting.
    CONT. How?
    LEON. In hote weather,

The painting on their face has been so mellow,
They have left the poore man harder worke by halfe,
To mend the Copie he wrought by: but indeed,
If ever I would have mine drawen to'th life,
I would have a Paynter steale it, at such a time,
190 I were devoutly kneeling at my prayers—
There is then a heavenly beautie in't, the Soule
Mooves in the Superficies.
    CONT. Excellent Lady,
Now you teach Beautie a preservative,
More then 'gainst fading Colours; and your judgement
Is perfect in all things.
    LEON. Indeed Sir, I am a Widdow,
And want the addition to make it so:
For mans Experience has still been held
200 Womans best eyesight. I pray sir tell mee,
You are about to sell a piece of Land
To my sonne, I heare.
    CONT. Tis truth.
    LEON. Now I could rather wish,
That Noblemen would ever live ith Countrey,
Rather then make their visits up to'th Citie
About such businesse: Oh Sir, Noble Houses
Have no such goodly Prospects any way,
As into their owne Land: the decay of that,
210 Next to their begging Churchland, is a ruine
Worth all mens pitie. Sir, I have forty thousand crownes
Sleepe in my Chest, shall waken when you please,
And flie to your commands. Will you stay supper?
    CONT. I cannot, worthy Lady.
    LEON. I would not have you come hither sir, to sell,
But to settle your Estate. I hope you understand
Wherefore I make this proffer: so I leave you.
    CONT. What a Treasury have I pearch'd! "I hope   *Exit*
You understand wherefore I make this proffer."   *Leon.*
220 Shee has got some intelligence, how I intend to marry
Her daughter, and ingenuously perceived,
That by her Picture, which I begged of her,
I meant the faire *Jolenta*: here's a Letter,
Which gives expresse charge, not to visit her

Till midnight: [reads]
"*Faile not to come, for tis a businesse*
   That concernes both our honors.
                    Yours in danger to be lost, Jolenta."
Tis a strange Injunction; what should be the businesse?
She is not chang'd I hope. Ile thither straight: 230
For womens Resolutions in such deeds,
Like Bees, light oft on flowers, and oft on weeds.   *Exit.*

[ACTUS PRIMUS, SCENA SECUNDA.]

[*The same.*]

Enter Ercole, Romelio, Jolenta.

ROM. Oh sister, come, the Taylor must to worke,
To make your wedding Clothes.
   JOL. The Tombe-maker,
To take measure of my coffin.
   ROM. Tombe-maker?
Looke you, the king of Spaine greets you.   [*gives her a paper.*]
   JOL. What does this meane,
Do you serve Proces on me?
   ROM. Proces? come
You would be wittie now.   10
   JOL. Why, what's this, I pray?
   ROM. Infinite grace to you: it is a Letter
From his Catholike Majestie, for the commends
Of this Gentleman for your Husband.
   JOL. In good season:
I hope he will not have my Allegiance stretcht
To the undoing of my selfe.
   ROM. Undoe your selfe? he does proclaime him here—
   JOL. Not for a Traytor, does he?
   ROM. You are not mad?   20
For one of the Noblest Gentlemen.
   JOL. Yet Kings many times
Know meerly but mens outsides; was this commendation
Voluntary, thinke you?
   ROM. Voluntary: what meane you by that?
   JOL. Why I do not thinke but he beg'd it of the King,

And it may fortune to be out of's way:
Some better suite—that woo'd have stood his Lordship
In farre more stead: Letters of Commendations—
30 Why tis reported that they are growen stale,
When places fall i'th Universitie.
I pray you returne his Passe: for to a Widdow
That longs to be a Courtier, this Paper
May doe Knights service.
    ERCO. Mistake not excellent Mistres, these commends
Expresse, his Majestie of Spaine has given me
Both addition of honour, as you may perceive
By my habit, and a place heere to command
Ore thirtie Gallies; this your brother shewes,
40 As wishing that you would be partner in my good Fortune.
    ROM. I pray come hither,
Have I any interest in you?
    JOL. You are my Brother.
    ROM. I would have you then use me with that respect
You may still keepe me so, and to be swayed
In this maine businesse of life, which wants
Greatest consideration, your Marriage,
By my direction: Here's a Gentleman——
    JOL. Sir, I have often told you,
50 I am so little my owne to dispose that way,
That I can never be his.
    ROM. Come, too much light
Makes you Moone-eyed—are you in love with title?
I will have a Herauld, whose continuall practise
Is all in pedigree, come a-wooing to you,
Or an Antiquary in old Buskins.
    ERCO. Sir, you have done me
The maynest wrong that ere was offred to
A Gentleman of my breeding.
60   ROM. Why sir? ERCO. You have led me
With a vaine confidence, that I should marry
Your sister—have proclaim'd it to my friends,
Employd the greatest Lawyers of our State
To settle her a joynture—and the issue
Is, that I must become ridiculous
Both to my friends and enemies: I will leave you,

Till I call to you for a strict account
Of your unmanly dealing.
    ROM. Stay my Lord!
[*aside to Jolenta*] Doe you long to have my throat cut?—Good
      my Lord,   70
Stay but a little, till I have remooved
This Court-mist from her eyes, till I wake her
From this dull sleepe, wherein sheele dreame herselfe
To a deformed Begger: [*to Jolenta*] you would marry
The great Lord *Contarino*.   *Enter Leonora.*
    LEON. *Contarino*
Were you talking of? he lost last night at Dice
Five thousand Duckets; and when that was gone,
Set at one throw a Lordship, that twice trebled
The former losse.   80
    ROM. And that flew after. LEON. And most carefully
Carried the Gentleman in his Carroch
To a Lawyers Chamber, there most Legally
To put him in possession: was this wisedome?
    ROM. O yes, their credit in the way of gaming
Is the mayne thing they stand on—that must be paid,
Tho the Brewer bawle for's money; and this Lord
Does shee preferre i'th way of marriage,
Before our Choyce ∧ here, noble *Ercole*!
    LEON. Youle be advis'd I hope: Know for your sakes   90
I married, that I might have children;
And for your sakes, if youle be rul'd by me,
I will never marry agen. Here's a Gentleman
Is noble, rich, well featur'd, but 'bove all,
He loves you intirely; his intents are aymed
For an Expedition 'gainst the Turke,
Which makes the Contract cannot be delayed.
    JO. Contract! you must do this without my knowledge;
Give me some potion to make me mad,
And happily not knowing what I speake,   100
I may then consent [to]'t.
    ROM. Come, you are mad already,
And I shall never heare you speake good sense,
Till you name him for Husband.
    ERCO. Lady, I will doe

A manly Office for you, I will leave you,
To the freedome of your owne soule—may it move whither
Heaven and you please.
    JOL. Now you expresse your selfe
110 Most nobly.
    ROM. Stay sir, what doe you meane to doe?
    LEON. [*kneels*] Heare me, if thou dost marry *Contarino*,
All the misfortune that did ever dwell
In a parents curse, light on thee!
    ERC. Oh rise Lady, certainly heaven never
Intended kneeling to this fearefull purpose.
    JOL. Your Imprecation has undone me for ever.
    ERC. Give me your hand.
    JOL. No sir.
120   ROM. Giv't me then: [*He takes her hand.*]
Oh what rare workmanship have I seene this
To finish with your needle, what excellent musicke
Have these strucke upon the Violl! Now Ile teach
A piece of Art.
    JOL. Rather a damnable cunning,
To have me goe about to giv't away,
Without consent of my soule.
    ROM. Kisse her my Lord,
If crying had been regarded, Maidenheads
130 Had nere been lost—at least some appearance of crying,
As an Aprill showre i'th Sunshine.
    LEON. Shee is yours.
    ROM. Nay, continue your station, and deale you in dumbe
        shew;
Kisse this doggednesse out of her.
    LEON. To be contracted
In teares, is but fashionable.
    ROM. Yet suppose
That they were heartie. . .
    LEON. Virgins must seeme unwilling.
140   ROM. Oh what else? And you remember, we observe
The like in greater Ceremonies then these Contracts—
At the Consecration of Prelates, they use ever
Twice to say nay, and take it.
    JOLEN. Oh Brother! [*He seizes her hand and lays it in Ercole's.*]

RO. Keep your possession, you have the dore bith'ring,
That's Livery and Seasin in England; but my Lord,
Kisse that teare from her lip—youle find the Rose
The sweeter for the dewe.

    JOLEN. Bitter as gall.

    ROM. I, I, all you women,   150
Although you be of never so low stature,
Have gall in you most abundant—it exceeds
Your braines by two ounces. I was saying somewhat;
Oh doe but observe ith Citie, and youle finde
The thriftiest bargaines that were ever made—
What a deale of wrangling ere they could be brought
To an upshot!

    LEON. Great persons doe not ever come together...

    ROM. With revelling faces, nor is it necessary
They should; the strangenesse and unwillingnesse   160
Weares the greater state, and gives occasion that
The people may buzz and talke of't, tho the Bells
Be tongue-tide at the Wedding.

    LEON. And truely I have heard say,
To be a little strange to one another,
Will keepe your longing fresh.

    ROM. I, and make you beget
More children when y'are maried: some Doctors
Are of that opinion. You see my Lord, we are merry
At the Contract—your sport is to come hereafter.   170

    ERCOL. I will leave you excellent Lady, and withall
Leave a heart with you so entirely yours,
That I protest, had I the least of hope
To enjoy you, tho I were to wayt the time
That Schollers doe in taking their degree
In the noble Arts, 'twere nothing—howsoere,
He parts from you, that will depart from life,
To doe you any service, and so humbly
I take my leave.

    JOL. Sir, I will pray for you.   *Exit Ercole.* 180

    RO. Why thats well, 'twill make your prayer compleat,
To pray for your Husband.

    JOL. Husband!

    LEON. This is

The happiest houre that I ever arrived at. [Exit.]

Rom. Husband, I, husband! come you peevish thing,
Smile me a thanke for the paynes I have tane.

Jol. I hate my selfe for being thus enforst,
You may soone judge then what I thinke of you
190 Which are the cause of it.

Enter [Winifrid, the] Wayting-woman.

Rom. You Lady of the Laundry, come hither.

Wayt. Sir?

Rom. Looke as you love your life, you have an eye
Upon your Mistresse; I doe henceforth barre her
All Visitants: I do heare there are Bawds abroad,
That bring Cut-works, & Man-toons, & convey Letters
To such young Gentlewomen, and there are others
That deale in Corne-cutting, and Fortune-telling—
Let none of these come at her on your life,
200 Nor *Dewes-ace* the wafer-woman, that prigs abroad
With Muskmeloons, and Malakatoones;
Nor the Scotchwoman with the Citterne, do you marke,
Nor a Dancer by any meanes, tho he ride on's foot-cloth,
Nor a Hackney Coachman, if he can speake French.

Wayt. Why sir?

Rom. By no meanes: no more words;
Nor the woman with Maribone puddings. I have heard
Strange jugling tricks have been conveyed to a woman
In a pudding: you are apprehensive?
210 Wayt. Oh good sir, I have traveld.

Rom. When you had a Bastard, you traveld indeed:
But my precious Chaperoones[s],
I trust thee the better for that; for I have heard,
There is no warier Keeper of a Parke,
To prevent Stalkers, or your Night-walkers,
Then such a man, as in his youth has been
A most notorious Deare-stealer.

Wayt. Very well sir,
You may use me at your pleasure.
220 Rom. By no meanes *Winifrid*, that were the way
To make thee travell agen: Come be not angry,
I doe but jest—thou knowest, wit and a woman

Are two very fraile things—and so I leave you. *Exit.*

WAYT. I could weepe with you, but tis no matter,
I can doe that at any time—I have now
A greater mind to rayle a little: Plague of these
Unsanctified Matches; they make us lothe
The most naturall desire our grandame *Eve* ever left us.
Force one to marry against their will!—why 'tis
A more ungodly worke, then inclosing the Commons.   230

JOLEN. Prethee peace;
This is indeed an argument so common,
I cannot thinke of matter new ynough,
To expresse it bad enough.

WAYT. Heere's one I hope
Will put you out of't.   *Enter Contarino.*

CONT. How now sweet Mistris?
You have made sorrow looke lovely of late,
You have wept.

WAIT. She has done nothing else these th[r]ee dayes; had 240
you stood behinde the Arras, to have heard her shed so much
salt water as I have done, you would have thought she had been
turn'd Fountaine.

CON. I would faine know the cause can be worthy this
Thy sorrow.

JOL. Reach me the Caskanet, I am studying Sir,
To take an Inventory of all that's mine.

CON. What to doe with it Lady?

JOL. To make you a Deed of gift.

CON. That's done already; you are all mine.   250

WAI. Yes, but the Devil would faine put in for's share,
In likenesse of a Separation.

JOL. Oh sir, I am bewitcht.

CON. Ha?

JOL. Most certaine, I am forespoken,
To be married to another: can you ever thinke
That I shall ever thrive in't? Am I not then bewitcht?
All comfort I can teach my selfe is this,
There is a time left for me to dye nobly,
When I cannot live so.   260

CON. Give me in a word, to whom, or by whose meanes
Are you thus torne from me?

Jol. By Lord *Ercole*, my Mother, and [m]y Brother.
   Cont. Ile make his bravery fitter for a grave,
Then for a wedding.
   Jolen. So you will beget
A farre more dangerous and strange disease
Out of the cure; you must love him agen
For my sake: for the noble *Ercole*
270 Had such a true compassion of my sorrow...
Harke in your eare, Ile shew you his right worthy
Demeanour to me.   [*As she speaks in his ear, he turns and*
   Wayt. [*aside*] Oh you pretty ones!—   *kisses her.*]
I have seene this Lord many a time and oft
Set her in's lap, and talke to her of Love
So feelingly, I doe protest it has made me
Run out of my selfe to thinke on't;
Oh sweet-breath'd monkey—how they grow together!
Well, tis my opinion,
280 He was no womans friend that did invent
A punishment for kissing.
   Cont. If he beare himselfe so nobly,
The manliest office I can doe for him,
Is to affoord him my pitie, since hee's like
To faile of so deare a purchase: for your mother,
Your goodnesse quits her ill; for your brother,
He that vowes friendship to a man, and prooves
A traytor, deserves rather to be hang'd,
Then he that counterfets money; yet for your sake
290 I must signe his pardon too. Why doe you tremble?
Be safe, you are now free from him.
   Jolen. Oh but sir,
The intermission from a fit of an ague
Is grievous: for indeed it doth prepare us,
To entertaine torment next morning.
   Cont. Why hee's gone to sea.
   Jol. But he may returne too soone.
   Con. To avoyd which, we will instantly be maried.
   Wa. To avoid which, get you instantly to bed together—
300 Doe, and I thinke no Civill Lawyer for his fee
Can give you better Councell.
   Jol. Fye upon thee, prethee leave us. [*Exit Waiting Woman.*]

CON. Be of comfort sweet Mistris.

JOL. On one condition, we may have no quarrell
About this.

CON. Upon my life—none.

JOL. None,
Upon your honour?

CON. With whom? with *Ercole?*
You have delivered him guiltlesse. With your Brother?   310
Hee's part of your selfe. With your complementall Mother?
I use not fight with women. To-morrow weele
Be married: Let those that would oppose this union,
Grow nere so subtill, and intangle themselves
In their owne worke like Spiders, while we two
Haste to our noble wishes, and presume,
The hindrance of it will breed more delight,
As black copartaments shewes gold more bright.   *Exeunt.*

Finis Actus primi.

ACTUS SECUNDUS, SCENA PRIMA.

[A public place.]

Enter Crispiano [disguised], Sanitonella.

CRISP. Am I well habited?

SAN. Exceeding well; any man would take you for a
Merchant: but pray sir resolve me, what should bee the reason,
that you being one of the most eminent Civill Lawyers in
Spaine, and but newly arrived from the East Indies, should take
this habit of a Marchant upon you?

CRISP. Why my sonne lives here in Naples, & in's riot
Doth farre exceed the exhibition I allowed him.

SAN. So then, & in this disguise you meane to trace him?

CRI. Partly for that, but there is other businesse   10
Of greater consequence.

SAN. Faith for his expence, tis nothing to your estate—What,
to *Don Crispiano,* the famous Corrigidor of Civill, who by his
meere practise of the Law, in lesse time then halfe a Jubile,
hath gotten thirtie thousand Duckets a yeare!

CRISP. Well, I will give him line,

Let him run on in's course of spending.

 SAN. Freely?

 CRISP. Freely:

20 For I protest, if that I could conceave

My sonne would take more pleasure or content,

By any course of ryot, in the expence,

Then I tooke joy, nay soules felicitie,

In the getting of it, should all the wealth I have

Waste to as small an atomy as Flies

I'th Sunne, I doe protest on that condition,

It should not moove mee.

 SAN. How's this? Cannot hee take more p[l]easure in spending

it ryotously, then you have done by scraping it together? O ten

30 thousand times more, and I make no question, five hundred

yong gallants wil be of my opinion.

Why all the time of your Collectionship

Has bene a perpetuall Callender—begin first

With your melancholly studie of the Law

Before you c[a]me to finger the Ruddocks—after that,

The tyring importunitie of Clyents,

To rise so early, and sit up so late,

You made your selfe halfe ready in a dreame,

And never prayed but in your sleepe: Can I thinke,

40 That you have halfe your lungs left with crying out

For Judgements, and dayes of Tryall? Remember sir,

How often have I borne you on my shoulder,

Among a shoale or swarme of reeking Night-caps,

When that your Worship has bepist your selfe,

Either with vehemency of Argument,

Or being out from the matter. I am merry.

 CRISP. Be so.

 SAN. You could [not] eat like a Gentleman, at leasure,

But swallow['d] it like Flap-dragons, as if you had lived

50 With chewing the Cud after.

 CRISP. No pleasure in the world was comparable [to]'t.

 SAN. Possible?

 CRISP. He shall never taste the like,

Unlesse he study law.

 SAN. What, not in wenching sir?

'Tis a Court game, beleeve it, as familiar

As Gleeke or any other.

CRISP. Wenching? O fie, the Disease followes it:
Beside, can the fingring Taffaties, or Lawnes,
Or a painted hand, or a Brest, be like the pleasure   60
In taking Clyents fees, and piling them
In severall goodly rowes before my Deske?
And according to the bignesse of each heape,
Which I tooke by a leare (for Lawyers do not tell them)
I vayl'd my cap, and withall gave great hope
The Cause should goe on their sides.
    SAN. What thinke you then
Of a good crie of Hounds? It has bene knowen
Dogs have hunted Lordships to a fault.
    CRISP. Cry of Curres?   70
The noyse of Clyents at my Chamber doore,
Was sweeter Musicke farre, in my conceit,
Then all the Hunting in Europe.
    SAN. Pray stay sir,
Say he should spend it in good House-keeping?
    CRISP. I, marry sir, to have him keepe a good house,
And not sell't away—Ide find no fault with that:
But his Kitchin, Ide have no bigger then a Saw-pit;
For the smalnesse of a Kitchin, without question,
Makes many Noblemen in France and Spaine,   80
Build the rest of the house the bigger.
    SAN. Yes, Mock-beggers.
    CRISP. Some sevenscore Chimneyes,
But halfe of them have no Tonnels.
    SAN. A pox upon them—Cuckshawes—that beget
Such monsters without fundaments.
    CRISP. Come, come, leave citing other vanities;
For neither Wine, nor Lust, nor riotous feasts,
Rich cloathes, nor all the pleasure that the Devill
Has ever practis'd with, to raise a man   90
To a Devils likenesse, ere brought man that pleasure
I tooke in getting my wealth: so I conclude.
If he can out-vie me, let it flie to'th Devill.
Yon's my sonne, what company keepes he?
    SAN. The Gentleman   *Enter Rom., Julio,*
He talks with, is *Romelio* the Merchant.   *Ariosto, Baptista.*

CRISP. I never saw him till now,
A has a brave sprightly looke, I knew his father,
And sojourn'd in his house two yeares together,
100 Before this young mans birth: I have newes to tell him
Of certaine losses happened him at Sea,
That will not please him.

SAN. What['s] that dapper fellow
In the long stocking? I doe thinke 'twas he
Came to your lodging this morning.

CRISP. Tis the same,
There he stands, but a little piece of flesh,
But he is the very myracle of a Lawyer,
One that perswades men to peace, & compounds quarrels
110 Among his neighbours, without going to law.

SAN. And is he a Lawyer?

CRISP. Yes, and will give counsell
In honest causes gratis—never in his life
Tooke fee, but he came and spake for't—is a man
Of extreame practise, and yet all his longing
Is to become a Judge.

SAN. Indeed that's a rare longing with men of his profession
I think heel prove the miracle of a lawier indeed.

ROM. Heere's the man brought word your father dyed i'th
120 Indies.

JUL. He died in perfect memory I hope,
And made me his heyre. CRI. Yes sir.

JUL. He's gone the right way then without question: Friend,
in time of mourning, we must not use any action, that is but
accessary to the making men merry, I doe therefore give you
nothing for your good tidings.

CRIS. Nor doe I looke for it sir.

JUL. Honest fellow, give me thy hand, I doe not thinke
but thou hast carried New-yeares gifts to'th Court in thy dayes,
130 and learndst there to be so free of thy paynes-taking.

ROM. Here's an old Gentleman sayes he was chamber-
fellow to your father, when they studied the Law together at
Barcellona.

JUL. Doe you know him?

ROM. Not I, he's newly come to Naples.

JUL. And what's his businesse?

ROM. A sayes he's come to read you good counsell.

CRISP. To him, rate him soundly.   *This is spoke aside* [*to*

JUL. And what's your counsell?   *Ariosto*].

ARI. Why, I would have you leave your whoring.   140

JUL. He comes hotly upon me at first: whoring?

ARI. O yong quat, incontinence is plagued
In all the creatures of the world.

JUL. When did you ever heare, that a Cockesparrow
Had the French poxe?

ARI. When did you ever know any of them fat, but in the
nest? aske all your Cantaride-mongers that question; remember
your selfe sir.

JUL. A very fine Naturallist!—a Phisician, I take you, by
your round slop; for tis just of the bignes, and no more, of the 150
case for a Urinall: tis concluded, you are a Phisician. [*Ariosto
takes off his hat.*] What doe you meane sir?—youle take cold.

ARI. Tis concluded, you are a foole, a precious one—you
are a meere sticke of Sugar Candy, a man may looke quite thorow
you.

JUL. You are a very bold gamester.   [*Julio takes off his hat.*]

AR. I can play at chesse, & know how to handle a rook.

JUL. Pray preserve your velvet from the dust.

ARI. Keepe your hat upon the blocke sir,
'Twill continue fashion the longer.   160

JUL. I was never so abused with the hat in the hand
In my life.

ARI. I will put on—why looke you,
Those lands that were the Clyents, are now become
The Lawyers; and those tenements that were
The Countrey Gentlemans, are now growen
To be his Taylors.

JUL. Taylors?

ARIO. Yes, Taylors in France, they grow to great abominable
purchase, and become great officers. How many Duckets thinke 170
you he has spent within a twelvemonth, besides his fathers
allowance?

JUL. Besides my fathers allowance? Why Gentleman, doe
you thinke an Auditor begat me? Would you have me make
even at yeares end?

ROM. A hundred duckets a month in breaking Venice glasses.

Ario. He learnt that of an English drunkard, and a Knight too, as I take it. This comes of your numerous Wardrobe.

Rom. I, and wearing Cut-worke, a pound a Purle.

180 Ario. Your daintie embroydered stockings, with overblowne Roses, to hide your gowtie anckles.

Ro. And wearing more taffaty for a garter, then would serve the Gally dung-boat for streamers.

Ari. Your switching up at the horse-race, with the Illustrissimi.

Rom. And studying a pusling Arithmatick at the cock-pit.

Ari. Shaking your elbow at the Taule-boord.

Rom. And resorting to your whore in hir'd velvet, with a spangled copper fringe at her netherlands.

190 Ari. Whereas if you had staid at Padua, and fed upon Cowtrotters, and fresh beefe to Supper...

Jul. How I am bayted!

Ari. Nay, be not you so forward with him neither, for tis thought, youle prove a maine part of his undoing.

Jul. [aside] I thinke this fellow is a witch.

Rom. Who—I sir?

Ari. You have certaine rich citie Chuffes, that when they have no acres of their owne, they will goe and plow up fooles, and turne them into excellent meadow; besides some Inclosures

200 for the first Cherries in the Spring, and Apricocks to pleasure a friend at Court with. You have Potecaries deal in selling commodities to yong Gallants, will put foure or five coxcombs into a sieve, and so drumme with them upon their Counter; theyle searse them through like Ginny Pepper—they cannot endure to finde a man like a payre of Tarriers, they would undoe him in a trice.

Rom. May be there are such.

Ari. O terrible exactors, fellowes with six hands, and three heads.

210 Jul. I those are Hell-hounds.

Ari. Take heed of them, theyle rent thee like Tenterhookes. Hearke in your eare, there is intelligence upon you; the report goes, there has been gold conveyd beyond the Sea in hollow Ancres. Farewell, you shall know mee better, I will doe thee more good, then thou art aware of. *Exit Ar.*

Jul. Hee's a mad fellow.

SAN. He would have made an excellent Barber, he does so
curry it with his tongue.   *Exit.*
  CRISP. Sir, I was directed to you.
  ROM. From whence?   220
  CRISP. From the East Indies.
  ROM. You are very welcome.
  CRI. Please you walke apart,
I shall acquaint you with particulars
Touching your Trading i'th East Indies.
  ROM. Willingly, pray walke sir.   *Ex. Cris. Rom.*

                    Enter Ercole.

  ERC. Oh my right worthy friends, you have staid me long—
One health, and then aboord; for all the Gallies
Are come about.   *Enter Contarino.*
  CONT. Signior *Ercole*,   230
The wind has stood my friend sir, to prevent
Your putting to Sea. ERC. Pray why sir?
  CONT. Onely love sir—
That I might take my leave sir, and withall
Intreat from you a private recommends
To a friend in Malta—'twould be delivered
To your bosome, for I had no time to write.
  ERC. Pray leave us Gentlemen. *Exeunt [Julio & Baptista].*
Wilt please you sit?   *They sit downe.*
  CON. Sir, my love to you has proclaim'd you one,   240
Whose word was still led by a noble thought,
And that thought followed by as faire a deed:
Deceive not that opinion—we were Students
At Padua together, and have long
To'th worlds eye shewen like friends—
Was it hartie on your part to me?
  ERC. Unfained.
  CON. You are false
To the good thought I held of you, and now
Joyne the worst part of man to you, your malice,   250
To uphold that falsehood—sacred innocence
Is fled your bosome. Signior, I must tell you,
To draw the picture of unkindnesse truely,
Is to expresse two that have dearly loved,

And falne at variance; tis a wonder to me,
Knowing my interest in the fayre *Jolenta*,
That you should love her.
    Erc. Compare her beauty, and my youth together,
And you will find the faire effects of love
260 No myracle at all.
    Con. Yes, it will prove
Prodigious to you. I must stay your Voyage.
    Erc. Your Warrant must be mightie.
    Con. 'Tis a Seale
From heaven to doe it, since you would ravish from me
What's there entitled mine: and yet I vow,
By the essentiall front of spotlesse Vertue,
I have compassion of both our youths:
To approve which, I have not tane the way,
270 Like an Italian, to cut your throat
By practise, that had given you now for dead,
And never frownd upon you.
    Erc. You deale faire, sir.
    Con. Quit me of one doubt, pray sir.
    Erc. Move it.
    Con. Tis this,
Whether her Brother were a maine Instrument
In her designe for Marriage.
    Erc. If I tell truth,
280 You will not credit me.
    Con. Why?
    Erc. I will tell you truth,
Yet shew some reason you have not to beleeve me:
Her Brother had no hand in't—ist not hard
For you to credit this? for you may thinke,
I count it basenesse to ingage another
Into my quarrell; and for that take leave
To dissemble the truth. Sir, if you will fight
With any but my selfe, fight with her Mother,
290 Shee was the motive.
    Con. I have no enemy in the world then, but your selfe;
You must fight with me.
    Erc. I will sir. Con. And instantly.
    Erc. I will haste before you—poynt whither.

CON. Why you speake nobly, and for this faire dealing,
Were the rich Jewell which we vary for,
A thing to be divided, by my life,
I would be well content to give you halfe:
But since tis vaine to thinke we can be friends,
Tis needfull one of us be tane away,   300
From being the others enemy.

ERC. Yet me thinks,
This looks not like a quarrell.

CON. Not a quarrell?

ERC. You have not apparelled your fury well,
It goes too plaine like a Scholler.

CON. It is an ornament
Makes it more terrible, and you shall finde it
A weightie injury, and attended on
By discreet valour; because I doe not strike you,   310
Or give you the lye—such foule preparatives
Would show like the stale injury of Wine—
I reserve my rage to sit on my swords poynt,
Which a great quantitie of your best blood
Cannot satisfie.

ERC. You promise well to your selfe.
Shall's have no Seconds?

CON. None, for feare of prevention.

ERC. The length of our weapons?

CON. Weele fit them by the way: 320
So whether our time calls us to live or dye,
Let us doe both like noble Gentlemen,
And true Italians.

ERC. For that let me embrace you:

CON. Me thinks, being an Italian, I trust you
To come somewhat too neere me:
But your Jelousie gave that embrace to trie
If I were armed, did it not?

ERC. No beleeve me,
I take your heart to be sufficient proofe,   330
Without a privie coat; and for my part,
A Taffaty is all the shirt of Mayle
I am armed with.

CONT. You deale equally.   *Exeunt.*

Enter Julio, and Servant.

JUL. Where are these Gallants, the brave *Ercole*,
And noble *Contarino*?
      SER. They are newly gone sir,
And bade me tell you, that they will returne
Within this halfe houre.   *Enter Romelio.*
340   JUL. Met you the Lord *Ercole*?
      ROM. No, but I met the devill in villanous tydings.
      JUL. Why, what's the matter?
      ROM. Oh I am powr'd out
Like water, the greatest Rivers i'th world
Are lost in the Sea, and so am I: pray leave me.
Where's Lord *Ercole*?
      JU. You were scarse gone hence,
But in came *Contarino*.
      ROM. *Contarino*?
350   JU. And intreated some private conference with *Ercole*,
And on the sudden they have giv'n's the slip.
      ROM. One mischiefe never comes alone:
They are gone to fight.
      JUL. To fight?
      ROM. And you be Gentlemen,
Doe not talke, but make haste after them.
      JUL. Let's take severall wayes then,
And if't be possible, for womens sakes,
For they are proper men, use our endeavours,
360 That the pricke doe not spoyle them.   *Exeunt.*

[ACTUS SECUNDUS, SCENA SECUNDA.]

[A field.]

Enter Ercole, Contarino.

CON. Youle not forgoe your interest in my Mistris?
ERC. My sword shall answer that; come, are you ready?
CON. Before you fight sir, thinke upon your cause,
It is a wondrous foule one, and I wish,
That all your exercise these foure dayes past,
Had been imploy'd in a most fervent prayer,

And the foule sinne for which you are to fight
Chiefly remembered in't.

   E R C. Ide as soone take
Your counsell in Divinitie at this present,   10
As I would take a kind direction from you
For the managing my weapon; and indeed,
Both would shew much alike.
Come are you ready?

   C O N. Bethinke your selfe,
How faire the object is that we contend for.

   E R C. Oh, I cannot forget it.   *They fight.*

   C O N. You are hurt.

   E R C. Did you come hither only to tell me so,
Or to doe it? I meane well, but 'twill not thrive.   20

   C O N. Your cause, your cause sir:
Will you yet be a man of Conscience, and make
Restitution for your rage upon your death-bed?

   E R. Never, till the grave gather one of us.   *Fight.*

   C O N. That was faire, and home I thinke. [*Wounds Ercole.*]

   E R. You prate as if you were in a Fence-schoole.

   C O N. Spare your youth, have compassion on your selfe.

   E R. When I am all in pieces—I am now unfit
For any Ladies bed; take the rest with you.

                       Contarino wounded, fals upon Ercole.

   C O N. I am lost in too much daring: yeeld your sword.   30

   E R. To the pangs of death I shall, but not to thee.

   C O N. You are now at my repayring, or confusion:
Begge your life.

   E R C. Oh most foolishly demaunded,
To bid me beg that which thou canst not give.

             Enter Romelio, Prosp., Bapt., Ario., Julio.

   P R O. See both of them are lost; we come too late.

   R O M. Take up the body, and convey it
To Saint *Sebastians* Monastery.

   C O N. I will not part with his sword, I have won't.

   J U L. You shall not: 40
Take him up gently: so—and bow his body,
For feare of bleeding inward.
Well, these are perfect lovers. P R O S. Why, I pray?

   J U L. It has been ever my opinion,

That there are none love perfectly indeed,
But those that hang or drowne themselves for love:
Now these have chose a death next to Beheading,
They have cut one anothers throats,
Brave valiant Lads.

50   PRO. Come, you doe ill, to set the name of valour
Upon a violent and mad despaire.
Hence may all learne, that count such actions well,
The roots of fury shoot themselves to hell.   *Exeunt.*

[ACTUS SECUNDUS, SCENA TERTIA.]

[*Leonora's house.*]

Enter Romelio, Ariosto.

ARIO. Your losses I confesse, are infinite,
Yet sir, you must have patience.
    ROM. Sir, my losses
I know, but you I doe not.
    ARI. Tis most true,
I am but a stranger to you, but am wisht
By some of your best friends, to visit you,
And out of my experience in the world,
To instruct you patience.

10   ROM. Of what profession are you?
    ARIO. Sir, I am a Lawyer.
    ROM. Of all men living,
You Lawyers I account the onely men
To confirme patience in us—your delayes
Would make three parts of this little Christian world
Run out of their wits else. Now I remember,
You read Lectures to *Julio*—are you such a Leech
For patience?
    ARI. Yes sir, I have had some crosses.

20   ROM. You are married then I am certaine.
    ARI. That I am sir.
    ROM. And have you studied patience?
    ARIO. You shall find I have.
    ROM. Did you ever see your wife make you Cuckold?
    ARIO. Make me Cuckold?

Rom. I aske it seriously—and you have not seene that,
Your patience has not tane the right degree
Of wearing Scarlet; I should rather take you
For a Batchelor in the Art, then for a Doctor.

Ari. You are merry.   30

Rom. No sir, with leave of your patience, I am horrible angry.

Ari. What should moove you
Put forth that harsh Interrogatory, if these eyes
Ever saw my wife doe the thing you wot of?

Rom. Why Ile tell you—
Most radically to try your patience,
And the meere question shewes you but a Dunse in't.
It has made you angry; there's another Lawyers beard
In your forehead, you doe brissle.

Ari. You are very conceited: 40
But come, this is not the right way to cure you.
I must talke to you like a Divine.

Rom. I have heard
Some talke of it very much, and many times
To their Auditors impatience; but I pray,
What practise doe they make of't in their lives?
They are too full of choller with living honest,
And some of them not onely impatient
Of their owne sleightest injuries, but starke mad,
At one anothers preferment: now to you sir—   50
I have lost three goodly Carracks. Ari. So I heare.

Rom. The very Spice in them,
Had they been shipwrackt heere upon our coast,
Would have made all our Sea a Drench.

Ario. All the sicke horses in Italy
Would have been glad of your losse then.

Rom. You are conceited too.

Ario. Come, come, come,
You gave those ships most strange, most dreadfull, and
Unfortunate names—I never lookt they'd prosper.   60

Rom. Is there any ill Omen in giving names to ships?

Ario. Did you not call one, *The Stormes Defiance*;
Another, *The Scourge of the Sea*; and the third, *The Great
Leviathan*? Rom. Very right sir.

Ari. Very devillish names

All three of them: and surely I thinke, they were curst
In their very cradles, I doe meane, when they were
Upon their Stockes.

    R o m. Come, you are superstitious,
70 Ile give you my opinion, and tis serious:
I am perswaded there came not Cuckolds enow
To the first Launching of them, and 'twas that
Made them thrive the worse for't. Oh your Cuckolds hansell
Is praid for i'th Citie.

    A r i. I will heare no more,
Give me thy hand—my intent of comming hither,
Was to perswade you to patience; as I live,
If ever I doe visit you agen,
It shall be to intreat you to be angry, sure I will,
80 Ile be as good as my word, beleeve it.   *Exit.*

    R o m. So sir: how now?   *Enter Leonora.*
Are the Scritch-owles abroad already?

    L e o n. What a dismall noyse yon bell makes,
Sure some great person's dead. R o m. No such matter,
It is the common Bell-man goes about,
To publish the sale of goods.

    L e o n. Why doe they ring
Before my gate thus? Let them into'th Court,
I cannot understand what they say.

                 Enter two Belmen and a Capouchin.
90   C a p. For pities sake, you that have teares to shed,
Sigh a soft Requiem, and let fall a Bead,
For two unfortunate Nobles, whose sad fate
Leaves them both dead, and excommunicate:
No Churchmans prayer to comfort their last groanes,
No sacred s[o]d of earth to hide their bones;
But as their fury wrought them out of breath,
The Canon speakes them guiltie of their owne death.

    L e o n. What Noblemen I pray sir?

    C a p. The Lord *Ercole,*
100 And the noble *Contarino,* both of them
Slaine in single combat.

    L e o. O, I am lost for ever.

    R o m. Denide Christian buriall—I pray what does that,
Or the dead lazy march in the Funerall,

Or the flattery in the Epitaphs, which shewes
More sluttish farre then all the Spiders webs
Shall ever grow upon it: what doe these
Adde to our well-being after death?
   CAPU. Not a scruple.
   ROM. Very well then,   110
I have a certaine Meditation,
If I can thinke of['t], somewhat to this purpose—
Ile say it to you, while my mother there
Numbers her Beades.
   You that dwell neere these graves and vaults,
Which oft doe hide Physicions faults,
Note what a small Roome does suffice,
To expresse mens good—their vanities
Would fill more volume in small hand,
Then all the Evidence of Church-land.   120
Funerals hide men in civill wearing,
And are to the Drapers a good hearing,
Make the Heraulds laugh in their blacke rayment,
And all die Worthies die worth payment
To the Altar Offerings, tho their fame,
And all the charitie of their name,
'Tweene heaven and this yeeld no more light,
Then rotten trees, which shine i'th night.
Oh looke the last Act be the best i'th Play,
And then rest gentle bones—yet pray,   130
That when by the precise you are vewed,
A Supersedeas be not sued,
To remoove you to a place more ayrie,
That in your stead they may keepe chary
Stockfish, or Seacole, for the abuses
Of sacriledge have turn'd graves to vilder uses.
How then can any Monument say,
Here rest these bones, till the last day,
When time swift both of foot and feather,
May beare them the Sexton kens not whither?   140
What care I then, tho my last sleepe,
Be in the Desart, or in the deepe,
No Lampe, nor Taper, day and night,
To give my Charnell chargeable light?

I have there like quantitie of ground,
And at the last day I shall be found.
Now I pray leave me.
    CAPU. I am sorry for your losses.
    ROM. Um sir—the more spatious that the Tennis court is,
150 The more large is the Hazard.
I dare the spitefull Fortune doe her worst,
I can now feare nothing.
    CAPU. Oh sir, yet consider,
He that is without feare, is without hope,
And sins from presumption; better thoughts attend you!
                                        Exit Ca. [*& Bellmen.*]
    RO. Poore *Jolenta*, should she heare of this!
Shee would not after the report keepe fresh,
So long as flowers in graves.   *Enter Prospero.*
How now *Prospero*?
160 PRO. *Contarino* has sent you here his Will,
Wherein a has made your sister his sole heire.
    ROM. Is he not dead? PRO. Hee's yet living.
    ROM. Living? the worse lucke.
    LEO. The worse? I doe protest it is the best,
That ever came to disturbe my prayers.
    ROM. How!
    LEON. Yet I would have him live
To satisfie publique Justice for the death
Of *Ercole*: oh goe visit him for heavens sake.
170 I have within my Closet a choyce Relicke,
Preservative 'gainst swounding, and some earth,
Brought from the Holy Land, right soveraigne
To staunch bloud: has he skilfull Surgeons, thinke you?
    PRO. The best in Naples?
    ROM. How oft has he been drest?
    PRO. But once.
    LEO. I have some skill this way:
The second or third dressing will shew clearely,
Whether there be hope of life: I pray be neere him,
180 If there be any soule can bring me word,
That there is hope of life.
    ROM. Doe you prise his life so?
    LEO. That he may live, I meane,

To come to his tryall, to satisfie the Law.

    Rom. Oh, ist nothing else?

    Leo. I shall be the happiest woman.   *Exeunt Le. Pro.*

    Rom. Here is cruelty appareled in kindnesse.

I am ful of thoughts, strange ones, but they'r no good ones.

I must visit *Contarino,* upon that

Depends an Engine shall weigh up my losses,   190

Were they sunke as low as hell; yet let me thinke,

How I am impayred in a houre, and the cause of't—

Lost in securitie: oh how this wicked world bewitches,

Especially made insolent with riches!

So Sayles with fore-winds stretcht, doe soonest breake,

And Piramides ath top, are still most weake.   *Exit.*

[ACTUS SECUNDUS, SCENA QUARTA.]

[A street.]

Enter Capuchin, Ercole led betweene two.

    Cap. Looke up sir,

You are preserved beyond naturall reason—

You were brought dead out a'th field, the Surgeons

Ready to have embalmed you.

    Erc. I do looke on my action with a thought of terror—

To doe ill and dwell in't, is unmanly.

    Cap. You are divinely informed sir.

    Erc. I fought for one, in whom I have no more right,

Then false executors have in Orphans goods,

They cozen them of; yet tho my cause were naught,   10

I rather chose the hazard of my soule,

Then foregoe the complement of a chollerick man.

I pray continue the report of my death, and give out,

'Cause the Church denyed me Christian buriall,

The Viceadmirall of my Gallies tooke my body,

With purpose to commit it to the earth,

Either in [S]icil, or Malta.

    Cap. What ayme you at

By this rumour of your death?

    Erc. There is hope of life   20

In *Contarino*; and he has my prayers,

That he may live to enjoy what is his owne,
The faire *Jolenta*; where, should it be thought
That I were breathing, happily her friends
Would oppose it still.
    CAPU. But if you be supposed dead,
The Law will strictly prosecute his life
For your murder.
    ERC. That's prevented thus—
30 There does belong a noble Priviledge
To all his Family, ever since his father
Bore from the worthy Emperour *Charles* the fift
An answere to the French Kings challenge, at such time
The two noble Princes were ingag'd to fight,
Upon a frontier arme o'th sea in a flat-bottom'd Boat—
That if any of his Family should chance
To kill a man i'th Field, in a noble cause,
He should have his Pardon; now sir, for his cause,
The world may judge if it were not honest.
40 Pray helpe me in speech, tis very painfull to me.
    CAPU. Sir I shall.
    ERC. The guilt of this lyes in *Romelio*,
And as I heare, to second this good Contract,
He has got a Nun with child.
    CAP. These are crimes
That either must make worke for speedy repentance,
Or for the Devill.
    ERC. I have much compassion on him,
For sinne and shame are ever tyde together,
50 With Gordi[a]n knots, of such a strong threed spun,
They cannot without violence be undone.   *Exeunt.*
        Explicit Actus secund[us].

ACTUS TERTIUS, SCENA PRIMA.

[*The same.*]

Enter Ariosto, Crispiano.

    ARIOST. Well sir, now I must claime
Your promise, to reveale to me the cause
Why you live thus clouded.

CRISP. Sir, the King of Spaine
Suspects, that your *Romelio* here, the Merchant
Has discover'd some Gold-myne to his owne use,
In the West Indies, and for that employes me,
To discover in what part of Christendome
He vents this Treasure: Besides, he is informed
What mad tricks has bin plaid of late by Ladies.   10
     ARI. Most true, and I am glad the King has heard on't:
Why they use their Lords, as if they were their Wards;
And as your Dutchwomen in the Low Countries,
Take all and pay all, and doe keepe their Husbands
So silly all their lives of their owne estates,
That when they are sicke, and come to make their Will,
They know not precisely what to give away
From their wives, because they know not what they are worth:
So heare should I repeat what factions,
What Bat-fowling for Offices—   20
As you must conceive their Game is all i'th night—
What calling in question one anothers honesties,
Withall what sway they beare i'th Viceroyes Court,
You'd wonder at it:
Twill doe well shortly, can we keepe them off
From being of our Councell of Warre.
     CRISP. Well, I have vowed,
That I will never sit upon the Bench more,
Unlesse it be to curbe the insolencies
Of these women.   30
     ARIO. Well, take it on my word then,
Your place will not long be emptie.   *Exeunt.*

[ACTUS TERTIUS, SCENA SECUNDA.]

[*The same—before a Surgeon's house.*]

Enter Romelio in the habit of a Jew.

ROM. Excellently well habited!—why me thinks,
That I could play with mine owne shaddow now,
And be a rare Italienated Jew;
To have as many severall change of faces,
As I have seene carv'd upon on[e] Cherrystone;

To winde about a man like rotten Ivie,
Eate into him like Quicksilver, poyson a friend
With pulling but a loose haire from's beard, or give a drench,
He should linger of't nine yeares, and nere complaine,
10 But in the Spring and Fall, and so the cause
Imputed to the disease naturall; for sleight villanies,
As to coyne money, corrupt Ladies Honours,
Betray a Towne to'th Turke, or make a Bonefire
A'th Christian Navy, I could settle [to]'t,
As if I had eate a Politician,
And disgested him to nothing but pure blood.
But stay, I loose my selfe, this is the house.
Within there!　　　　　　　　[*He knocks.*] *Enter two Surgeons.*

　　1. SUR. Now sir?
20 ROM. You are the men of Art, that as I heare,
Have the Lord *Contarino* under cure.

　　2. SUR. Yes sir, we are his Surgeons,
But he is past all Cure.

　　ROM. Why, is he dead?

　　1. SUR. He is speechlesse sir, and we doe find his wound
So fester'd neere the vitals, all our Art
By warme drinks, cannot cleare th'impostumation,
And hee's so weake, to make [incision]
By the Orifix were present death to him.

30 ROM. He has made a Will I heare. 1. SUR. Yes sir.

　　ROM. And deputed *Jolenta* his heyre.

　　2. SUR. He has, we are witnesse [to]'t.

　　ROM. Has not *Romelio* been with you yet,
To give you thanks, and ample recompence
For the paines you have tane? 1. SUR. Not yet.

　　ROM. Listen to me Gentlemen, for I protest,
If you will seriously mind your owne good,
I am come about a businesse shall convey
Large legacies from *Contarino's* Will
40 To both of you.

　　2. SUR. How sir? Why *Rom*[*elio*] has the wil,
And in that he has given us nothing.

　　ROM. I pray attend me: I am a Phisician.

　　2. SUR. A Phisician? where doe you practise?

　　ROM. In Rome.

   1. Sur. O then you have store of Patients.
   Rom. Store? why looke you, I can kill my 20. a month
And worke but i'th forenoones: (you will give me leave
To jest and be merry with you); but as I said,
All my study has been Phisicke—I am sent   50
From a noble Roman that is neere a-kinne
To *Contarino*, and that ought indeed,
By the Law of alliance, be his onely heyre,
To practise his good and yours.
   Both. How, I pray sir?
   Rom. I can by an Extraction which I have,
Tho he were speechlesse, his eyes set in's head,
His pulses without motion, restore to him
For halfe an houres space the use of sense,
And perhaps a little speech: having done this,   60
If we can worke him, as no doubt we shall,
To make anothe[r] Will, and therein assigne
This Gentleman his Heyre, I will assure you,
Fore I depart this house, ten thousand Duckets,
And then weele pull the pillow from his head,
And let him eene goe whither the Religion sends him
That he died in.
   1. Sur. Will you give's ten thousand Duckets?
   Rom. Upon my Jewisme.
   2. Sur. Tis a bargaine sir, we are yours: 70
     [*They draw the traverse, discovering*] *Contarino in a bed.*
Here is the Subject you must worke on.
   Rom. Well said, you are honest men,
And goe to the businesse roundly: but Gentlemen,
I must use my Art singly.
   1. Sur. Oh sir, you shall have all privacy—
   Rom. And the doores lockt to me.
   2. Sur. At your best pleasure.
[*aside*] Yet for all this, I will not trust this Jew.
   1. Sur. [*aside*] Faith, to say truth,
I doe not like him neither, he looks like a rogue.   80
This is a fine toy, fetch a man to life,
To make a new Will—there's some tricke in't.
Ile be neere you, Jew.   *Exeunt Surgeons.*
   Rom. Excellent!—as I would wish: these credulous fooles

Have given me freely what I would have bought
With a great deale of money.——Softly, her[e]'s breath yet;
Now *Ercole*, for part of the Revenge,
Which I have vow'd for thy untimely death:
Besides this politique working of my owne,
90 That scornes Pre[ce]dent—why, should this great man live,
And not enjoy my sister, as I have vowed
He never shall, Oh, he may alter's will
Every New Moone if he please; to prevent which,
I must put in a strong Caveat. Come forth then
My desperate Steeletto, that may be worne
In a womans haire, and nere discover'd,
And either would be taken for a Bodkin,
Or a curling yron at most; why tis an engine,
That's onely fit to put in execution
100 Barmotho Pigs—a most unmanly weapon,
That steales into a mans life he knowes not how:
O [that] great *Cæsar*, he that past the shocke
Of so many armed Pikes, and poyson'd Darts,
Swords, Slings, and Battleaxes, should at length
Sitting at ease on a cushion, come to dye
By such a Shoo-makers aule as this, his soule let forth
At a hole no bigger then the incision
Made for a wheale! uds foot, I am horribly angry,
That he should dye so scurvily: yet wherefore
110 Doe I condemne thee thereof so cruelly,
Yet shake him by the hand?—tis to expresse,
That I would never have such weapons used,
But in a plot like this, that's treacherous:
Yet this shall proove most mercifull to thee,
For it shall preserve thee
From dying on a publique Scaffold, and withall
Bring thee an absolute Cure, thus.   *Stabs him.*
                    So, tis done:
And now for my escape.   *Enter Surgeons.*
120   1. SUR. You Rogue Mountebanke,
I will try whether your inwards can indure
To be washt in scalding lead.
    ROM. Hold, I turne Christian.
    2. SUR. Nay prethee bee a Jew still;

I would not have a Christian be guiltie
Of such a villanous act as this is.

  Rom. I am *Romelio* the Marchant.

  1. Sur. *Romelio!* you have prooved your selfe
A cunning Marchant indeed.

  Rom. You may reade why   130
I came hither.

  2. Sur. Yes, in a bloudy Roman Letter.

  Rom. I did hate this man, each minute of his breath
Was torture to me.

  1. Sur. Had you forborne this act, he had not liv'd
This two houres.

  Rom. But he had died then,
And my revenge unsatisfied: here's gold;
Never did wealthy man purchase the silence
Of a terrible scolding wife at a dearer rate,   140
Then I will pay for yours: here's your earnest
In a bag of double Duckets.

  2. Sur. Why looke you sir, as I do weigh this busines,
This cannot be counted murder in you by no meanes.
Why tis no more, then should I goe and choke
An Irishman, that were three quarters drownd,
With powring Usquebath in's throat.

  Ro. You will be secret? 1. Su. As your soule.

  Rom. The West Indies shall sooner want gold, then you then.

  2. Su. That protestation has the musick of the Mint in't.   150

  Ro. *[aside]* How unfortunatly was I surpriz'd!—
I have made my selfe a slave perpetually
To these two beggars.   *Exit.*

  1. Su. Excellent; by this act he has made his estate ours.

  2. Su. Ile presently grow a lazy Surgeon, & ride on my foot-
cloth; Ile fetch from him every eight dayes a policy for a hundred
double Duckets; if hee grumble, Ile peach.

  1. Sur. But let's take heed he doe not poyson us.

  2. Sur. Oh, I will never eate nor drinke with him,
Without Unicornes Horne in a hollow tooth.   160

  Cont. Oh! 1. Sur. Did he not groane?

  2. Sur. Is the wind in that doore still?

  1. Sur. Ha! come hither, note a strange accident:
His Steele has lighted in the former wound,

And made free passage for the congealed blood;
Observe in what abundance it delivers
The putrifaction.
    2. SUR. Me thinks he fetches
His breath very lively.
170   1. SUR. The hand of heaven is in't,
That his entent to kill him should become
The very direct way to save his life.
    2. SUR. Why this is like one I have heard of in England,
Was cured a'th Gowt, by being rackt i'th Tower.
Well, if we can recover him, here's reward
On both sides: howsoever, we must be secret.
    1. SUR. We are tyde [to]'t,
When we cure Gentlemen of foule diseases,
They give us so much for the cure, and twice as much,
180 That we doe not blab on't. Come lets to worke roundly,
Heat the Lotion, and bring the Searing.   *Exeunt.*

[ACTUS TERTIUS, SCENA TERTIA.]

[*Leonora's House.*]

*A Table set forth with two Tapers, a Deaths head, a
Booke. Jolenta in mourning, Romelio sits by her.*

ROM. Why do you grieve thus? take a Looking-glasse,
And see if this sorrow become you; that pale face
Will make men thinke you usde some Art before,
Some odious painting: *Contarino's* dead.
    JOL. Oh that he should dye so soone!
    ROM. Why, I pray tell me,
Is not the shortest fever the best? and are not bad Playes
The worse for their length?
    JOLEN. Adde not to'th ill y'ave done
10 An odious slander; he stuck i'th eyes a'th Court,
As the most choyce jewell there.
    ROM. Oh be not angry;
Indeed the Court to well composed nature
Addes much to perfection: for it is or should be,
As a bright Christall Mirrour to the world,
To dresse it selfe; but I must tell you sister,

If th'excellency of the place could have wroght salvation,
The Devill had nere falne from heaven; he was proud—

          [*Jolenta rises angrily to go away.*]

Leave us, leave us?
Come, take your seat agen, I have a plot,   20
If you will listen to it seriously,
That goes beyond example—it shall breed
Out of the death of these two Noblemen,
The advancement of our House.

    J o l. Oh take heed,
A grave is a rotten foundation.

    R o m. Nay, nay, heare me.
Tis somewhat indirectly, I confesse:
But there is much advauncement in the world,
That comes in indirectly. I pray mind me: 30
You are already made by absolute Will,
Contarino's heyre: now, if it can be prooved,
That you have issue by Lord *Ercole*,
I will make you inherite his Land too.

    J o l. How's this?
Issue by him, he dead, and I a Virgin!

    R o m. I kn[e]w you would wonder how it could be done,
But I have layd the case so radically,
Not all the Lawyers in Christendome
Shall finde any the least flaw in't: I have a Mistris   40
Of the Order of Saint *Clare*, a beautious Nun,
Who being cloystred ere she knew the heat
Her blood would arrive to, had onely time enough
To repent, and idlenesse sufficient
To fall in love with mee; and to be short,
I have so much disordered the holy Order,
I have got this Nun with child.

    J o l. Excellent worke made for a dumbe Mid-wife!

    R o m. I am glad you grow thus pleasant.
Now will I have you presently give out,   50
That you are full two moneths quickned with child
By *Ercole*, which rumour can beget
No scandall to you, since we will affirme,
The Precontract was so exactly done,
By the same words usde in the forme of mariage,

                        18-2

That with a little Dispensation,
A money matter, it shall be registred
Absolute Matrimony.
    J o l. So—then I conceave you,
60 My conceaved child must prove your Bastard.
    R o m. Right:
For at such time my Mistris fals in labour
You must faine the like.
    J o l. Tis a pretty feat this,
But I am not capable of it.
    R o m. Not capable?
    J o l. No, for the thing you would have me counterfet,
Is most essentially put in practise: nay, tis done,
I am with child already. R o m. Ha, by whom?
70   J o l. By *Contarino*—doe not knit the brow,
The Precontract shall justifie it, it shall:
Nay, I will get some singular fine Churchman,
Or tho he be a plurall one, shall affirme,
He coupled us together.
    R o m. Oh misfortune!
Your child must then be reputed *Ercoles*.
    J o l. Your hopes are dasht then, since your Votaries issue
Must not inherit the land.
    R o m. No matter for that,
80 So I preserve her fame. I am strangely puzled:
Why, suppose that she be brought abed before you,
And we conceale her issue till the time
Of your delivery, and then give out,
That you have two at a birth; ha, wert not excellent?
    J o l. And what resemblance think you, would they have
To one another? Twinnes are still alike:
But this is not your ayme, you would have your child
Inherite *Ercoles* Land—Oh my sad soule,
Have you not made me yet wretched ynough,
90 But after all this frostie age in youth,
Which you have witcht upon me, you will seeke
To poyson my Fame?
    R o m. That's done already.
    J o l. No sir, I did but faine it,
To a fatall purpose, as I thought.

Rom. What purpose?

Jol. If you had lov'd or tendred my deare honour,
You would have lockt your ponyard in my heart,
When I nam'd I was with child; but I must live
To linger out, till the consumption   100
Of my owne sorrow kill me.

Rom. [aside] This will not doe;
The Devill has on the sudden furnisht mee
With a rare charme, yet a most unnaturall falshood:
No matter so 'twill take.
Stay sister, I would utter to you a businesse,
But I am very loath: a thing indeed,
Nature would have compassionately conceal'd,
Till my mothers eyes be closed.

Jol. Pray what's that sir?   110

Rom. You did observe,
With what a deare regard our mother tendred
The Lord *Contarino*, yet how passionately
Shee sought to crosse the match: why this was meerely
To blind the eye o'th world; for she did know
That you would marry him, and he was capable.
My mother doated upon him, and it was plotted
Cunningly betweene them, after you were married,
Living all three together in one house—
A thing I cannot whisper without horrour: 120
Why, the malice scarse of Devils would suggest,
Incontinence 'tweene them two.

Jol. I remember since his hurt,
Shee has bene very passionately enquiring,
After his health.

Rom. Upon my soule, this Jewell,
With a piece of the holy Crosse in't, this relicke,
Vallewed at many thousand crownes, she would have sent him,
Lying upon his death-bed.

Jol. Professing as you say,   130
Love to my mother: wherefore did he make
Me his heyre?

Rom. His Will was made afore he went to fight,
When he was first a Suitor to you.

Jol. To fight: oh well remembred!—

If he lov'd my mother, wherefore did he loose
His life in my quarrell?

    ROM. For the affront sake, a word you understand not—
Because *Ercole* was pretended Rivall to him,
140 To cleare your suspition; I was gulld in't too:
Should he not have fought upon't,
He had undergone the censure of a Coward.

    JOL. How came you by this wretched knowledge?

    ROM. His Surgeon over-heard it,
As he did sigh it out to his Confessor,
Some halfe houre fore hee died.

    JOL. I would have the Surgeon hang'd
For abusing Confession, and for making me
So wretched by'th report. Can this be truth?

150   ROM. No, but direct falshood,
As ever was banisht the Court: did you ever heare
Of a mother that has kept her daughters husband
For her owne tooth? He fancied you in one kind,
For his lust,
And he loved our mother in another kind,
For her money—
The Gallants fashion right. But come, nere thinke on't,
Throw the fowle to the Devill that hatcht it, and let this
Bury all ill that's in't—shee is our mother.

160   JOL. I never did find any thing ith world,
Turne my blood so much as this: here's such a conflict,
Betweene apparant presumption, and unbeleefe,
That I shall dye in't.
Oh, if there be another world i'th Moone,
As some fantasticks dreame, I could wish all men,
The whole race of them, for their inconstancy,
Sent thither to people that. Why, I protest,
I now affect the Lord *Ercoles* memory,
Better then the other's.

170   ROM. But were *Contarino* living?

    JOL. I doe call any thing to witnesse,
That the divine Law prescribed us to strengthen
An oath, were he living and in health, I would never
Mary with him. Nay, since I have found the world
So false to me, Ile be as false to it;

I will mother this child for you. ROM. Ha?

JOL. Most certainly it will beguile part of my sorrow.

ROM. Oh most assuredly—make you smile to thinke,
How many times ith world Lordships descend
To divers men, that might, and truth were knowne,   180
Be heyre, for any thing belongs to'th flesh,
As well to the Turkes richest Eunuch.

JOL. But doe you not thinke
I shall have a horrible strong breath now?

ROM. Why?

JOL. Oh, with keeping your counsel, tis so terrible foule

ROM. Come, come, come,
You must leave these bitter flashes.

JOL. Must I dissemble dishonestie? you have divers
Counterfeit honestie: but I hope here's none   190
Will take exceptions; I now must practise
The art of a great-bellyed woman, and goe faine
Their qualmes and swoundings.

ROM. Eat unripe fruit, and Oatmeale,
To take away your colour.

JOL. Dine in my bed
Some two houres after noone.

ROM. And when you are up,
Make to your petticoat a quilted preface,
To advance your belly.   200

JOL. I have a strange conceit now.
I have knowen some women when they were with child,
Have long'd to beat their Husbands: what if I,
To keepe decorum, exercise my longing
Upon my Taylor that way, and noddle him soundly?—
Heele make the larger Bill for't.

ROM. Ile get one shall be as tractable [to]'t as Stockfish.

JOL. Oh my phantasticall sorrow!—Cannot I now
Be miserable enough, unlesse I weare
A pyde fooles coat? Nay worse, for when our passions   210
Such giddy and uncertaine changes breed,
We are never well, till we are mad indeed.   *Exit.*

ROM. So—nothing in the world could have done this,
But to beget in her a strong distaste
Of the Lord *Contarino*: oh Jelousie,

How violent, especially in women,
How often has it raisd the devil up
In forme of a law-case! My especiall care
Must be, to nourish craftily this fiend,
220 Tweene the mother and the daughter, that the deceit
Be not perceived. My next taske, that my sister,
After this supposed child-birth, be perswaded
To enter into Religion: tis concluded,
Shee must never marry; so I am left guardian
To her estate: and lastly, that my two Surgeons
Be waged to the East Indies: let them prate,
When they are beyond the Lyne; the Callenture,
Or the Scurvy, or the Indian Pox, I hope,
Will take order for their comming backe.   *Enter Leon.*
230 Oh heere's my mother: I ha strange newes for you—
My sister is with child.
          L e o. I doe looke now
For some great misfortunes to follow: for indeed mischiefes
Are like the Visits of Franciscan Fryers,
They never come to pray upon us single.
In what estate left you *Contarino*?
          R o m. Strange, that you
Can skip from the former sorrow to such a question!
Ile tell you—in the absence of his Surgeon,
240 My charitie did that for him in a trice,
They would have done at leasure, and been paid for't.
I have killed him.
          L e o n. I am twentie yeares elder
Since you last opened your lips. R o m. Ha?
          L e o n. You have given him the wound you speake of
Quite thorow your mothers heart.
          R o m. I will heale it presently mother: for this sorrow
Belongs to your errour: you would have him live,
Because you thinke hee's father of the child;
250 But *Jolenta* vowes by all the rights of Truth,
Tis *Ercole's*: it makes me smile to thinke,
How cunningly my sister could be drawne
To the Contract, and yet how familiarly
To his bed. Doves never couple without
A kind of murmur. L e o. Oh, I am very sicke.

Rom. Your old disease—when you are griev'd, you are
　　troubled
With the Mother.
　　Leo. [*aside*] I am rapt with the Mother indeed,
That I ever bore such a sonne.
　　Rom. Pray tend my sister,　　　　　　　　　　　260
I am infinitely full of businesse.
　　Leo. Stay, you will mourne
For *Contarino*? Ro. Oh by all meanes, tis fit—
My sister is his heire.　　　　　　　　　　　　　*Exit.*
　　Leo. I will make you chiefe mourner, beleeve it.
Never was woe like mine: oh that my care,
And absolute study to preserve his life,
Should be his absolute ruine! Is he gone then?
There is no plague i'th world can be compared
To impossible desire, for they are plagued　　　　270
In the desire it selfe: never, oh never
Shall I behold him living, in whose life
I lived farre sweetlier then in mine owne.
A precise curiositie has undone me; why did I not
Make my love knowne directly? 't had not been
Beyond example, for a Matron to affect
I'th honourable way of Marriage,
So youthfull a person: oh I shall runne mad,
For as we love our youngest children best:
So the last fruit of our affection,　　　　　　　　280
Where ever we bestow it, is most strong,
Most violent, most unresistable,
Since tis indeed our latest Harvest-home,
Last merryment fore Winter; and we widdowes,
As men report of our best Picture-makers,
We love the piece we are in hand with better,
Then all the excellent worke we have done before—
And my sonne has depriv'd me of all this. Ha my sonne!—
Ile be a fury to him—like an Amazon Lady,
Ide cut off this right pap, that gave him sucke,　　290
To shoot him dead. Ile no more tender him,
Then had a Wolfe stolne to my teat i'th night,
And robb'd me of my milke: nay, such a creature
I should love better farre.——Ha, ha, what say you?

I doe talke to somewhat, me thinks; it may be
My evill Genius. Doe not the Bells ring?
I have a strange noyse in my head: oh, fly in pieces!—
Come age, and wither me into the malice
Of those that have been happy; let me have
300 One propertie more then the Devill of Hell,
Let me envy the pleasure of youth heartily,
Let me in this life feare no kinde of ill,
That have no good to hope for: let me dye
In the distraction of that worthy Princesse,
Who loathed food, and sleepe, and ceremony,
For thought of loosing that brave Gentleman,
She would faine have saved, had not a false convayance
Exprest him stubborne-hearted. Let me sinke,
Where neither man, nor memory may ever find me.
                    Falls downe. [*Enter Capuchin & Ercole.*]
310   CAP. This is a private way which I command,
As her Confessor. I would not have you seene yet,
Till I prepare her. [*Ercole withdraws.*] Peace to you Lady.
    LEO. Ha?
    CAP. You are wel imployd, I hope; the best pillow i'th world
For this your contemplation, is the earth,
And the best object heaven.
    LEO. I am whispering to a dead friend.
    CAP. And I am come
To bring you tidings of a friend was dead,
320 Restored to life againe. LEO. Say sir?
    CAP. One whom I dare presume, next to your children,
You tendred above life.
    LEO. Heaven will not suffer me
Utterly to be lost.
    CAP. For hee should have been
Your sonne in Law—miraculously saved,
When Surgery gave him ore. LEON. Oh, may you live
To winne many soules to heaven, worthy sir,
That your crowne may be the greater. Why my sonne
330 Made me beleeve he stole into his chamber,
And ended that which *Ercole* began
By a deadly stabb in's heart.
    ERCO. [*aside*] Alas, shee mistakes,

Tis *Contarino* she wishes living; but I must fasten
On her last words, for my owne safetie.
    L E O. Where,
Oh where shall I meet this comfort?
    E R C O. [*revealing himself*] Here in the vowed comfort of your
        daughter.
    L E O. Oh I am dead agen—instead of the man, you present me
The grave swallowed him.   340
    E R C O. Collect your selfe, good Lady,
Would you behold brave *Contarino* living?
There cannot be a nobler Chronicle
Of his good then my selfe: if you would view him dead,
I will present him to you bleeding fresh,
In my penitency.   L E O. Sir, you doe onely live,
To redeeme another ill you have committed,
That my poore innocent daughter perish not,
By your vild sinne, whom you have got with child.
    E R C O. Here begin all my compassion: oh poore soule!   350
Shee is with child by *Contarino*, and he dead,
By whom should she preserve her fame to'th world,
But by my selfe that loved her bove the world?
There never was a way more honourable,
To exercise my vertue, then to father it,
And preserve her credit, and to marry her.
Ile suppose her *Contarino's* widdow, bequeath'd to me
Upon his Death: for sure shee was his wife,
But that the Ceremony a'th Church was wanting.
Report this to her, Madam, and withall,   360
That never father did conceave more joy
For the birth of an heyre, then I to understand,
Shee had such confidence in me. I will not now
Presse a Visit upon her, till you have prepar'd her:
For I doe reade in your distraction,
Should I be brought a'th sudden to her presence,
Either the hastie fright, or else the shame
May blast the fruit within her. I will leave you,
To commend as loyall faith and service to her,
As ere heart harbour'd—by my hope of blisse,   370
I never liv'd to doe good act but this.
    C A P. [*aside to Ercole*] Withall, and you be wise,

Remember what the mother has reveal'd
Of *Romelio's* treachery.   *Exeunt Ercole, Capuchin.*
   L E O N. A most noble fellow! In his loyaltie
I read what worthy comforts I have lost
In my deare *Contarino*, and all addes
To my dispayre.——Within there!   *Enter Winifrid.*
Fetch the picture
380 Hangs in my inner closet. I remember,
I let a word slip of *Romelio's* practise   *Exit Win.*
At the Surgeons': no matter, I can salve it,
I have deeper vengeance that's preparing for him—
To let him live and kill him, that's revenge
I meditate upon.   *Enter Win. and the Picture.*
   L E O. So, hang it up.
I was enjoyned by the partie ought that picture,
Fortie yeares since, ever when I was vext,
To looke upon that: what was his meaning in't,
390 I know not, but me thinkes upon the sudden,
It has furnisht me with mischiefe—such a plot,
As never mother dreamt of. Here begines
My part i'th play: my sonnes estate is sunke,
By losse at sea, and he has nothing left,
But the Land his father left him. Tis concluded,
The Law shall undoe him. Come hither,
I have a weightie secret to impart,
But I would have thee first confirme to mee,
How I may trust, that thou canst keepe my counsell,
400 Beyond death.
   W I N. Why Mistris, tis your onely way,
To enjoyne me first that I reveale to you
The worst act I ere did in all my life:
So one secret shall bind ˄ another.
   L E O. Thou instru[ct]'st me
Most ingenuously—for indeed it is not fit,
Where any act is plotted, that is nought,
Any of counsell to it should be good,
And in a thousand ils have hapt i'th world,
410 The intelligence of one anothers shame
Have wrought farre more effectually then the tye
Of Conscience, or Religion.

WIN. But thinke not, Mistris,
That any sinne which ever I committed,
Did concerne you—for prooving false in one thing,
You were a foole, if ever you would trust me
In the least matter of weight.
LEO. Thou hast lived with me
These fortie yeares; we have growne old together,
As many Ladies and their women doe,   420
With talking nothing, and with doing lesse:
We have spent our life in that which least concernes life,
Only in putting on our clothes; and now I thinke on't,
I have been a very courtly Mistris to thee,
I have given thee good words, but no deeds—now's the time,
To requite all; my sonne has sixe Lordships left him.
WIN. Tis truth.
LEO. But he cannot live foure dayes to enjoy them.
WIN. Have you poysoned him?
LEO. No, the poyson is yet but brewing.   430
WIN. You must minister it to him with all privacie.
LEO. Privacie? It shall be given him
In open Court—Ile make him swallow it
Before the Judges face: if he be Master
Of poore ten arpines of land fortie houres longer,
Let the world repute me an honest woman.
WIN. So 'twill I hope.
LEO. Oh thou canst not conceive
My unimitable plot; let's to my ghostly Father,
W[h]ere first I will have thee make a promise   440
To keepe my counsell, and then I will employ thee
In such a subtill combination,
Which will require to make the practise fit,
Foure Devils, five Advocats, to one womans wit.   *Exeunt.*

Explicit Act[us] Terti[us].

ACTUS QUARTUS, SCENA PRIMA.

[The antechamber of a Court of Justice.]

Enter Leonora, Sanitonella at one doore, Winifrid,
Register: at the other, Ariosto.

SAN. *[to Register]* Take her into your Office sir, shee has
 that in her Belly,
Will drie up your inke I can tell you.
         [Exeunt Winifrid, Register.]
[to Leonora] This is the man that is your learned Councell,
A fellow that will trowle it off with tongue:
He never goes without Restorative powder
Of the lungs of Fox in's pocket, and Malligo Reasins
To make him long-winded. Sir, this Gentlewoman
Intreats your Counsell in an honest cause,
Which please you sir, this Briefe, my owne poore labor
10 Will give you light of.   *[Gives brief.]*
 ARIO. Doe you call this a Briefe?
Here's as I weigh them, some fourescore sheets of paper.
What would they weigh if there were cheese wrapt in them,
Or Figdates!   *[Reads.]*
 SAN. Joy come to you, you are merry;
We call this but a Briefe in our Office.
The scope of the businesse lyes i'th Margent.
 ARIO. Me thinks you prate too much.
I never could endure an honest cause
20 With a long Prologue [to]'t.
 LEON. You trouble him.
 AR. Whats here? oh strange; I have lived this 60 yeres,
Yet in all my practise never did shake hands
With a cause so odious. Sirrah, are you her knave?
 SAN. No sir, I am a Clarke.
 ARI. Why you whorson fogging Rascall,
Are there not whores enow for Presentations,
Of Overseers, wrong the will o'th Dead,
Oppressions of Widdowes, or young Orphans,
30 Wicked Divorces, or your vicious cause
Of *Plus quam satis*, to content a woman,
But you must find new stratagems, new pursnets?—

Oh women, as the Ballet lives to tell you,
What will you shortly come to?
   SAN. Your Fee is ready sir.
   ARI. The Devill take such Fees,
And all such Suits i'th tayle of them; see the slave
Has writ false Latine: sirrah Ignoramus,
Were you ever at the Universitie?
   SAN. Never sir: 40
But tis well knowne to divers I have Commenc't
In a Pewe of our Office.
   ARI. Where?—in a Pew of your Office!
   SAN. I have been dry-foundred in't this foure yeares,
Seldome found Non-resident from my deske.
   ARI. Non-resident Subsumner!
Ile teare your Libell for abusing that word,
By vertue of the Clergie.   [*Tears the brief.*]
   SAN. What doe you meane sir?
It cost me foure nights labour.   50
   ARIO. Hadst thou been drunke
So long, th'adst done our Court better Service.
   LEO. Sir,
You doe forget your gravitie, me thinks.
   ARIO. Cry ye mercy, doe I so?
And as I take it, you doe very little remember
Either womanhood, or Christianitie:
Why doe ye meddle
With that seducing knave, that's good for nought,
Unlesse 't be to fill the Office full of Fleas,   60
Or a Winter itch—weares that spatious Inkehorne
All a Vacation onely to cure Tetters,
And his Penknife to weed Cornes from the splay toes
Of the right worshipfull of the Office?
   LEO. You make bold with me sir.
   ARIO. Woman, y'are mad, Ile swear't, & have more need
Of a Physician then a Lawyer.
The melancholly humour flowes in your face,
Your painting cannot hide it: such vild suits
Disgrace our Courts, and these make honest Lawyers   70
Stop their own eares, whilst they plead, & thats the reason
Your yonger men that have good conscience,

Weare such large Night-caps; go old woman, go pray,
For Lunacy, or else the Devill himselfe
Has tane possession of thee; may like cause
In any Christian Court never find name:
Bad Suits, and not the Law, bred the Lawes shame.   *Exit.*
   L E O N. Sure the old man's franticke.
   S A N. Plague on's gowtie fingers,
80 Were all of his mind, to entertaine no suits,
But such they thought were honest, sure our Lawyers
Would not purchase halfe so fast:
But here's the man,   *Enter Contilupo, a spruce Lawyer.*
Learned Seignior *Contilupo*—[*aside*] here's a fellow
Of another piece, beleeve't—I must make shift
With the foule Copie. C O N. Businesse to me?
   S A N. To you sir, from this Lady. C O N. She is welcom.
   S A N. Tis a foule Copy sir, youle hardly read it—
There's twenty double duckets, can you reade sir?
90   C O N. Exceeding well, very, very exceeding well.
   S A N. [*aside*] This man will be saved, he can read; Lord, Lord,
     to see,
What money can doe!—be the hand never so foule,
Somewhat will be pickt out on't.
   C O N. Is not this
Vivere honeste?
   S A N. No, that's strucke out sir;
And where ever you find *vivere honeste* in these papers,
Give it a dash sir. C O N. I shall be mindfull of it:
In troth you write a pretty Secretary—
100 Your Secretary hand ever takes best
In mine opinion.
   S A N. Sir, I have been in France,
And there beleeve't your Court hand generally,
Takes beyond thought.
   C O N. Even as a man is traded in't.
   S A. [*aside*] That I could not think of this vertuous Gentleman
Before I went to'th tother Hogg-rubber!
Why this was wont to give young Clerkes halfe fees,
To helpe him to Clyents. Your opinion in the Case sir?
110   C O N. I am strucke with wonder—almost extaside,
With this most goodly Suite.

LEON. It is the fruit
Of a most heartie penitence.
    CON. Tis a Case
Shall leave a Pre[ce]dent to all the world,
In our succeeding Annals, and deserves
Rather a spatious publike Theater,
Then a pent Court for Aud[i]ence; it shall teach
All Ladies the right path to rectifie
Their issue.   120
    SAN. Loe you, here's a man of comfort.
    CON. And you shall goe unto a peacefull grave,
Discharg'd of such a guilt, as would have layne
Howling for ever at your wounded heart,
And rose with you to Judgement.
    SAN. Oh give me such a Lawyer, as wil think
Of the day of Judgment!
    LEO. You must urge the businesse against him
As spightfully as may be.
    CON. Doubt not. What, is he summon'd?   130
    SAN. Yes & the Court will sit within this halfe houre.
Peruse your Notes, you have very short warning.
    CON. Never feare you that:
Follow me worthy Lady, and make account
This Suite is ended already.   *Exeunt.*

[ACTUS QUARTUS, SCENA SECUNDA.]

[A Court of Justice.]

*Enter Officers preparing seats for the Judges,
to them Ercole muffled.*

    1. OF. You would have a private seat sir?
    ERC. Yes sir.
    2. OF. Here's a Closset belongs to'th Court,
Where you may heare all unseene.
    ER. I thank you; there's money.
    2. OF. I give you your thanks agen sir. *Enter Contarino, the*
    CONT. Ist possible *Romelio*'s perswaded, *Surgeons, disguised,*
You are gone to the East Indies?   *[Contarino, as a Dane].*
    1. SUR. Most confidently.

10   Con. But doe you meane to goe?

2. Su. How? goe to the East Indies? And so many Hollanders
gone to fetch sauce for their pickeld Herrings: some have bene
pepperd there too lately—but I pray, being thus well recoverd
of your wounds, why doe you not reveale your selfe?

Con. That my fayre *Jolenta* should be rumor'd
To be with child by noble *Ercole*,
Makes me expect to what a violent issue
These passages will come. I heare her brother
Is marying the Infant shee goes with,
20 Fore it be borne—as, if it be a Daughter,
To the Duke of *Austrias* Nephew; if a Sonne,
Into the Noble ancient Family
Of the *Palavafini*: Hee's a subtill Devill.
And I doe wonder what strange Suite in Law,
Has hapt betweene him and's mother.

1. Sur. Tis whisperd 'mong the Lawyers,
'Twill undoe him for ever.   *Enter Sanit. Win.*

San. Doe you heare, Officers?
You must take speciall care, that you let in
30 No *Brachigraphy* men, to take notes.

1. Of. No sir? San. By no meanes—
We cannot have a Cause of any fame,
But you must have scurvy pamphlets, and lewd Ballets
Engendred of it presently.

San. Have you broke fast yet? Win. Not I sir.

San. 'Twas very ill done of you:
For this cause will be long a-pleading; but [no] matter,
I have a modicum in my Buckram bagg,
To stop your stomacke.

40 Win. What ist? Greene ginger?

San. Greene ginger, nor Pellitory of Spaine neither,
Yet 'twill stop a hollow tooth better then either of them.

Win. Pray what ist?

San. Looke you,
It is a very lovely Pudding-pye,
Which we Clerkes find great reliefe in.

Win. I shall have no stomacke.

San. No matter and you have not, I may pleasure
Some of our Learned Councell with't; I have done it

Many a time and often, when a Cause 50
Has prooved like an after-game at Irish.

Enter Crispiano like a Judge, with another Judge; Contilupo,
and another Lawyer at one Barre; Romelio, Ariosto, at
another; Leonora with a blacke vaile over
her, and Julio.

CRISP. Tis a strange Suite—is *Leonora* come.
CONTI. She's here my Lord; make way there for the Lady.
CRISP. Take off her Vaile: it seemes she is ashamed
To looke her cause i'th face.
CONTIL. Shee's sicke, my Lord.
ARI. Shee's mad my Lord, & would be kept more dark.
[*to Romelio*] By your favour sir, I have now occasion
To be at your elbow, and within this halfe houre
Shall intreat you to bee angry, very angry. 60
CRISP. Is *Romelio* come?
ROM. I am here my Lord, and call'd, I doe protest,
To answer what I know not, for as yet
I am wholly ignorant, of what the Court
Will charge me with.
CRISP. I assure you, the proceeding
Is most unequall then, for I perceive,
The Councell of the adverse partie furnisht
With full Instruction.
ROM. Pray my Lord, 70
Who is my accuser?
CRISP. Tis your mother.
ROM. [*aside*] Shee has discovered *Contarino's* murder:
If shee proove so unnaturall, to call
My life in question, I am arm'd to suffer
This to end all my losses.
CRISP. Sir, we will doe you
This favour—you shall heare the Accusation,
Which being knowne, we will adjourne the Court,
Till a fortnight hence—you may provide your Counsell. 80
ARIO. I advise you, take their proffer,
Or else the Lunacy runnes in a blood,
You are more mad then shee. ROM. What are you sir?
ARIO. An angry fellow that would doe thee good,

19-2

For goodnesse sake it selfe, I doe protest,
Neither for love nor money.
    ROM. Prethee stand further, I shal gall your gowt else.
    AR. Come, come, I know you for an East Indy Marchant,
You have a spice of pride in you still.
90   ROM. My Lord,
I am so strengthned in my innocence,
For any the least shaddow of a crime,
Committed gainst my mother, or the world,
That shee can charge me with, here doe I make it
My humble suite, onely this houre and place,
May give it as full hearing, and as free,
And unrestrain'd a Sentence.
    CRI. Be not too confident—you have cause to feare.
    ROM. Let feare dwell with Earth-quakes,
100 Shipwracks at Sea, or Prodegies in heaven,
I cannot set my selfe so many fathome
Beneath the haight of my true heart, as feare.
    ARI. Very fine words I assure you, if they were
To any purpose.
    CRI. Well, have your intreatie:
And if your owne credulitie undoe you,
Blame not the Court hereafter: fall to your Plea.
    CON. May it please your Lordsh[ip] & the reverend Court,
To give me leave to open to you a Case
110 So rare, so altogether voyd of Pre[ce]dent,
That I doe challenge all the spacious Volumes,
Of the whole Civill Law to shew the like.
We are of Councell for this Gentlewoman,
We have receiv'd our Fee, yet the whole course
Of what we are to speake, is quite against her,
Yet weele deserve our fee too. There stands one,
Romelio the Marchant; I will name him to you,
Without either title or addition:
For those false beames of his supposed honour,
120 As voyd of true heat, as are all painted fires,
Or Glow-wormes in the darke, suite him all basely,
As if he had bought his Gentry from the Herauld,
With money got by extortion: I will first
Produce this *Æsops* Crow, as he stands forfeit

For the long use of his gay borrowed plumes,
And then let him hop naked: I come to'th poynt—
T'as been a Dreame in Naples, very neere
This eight and thirtie yeares, that this *Romelio*
Was nobly descended—he has rankt himselfe
With the Nobilitie, shamefully usurpt   130
Their place, and in a kind of sawcy pride,
Which like to Mushromes, ever grow most ranke,
When they do spring from dung-hills, sought to oresway
The [*Fieschi*], the *Grimaldi, Dori[a]*,
And all the ancient pillars of our State;
View now what he is come to: this poore thing
Without a name, this Cuckow hatcht ith nest
Of a Hedge-sparrow.
    Rom. Speakes he all this to me?
    Ari. Onely to you sir.   140
    Rom. I doe not aske thee, prethee hold thy prating.
    Ari. Why very good!—you will be presently
As angry as I could wish.
    Contil. What title shall I set to this base coyne?—
He has no name, and for's aspect he seemes
A Gyant in a May-game, that within
Is nothing but a Porter: Ile undertake,
He had as good have traveld all his life
With Gypsies: I will sell him to any man
For an hundred Chickeens, and he that buyes him of me,   150
Shall loose byth hand too.
    Ari. Loe, what you are come [to]:
You that did scorne to trade in any thing,
But Gold or Spices, or your Cochineele—
He rates you now at poore John.
    Rom. Out upon thee,
I would thou wert of his side—
    Ari. Would you so?
    Rom. The devill and thee together on each hand,
To prompt the Lawyers memory when he founders.   160
    Cris. Signior *Contilupo*, the Court holds it fit,
You leave this stale declaiming 'gainst the person,
And come to the matter.
    Cont. Now I shall my Lord.

CRIS. It showes a poore malicious eloquence,
And it is strange, men of your gravitie
Will not forgoe it: verely, I presume,
If you but heard your selfe speaking with my eares,
Your phrase would be more modest.
170   CONTIL. Good my Lord, be assured,
I will leave all circumstance, and come toth purpose:
This *Romelio* is a Bastard.
      ROM. How, a Bastard?
Oh mother, now the day begins grow hote
On your side.
      CONTIL. Why shee is your accuser.
      ROM. I had forgot that; was my father maried
To any other woman, at the time
Of my begetting?
180   CONTIL. That's not the businesse.
      ROM. I turne me then to you that were my mother,
But by what name I am to call you now,
You must instruct me: were you ever marryed
To my father?
      LEON. To my shame I speake it, never
      CRISP. Not to *Fra[nc]isco Romelio?*
      LEO. May it please your Lordships,
To him I was, but he was not his father.
      CONT. Good my Lord, give us leave in a few words,
190 To expound the Riddle, and to make it plaine,
Without the least of scruple: for I take it,
There cannot be more lawfull proofe i'th world,
Then the oath of the mother.
      CRIS. Well then, to your proofes,
And be not tedious.
      CONTIL. Ile conclude in a word:
Some nine and thirtie yeares since, which was the time,
This woman was maryed, *Francisco Romelio,*
This Gentlemans putative father, and her husband,
200 Being not married to her past a fortnight,
Would needs goe travell; did so, and continued
In *France* and the *Low-Countries* eleven monthes:
Take speciall note o'th time; I beseech your Lordship,
For it makes much to'th businesse: in his absence

He left behind to sojourne at his house
A Spanish Gentleman, a fine spruce youth
By the Ladies confession, and you may be sure
He was no Eunuch neither; he was one
Romelio loved very dearely, as oft haps,
No man alive more welcome to the husband   210
Then he that makes him Cuckold.
This Gentleman I say,
Breaking all Lawes of Hospitalitie,
Got his friends wife with child, a full two moneths
Fore the husband returned.
     SAN. *[aside]* Good sir, forget not the Lambskin.
     CONTIL. *[aside]* I warrant thee.
     SA. *[aside]* I wil pinch by the buttock,
To put you in mind of't.
     CONTIL. *[aside]* Prethee hold thy prating.   220
What's to be practis'd now my Lord? Marry this—
Romelio being a yong novice, not acquainted
With this precedence, very innocently
Returning home from travell, finds his wife
Growne an excellent good Huswife, for she had set
Her women to spin Flax, and to that use,
Had in a study which was built of stone,
Stor'd up at least an hundreth waight of flaxe:
Marry such a threed as was to be spun from the flax,
I thinke the like was never heard of.   230
     CRISP. What was that?
     CONTIL. You may be certaine, shee would lose no time,
In braging that her Husband had got up
Her belly: to be short, at seven moneths end,
Which was the time of her delivery,
And when shee felt her selfe to fall in travell,
Shee makes her Wayting woman, as by mischance,
Set fire to the flax, the frright whereof,
As they pretend, causes this Gentlewoman
To fall in paine, and be delivered   240
Eight weekes afore her reckoning.
     SAN. *[aside]* Now sir, remember the Lambeskin.
     CON. The Midwife strait howles out, there was no hope
Of th'infants life, swaddles it in a flead Lambeskin,

As a Bird hatcht too early, makes it up
With three quarters of a face, that made it looke
Like a Changeling, cries out to *Romelio*,
To have it Christned, least it should depart
Without that it came for: and thus are many serv'd,
250 That take care to get Gossips for those children,
To which they might be Godfathers themselves,
And yet be no arch-Puritans neither.
　　　CRISP. No more!
　　　AR. Pray my Lord give him way, you spoile his oratory else:
Thus would they jest were they fee'd to open
Their sisters cases. CRISP. You have urged enough;
You first affirme, her husband was away from her
Eleven moneths? CONTIL. Yes my Lord.
　　　CRISP. And at seven moneths end,
260 After his returne shee was delivered
Of this *Romelio*, and had gone her full time?
　　　CONTIL. True my Lord.
　　　CRISP. So by this account this Gentleman was begot
In his supposed fathers absence.
　　　CONTIL. You have it fully.
　　　CRISP. A most strange Suite this, tis beyond example,
Either time past, or present, for a woman,
To publish her owne dishonour voluntarily,
Without being called in question, some fortie yeares
270 After the sinne committed, and her Councell
To inlarge the offence with as much Oratory,
As ever I did heare them in my life
Defend a guiltie woman; tis most strange:
Or why with such a poysoned violence
Should shee labour her so[n]nes undoing? we observe
Obedience of creatures to the Law of Nature
Is the stay of the whole world; here that Law is broke,
For though our Civill Law makes difference
Tween the base, and the ligitimate; compassionat Nature
280 Makes them equall, nay, shee many times preferres them.
I pray resolve me sir, have not you and your mother
Had some Suite in Law together lately?
　　　ROM. None my Lord.
　　　CRIS. No? no contention about parting your goods?

ROM. Not any. CRIS. No flaw, no unkindnesse?
ROM. None that ever arrived at my knowledge.
CRIS. Bethink your selfe, this cannot chuse but savour
Of a womans malice deeply; and I feare,
Y'are practiz'd upon most devillishly.
How hapt Gentlewoman, you reveal'd this no sooner?   290
     LEO. While my husband lived, my Lord, I durst not.
     CRIS. I should rather aske you, why you reveale it now?
     LEO. Because my Lord, I loath'd that such a sinne
Should lie smotherd with me in my grave; my penitence,
Though to my shame, preferres the revealing of it
Bove worldly reputation. CRIS. Your penitence?
Might not your penitence have beene as hartie,
Though it had never summon'd to the Court
Such a conflux of people?
     LEON. Indeed I might have confest it,   300
Privately toth Church, I grant; but you know repentance
Is nothing without satisfaction.
     CRISP. Satisfaction? why your Husbands dead,
What satisfaction can you make him?
     LEO. The greatest satisfaction in the world, my Lord,
To restore the land toth right heire, & thats
My daughter.
     CRISP. Oh shee's straight begot then?
     ARIO. Very well, may it please this honourable Court,
If he be a bastard, and must forfeit his land for't,   310
She has prooved her selfe a strumpet, and must loose
Her Dower—let them goe a-begging together.
     SAN. Who shall pay us our Fees then?
     CRIS. Most just.
     ARIO. You may see now what an old house
You are like to pull over your head, Dame.
     ROM. Could I conceive this Publication
Grew from a heartie penitence, I could beare
My undoing the more patiently; but my Lord,
There is no reason, as you sayd even now,   320
To satisfie me but this suite of hers
Springs from a devillish malice, and her pretence,
Of a grieved Conscience, and Religion,
Like to the horrid Powder-Treason in England,

Has a most bloody unnaturall revenge
Hid under it: Oh the violencies of women!
Why, they are creatures made up and compounded
Of all monsters, poysoned Myneralls,
And sorcerous Herbes that growes.

330   ARIO. Are you angry yet?

    ROM. Would m[a]n expresse a bad one, let him forsake
All naturall example, and compare
One to another; they have no more mercy,
Then ruinous fires in great tempests.

    ARIO. Take heed you doe not cracke your voice sir.

    ROM. Hard-hearted creatures, good for nothing else,
But to winde dead bodies.

    ARI. Yes, to weave seaming lace
With the bones of their husbands that were long since buried,

340 And curse them when they tangle. ROM. Yet why doe I
Take Bastardy so distastfully, when i'th world,
A many things that are essentiall parts
Of greatnesse, are but by-slips, and are father'd
On the wrong parties?
Preferment in the world a many times,
Basely begotten? nay, I have observ'd
The immaculate Justice of a poore mans cause,
In such a Court as this, has not knowen whom
To call Father, which way to direct it selfe

350 For Compassion: but I forget my temper—
Onely that I may stop that Lawyers throat,
I doe beseech the Court, and the whole world,
They will not thinke the baselyer of me,
For the vice of a mother: for that womans sinne,
To which you all dare sweare when it was done,
I would not give my consent.

    CRIS. Stay, heere's an Accusation,
But here's no proofe; what was the Spanyards name
You accuse of adultery? CON. *Don Crispiano*, my Lord.

    CRISP. What part of Spaine was he borne in? CONTIL. In

360   Castile.

    JUL. [*aside*] This may prove my father.

    SAN. [*aside*] And my Master—my Clyent's spoyl'd then.

    CRIS. I knew that Spanyard well: if you be a Bastard,

Such a man being your father, I dare vouch you
A Gentleman; and in that, Signiour *Contilupo*,
Your Oratory went a little too farre.
When doe wee name *Don John* of *Austria*,
The Emperours sonne, but with reverence?
And I have knowne in divers Families,
The Bastards the greater spirits; but to'th purpose—   370
What time was this Gentleman begot? And be sure
You lay your time right.
    ARIO. Now the mettall comes
To the Touchstone.
    CONTIL. In *Anno* seventie one, my Lord.
    CRISP. Very well, seventie one: the Battell of *Lepanto*
Was fought in't—a most remarkeable time,
'Twill lye for no mans pleasure: and what proofe is there
More then the affirmation of the mother,
Of this corporall dealing?   380
    CONTIL. The deposition
Of a Wayting-woman served her the same time
    CRISP. Where is shee?
    CON. Where is our Solicitor
With the Waitingwoman?
    ARIO. Roome for the bagge and baggage!
    SAN. Here my Lord, *Ore tenus*.
    CRISP. And what can you say Gentlewoman?
    WIN. Please your Lordship, I was the partie that dealt in
the businesse, and brought them together.   390
    CRISP. Well.
    WIN. And conveyed letters betweene them.
    CR. What needed letters, when tis said he lodg'd in her house?
    WIN. A running Ballad now and then to her Violl—for he
was never well, but when he was fidling.
    CRISP. Speake to the purpose, did you ever know them bed
together? WIN. No my Lord, but I have brought him to the
bed side.
    CRISP. That was somewhat neere to the busines; and what—
did you helpe him off with his shooes?   400
    WIN. He wore no shooes, an't please you my Lord.
    CRIS. No? what then, Pumpes? WIN. Neither.
    CRISP. Boots were not fit for his journey.

WIN. He wore Tennis-court woollen slippers, for feare of creaking sir, and making a noyse, to wake the rest o'th house.

CRISP. Well, and what did he there, in his Tennis-court woollen slippers?

WIN. Please your Lordship, question me in Latin, for the cause is very foule; the Examiner o'th Court was faine to get 410 it out of me alone i'th Counting-house, cause he would not spoyle the youth o'th Office.

ARI. Here's a Latin spoone, and a long one, to feed with the Devill.

WIN. Ide be loth to be ignorant that way, for I hope to marry a Proctor, & take my pleasure abroad at the Commencements with him.

ARIO. Come closer to the businesse.

WIN. I will come as close as modesty will give me leave. Truth is, every morning when hee lay with her, I made a 420 Caudle for him, by the appoyntment of my Mistris, which he would still refuse, and call for small drinke.

CRISP. Small drinke? ARIO. For a Julipe.

WIN. And said he was wondrous thirstie.

CRISP. What's this to the purpose?

WIN. Most effectuall, my Lord—I have heard them laugh together extreamely, and the Curtaine-rods fall from the tester of the bed, and he nere came from her, but hee thrust money in my hand; and once in truth, he would have had some dealing with mee; which I tooke he thought 'twould be the onely way 430 ith world to make me keepe counsell the better.

SAN. [aside] That's a stinger, tis a good wench, be not daunted.

CRI. Did you ever find the print of two in the bed?

WIN. What a questions that to be askt!—may it please your Lordsh[ip], tis to be thought he lay nearer to her then so.

CRISP. What age are you of, Gentlewoman?

WIN. About six and fortie, my Lord.

CRISP. *Anno* seventie one,
And *Romelio* is thirty eight: by that reckoning,
You were a Bawd at eight yeare old: now verily,
440 You fell to the Trade betimes.

SAN. [aside] There y'are from the Byas.

WIN. I doe not know my age directly; sure I am elder—I can remember two great frosts, and three great plagues, and the

losse of Callis, and the first comming up of the Breeches with
the great Codpiece—and I pray what age doe you take me of
then?

SAN. [aside] Well come off agen!

ARI. An old hunted Hare, she has all her doubles.

ROM. For your owne gravities,
And the reverence of the Court, I doe beseech you,   450
Rip up the cause no further, but proceed
To Sentence.

CRISP. One question more and I have done:
Might not this *Crispiano*, this Spanyard,
Lye with your Mistris at some other time,
Either afore or after, then ith absence
Of her husband?

LEO. Never. CRIS. Are you certaine of that?

LEO. On my soule, never.

CRIS. That's well—he never lay with her,   460
But in *anno* seventy one, let that be remembred.
Stand you aside a while. Mistris, the truth is,
I knew this *Crispiano*, lived in Naples
At the same time, and loved the Gentleman
As my bosome friend; and as I doe remember,
The Gentleman did leave his Picture with you,
If age or neglect have not in so long time ruin'd it.

LEO. I preserve it still my Lord.

CRIS. I pray let me see't,
Let me see the face I then loved so much to looke on.   470

LEO. Fetch it. WIN. I shall, my Lord.

CRIS. No, no, Gentlewoman,
I have other businesse for you.   [*Exit one for the Picture.*]

1. SUR. [aside] Now were the time to cut *Romelio's* throat,
And accuse him for your murder.

CONTAR. [aside] By no meanes.

2. SUR. [aside] Will you not let us be men of fashion,
And downe with him now hee's going?

CONTAR. [aside] Peace, lets attend the sequell.

CRIS. I commend you Lady,   480
There was a maine matter of Conscience—
How many ills spring from Adultery!
First, the supreame Law that is violated,

Nobilitie oft stain'd with Bastardy,
Inheritance of Land falsly possest,
The husband scorn'd, wife sham'd, and babes unblest.
So, hang it up i'th Court; you have heard,   . *The Picture* [is
What has been urged gainst *Romelio*.   *brought in*].
Now my definitive sentence in this cause,
490 Is, I will give no sentence at all. ARIO. No?
        CRIS. No, I cannot, for I am made a partie.
        SAN. [*aside*] How, a party? here are fine crosse trickes,
What the devill will he doe now?
        CRISP. Signior *Ariosto*, his Majestie of Spaine,
Conferres my Place upon you by this Patent,
Which till this urgent houre I have kept
From your knowledge: may you thrive in't, noble sir,
And doe that which but few in our place doe—
Goe to their grave uncurst. ARIO. This Law businesse
500 Will leave me so small leasure to serve God,
I shall serve the King the worse.
        SAN. [*aside*] Is hee a Judge?
We must then looke for all Conscience, and no Law,
Heele begger all his followers.
        CRIS. [*to Romelio*] Sir, I am of your Counsell, for the cause
        in hand
Was begun at such a time, fore you could speake;
You had need therefore have one speake for you.
        ARIO. Stay, I doe here first make protestation,
I nere tooke fee of this *Romelio*,
510 For being of his Councell—which may free me,
Being now his Judge, for the imputation
Of taking a Bribe. Now sir, speake your mind.
        CRISP. I do first intreat, that the eyes of all here present,
May be fixt upon this.
        LEO. [*aside*] Oh, I am confounded: this is *Crispiano*.
        JUL. [*aside*] This is my father—how the Judges have blea[r]ed
        him!
        WIN. [*aside*] You may see truth will out in spite of the Devill.
        CRIS. Behold, I am the shadow of this shadow,
Age has made me so; take from me fortie yeares,
520 And I was such a Summer fruit as this,
At least the Paynter fayned so: for indeed,

Painting and Epitaphs are both alike,
They flatter us, and say we have been thus:
But I am the partie here, that stands accused,
For Adultery with this woman, in the yeare
Seventie one: now I call you my Lord to witnesse,
Foure yeares before that time I went to'th Indies,
And till this month, did never set my foot since
In Europe; and for any former incontinence,
She has vowed there was never any: what remaines then,   530
But this is a meere practise 'gainst her sonne?—
And I beseech the Court it may be sifted,
And most severely punisht.
     SAN. [*aside*] Uds foot, we are spoyled—
Why my Clyent's prooved an honest woman.
     WIN. [*aside*] What doe you thinke will become of me now?
     SAN. [*aside*] You'l be made daunce *lachrimæ* I feare
At a Carts tayle.
     ARI. You, Mistris, where are you now?
Your Tennis-court slip[per]s, and your tane drinke   540
In a morning for your hote liver; where's the man,
Would have had some dealing with you, that you might
Keepe counsell the better?
     WIN. May it please the Court, I am but a yong thing, and
was drawne arsie varsie into the businesse.
     ARIO. How young? of five and fortie?
     WIN. Five and fortie! And shall please you, I am not five
and twentie: shee made me colour my haire with Bean-flower,
to seeme elder then I was; and then my rotten teeth, with
eating sweet-meats...why, should a Farrier looke in my 550
mouth, he might mistake my age. Oh Mistris, Mistris, you are
an honest woman, and you may be asham'd on't, to abuse the
Court thus.
     LEO. Whatsoere I have attempted,
Gainst my owne fame, or the reputation
Of that Gentleman my sonne, the Lord *Contarino*
Was cause of it. CONTA. [*aside*] Who—I?
     ARIO. He that should have married your daughter?
It was a plot belike then to conferre
The land on her that should have bin his wife?   560
     LEO. More then I have said already, all the world

Shall nere extract from me; I intreat from both
Your equall pardons. JUL. And I from you sir.
    CRISP. Sirrah, stand you aside,
I will talke with you hereafter.
    JUL. I could never away with after reckonings.
    LEO. And now my Lords, I doe most voluntarily
Confine my selfe unto a stricter prison,
And a severer penance, then this Court
570 Can impose—I am entred into Religion.
    CON. *[aside]* I the cause of this practise!...this ungodly
        woman
Has sold her selfe to falshood: I wil now
Reveale my selfe.
    ERCO. *[revealing himself, to Ariosto]* Stay my Lord, here's a
        window
To let in more light to the Court.
    CONT. *[aside]* Mercy upon me! oh, that thou art living
Is mercy indeed!
    I. SUR. *[aside]* Stay, keepe in your shell
A little longer.
580 ERCO. I am *Ercole*.
    ARIO. A guard upon him for the death of *Contarino*.
    ERCO. I obey the arrest o'th Court.
    ROM. Oh sir, you are happily restored to life,
And to us your friends!
    ERCO. Away, thou art the Traytor,
I onely live to challenge; this former suite,
Toucht but thy fame—this accusation
Reaches to thy fame and life: the brave *Contarino*
Is generally supposed slaine by this hand.
590   CON. *[aside]* How knowes he the contrary? ERC. But truth is,
Having received from me some certaine wounds,
Which were not mortall, this vild murderer,
Being by Will deputed Overseer
Of the Noblemans Estate, to his sisters use,
That he might make him sure from surviving,
To revoke that Will, stole to him in's bed, and kild him.
    ROM. Strange, unheard of!—more practise yet!
    ARI. What proofe of this?
    ERCO. The report of his mother delivered to me,

In distraction for *Contarino's* death.   600
   Con. *[aside]* For my death? I begin to apprehend,
That the violence of this womans love to me
Might practise the disinheriting of her sonne.
   Ario. What say you to this, *Leonora?*
   Leo. Such a thing I did utter out of my distraction:
But how the Court will censure that report,
I leave to their wisdomes. Ario. My opinion is,
That this late slaunder urged against her sonne,
Takes from her all manner of credit:
Shee that would not sticke to deprive him of his living,   610
Will as little tender his life. Leo. I beseech the Court,
I may retire my selfe to my place of pennance,
I have vowed my selfe and my woman.
   Ario. Goe when you please: *[to Ercole]* what should move
      you be thus forward   *[Exeunt Leon. & Win.]*
In the accusation?
   Erco. My love to *Contarino.*
   Ari. Oh, it bore very bitter fruit at your last meeting.
   Erco. Tis true: but I begun to love him,
When I had most cause to hate him—when our bloods
Embrac'd each other, then I pitied,   620
That so much valour should be hazarded
On the fortune of a single Rapier,
And not spent against the Turke.
   Ario. Stay sir, be well advised,
There is no testimony but your owne,
To approve you *[turning to Rom.]* slew him, therefore no other way
To decide it, but by Duell.
   Con. Yes my Lord, I dare affirme gainst all the world,
This Nobleman speakes truth.
   Ari. You will make your selfe a party in the Duell.   630
   Rom. Let him, I will fight with them both, sixteen of them.
   Erco. Sir, I doe not know you.
   Cont. Yes, but you have forgot me,
You and I have sweat in the Breach together
At Malta.
   Erco. Cry you mercy, I have knowne
Of your Nation brave Souldiers. Julio. *[aside]* Now if my father
Have any true spirit in him, Ile recover

His good opinion. *[to Contarino]* Doe you heare? doe not sweare sir,
640 For I dare sweare, that you will sweare a lye,
A very filthy, stinking, rotten lye:
And if the Lawyers thinke not this sufficient,
Ile give the lye in the stomacke—
That's somewhat deeper then the throat...
Both here, and all France over and over,
From Marselys, or Bayon, to Callis Sands,
And there draw my Sword upon thee,
And new scoure it in the gravell of thy kidneys.
     ARI. You the Defendant charged with the murder,
650 And you Second there,
Must be committed to the custody
Of the Knight-Marshall; and the Court gives charge,
They be to-morrow ready in the Listes
Before the Sunne be ⌈risen⌉.
     ROM. I doe entreat the Court, there be a guard
Placed ore my Sister, that shee enter not
Into Religion: shee's rich my Lords,
And the perswasions of Fryers, to gaine
All her possessions to their Monasteries,
660 May doe much upon her.
     ARIO. Weele take order for her.
     CRISP. There's a Nun too you have got with child,
How will you dispose of her?
     ROM. You question me, as if I were grav'd already,
When I have quencht this wild-fire in *Ercoles*
Tame blood, Ile tell you.   *Exit.*
     ERCO. You have judged to-day
A most confused practise, that takes end
In as bloody a tryall, and we may observe
670 By these great persons, and their indirect
Proceedings, shaddowed in a vaile of State,
Mountaines are deformed heaps, sweld up aloft;
Vales wholsomer, though lower, and trod on oft.
     SAN. Well, I will put up my papers,
And send them to France for a Pre⌈ce⌉dent,
That they may not say yet but, for one strange Law-suite,
We come somewhat neere them.   *Exeunt.*
                 Explicit Act⌈us⌉ quart⌈us⌉.

ACTUS QUINTUS, SCENA PRIMA.

[*A Nunnery.*]

Enter Jolenta, and Angiolella great-bellied.

JOLEN. How dost thou friend? welcome, thou and I
Were play-fellowes together, little children,
So small a while agoe, that I presume,
We are neither of us wise yet.
   ANGI. A most sad truth
On my part.
   JOLEN. Why doe you plucke your vaile
Over your face?
   ANGIO. If you will beleeve truth,
There's nought more terrible to a guiltie heart,   10
[Then] the eye of a respected friend.
   JOL. Say friend,
Are you quicke with child?
   ANGI. Too sure. JOL. How could you know
[First of your] child when you quickned?
   ANGIO. How could you know, friend?
Tis reported you are in the same taking.
   JOLEN. Ha, ha, ha, so tis given out:
But *Ercoles* comming to life againe has shrunke,
And made invisible my great belly; yes faith,   20
My being with child was meerely in supposition,
Not practise.
   ANGIO. You are happy—what would I give,
To be a Mayd againe!
   JOLEN. Would you?—to what purpose?
I would never give great purchase for that thing
Is in danger every houre to be lost: pray thee laugh.
A Boy or a Girle for a wager?
   ANGIO. What heaven please.
   JOLEN. Nay, nay, will you venter   30
A chaine of Pearle with me whether?
   ANGIO. Ile lay nothing,
I have ventur'd too much for't already—my fame.
I make no question sister, you have heard
Of the intended combate.

20-2

J OLEN. O what else?
I have a sweet-heart in't, against a brother.
A NGIO. And I a dead friend, I feare; what good counsell
Can you minister unto me?
40 J OLEN. Faith onely this—
Since there's no meanes i'th world to hinder it,
Let thou and I, wench, get as farre as we can
From the noyse of it. A NGIO. Whither?
J OLEN. No matter, any whither.
A NGIO. Any whither, so you goe not by sea:
I cannot abide rough water.
J OLEN. Not indure to be tumbled? say no more then,
Weele be land-Souldiers for that tricke: take heart,
Thy boy shall be borne a brave Roman.
50 A NGIO. O you meane
To goe to Rome then.
J OL. Within there! Beare this Letter   *Enter a servant.*
To the Lord *Ercole.* Now wench, I am for thee
All the world over.
A NGIO. I like your shade pursue you.   *Exeunt.*

[A room.]

Enter Prospero, and Sanitonella.

PROS. Well, I do not thinke but to see you as pretty a piece
of Law-flesh... SAN. In time I may—Marry I am resolved
to take a new way for't. You have Lawyers take their Clients
fees, & their backs are no sooner turn'd, but they call them
fooles, and laugh at them. PROSP. That's ill done of them.
SAN. There's one thing too that has a vild abuse in't.
PRO. What's that? SAN. Marry this—that no Proctor in
the Terme time be tollerated to go to the Taverne above six
times i'th forenoone.
10 PROS. Why, man?
SAN. Oh sir, it makes their Clients overtaken, and become
friends sooner then they would be.

Enter Ercole with a letter, and Contarino, comming in
Friers habits, as having bin at the Bathanites,
a Ceremony used afore these Combates.

ERCO. Leave the Roome, Gentlemen. [*Exeunt Pros. & San.*]

CON. Wherefore should I with such an obstinacy,
Conceale my selfe any longer? I am taught,   *Con. speaks*
That all the blood which wil be shed to-morrow,   *aside.*
Must fall upon my head; one question
Shall fix it or untie it: [*to Ercole*] Noble brother,
I would faine know how it is possible,
When it appeares you love the faire *Jolenta*   20
With such a height of fervor, you were ready
To father anothers child, and marry her,
You would so suddenly ingage your selfe,
To kill her brother, one that ever stood,
Your loyall and firme friend?

ERCO. Sir, Ile tell you—
My love, as I have formerly protested,
To *Contarino*, whose unfortunate end
The traytor wrought: and here is one thing more,
Deads all good thoughts of him, which I now receiv'd   30
From *Jolenta*. CONT. In a Letter?

ERCO. Yes, in this Letter:
For having sent to her to be resolved
Most truely, who was father of the child,
Shee writes backe, that the shame she goes withall,
Was begot by her brother.

CONT. O most incestious villaine!

ERC. I protest,
Before, I thought 'twas *Contarinos* Issue,
And for that would have vail'd her dishonour.   40

CONT. No more.
Has the Armorer brought the weapons?

ERCO. Yes sir.

CONT. I will no more thinke of her.

ERCO. Of whom?

CON. Of my mother—I was thinking of my mother.
Call the Armorer.   *Exeunt.*

[ACTUS QUINTUS, SCENA TERTIA.]

[*The Surgeon's House.*]

Enter Surgeon, and Winifrid.

WIN. You doe love me sir, you say?

SUR. O most intirely.

WIN. And you will marry me?

SUR. Nay, Ile doe more then that.
The fashion of the world is many times,
To make a woman naught, and afterwards
To marry her: but I a'th contrary,
Will make you honest first, and afterwards
Proceed to the wedlocke.

10 WIN. Honest!—what meane you by that?

SUR. I meane, that your suborning the late Law-suite,
Has got you a filthy report: now there's no way,
But to doe some excellent piece of honesty,
To recover your good name. WIN. How sir?

SUR. You shall straight goe, and reveale to your old Mistris,
For certaine truth, *Contarino* is alive.

WIN. How, living? SUR. Yes, he is living.

WIN. No, I must not tell her of it.

SUR. No?—why?

20 WIN. For shee did bind me yesterday by oath,
Never more to speake of him.

SUR. You shall reveale it then
To *Ariosto* the Judge.

WIN. By no meanes, he has heard me
Tell so many lyes ith Court, hee'l nere beleeve mee.
What if I told it to the *Capuchin*?

SUR. You cannot
Think of a better; [as for] your yong [Mistris],
Who as you told me, has perswaded you,

30 To runne away with her: let her have her humour.
I have a suite *Romelio* left i'th house,
The habit of a Jew, that Ile put on,
And pretending I am robb'd, by breake of day,
Procure all Passengers to be brought backe,
And by the way reveale my selfe, and discover

The Commicall event. They say shee's a little mad,
This will helpe to cure her: goe, goe presently,
And reveale it to the *Capuchin.*
   WIN. Sir, I shall.   *Exeunt.*

        [ACTUS QUINTUS, SCENA QUARTA.]

          [*A room in Castel Nuovo.*]

      Enter Julio, Prospero, and Sanitonella.

   JUL. A pox ont,
I have undertaken the challenge very foolishly:
What if I doe not appeare to answer it?
   PRO. It would be absolute conviction
Of Cowardice, and Perjury; and the Dane
May to your publike shame, reverse your Armes,
Or have them ignom[in]iously fastned
Under his horse tayle.
   JUL. I doe not like that so well.
I see then I must fight whether I will or no.   10
   PROSP. How does *Romelio* beare himselfe? They say,
He has almost brain'd one of our cunningst Fencers,
That practisd with him.
   JUL. Very certaine; and now you talke of fencing,
Doe not you remember the Welsh Gentleman,
That was travailing to Rome upon returne?
   PROS. No, what of him?
   JUL. There was a strange experiment of a Fencer.
   PR[O]S. What was that?
   JUL. The Welshman in's play, do what the Fencer could,   20
Hung still an arse; he could not for's life
Make him come on bravely: till one night at supper,
Observing what a deale of Parma cheese
His Scholler devoured, [a] goes ingeniously
The next morning, and makes a spacious button
For his foyle, of tosted cheese, and as sure as you live,
That made him come on the braveliest.
   PROS. Possible!
   JUL. Marry it taught him an ill grace in's play,
It made him gape still, gape as he put in for't,   30

As I have seene some hungry Usher.

SAN. The tosting of it belike,
Was to make it more supple, had he chanc'd
To have hit him a'th chaps.

JUL. Not unlikely. Who can tell me,
If we may breath in the Duell? PRO. By no meanes.

JUL. Nor drinke? PROS. Neither.

JUL. That's scurvy—anger will make me very dry.

PROS. You mistake sir, tis sorrow that is very dry.

40 SAN. Not alwayes sir, I have knowne sorrow very wet.

JUL. In rainy weather?

SAN. No, when a woman has come dropping wet
Out of a Cuckingstoole. JUL. Then twas wet indeed sir.

Enter Romelio very melancholly, and the Capuchin.

CAP. [aside] Having from *Leonoras* Wayting-woman
Deliver'd a most strange Intelligence
Of *Contarino's* recovery, I am come
To sound *Romelio's* penitence; that perform'd,
To end these errours by discovering,
What shee related to me. [to *Romelio*] Peace to you sir—
50 Pray Gentlemen, let the freedome of this Roome
Be mine a little. [to *Julio*] Nay sir, you may stay. *Exeunt*
Will you pray with me?   *Pro. San.*

ROM. No, no, the world and I
Have not made up our accounts yet.

CAP. Shall I pray for you?

ROM. Whether you doe or no, I care not.

CAP. O you have a dangerous voyage to take.

ROM. No matter, I will be mine owne Pilot:
Doe not you trouble your head with the businesse.

60 CAP. Pray tell me, do not you meditate of death?

ROM. Phew, I tooke out that Lesson,
When I once lay sicke of an Ague: I doe now
Labour for life, for life! Sir, can you tell me,
Whether your Tolledo, or your Millain Blade
Be best temper'd?

CAP. These things you know,
Are out of my practice.

ROM. But these are things you know,

I must practice with to-morrow.

    CAP. Were I in your case,   70
I should present to my selfe strange shaddowes.

    ROM. Turne you, were I in your case, I should laugh
At mine o[w]ne shadow.
Who has hired you to make me Coward?

    CAP. I would make you
A good Christian.

    ROM. Withall, let me continue
An honest man, which I am very certaine,
A coward can never be; you take upon you
A Phisicians place, rather then a Divines.   80
You goe about to bring my body so low,
I should fight i'th Lists to-morrow like a Dormouse,
And be made away in a slumber.

    CAP. Did you murder *Contarino?*

    ROM. That's a scurvy question now.   CAP. Why sir?

    ROM. Did you aske it as a Confessor, or as a spie?

    CAP. As one that faine would justle the devill
Out of your way.

    ROM. Um, you are but weakly made for't:
Hee's a cunning wrastler, I can tell you, and has broke   90
Many a mans necke.

    CAP. But to give him the foyle,
Goes not by strength.

    ROM. Let it goe by what it will,
Get me some good victuals to breakfast, I am hungry.

    CAP. Here's food for you.   *Offering him a Booke.*

    ROM. Pew, I am not to commence Doctor:
For then the word, Devoure that booke, were proper.
I am to fight, to fight sir, and Ile doo't,
As I would feed, with a good stomacke.   100

    CAP. Can you feed,
And apprehend death?

    ROM. Why sir? Is not Death
A hungry companion? Say? is not the grave
Said to be a great devourer? Get me some victuals.
I knew a man that was to loose his head,
Feed with an excellent good appetite,
To strengthen his heart, scarce halfe an houre before.

And if he did it, that onely was to speake,
110 What should I, that am to doe?
    Cap. This confidence,
If it be grounded upon truth, tis well.
    Rom. You must understand, that Resolution
Should ever wayt upon a noble death,
As Captaines bring their Souldiers out o'th field,
And come off last: for, I pray, what is death?
The safest Trench i'th world to keepe man free
From Fortunes Gunshot; to be afraid of that,
Would prove me weaker then a teeming woman,
120 That does indure a thousand times more paine
In bearing of a child. Cap. O, I tremble for you:
For I doe know you have a storme within you,
More terrible then a Sea-fight, and your soule
Being heretofore drown'd in securitie,
You know not how to live, nor how to dye:
But I have an object that shall startle you,
And make you know whither you are going.
    Rom. I am arm'd for't.

Enter Leonora with two Coffins borne by her servants, and two
Winding-sheets stucke with flowers—presents one to her sonne,
and the other to Julio.

Tis very welcome, this is a decent garment
130 Will never be out of fashion. I will kisse it.
All the Flowers of the Spring
Meet to perfume our burying:
These have but their growing prime,
And man does flourish but his time.
Survey our progresse from our birth,
We are set, we grow, we turne to earth.
Courts adieu, and all delights,   *Soft Musicke.*
All bewitching appetites;
Sweetest Breath, and clearest eye,
140 Like perfumes goe out and dye;
And consequently this is done,
As shadowes wait upon the Sunne.
Vaine the ambition of Kings,
Who seeke by trophies and dead things,

To leave a living name behind,
And weave but nets to catch the wind:
O you have wrought a myracle, and melted
A heart of Adamant, you have compris'd
In this dumbe Pageant, a right excellent forme
Of penitence. CAP. I am glad you so receive it.   150
   RO. This object does perswade me to forgive
The wrong she has don me, which I count the way
To be forgiven yonder: and this Shrowd
Shewes me how rankly we doe smel of earth,
When we are in all our glory. Will it please you   *to his*
Enter that Closet, where I shall confer   *mother*.
Bout matters of most waightie consequence,
Before the Duell?   *Exit Leonora* [*into Closet*].
   JUL. Now I am right in the Bandileere for th' gallows.
What a scurvy fashion tis, to hang ones coffin in a scarfe!   160
   CAP. Why this is well:
And now that I have made you fit for death,
And brought you even as low as is the grave,
I will raise you up agen, speake comforts to you
Beyond your hopes, turne this intended Duell
To a triumph. ROM. More Divinitie yet?
Good sir, doe one thing first, there's in my Closet
A Prayer-booke that is cover'd with guilt Vellom—
Fetch it, and pray you certifie my mother,
Ile presently come to her.   [*Exit Capuchin into Closet*.] 170
So now you are safe.   *Lockes him in.*
   JUL. What have you done?
   ROM. Why I have lockt them up
Into a Turret of the Castle, safe enough
For troubling us this foure houres; and he please,
He may open a Casement, and whistle out to'th Sea,
Like a Boson, not any creature can heare him.
Wast not thou a-weary of his preaching?
   JUL. Yes, if he had had an houre-glasse by him,
I would have wisht ‸ he would have joggd it a little.   180
But your mother—your mother's lockt in to[o].
   ROM. So much the better,
I am rid of her howling at parting.
   JUL. Harke, he knocks to be let out and he were mad.

Rom. Let him knocke till his Sandals flie in pieces.
Jul. Ha, what sayes he? *Contarino* living?
Rom. I, I, he meanes he would have *Contarino's* living
Bestowed upon his Monastery, 'tis that
He onely fishes for. So, 'tis breake of day,
190 We shall be call'd to the combate presently.
    Jul. I am sory for one thing. Rom. What's that?
    Jul. That I made not mine owne Ballad: I doe feare
I shall be roguishly abused in Meeter,
If I miscarry. Well, if the young *Capuchin*
Doe not talke a'th flesh as fast now to your mother,
As he did to us a'th spirit! if he doe,
Tis not the first time that the prison royall
Has been guiltie of close committing.
    Rom. Now to'th Combate.   [*Exeunt.*]

Enter Capuchin and Leonora above at a window.

200 Leon. *Contarino* living?
    Cap. Yes Madam, he is living and *Ercoles* Second.
    Leo. Why has he lockt us up thus?
    Cap. Some evill Angell
Makes him deafe to his owne safetie—we are shut
Into a Turret, the most desolate prison
Of all the Castle, and his obstinacy,
Madnesse, or secret fate, has thus prevented
The saving of his life. Leo. Oh the saving *Contarino's*—
His is worth nothing: for heavens sake call lowder.
210 Cap. To little purpose.
    Leo. I will leape these Battlements,
And may I be found dead time enough,
To hinder the combate! Cap. Oh looke upwards rather,
Their deliverance must come thence: to see how heaven
Can invert mans firmest purpose! his intent
Of murthering *Contarino*, was a meane
To worke his safety, and my comming hither
To save him, is his ruine: wretches turne
The tide of their good fortune, and being drencht
220 In some presumptuous and hidden sinnes,
While they aspire to doe themselves most right,
The devil that rules ith ayre, hangs in their light.

LEO. Oh they must not be lost thus: some good christian
Come within our hearing! ope the other casement
That looks into the citie.   CAP. Madam, I shall.   *Exeunt.*

[ACTUS QUINTUS, SCENA QUINTA.]

The Lists set up. Enter the Marshall, Crispiano, and
Ariosto as Judges, they sit. [With them Sanitonella.]

MAR. Give the Appealant his Summons, doe the like
To the Defendant.   *Two Tuckets by severall Trumpets.*

Enter at one doore, Ercole and Contarino, at the
other, Romelio and Julio.

Can any of you alledge ought, why the Combate
Should not proceed?   COMBATANTS. Nothing.
    ARIO. Have the Knights weighed,
And measured their weapons?   MAR. They have.
    ARIO. Proceed then to the battell, and may heaven
Determine the right.
    HERAULD. *Soit [la] Battaile, et [Victoire] à ceux qu[i ont] droit.*
    ROM. Stay, I doe not well know whither I am going: 10
'Twere needfull therefore, though at the last gaspe,
To have some Church-mans prayer. Run I pray thee,
To Castle Novo; this key will release
A *Capuchin* and my mother, whom I shut
Into a Turret—bid them make hast, and pray—
I may be dead ere he comes.   [*Exit Attendant.*]
Now, *[Victoire] à ceux qu[i ont] droit.*
    ALL THE CHAMP. *[Victoire] à ceux qu[i ont] droit.*

The Combate continued to a good length, when
enters Leonora, and the Capuchin.

LEON. Hold, hold, for heavens sake hold!
    ARI. What are these that interrupt the combate?   20
Away to prison with them.
    CAP. We have been prisoners too long:
Oh sir, what meane you? *Contarino's* living.
    ERCO. Living!   CAP. Behold him living.
    ERCO. You were but now my second, now I make you
My selfe for ever.   [*They embrace.*]

LEON. Oh here's one betweene,
Claimes to be neerer.
    CONT. And to you deare Lady,
30 I have entirely vowed my life.
    ROM. If I doe not
Dreame, I am happy to[o].
    ARIO. How insolently
Has this high Court of Honor beene abused!

*Enter Angiolella vail'd, and Jolenta, her face colour'd like a
Moore, the two Surgeons, one of them like a Jew.*

    ARIO. How now, who are these?
    2. SUR. A couple of strange Fowle, and I the Falconer,
That have sprung them. This is a white Nun,
Of the Order of Saint *Clare*; and this a blacke one,
Youle take my word for't.   *Discovers Jolenta.*
40   ARIO. Shee's a blacke one indeed.
    JOLEN. Like or dislike me, choose you whether—
The Downe upon the Ravens feather
Is as gentle and as sleeke,
As the Mole on *Venus* cheeke.
Hence vaine shew!—I onely care,
To preserve my Soule most faire.
Never mind the outward skin,
But the Jewell that's within:
And though I want the crimson blood,
50 Angels boast my Sister-hood.
Which of us now judge you whiter,
Her whose credit proves the lighter,
Or this blacke, and Ebon hew,
That unstain'd, keeps fresh and true?
For I proclaim't without controle,
There's no true beauty, but ith Soule.
    ERCO. Oh tis the faire *Jolenta*; to what purpose
Are you thus ecclipst? JOL. Sir, I was running away
From the rumour of this Combate: I fled likewise,
60 From the untrue report my brother spread
To his politike ends, that I was got with child.
    LEON. Cease here all further scruteny, this paper
Shall give unto the Court each circumstance,
Of all these passages.

ARIO. No more: attend the Sentence of the Court.
Rarenesse and difficultie give estimation
To all things are i'th world: you have met both
In these severall passages: now it does remaine,
That these so Comicall events be blasted
With no severitie of Sentence: You *Romelio*,   70
Shall first deliver to that Gentleman,
Who stood your Second, all those Obligations,
Wherein he stands engaged to you, receiving
Onely the principall.
     ROM. I shall my Lord. JUL. I thanke you,
I have an humour now to goe to Sea
Against the Pyrats; and my onely ambition
Is to have my Ship furnisht with a rare consort
Of Musicke; and when I am pleased to be mad,
They shall play me *Orlando*.   80
     SAN. You must lay wait for the Fidlers,
Theyle flye away from the presse like Watermen.
     ARIO. Next, you shall marry that Nun.
     ROM. Most willingly.
     ANGIO. Oh sir, you have been unkind;
But I doe onely wish, that this my shame
May warne all honest Virgins, not to seeke
The way to Heaven, that is so wondrous steepe,
Th[o]rough those vowes they are too fraile to keepe.
     ARIO. *Contarino*, and *Romelio*, and your selfe,   90
Shall for seven yeares maintaine against the Turke,
Six Gallies. *Leonora*, *Jolenta*,
And *Angiolella* there, the beautious Nun,
For their vowes breach unto the Monastery,
Shall build a Monastery. Lastly, the two Surgeons,
For concealing *Contarino's* recovery,
Shall exercise their Art at their owne charge,
For a twelvemonth in the Gallies: so we leave you,
Wishing your future life may make good use
Of these events, since that these passages,   100
Which threatned ruine, built on rotten ground,
Are with success beyond our wishes crown'd.
                        Exeunt Omnes.

F I N I S.

COMMENTARY

THE DEVIL'S LAW-CASE

TITLE-PAGE

Non quam diu, fed quam bene. From Seneca, *Epistles*, 77 (end): "Quomodo fabula, sic vita, non quam diu sed quam bene acta sit, refert". "With life, as with a play, it matters, not how long, but how good the performance is."
A. M.: Augustine Matthews, printer, 1619–53.
Iohn Grifmand: bookseller and printer, 1618–38.

DEDICATION

Sir Thomas Finch: son of Sir Moyle Finch and Elizabeth, daughter of Sir T. Heneage, vice-chamberlain of the Queen's household, who died in 1595 after thirty years in high favour with his mistress. In 1628, in recognition of her father's services, Elizabeth Finch was made Countess of Winchilsea, and transmitted the title to her son, Webster's patron. His grandson Heneage Finch was the husband of the poetic Countess of Winchilsea (d. 1720), whose "Nocturnal Reverie" justly seemed to Wordsworth an anticipation of his own nature-poetry, unique in the period when it was written.

6. *Guise*: a lost play, called a comedy in Archer's play-list (1656), a tragedy (as it surely must have been) in Kirkman's lists of 1661 and 1671. J. P. Collier made a forged insertion of Webster's name in Henslowe's Diary for Nov. 3rd 1601, in an entry which records an advance made for "the Gwisse"—probably a revival of Marlowe's *Massacre at Paris*. (See Chambers, *Eliz. Stage*, III. 511–2.) That Webster's play had the same subject—the assassination of the Duke of Guise—is likely enough: and we may perhaps assign its date to the gap in Webster's career which follows *The Duchess of Malfi*—not only because he here mentions *W.D.*, *D.M.*, and *Guise* in what may be their chronological order, but also because of the curiously Marlowesque tone of a passage in the present play, with its unmistakable reference to *The Jew of Malta* (III. 2. 1 ff.). But of course all we can say for certain is that *The Guise* was written before 1623.

TO THE JUDITIOUS READER

1. *that of Horace*: a seventeenth-century Latinism, based on the Latin construction of the type "illud Solonis"—"that saying of Solon" (Cic. *de Sen.* XIV. 50). So Stillingfleet (1662—the earliest instance in *N.E.D.*): "according to that of Macrobius".

1–2. *Sapientia prima...caruisse*: "the beginning of wisdom is freedom from folly" (Horace, *Epist.* I. I. 41–2).

5. *Locus... Umbris*: "there is room also for a number of unbidden guests" (Hor. *Epist.* I. 5. 28). An *umbra* (*lit.* "shadow") was the Latin term for a hanger-on who followed some more distinguished personage, like his shadow. Cf. Lyly, *Euphues*, 52: "I was the bolder to bring my shadow with me".

8. *Auriculas... dolentes*: (it would give no more pleasure to them than) "the music of lyres to ears afflicted with the dirt of ages" (Hor. *Epist.* I. 2. 53). *Citherae* should, of course, strictly be *Citharae*.

16. *approoved*: made trial of. Cf. I *Hen. IV*, IV. I. 9.

I. I.

Outer stage?

It is worth noting from the first moment of the scene how totally and irreconcilably, though at first unconsciously, Romelio and Contarino differ in their attitude towards money. The contrast between merchant and nobleman is stressed from the outset of this admirable first act.

5–6. *and discharge My yearely Custome*: *i.e.* presumably, if I gave the King of Spain 10,000 ducats a year, that would be about the equivalent of the customs-dues I pay; and that will give some idea of the volume of my trade.

6. *The Hollanders*: English sympathy with the Netherlands as the victims of Spain had changed by this time to jealous alarm at the growth of their trade, especially in the East Indies.

8. *Shaperoones*: chaperons, a kind of fashionable hood, which Dekker mentions (*Dream*, 49) as worn by "gay women" along with powdered hair (which was just coming in).

10. *Belvidears*: belvederes, raised turrets or lanterns on the roofs of houses or summer-houses, with a commanding view. That of the Vatican was famous; cf. Burton, *Anat.* II. 2. 4, where he mentions among pleasing sights to cure melancholy—"the pope's Belvedere in Rome, as pleasing as those *horti pensiles* in Babylon, or the Indian king's delightsome garden in Aelian".

11. *musicall Water-workes*: artificial cascades, fountains, and streams of water contrived to make imitation birds sing, etc. Cf. Sidney, *Arcadia*, I. (*Wks.* I. 92) (a passage which Webster must have known): "The table was set neere to an excellent water-worke" (which was contrived to throw a rainbow). "There were birds also made so finely, that they did not onely deceive the sight with their figure, but the hearing with their songs; which the watrie instruments did make their gorge deliver." Cf. Nash, *Unfort. Traveller* (ed. Brett-Smith), pp. 79–80; Davenant's *Love and Honour*, II. I. 105.

     H.D.S. cites also an amusing article in *N.Q.* 12. I. 221, on Mortoft's travels (1658–9). The water-works at the *Belvedere* gardens and at

Frascati delighted him extremely. He mentions a grotto containing "a pair of organs which are made with such art y^t noe man can play and keep better tyme on a paire of organs than the water does upon these. Also Apollo and the Nine Muses having all sorts of Instruments at their mouths, they make different Musicke according to ye Instruments they represent".

17. *Lotterie*: several times alluded to by Webster. The first in England was drawn in 1569; but probably the one in Webster's mind was that conducted for the benefit of Virginia in 1612. In 1620 (note date) they were suspended in England; though we find another being held in 1627. (See J. Ashton, *History of Eng. Lotteries*, 1893.)

40–1. *What tell you me of Gentrie?...time past.* Cf. *D.M.* Dedicat. ll. 9–10 and II. I. 101 ff.

44–5. *colour Of visiting...to sell land*: "he makes it an excuse for visiting us that he wants to sell land".

54. *Gilthead*: of the various fishes of this name, *Crenilabrus melops*, the gilt-head or Golden Maid is probably meant. (Yarrell, *Brit. Fishes*, I. 325.)

55. *draw up a Gudgeon*: the usual phrase is "to *swallow* a gudgeon", *i.e.* "be taken in", since the gudgeon was a small fish used for *bait*. Webster seems here to have confused fish and fisherman; there was perhaps also an association in his mind between "gudgeon" and "gilt-*tail*", a small worm used to catch the gudgeon. Cf. T. Barker, *Art of Angling* (1651–7):

> The greedy Gudgeon doth love the Gildtaile.

57. *Evidence*: title-deeds.

58. *motioned*: proposed.

62. *absolute*: perfect, finished, complete.

64. *passing of the Alpes*: since the scene is Naples, this would naturally mean travelling *north* of the Alps; but the audience certainly thought of the young Englishman crossing them *southward* into Italy; to the doubtful improvement of his morals, in the opinion of Ascham and many another. H.D.S. quotes Burleigh's *Advice to his Son*: "Suffer not thy sons to pass the Alps, for they shall learn nothing there but pride, blasphemy and atheism".

70–2. From *Arcadia*, I. (*Wks.* I. 58): "the gods would not have delivered a soule into the body, which hath armes and legges, only instruments of doing, but that it wer intended the mind should imploy them". (H.D.S.)

72. *Mathematicall*: precise and exact, like an intricate mechanism.

92–4. From *Arcadia*, I. (*Wks.* I. 86): "thinking it a lesse fault in friendship to do a thing without your knowledge, then against your wil". (H.D.S.)

97–8. *Myne...mine*: the same quibble as probably occurs in *D.M.* I. I. 493.

116. *mainely*: mightily, extremely.

133. *without the greater grace*: into the bargain (*i.e.* without regarding it as an extra favour).

138. *presume*: of course, imperative—"you must presume".

146. *sweeter ayre...breath*. Cf. *Mon. Col.* 222. From *Arcadia*, II: "His fame could by no meanes get so sweete and noble an aire to flie in, as in your breath". (C.)

147. *strange*: *i.e.* a stranger, not visiting us.

149. *th'Exchange Bell*. In Jonson's *Ev. Man in his H.*, III. 3. 45, where the Quarto (1601) reads: "past ten", the Folio (1616) has "Exchange time". This has been taken to show that the Exchange opened at ten: see however P. Simpson's note *ad loc.*, where, though *A Warning for Fair Women* (1599), sig. C *verso*, also supports ten o'clock, it appears that Nash, *Ret. of Pasquil* (1589), sig. D 2 *verso*, and Haughton, *Englishmen for my Money* (1616), sig. B, make the hour eleven (cf. Middleton quoted below).

Certainly Peter Eisenberg, who published an itinerary in 1614, says that the merchants met at the Exchange from eleven till twelve and from five till six. (Rye, *England as seen by foreigners*, p. 171.) The hours may have varied at different periods. Here it is clearly from eleven till twelve. Cf. Middleton, *Five Gallants* (licensed for printing March 1608), IV. 7. 1: "Why, how now, sirrah? Upon twelve of the clock, and not the cloth laid yet? Must we needs keep Exchange time still?" Similarly Harrison, *Descr. of Eng.* (1577): "The nobility, gentry, and students ordinarily go to dinner at 11 before noon. The merchants dine seldom before 12 at noon". (Quoted in Sugden.)

150. *from us*: with emphasis on *us*; for one would naturally have expected the *bourgeoisie* to copy the Court, not *vice versa*. For the late rising of citizens' wives cf. Dekker, *Jests to make you merry* (1607; Grosart II. 324): "'Tis growne of fashion amongst them to eate their breakfasts in their beds and not to be ready (dressed) till halfe an houre after noone: about which time their husbands are to returne from the Bursse, and they make it their dinner time".

154. *the New Burse*: the New Exchange was built by the Earl of Salisbury in the Strand and opened by James I in 1609 as a rival to the Old Exchange erected by Gresham on Cornhill in 1566-7. It is described as "being furnished with shops on both sides the walls, both below and above stairs for milleners, sempstresses, and other trades, that furnished dresses". It did not flourish at first (cf. "thinly furnisht") and soon after the date of this play there was talk of selling it (Dec. 20th 1623)—"Lady Hatton is said to have bought Britain's Burse for £6000, and means to make the upper part her dwelling house" (*Cal. State Papers (Domestic)* 1623-5, p. 132, quoted in Wheatley's *London Past and Present*, II. 582). At the Restoration however the New Exchange became popular and supplanted the Old, though it fell into decay after the death of Queen Anne.

155. *Tyers*: dresses.
161. *Shaddowes*: regularly used to mean "pictures"; cf. *Two Gent. of Ver*. IV. 2. 128 (of Silvia's portrait):
    And to your shadow will I make true love.
167. *the Cuckow* arrives in April and, "too quick despairer", departs in July. Here, of course, there is the usual reference to cuckoldry.
174. *compeld*: constrained.
185. *mellow*: soft.
192. *Mooves in the Superficies*: reveals itself outwardly in the face.
198. *the addition*: i.e. of a man's, a husband's, experience.
    With all its differences, the scene faintly but unmistakably recalls the far greater passage in *The Duchess of Malfi*, where another widow ambiguously woos a backward lover.
199–200. *mans Experience... Womans best eyesight*: from *Arcadia*, III. (*Wks*. I. 380): "mans experience is womans best eie-sight". (C.)
205 ff. Repeated attempts were being made in England at this time to make the nobility and gentry stay in their country homes instead of flocking to London. In April 1617 James I issued a proclamation on the subject. The actual words of a speech from the throne are not without interest in this connection: "One of the greatest causes of all gentlemen's desire, that have no call or errand, to dwell in London is apparently the pride of the women, for if they be wives, then their husbands, if they be maids, then their fathers, must bring them up to London.... It is the fashion of Italy...that all the gentry dwell in the principal towns, and so the whole country is empty; even so now in England, all the country is gotten into London, so as with time England will be only London, and the whole country be left waste.... But let us in God's name leave these idle foreign toys and keep the old fashion of England". However all this seems to have had little effect, for six years later Chamberlain writes to Carleton (April 5th 1623): "Here is a third strict proclamation come forth for gentlemen of quality to avoid this town.... It is nothing pleasing to all; but least of all to the women". The ascription of the abuse largely to women is an additional link with this anti-feminist play.
208–9. Cf. "Overbury", *Characters*, "Newes from my Lodging" (by "B.R.": Rimbault, p. 187): "the best prospect is to look inward".
210. *Next to their begging Churchland*: the greedy appropriation of Church-property at the Reformation, which all the zeal of Mary could not undo, was often superstitiously believed to have brought retribution on the spoilers and detainers of holy things, just as (to quote Cardinal Pole's parallel) the profanation of the vessels of the Temple brought ruin on Belshazzar.
218. *pearch'd*: old spelling of "pierc'd", i.e. "*penetrated*". See *N.E.D* and Text. Note.
221. *ingenuously*: ingeniously.

230. *Ile thither straight*: whither? It might be explained that Jolenta is living for the moment not at home, but in a convent; but this would create more difficulties than it solves. Webster is merely heedless.

I. 2.

It is possible that here the curtain of the inner stage is drawn as if revealing Jolenta's room.

3. *Tombe-maker*. Cf. *D.M.* IV. 2. 145, where Bosola masquerades as an Old Mortality.

6. *the king of Spaine greets you*: I suppose Romelio hands his sister, as if it were a letter addressed to her in person, the commission in which the King of Spain names Ercole the commander of thirty galleys. The document may well have begun with a general official greeting to all whom the appointment might concern, like a modern passport.

8. *Proces*: an official document of another sort—a summons before a court of justice.

29–31. *Letters of Commendations... Universitie*: *i.e.* "*even* for filling places in the University such letters have ceased to carry weight". Such letters were naturally disliked by the Universities themselves: thus in 1579 the Vice-Chancellor of Cambridge and the Heads of Colleges wrote to Lord Burghley "complaining of the frequency of letters mandatory from the Queen for the admission of Fellows and Scholars in Colleges, whereby the right of free election was taken away, and the scholars were induced to look for preferment to the favour of courtiers, rather than to diligence and proficiency in their studies". (Cooper, *Annals of Cambridge*, 1843, II. 368.)

32. *Passe*: "testimonial"; it may not be accidental that the word is used of the testimonial given by magistrates to vagrants and beggars to authorize them to beg their way home again. Cf. *W.D.* v. 6. 16.

34. *Knights service*: "good service"; cf. the still current "yeoman service". There is also a hit at the proverbial frequency of weddings between wealthy widows wanting rank and poor knights wanting money. Cf. W. Fennor, *Compter's Commonwealth* (1617): "with more fervency and protestation wooe...then many decayed K^{ts} will rich widowes, to inherit their possessions".

37. *addition*: rank, title.

40. Scan: "As wish|ing that *you* | would be part|ner in *my* | good Fortune".

42. *interest in you*: influence with you.

52–3. *too much light...Moone-eyed*: too much gazing on the glitter of worldly greatness has dazzled and half blinded you. Cf. *D.M.* IV. 1. 50 (where the Duke similarly rebukes his sister): "You were too much i'th' light".

Moone-eyed is originally a term of farriery applied to animals suffering from an intermittent blindness, called "moon-blindness" because attributed to the moon's influence. Cf. Markham, *Masterpiece Revived* (1688 ed.), p. 171: "Now they be called Moon-eyes, because if the Farrier do observe them, he shall perceive that at some times of the Moon the horse will see very prettily, and at some times of the Moon he will see nothing at all". Topsell, *Four-footed Beasts* (1658 ed.; p. 279), brings a rival explanation that the eye seems sometimes covered with white, like a moon, sometimes clear.

At all events, helped perhaps by the other association between the moon and lunacy, the word becomes applied to mental blindness too, as here and in Dryden, *Brit. Redux*, 94:

> So manifest that even the moon-eyed sects
> See whom and what this Providence protects.

Note the Elizabethan use of the capital letter in the text for a technical term (see P. Simpson, *Eliz. Punctuation*, p. 104).

133. *station...dumbe shew*: the metaphor is apparently of a moveable "pageant" or stage on wheels, such as was used in the English mystery-cycles. The "stations" are the places where the pageants, in their procession through the town, stop and perform their "turn". So here, Ercole is not to make his *Exit* or "move on", but to continue acting, though only in dumb show—*i.e.* with silent wooing, not with words.

138. *That they were heartie*: *i.e.* that the virgins were really only too glad to be married (*not* "that the tears were from the heart").

142–3. *Prelates...Twice to say nay, and take it.* Chamberlayne, *Present State of England* (1689 ed. p. 15), says that it was the regular form for those offered bishoprics to reply "*Nolo episcopari*"—twice in any case, thrice if they were really unwilling.

Yet there is strangely little evidence for the custom: the only specific occasion of its use on record seems to be William Beveridge's (1637–1708) refusal of the see of Bath and Wells: cf., however, Dryden, *Limberham*, III. 1: "But you would be entreated and say *Nolo, Nolo, Nolo* three times, like any bishop, when your mouth waters at the diocese".

"To say nay and take it" occurs also (as H.D.S. points out) in the proverbial expression "Maids say nay and take it". Cf. *Rich. III*, III. 7. 50, etc.

145–6. *dore bith'ring...Livery and Seasin*: an allusion to the feudal form of conveyance of estates (practically abolished in 1845) called "feoffment with livery and seisin" (Fr. *saisir*). The feoffer and the feoffee (or their attorneys) went together to the place and, if it was land that was being conveyed, the feoffer gave the feoffee a turf or twig from it; if it was a house, the ring or latch of the door. At the same time he recited the formula—"I deliver these to you in the name of seisin of all the lands and tenements contained in this deed". When William the Conqueror landed, one of his men-at-arms is

said to have torn a piece of thatch from a cottage-roof and offered
it to him as seisin of the realm of England.
For this metaphorical use cf. Marston, 1 *Ant. and Mellida*, II. 1.
184–5:

> *Gal.* Thy lips and love are mine.
> *Mel.* You ne'er took seizin on them yet; forbear.

174–5. *the time...in taking their degree*: seven years, Jacob's term of
service for Rachel.

186. *peevish*: froward. Cf. *D.M.* III. 2. 32.

188–90. From *Arcadia*, III. (*Wks.* 1. 355): "Assure thyselfe, I hate
myselfe for being so deceived: judge then what I doo thee, for
deceiving me". (Not in C.)

191. *Lady of the Laundry*: laundresses had a poor reputation for virtue,
cf. *W.D.* IV. 1. 96.

193 ff. From Jonson's *The Devil is an Ass* (1616), II. 1 (Dyce):

> Be you sure, now,
> You have all your eyes about you; and let in
> No lace-woman, nor bawd that brings French masks
> And cut-works; see you? nor old crones with wafers,
> To convey letters; nor no youths, disguis'd
> Like country-wives, with cream and marrow-puddings.
> Much knavery may be vented in a pudding,
> Much bawdy intelligence; they are shrewd cyphers.

There is another borrowing from the same play at II. 1. 164 below.

196. *Cut-works*: stuff *cut* out into an open-work pattern, as contrasted
with lace.

196. *Man-toons*: large mantles (Ital. *mantone*).

200. *Dewes-ace*: "deuce-ace" is a throw in dice which turns up ace
on one side, deuce on the other, *i.e.* a poor throw. Hence applicable
to a woman of the poorer class.

200. *wafer-woman*: a seller of thin cakes and confectionery. As a class
they were notorious go-betweens. Cf. "Beaum. & Fl.", *Maid in the
Mill*, 1. 3:

> Am I not able, cousin,
> At my years and discretion to deliver
> A letter handsomely?...
> Why every wafer-woman will undertake it.

200. *prigs*: thieves' slang, meaning (1) steal, (2) chaffer, haggle, (3) ride
(cf. "to prick"). Here *abroad* rather suits "rides"; but Dewesace
probably walked and certainly "chaffered", so that sense (2) seems
likelier.

201. *Muskmeloons*: oriental melons with a musky taste (see on *D.M.*
II. 1. 145), which came to be confused with the ordinary melon.

201. *Malakatoones*: derived from Lat. *malum cotoneum*, Gk. μῆλον
κυδώνιον, which means "quince", *lit.* "apple of Cydonia" (in
Crete; cf. Pliny xv. 11: "Quinces which we call Cotonea, the Greeks
Cydonea, because they were first brought out of Candie"). There is

no connection such as Nares suggests, with cotton. "Malakatoon",
however, despite its derivation does not itself mean "quince", but
"peach grafted on a quince".

202. *Citterne*: musical instrument like a guitar.

203. *foot-cloth*: housing for horse or mule. For this sign of affluence
see on *W.D.* I. 2. 48.

207. *Maribone*: marrow-bone. In point here, like Jonson's corresponding "marrow-puddings", because supposed to be aphrodisiac.
Cf. Middleton, *A Mad World*, I. 2. 47: "Her wanton pamphlets, as
Hero and Leander, Venus and Adonis, oh two lushious mary-bone
pies, for a young married wife".

209. *apprehensive*: quick of apprehension, quick-witted.

210. *traveld*: (1) travelled; (2) travailed.

212. *Chaperoones*[s]: a nonce-word? (It is not in *N.E.D.*) *Chaperon*
(Fr. *chaperon*, a hood: *chaperone* is an incorrect attempt to add a
feminine ending to a word fem. already) means (1) a hood, thence
(2) a lady wearing one. And so here too the fem. ending -*ess* is re-
dundant.

214 ff. On this subject of chaperons with pasts, and setting a thief
to catch a thief, cf. Chaucer's *Physician's Tale* (which Webster may
have read for his *Appius and Virginia*), 83:

> A theef of venison, that hath forlaft
> His likerousnesse, and al his olde craft,
> Can kepe a forest best of any man.

222–3. Cf. "Overbury", *Characters*, "Newes from Court" (Rimbault,
171–2): "wit and a woman are two fraile things". But it looks
proverbial.

230. *inclosing the Commons*: for this political allusion see on *W.D.*
I. 2. 95–6.

246 ff. Cf. *D.M.* I. 1. 407 ff.

246. *Caskanet*: a word formed by confusion of "casket" and "carcanet"
and used to mean either: here the first.

255. *forespoken*: (1) bespoken beforehand; (2) bewitched. (Dyce.)

259–60. From *Arcadia*, III. (*Wks.* I. 508): "for then would be the time
to die nobly, when you cannot live nobly". (Not in C.) The same
sentiment recurs in the very different works of Nietzsche—"When
it is no longer possible to live proudly, we should die proudly".

264. *bravery*: finery.

278. Cf. *W.D.* I. 2. 204–5. For the monkey's sweet breath, cf.
Arcadia, I. (*Wks.* I. 135); where among the gifts contributed by the
beasts to woman, the monkey provides this one; and Herrick's
"Oberon's Palace":

> The breath of Munkies met to mix
> With Musk-flies, are th' Aromaticks.

See Text. Note.

280–1. *no womans friend...kissing*: perhaps an allusion to Cato the

Elder who degraded Manilius from the Senate for kissing his own
wife in the daytime in the presence of their daughter (Plutarch,
Cato, 17).

285. *purchase*: acquisition.

286. *quits her ill*: does not succeed in acquitting, absolving her.

293 ff. Cf. *D.M.* v. 4. 78–9.

300. *Civill Lawyer*: perhaps with a play on the sense of *civil* =
"obliging".

300–1. Cf. *W.D.* I. 2. 87, etc.

304. *On one condition, we may have no quarrell*: on the single condition
that we have no quarrel (between you and the others).

311. *complementall*: courtly, smooth-tongued. Cf. *D.M.* I. 1. 301.

318. *copartaments*: ornamental subdivisions or compartments in a larger
design, *e.g.* the sunk panels in a coffered ceiling.

II. 1.

Outer stage.

8. *exhibition*: money-allowance.

13. *Corrigidor of Civill*: *Corrigidor* (corregidor) normally means "the
chief Justice of a town"; but sometimes, as H.D.S. points out, simply
"advocate"; cf. Kyd, *Span. Trag.* III: "To plead in causes as
corrigidor". This may be the meaning here, for Crispiano had
certainly practised as an advocate, and it is not easy to combine his
being chief Justice of Seville with his last forty-two years having
been spent in the Indies (IV. 2. 525–9). In which case *of Civill*
can only mean "born in Seville", though we should naturally take
it closely with *Corrigidor*, as "chief Justice of Seville". (There is
perhaps too a play on Civill (Seville) and *Civill Lawyer* in 4 above.)
The alternative is to suppose that Webster was careless and provided
his Crispiano with two incompatible careers: which is perfectly
possible.

14. *a Jubile*: fifty years.

32. *Collectionship*: (not in *N.E.D.*) "accumulation, collecting of
wealth"? Baron Bourgeois (*N.Q.* 11. IX. 303) renders "time of
reading for a degree at the University" ("collections" being the
name of an Oxford exam. at the end of each term); but it is clearly
the whole period of Crispiano's amassing a fortune at the bar which
is meant here.

33. *a perpetuall Callender*: *i.e.* every single day in the year has been
marked by some business or other. Cf. *A.V.* III. 2. 12.

35. *Ruddocks*: (1) robin red-breast, (2) (slang) coin (from the idea of
"red" gold).

38. *made your selfe halfe ready*: "to make oneself ready" is simply "to
dress".

43. *Night-caps*: lawyers. See on *D.M.* II. 1. 21.

46. *out from the matter*: off the point, having lost your thread.

49. *swallow['d] it like Flap-dragons.* Drinkers used to amuse themselves by putting into their drink small burning objects, generally raisins, sometimes even candle-ends, which they then swallowed alight. Another variety consisted of snatching raisins out of burning brandy. The game was apparently of Dutch origin. Cf. *Winter's Tale*, III. 3. 99: "But to make an end of the ship: to see how the sea flap-dragoned it!"

57. *Gleeke*: (1) a card-game for three, (2) a scoff, (3) an ogle. Cf. Jonson, *Cynthia's Revels*, Palinode 10:

Coy glances, gleeks, cringes, and all such simpring humours.

There may be a play on sense (3) as well as (1). There *may* also be a particular point in *"familiar* as Gleeke": for its terminology, as given in Cotton's *Complete Gamester*, p. 90, is "familiar" in the extreme: "The Ace is called *Tib*, the Knave *Tom*, the four of Trumps *Tiddy*...the fifth *Towser*, the sixth *Tumbler*".

59. *Taffaties, or Lawnes*: silks or fine linens.

60 ff. A good instance of Elizabethan carelessness whether speeches are always in character or not. Crispiano is later drawn as a most sober and upright judge: here he is made to give the most cynical account of his own past so that Webster may have an extra gibe at lawyers.

64. *tooke by a leare*: took in by a stealthy glance.

65. *vayl'd*: doffed.

68. *crie of Hounds*: pack.

69. *hunted...to a fault*: i.e. "to a break in the scent", with the sense also of "ruin". The oldest meaning of *fault* is "scarcity", "want" (cf. "default" and Berners, *Froissart*, I. clix. 193: "they had gret faut in their hoost of vitayle"), and this idea was perhaps in Webster's mind. He may also have remembered the rationalizing explanation of the myth of Actaeon, as an allegory of a hunter eaten up by the expenses of his kennel.

82. *Mock-beggers*: with a pun on "bigger". This word was regularly applied to fine, but inhospitable houses. Nares says the name was also given to the masters of such houses, but this seems due to a mis-understanding of "Mock-beggars Hall" as "Mock-beggar's Hall". The name still clings not only to certain houses in various parts of England, but also to a rock near Bakewell in Derbyshire, which looked from the road deceptively like a house.

85. *Cuckshawes*: *quelquechoses*—originally a light dish of French cookery, regarded as frivolous in comparison with solid English diet (cf. "trifle"). Thence, in general, "frivolities", "frivolous persons"; so Milton (*Educat.*) speaks of Frenchified youths as "Mimicks, Apes, and Kickshoes".

142. *quat*: "pimple", hence "contemptible person". Cf. *Othello*, v. 1. 11:

I have rubb'd this young quat almost to the sense (*i.e.* to the quick)
And he grows angry.

144–5. *Cockesparrow...poxe.* Cf. "Overbury", *Characters,* "Newes from the verie Countrie" (signed "I.D."—perhaps John Donne, in the 1669 edition of whose poems it is reprinted; p. 177 in Rimbault): "that intemperance is not so unwholesome here; for none ever saw Sparrow sicke of the poxe". Burton would, however, have had an answer ready to this (*Anat.* II. 2. 2): "Aristotle gives instance in sparrows, which are *parum vivaces ob salacitatem,* short-lived because of their salacity".

147. *Cantaride-mongers:* cantharides, made from the Spanish Fly (*Cantharis vesicatoria*), a poison taken in minute doses as an aphrodisiac. Cf. on *W.D.* II. I. 285.

150. *slop:* wide breeches.

154–5. Cf. *D.M.* III. I. 51–2.

157. *rook:* (1) (in chess) a castle; (2) a gullible person. (A third meaning, "sharper", is out of place here.) Cf., for (2), Chapman, *May Day,* III. I. 187: "An arrant rook by this light...a man may carry him up and down by the ears like a pipkin".

159. *blocke:* the wooden block used to keep hats in shape; hence, here, Julio's wooden head.

163. *put on:* put on my hat. Perhaps also with the other sense of *put on* = "go ahead".

164–7. H.D.S. points out that this is another reminiscence (cf. I. 2. 193 above) of Jonson's *The Devil is an Ass* (1616), II. I:

> The fair lands
> That were the client's, are the lawyer's now
> And those rich manors there of goodman Taylor's
> Had once more wood upon them than the yard
> By which they were measured out for the last purchase.

169–70. Cf. *D.M.* III. I. 33.

176 ff. A bout of Webster's favourite form of dialogue "with two buckets", where two characters alternately break in upon each other in baiting and rating a third. Cf. *W.D.* I. I. 12 ff.; *D.M.* I. I. 318 ff.; *D.L.* I. 2. 135 ff.

179. *Cut-worke:* stuff cut or stamped out into open-work.

179. *Purle:* pleat or fold of a ruff or band. Cf. Jonson, *Ev. Man out of his H.,* IV. 4: "It graz'd on my shoulder, takes me away six purls of an Italian cut-work band I wore, cost me three pound in the Exchange but three days before".

180–1. *overblowne Roses:* silk rosettes on the shoes, a very expensive luxury. See on *W.D.* V. 3. 104.

182. *taffaty:* shining silk.

183. *Gally dung-boat. Gally* = "large row-boat". For the whole, cf. Cowley, "Answer to an invitation to Cambridge":

> I shall contemne the troubled *Thames,*
> On her chief *Holiday,* even when her streames
> Are with rich folly guilded, when

The *quondam Dung-boat* is made gay,
Just like the bravery of the men,
And graces with fresh paint that day.

184–5. *switching up...Illustrissimi*: galloping up with the best
society.

186. *pusling Arithmatick*: *i.e.* betting.

187. *Taule-boord*: table-board, *i.e.* backgammon-board (which has
folding leaves called the inner, and the outer, table). Whence the
old name for the game—"tables" (Lat. *tabularum lusus*, Fr. *tables*).

188. The *hir'd velvet* belongs to the whore, not the youth.

189. *spangled copper*: imitating gold lace. So we hear of gallants at the
theatre betting whether the actors' gold lace is real or gilt.

190. *Padua*: the university. Cf. 243–4: *W.D.* I. 2. 313.

197. *Chuffes*: (1) boors, (2) (as here) misers.

201–2. *selling commodities*: for this form of exorbitant usury see on
W.D. IV. 1. 54.

201–2. The construction is: "You have Potecaries *who* deal...*who*
will put...".

203. *Counter*: with a play on *Counter* = debtor's prison. See on
A.V. III. 2. 25.

204. *searse*: sift (Lat. *saeta*, bristle, used for making sieves).

204. *Ginny Pepper*: Guinea pepper or "grains of paradise" is not true
pepper, but the seed of a W. African plant of the ginger family,
used as a drug and spice in the Middle Ages, in hippocras for instance. It was finally driven from the market by eastern pepper at
the close of the eighteenth century.

205. *like a payre of Tarriers*: *i.e.* terriers (Lat. *terra*, because used in
burrows underground). "These usurers cannot bear to have a long
round-about pursuit of their victims (there is clearly a play on
"tarry", contrasted with "in a trice"); they do not want to be like
terriers burrowing laboriously through a labyrinthine earth; they long
only to leap at their quarry's throat in an instant. Cf. *Char.* "Petifogger", 4–5: "*Writs of error* are the *Tariers* that keepe his *Clyent*
undoing somewhat the longer". There the pun is clearer: but it is
certainly meant here too.

207. Cf. *W.D.* IV. 1. 58.

208–10. *three heads...Hell-hounds*: Cerberus, the classical Hound of
Hell, had three heads.

211–2. *Tenterhookes*: commonly as this metaphor is used, few realize
that tenterhooks are the bent nails to hold the cloth on the "tenter"
or wooden framework, upon which it is stretched, after milling, to
prevent shrinkage. Hence *rent*; with perhaps a pun on the economic
sense. Cf. "Overbury", *Characters*, "A Golden Asse": "Knaves
rent him like Tenter-hookes"; and "A Creditor": "Every term he
sets up a tenters in Westminster Hall, upon which he racks and
stretches gentlemen like English broad-cloth".

212. *gold conveyd beyond the Sea*: for such an offence see on *W.D.*
v. 3. 83. In 1618 it was found that foreign merchants, mainly
Dutch, had smuggled £7,000,000 out of England since the accession
of James. There was considerable excitement, and the case was tried
before the Star Chamber in the summer and autumn of 1619. Fines
totalling £140,000 were imposed, though only £29,000 or less was
exacted in the end. (Gardiner III. 323.)
    This warning is presumably addressed to Romelio.

217–8. *Barber...curry: curry* = (1) "to comb" (used of human beings
as well as of curry-combing animals); (2) "to scratch, claw" (here
of the stinging of Ariosto's tongue).

240 ff. This quarrel between Ercole and Contarino is, as Lamb justly
says (more justly indeed than in most of his criticism of Webster),
"the model of a gentleman-like and well-managed difference". The
scene must have had all the more interest for an Elizabethan audience
as duels were a comparative novelty in England. In France duelling
had been common for a century and two thousand noble persons are
said to have fallen its victims in the years 1601–9: but there are few
recorded on this side of the Channel before the reign of James I,
who himself so disapproved the practice that he regarded the murder
of Henri IV as a judgment on him for permitting it.

253 ff. Not less beautiful, though almost unknown, than Coleridge's
famous: For to be wroth with those we love
                Doth work like madness in the brain.

Webster's words are based on *Arcadia*, I. (*Wks.* I. 83): "They rested,
with their eyes placed one upon another, in such sort, as might well
paint out the true passion of unkindnes to be never aright, but betwixt
them that most dearely love". (Not in C.)

258–60. For these charming lines, also from the *Arcadia*, cf. *D.M.* v. 2.
174–5 and note.

261–2. You say it was "No myracle at all"; but it will certainly prove
a prodigy of evil omen for you.

271. *practise*: treachery.

290. *motive*: prime mover, instigator. Cf. *Authorized Version*, 1611,
Translators' Preface: "They were the principal motives of it".
    Though Ercole denies that he is influenced by the chivalrous
desire not to transfer the blame and the quarrel to Romelio's shoulders,
that appears to be in fact his only motive for deceiving Contarino.

296. *vary for*: are at variance about.

318. *prevention*: being anticipated before we can fight.

321–2. Cf. *D.M.* III. 2. 77–9 and note.

330. *sufficient proofe*: (1) "sufficiently stout", as in "armour of proof";
(2) "sufficient evidence".

331. *privie coat*: against the laws of duelling. Cf. Fynes Moryson's
account of Italy (*Shakespeare's Europe*, ed. by C. Hughes, 1903,
p. 159): "Myselfe have seene young Gentlemen, for feare of those

with whom they had some quarrells, weare continually an yron coate
of thirty pounds weight, next above their shirts".
332. *Taffaty*: silk doublet.
334. *equally*: fairly, justly.

II. 2.
Outer stage.

Those who are interested to see a description of a real duel of the
period, as recounted with extraordinary vividness by the survivor,
Edward Sackville, should turn to *The Guardian*, No. 133 (Aug. 13th
1713), where Steele has printed it, exactly a century after it was
written. Its resemblance to the present scene is very striking.
9–13. Cf. v. 4. 63–9.
20. *I meane well...thrive*: *i.e.* "I have the best intentions of hurting
you; only it does not succeed".
32. *at my repayring, or confusion*: at my mercy to kill or spare. For
"repayre" = "save" cf. Southwell, "Mary Magdalene's Funerall
Teares", 46: "Could thy love repaire thee from his rage?"

II. 3.

Whole stage (cf. "let them into' th Court" at 88—the outer stage
representing the courtyard of the house).
28. *Scarlet*: the colour of a doctor's robes.
40. *conceited*: full of conceits, witty.
43–5. See on *W.D.* v. 6. 69; *talk of it* refers, of course, to *patience*.
47. A perfect description of a familiar type of human being. That
vitriolic humour which is the vivid thing about Romelio, surpasses
itself here.
51. *Carracks*: large merchant-ships.
52–4. *Spice... Drench*: Markham in his *Masterpiece Revived* (1688 ed.
pp. 134–6) mentions as ingredients of such drenches, myrrh, pepper,
oil of spikenard, aloes, etc.
59 ff. A certain resemblance between these lines and a passage
of Sir R. Hawkins's *Voyage into the South Sea* (1622) was
pointed out in a note in *N.Q.* 3. iv. 225 (1863). See the *Hakluyt
Soc.* edit., 1847, pp. 8–10, where Hawkins writes: "Yet advise
I all persons ever (as neare as they can) by all meanes, and in all
occasions, to presage unto themselves the good they can, and in
giving names to terestriall workes (especially to ships), not to give
such as meerly[1] represent the celestial character; for few have I
knowne, or seen, come to a good end, which have had such attributes". He then instances the *Revenge*, whose career was one long
chapter of mishaps down to the magnificent disaster which closed it;
the *Thunderbolt*, again, "had her mast cleft with a thunderbolt, upon

---

[1] ? neerly (*i.e.* closely).

the coast of Barbary", then had her poop mysteriously blown up at Dartmouth, and was finally "burned with her whole companie in the river of Bourdieux". Similar misfortunes dogged the *Jesus* of Lubeck at St John de Ulua, and Hawkins's own *Repentance*. But of course other people besides Hawkins may well have shared a superstition of this sort: and we cannot postulate borrowing by Webster, which is indeed made most improbable by the dates, unless this passage is a later insertion in the play. And the names objected to in Webster are not representative of any "celestial character": it is rather that they show what a Greek would have called ὕβρις.

73. *hansell*: "first use of a thing"; hence, here, "inauguration". Cuckold's luck was proverbially good.

85. *common Bell-man*: town-crier. For such notices of sale, cf. Holinshed (1577), III. 1209: "Certeine houses in Cornehill, being first purchased by the citizens of London, were in the moneth of Februarie cried by a belman and afterward sold".

91. *Bead*: (1) prayer (cf. Germ. *beten*, to pray); thence (2) bead of a rosary.
Cf. Herrick, *Hesperides*:
> Be brief in praying,
> Few beads are best, when once we go a-maying.

97. *Canon*: Canon Law, which anciently denied Christian burial to those slain in duels, tilts, and tournaments (cf. Burn's *Ecclesiastical Law* (9th ed.), I. 265).

105–7. *Epitaphs...Spiders*. Cf. *W.D.* v. 6. 158–9.

111. *I have a certaine Meditation*: for this naïve introduction of a string of irrelevant common-places, cf. *D.M.* II. 1. 45–6.

115 ff. An interesting example of that *Christabel* metre (iambic octosyllables with free substitution) which Coleridge imagined he had invented, though it occurs in early poems like the metrical *Genesis* and *Exodus* of the thirteenth century, in Spenser's "The Oak and the Briar" (*Shep. Cal.* "February"), and again in Chatterton.

120. *Evidence*: title-deeds.

120. *Church-land*: see on I. 1. 210.

122. *a good hearing*: pleasant tidings.

124. *all die Worthies die worth payment*: i.e. all die Worthies *who* die worth payment.

128. *rotten trees...shine i'th night.* Cf. Hall, *Characters*, "Of the Hypocrite": "a rotten stick in a dark night".

132. *Supersedeas*: "a Writ signifying a Command to stay, or forbear the doing of that which in Appearance of law ought to be done, were it not for that Reason on which the Writ is granted"—Phillips, *New World of Words* (1696—quoted by H.D.S.). Hence, metaphorically, an interruption of the normal course of anything, here of their last sleep. Cf. Babington, *Works*, II. 127: "Sweet Death is a Supersedeas for all"; *A.Q.L.* II. 1. 121.

134. *chary*: charily, *i.e.* carefully, Cf. Shakesp., *Sonnets*, XXII:

> Which I will keep so chary
> As tender nurse her babe from faring ill.

136. *vilder uses*: Hazlitt explains "than that of burning men's bones for fuel"; but there is no question of burning anybody's bones, only of keeping coal in the vaults. For these yet *vilder uses*, cf. Marston, *Sophonisba*, IV. I. 157–60:

> Where tombs and beauteous urns of well-dead men
> Stood in assurèd rest, the shepherd now
> Unloads his belly, corruption most abhorr'd
> Mingling itself with their renownèd ashes.

141 ff. Cf. Lucan's famous "caelo tegitur qui non habet urnam" (VII. 819).

144. *Charnell*: this has been explained to mean here "corpse"; but that is a rare use, and the ordinary meaning of "burial vault" makes perfectly good sense.

144. *chargeable*: costly, expensive.

150. *the Hazard*: there are three openings of this name in the tennis-court, by striking the ball through which the player gains a point. See on *W.D.* v. I. 72.

151–2. Cf. *D.M.* IV. 2. 391–2.

156. An unexpected touch of tenderness in the brazen Romelio. As Ferdinand to Bosola, we may well exclaim: "Thy pity is nothing of kin to thee".

167. *Yet* must be temporal, not adversative,—"still, longer", with an emphatic echo of Prospero's "He's yet living"—'*Yet* I would have him live" (unless we should read *Yes*).

190. *Engine*: (1) plot, (2) piece of machinery. Cf. the double sense of the Gk. μηχανή.

190. *weigh up*: counterbalance.

195. *fore-winds*: not "winds blowing from the front", "head-winds", but "winds that blow the ship forward".

196. Cf. *D.M.* v. 5. 96–8.

II. 4.

Outer stage.

6. *dwell in't*: persist in it, unrepentantly.

7. *informed*: inspired. Cf. *Coriol.* v. 3. 70:

> The God of soldiers...inform
> Thy thoughts with nobleness.

12. *foregoe the complement*: give up, relinquish the reputation.

23. *where*: whereas. Cf. *W.D.* v. 6. 274.

24. *happily*: haply.

32 ff. This is an allusion to the famous and abortive exchange of cartels in 1528 between Francis I and Charles V, who had accused the

French king of breaking his faith "lâchement et méchamment" in violation of the Treaty of Madrid, accepted by him when a prisoner in Spain. The scene chosen by Charles for this single combat was "la rivière qui passe entre Fontarabie et Andaya", *i.e.* the Bidassoa, between Fuenterrabia and Hendaye (a spot on the coast half-way between Biarritz and St Sebastian). (See *Mém. de Martin du Bellay*, in *Collect. Univers. des Mém. relatifs a l'hist. de France* (London and Paris, 1786), xviii. 53; Gaillard, *Hist. de François I* (1819), ii. 347.)

With this Webster has combined another different challenge to which the Emperor made reference eight years later at a Papal Consistory in 1536. There Charles V rose and said (in the words of Montaigne i. 16): "he had challenged the King (Francis I) to fight with him, man to man, in his shirt, with Rapier and Dagger in a boat". Cf. *Collect. Univ. des Mém.* etc. xix. 79: "que le combat pouvoit se faire dans une isle, un pont, ou sur un bateau fait exprès au milieu d'une rivière... qu'il combattroit l'épée ou le poignard à la main, et en chemise, si on le vouloit".

45–7. *crimes...Devill.* Cf. "Overbury", *Characters*, "Newes of my morning Worke" (By "Mist. B.") (Rimbault, p. 189): "That sinne makes work for repentance, or the devill".

50. *Gordi[a]n knots:* see on *D.M.* i. 1. 549.

III. 1.

Outer stage, if the scene is still supposed to be in the street; or inner, if we imagine Crispiano calling on Ariosto, as Dyce. This seems less likely.

9. *vents:* spends. Cf. Jonson, *Alchem.* iii. 2: "that have vented Six times your fortunes".

11 ff. See on iv. 1. 33.

13–4. *Dutchwomen...Take all and pay all.* Cf. Fynes Moryson, *Itinerary*, Pt. iii. Bk. 4. ch. 6: "The wives of *Holland* buy and sell all things at home, and use to saile to *Hamburg* and into *England* for exercise of traffique.... And the Women not only take young Men to their Husbands, but those also which are most simple and tractable; so as by the foresaid priviledge of Wives to dispose goods by their last will...they keep their Husbands in a kind of awe, and almost alone, without their Husbands intermedling, not onely keepe their shops at home, but exercise trafficke abroad. My selfe have heard a Wife make answere to one asking for her Husband, that he was not at home, but had newly asked her leave to goe abroade...I may boldly say, that the Women of these parts, are above all other truly taxed with this unnatural dominering over their Husbands".

"Take all and pay all" is, H.D.S. points out, a regular phrase for such dominering wives. Cf. *W.Ho!* i. 2. p. 81; *Merry Wives of Windsor*, II. 2. 123: "do what she will, say what she will, take all, pay all, go to bed when she list, rise when she list, all is as she will".

15. *silly...of their owne estates*: ignorant about them.

20. *Bat-fowling*: catching birds by knocking them on the heads with wooden bats when roosting at night and dazed or attracted by a sudden glare of torches. This "sport" is described at length in Markham's *Hunger's Prevention* (1600). ("Bat-folding", "bird-batting" still occur in provincial English.) Hence the term is applied to dark practices in gulling the simple (cf. "coney-catching"); it was also used of a special form of fraud in which the swindler pretended about dusk to have dropped some valuable by a shop-door, and asked the shopman to lend his light in order to look for it. He would then drop this light, as by accident, and while his victim was fetching a new one, the thief snatched up what he could in the darkened shop and ran. The nocturnal association may have been strengthened by confusion with "bat" meaning "nocturnal animal".

III. 2.

Outer stage at first, as before; Contarino's bed is doubtless in "the study"; the curtains of which may be closed again a little before the end of this scene, to allow of the arrangement of the properties for the next one.

3. *Italienated Jew*: it seems clear that Webster had here in mind *The Jew of Malta*, and its Machiavellian villain Barabas (cf. "Betray a Towne to'th Turke"). Doubtless Romelio was disguised in the traditional way with a large false nose. Cf. W. Rowley, *A Search for Money* (1609: Percy Soc. reprint, 1840, p. 19); where Mounsier Money is described with "his visage (or vizard) like the artificiall Jewe of Maltaes nose...upon which nose, two casements were built, through which his eyes had a little ken of us".

8–11. See on *W.D.* v. 3. 157.

16. *disgested*: digested.

27. *impostumation*: gathering of septic matter.

29. *Orifix.* Cf. Markham, *Cheap Husbandry*: "Orifice is the mouth, hole, or open passage in any wound or ulcer"—the modern "sinus".

46. *store of Patients*: owing to the abundant crime and vice of Rome.

56. *Extraction*: extract, essence.

65. *pull the pillow.* Cf. *Volpone*, II. 3 (H.D.S.):

> 'Tis but to pull the pillow from his head
> And he is throttled.

94. *put in a...Caveat*: in law, "to call on a legal officer appointed to take certain action, not to take it, but stay proceedings till the caveator's objection has had a legal hearing".

100. *Barmotho Pigs*: the Bermudas were as famous for pigs as for tempests. Cf. *A.Q.L.* v. 1. 358; and see the Appendix to Furness's

Variorum edit. of *The Tempest*, pp. 308 ff. which quotes from various accounts of Sir George Somers' shipwreck there in 1609, *e.g.* Jourdan's *A Discovery of the Bermudas* (1610): "The country afforded such an abundance of hogs, that Sir George Somers brought in thirty-two at one time"; and again—"These islands of the Bermudos have ever been accounted as an inchaunted pile of rockes, and a desert inhabitation for divels; but all the fairies of the rocks were but flocks of birds, and all the divels that haunted the woods were but heards of swine" (cf. Ariel and Caliban).

108. *wheale*: blister.

110. *thee*: (he is addressing his dagger).

129. *A cunning Marchant*: *Marchant* being also slang for "fellow". Cf. Carleton, *Jurisdiction Regall, Episcopall, papall* (1610), VII. 172: "The King to hold fast this slippery Merchant... required all the Bishops to set to their approbation, and seales to those Lawes". H.D.S. points out the similar derivation of "chap" from "chapman".

132. *Roman Letter*: metaphor of Roman type in printing (Romelio had pretended to come from Rome).

138. *And my revenge unsatisfied*: *i.e. with* my revenge unsatisfied (καὶ ταῦτα δίκης μὴ τελεσθείσης, as a Greek might have said).

143. *as I do weigh this busines*: no doubt, as he speaks, the Surgeon weighs also the bag of ducats in his hand.

146. *drownd*: drunk.

147. *Usquebath*: whiskey. (Gaelic, *uisge-beatha*, "water of life" (Gk. βίος). Cf. *eau de vie*.)

155. *foot-cloth*: horse-housing, a sign of affluence, especially affected by physicians. See on *W.D.* I. 2. 48.

156. *policy* seems to mean simply "bond", *i.e.* as we should say to-day "a cheque for two hundred ducats". *N.E.D.* indeed gives no sense nearer to this than "a conditional promissory note, depending on the result of a wager". But there is nothing here "conditional"; and we must take it simply to mean what, after all, is meant by the Italian *polizza*, Span. *poliza* (med. Lat. *apodixa* from Gk. ἀπόδειξις)—"a bond".

160. *Unicornes Horne*: for this famous antidote see on *W.D.* II. 1. 14.

162. *Is the wind in that doore still?* An excellent example of the way authors are made to live up to their reputation (so that Webster's most innocent remarks assume a macabre eeriness—cf. on *W.D.* IV. 2. 21) is afforded by Rupert Brooke's comment on this line, as showing "something of the ghastliness of the midnight scene in the *Duchess of Malfi* or *Macbeth* or Jonson's additions to the *Spanish Tragedy*". It is indeed tempting to imagine the ghostly wail of the reviving Contarino sounding like wind moaning in a cranny. Unfortunately "is the wind in that door?" is a common old English idiom meaning simply "is the wind in that *quarter*?" *i.e.* "is that how the land lies?" It occurs repeatedly from Malory (*Arthur*, VII. 35) to

Dryden (*Evening's Love*, IV. 3). Cf. I *Hen. IV*, III. 3. 101: "How now, lad! Is the wind in that door i' faith? Must we all march?" Similarly *Much Ado*, II. 3. 108; Lyly, *Euphues*, 317; Fletcher, *Loyal Subject*, I. 2. Some may suppose that there is here, just possibly, a further association between *wind* and the breath in Contarino's body; but there is certainly no banshee-like wailing of wind in any literal door.

171–2. This *peripeteia* of a man's life being saved by an attempt to murder him is an old story. Langbaine pointed out that Val. Maximus (I. 8, *Ext*. 6) related a similar anecdote of Jason tyrant of Pherae, who was cured of a dangerous abscess by an assassin's dagger. But Stoll has undoubtedly found Webster's actual source in Goulart's *Histoires Admirables* (transl. by Grimeston 1607), which the dramatist had already used for the Duke's *licanthropia* in *D.M.* Goulart merely reproduces the case mentioned by the physician Reinerus Solenander (*Consilia Medicinalia*, V. 15. 9: Frankfort 1596). See p. 217 where it is quoted.

174. *cured a'th Gowt, by being rackt i'th Tower*: for this clearly topical allusion, cf. Jonson, *Volpone*, IV. 2:

> I have heard
> The rack hath cured the gout;

Marston, *Malcontent*, III. 1. 80: "All your empirics could never do the like cure upon the gout the rack did in England, or the Scotch boot".

It may have been a case of hysteria; for hysterical paralytics will generally succeed in running out of a burning house.

181. *Searing*: cauterizing iron.

III. 3.

Inner stage at first, then perhaps whole stage.

14–6. Cf. *D.M.* I. 1. 12–4, 208–9.

38. *radically*: thoroughly.

54. *The Precontract*: i.e. *per verba de presenti*, valid in civil law, though requiring to be ceremonially completed in church. See on *D.M.* I. 1. 548.

73. *plurall*: a reference to the ecclesiastical scandal of priests holding a plurality of benefices. Cf. *A.Q.L.* V. 1. 125–8.

104. *falshood*: it is important, for the understanding of the play, to realize that Romelio is unconscious that this falsehood of his about Leonora loving Contarino, is actually the truth; though, of course, the plot which he alleges to have been concerted between them is not true.

112. *tendred*: esteemed, held dear.

140. *To cleare your suspition*: to clear up any suspicion you might have formed that he was not really in love with you.

142. *censure*: repute.

150. *direct*: downright.

150–1. *No*...*Court*: these two lines are difficult. As they stand, it seems simplest to suppose that Romelio quibbles on his sister's question, and applies the term "falshood" to Contarino's treachery. "Is this truth?"—"No, it's as untrue and dishonest a piece of conduct as ever brought a man expulsion from the Court". It is indeed possible the words should be spoken "*aside*". But cf. the very similar quibble in *C.C.* v. 1. 170–1.

153. *For her owne tooth?* The force of the sentence becomes slightly clearer, if it is realized that the question-mark, as often in Elizabethan printing, might to-day be replaced by a mark of exclamation.

158. *fowle*: doubtless with a play on "foul".

162. *apparant*: manifest.

164. *another world i'th Moone*. Cf. *D.M.* II. 4. 26–7.

181. *for any thing belongs to'th flesh*: for aught that physical relation-ship has to do with it.

199. *preface*: "front", "facing", as if *preface* were connected with *face* (instead of Lat. *fari*, to speak). *N.E.D.*, with its usual neglect of Webster, gives no instance of the noun in this sense, though it gives three analogous uses of the verb: *e.g.* Cleveland, *Gen. Poems*, 24:

Not prefacing old Rags with Plush.

For this simulation of pregnancy with a cushion cf. *A.V.* IV. 1. 116–7 and T. May, *The Heir* (1620), v. where the whole *dénouement* of the sub-plot turns on this trick. See on IV. 1. 33 below.

204. *To keepe decorum*: "to lend consistency to my pretence of preg-nancy". Cf. the use of the word, in Elizabethan criticism, of artistic consistency and appropriateness.

205. *noddle*: beat (on the head?).

207. *tractable [to]'t as Stockfish*. Cf. Eden, *Decades* (Arber), 303, where stockfish are defined as "haddockes or hakes indurate and dryed with coulde, and *beaten with clubbes or stockes*, by reason whereof the Germayns caule them stockefysshe". Hence such phrases as Cotgrave gives in his *Dictionary* for "Je te frotteray à double carillon"—"I will beate thee like a stockfish, I will swinge thee while I may stand over thee". Cf. *Tempest*, III. 2. 81.

219. *nourish*...*fiend*: as witches give the devil suck (see on *D.M.* 1. 1. 345). But see Text. Note.

226. *waged to the East Indies*: hired to go there.

227. *Callenture*: a disease supposed to attack voyagers in tropical seas and make them try to jump in their delirium into the sea, imagining it to be green fields. Could this have suggested to Shakespeare Falstaff's dying babble "of green fields" (supposing Theobald's famous conjecture to be right)?

228. *Indian Pox*: syphilis, believed (though apparently wrongly) to have been brought by Columbus's men from the *West* (not the East) Indies.

234–5. *Franciscan Fryers . . . never . . . single*: Franciscans always wandered in pairs. There is of course a quibble on *prey* and *pray*.

243–4. Cf. *W.D.* v. 4. 47–8.

245–6. From *Arcadia*, III. (*Wks.* I. 361): (Pamela) "was grieved for his absence, having given the wound to him through her owne harte". (C.) Cf. *C.C.* IV. 2. 34.

252. *How cunningly . . . drawen*: *i.e.* what cunning she forced me to use in order to draw her, how cunningly she had to be drawn.

257. *Mother*: hysteria. Cf. on *D.M.* II. I. 118–9.

258. *rapt*: carried away, transported.

265 ff. Every time I read this speech, like several others in the play, it is with amazement at the genius Webster squandered even on his inferior works.

270. *they*: *i.e.* they who desire the impossible.

274. *precise curiositie*: over-scrupulous nicety of behaviour.

279 ff. Lowell (*Old Eng. Dramatists*, p. 68) compares these anguished lines with Balzac's treatment of the same theme of a middle-aged woman's last passion.

285. *Picture-makers*: for the metaphor from painting cf. *W.D.* v. 6. 299.

289. *Amazon*. This strange people already appears in Homer: their legend was perhaps based on the warlike prowess of the women of some tribes of the Caucasus. Others have identified them with the beardless Hittites.

290. *cut off this right pap*. This supposed custom of the Amazons is perhaps based on an etymological attempt to derive their name from ἀ-, "without" and μαζός, "breast" (Eustathius, *On Homer*, p. 402). At all events cf. Gautier de Châtillon, *Alexandreis* (ed. Mueldener), VIII. pp. 173–4:

> Laeva papilla manet et conservatur adultis,
> Cuius lacte infans sexus muliebris alatur.
> Non intacta manet sed aduritur altera, lentos
> Promptius ut tendant arcus.

Mandeville (XVIII) introduces a distinction between the Amazons of high estate who lose the left breast that they may the better bear a shield, and the meaner sort who lose the right breast to aid their archery.

297. *fly in pieces!*—like an overcharged cannon; as is clear from the parallel passage, *D.M.* III. 5. 121–2.

303 ff. Here we have a clear allusion to some form of the romantic legend which clings to the execution of Essex by the Queen who had loved him (Feb. 25th 1601).

To begin with certainties, it is known that his friends urged him after his condemnation to sue for pardon; and that he refused, though hoping to be pardoned notwithstanding. When Henri IV sent Admiral Biron (Chapman's hero) as envoy to England in Sept. 1601,

Elizabeth spoke to him of Essex's fate and warned him—vainly as the issue proved—to beware in his arrogance of a like end. The report of a speech supposed to have been made by her was published in French at the Hague in 1607; and there she says she would have pardoned Essex, had he but stooped to sue for mercy.

A similar statement is made in a speech attributed to Biron in Grimeston's *Inventory of the History of France* (1607—a translation of de Serres), p. 984: and Grimeston's prose reappears with little change in the blank verse of Chapman's *Byron's Tragedy*, v. 3. 139 ff.:

> The Queen of England
> Told me that if the wilful Earl of Essex
> Had used submission and but asked her mercy,
> She would have given it past resumption.
> She, like a gracious princess, did desire
> To pardon him, even as she prayed to God
> He would let down a pardon unto her.

But so far we have had nothing about *false convayance*; here we come to the tale of the Countess of Nottingham and the Ring. For the legend will have it that Essex *did* sue for pardon: only his message never reached its destination. The Queen had once given him a ring, promising, if he ever sinned against her, at the sight of that token to forgive him all. Accordingly just before his execution Essex, as his last hope, sent it to Lady Scrope to give the Queen; but the boy who carried it, gave it by mistake to Lady Scrope's sister, the Countess of Nottingham, whose husband forbade her to do anything with it. On her death-bed however the Countess sent for Elizabeth and confessed her "false convayance"; stricken with remorse the Queen too took to her bed and soon after died broken-hearted. Such is the story: ring or no ring, the last days of Elizabeth were certainly embittered with regret for the favourite she had sent to his death.

This tale (rejected by Lord Clarendon in his *Difference between Buckingham and Essex*—about 1641?) was given wide currency by a romance published about 1650, called "A History of the most renowned Queen Elizabeth and her great Favourite, the Earl of Essex". And it was repeated with variations by Francis Osborn in his *Traditionall Memoires of Elizabeth* (1658), by Louis Aubery in *Mémoires pour servir à l'Histoire d'Hollande* (1680, 1688), and again, towards the close of the century, by Lady Elizabeth Spelman who purported to have it from her great-grandfather Sir Robert Carey (1560?–1639), who had been with the Queen and on intimate terms with her during her last illness. Webster's allusion has thus a special interest, which has not been recognized, as our earliest evidence of a popular belief in the story sufficiently widespread to make a reference like this intelligible. (See *D.N.B.* "Robert Devereux"; Brewer in *Quarterly Review*, 1876, 1. 23; Ranke, *Hist. of Eng.* (Oxford transl.), 1. 352; Devereux, *Lives of the Earls of Essex*, II. 178 ff.)

308. *Exprest him stubborne-hearted*: gave him the appearance of being so.

334–5. *fasten On her last words*: *i.e.* not to let escape her involuntary confession (that Romelio has murdered Contarino).

338. *vowed comfort*: "betrothed comforter". But see Text. Note.

372. *and*: if.

387. *the partie ought*: the person *who* owned.

406. *ingenuously*: ingeniously.

407. *nought*: naughty, good-for-nothing, wicked.

435. *arpines*: Fr. *arpent* (from a Gallic word *arepennis* = Lat. *semi-jugerum*); an old French measure = 100 sq. perches = $\frac{5}{6}$ to $1\frac{1}{2}$ acres (according to the amount of a perch).

436. Cf. below, IV. 2. 535.

IV. 1.

Outer stage.

4. *trowle*: "troll", a curious word, perhaps from the Fr. *troller* "to hunt aimlessly". Hence "troll" means "to move something, or to move about", "to pass (the drinking-bowl)", "to wag the tongue", "to utter volubly" (as here).

6. *lungs of Fox*: used, by a sort of sympathetic magic, for consumption, asthma, and other lung diseases. Cf. *Luminare maius, lumen apothecariorum*, etc., Venice (1561), p. 44; *Pharmacopoeia Londinensis* (1618)—"Pulmonum Vulpis Praeparatio. Pulmones Vulpis recentes, exemptâ prius asperâ arteriâ, Vino albo cui Hyssopus et Scabiosa prius incoctae, deinde in fumo temperati calido sicco, ita tamen ut non comburantur, postea reponantur involuti Absinthio, Massubio, vel Hyssopo siccis".

In *N.Q.* 11. IX. 324, Baron A. F. Bourgeois explains *lungs of Fox* as simply "lung-wort" (*Pulmonaria officinalis*). It is true that several plants are sometimes called "lung-wort"; and some plants are used for the lungs, as Mullein, Lungs of Oak (*Sticta pulmonacea*), Angelica, and Tooth-wort (*Lathraea Squamaria*). But there is no evidence for calling any of these "lungs of fox"; and Baron Bourgeois' suggestion cannot stand against the evidence of the pharmacopoeias.

6. *Malligo Reasins*: Malaga raisins, from the sea-port of that name in S. Spain, famous for the export of white wine. For the medical use of raisins, cf. Gerard, *Herball* (1633 ed.), p. 877: "They are good for the chest, lungs, winde-pipe . . . for they make smooth the roughnesse of the winde-pipe, and are good against hoarsenesse, shortnesse of breathe, or difficulty of breathing".

10. *give you light of*. Probably on the stage, as Sanitonella handed over his ponderous mass of papers, *light* suggested an ironic quibble on its weight (cf. next note).

11. *Briefe*: with reference, of course, to "brief" = "short". A lawyer's brief (Lat. *breve*) is indeed in its origin a short summary of the facts of a case.

14. *Figdates*: a variant spelling (helped doubtless by popular association with "date", the fruit) of "fig-dote", probably from the Portuguese *figo doudo*, "mad (*i.e.* wild) fig" (cf. Fr. *figue folle*), an inferior sort of fig.

17. *scope*: gist.

23–4. *shake hands With*: meet with. Cf. 3 *Hen. VI*, i. 4. 102:

> Till our King Henry had shook hands with death.

Contrast the sense "say farewell to" as in *D.M.* iii. 2. 157:

> Shooke hands with Reputation.

24. *knave*: servant.

26. *fogging*: pettifogging. "Fogger" seems to be a corruption of "Fugger", the name of the famous Augsburg financiers (there are similar words in German, Flemish, Spanish). Hence the meaning "usurer, swindler"; then "petty fogger", "swindler on a mean scale", somehow became restricted to lawyers.

27. *Presentations*: obscure here. Usually of presentations to livings: but it is not clear what "whores" have to do with that. See Text. Note.

28. *Overseers*: executors. See on *D.M.* i. 1. 435.

28. *Of Overseers, wrong*: of course "Enow of Overseers *who* wrong".

31. *Plus quam satis*: after days of search, and consultation of lawyers, I cannot certainly explain this phrase. The only passage known to me that seems to throw light on it is Ford's *Love's Sacrifice*, i. 2, where the wanton Ferentes answers the reproaches of one of his many mistresses—"I hope I neglect no opportunity to your *nunquam satis*, to be called in question for". The words "*nunquam satis*" look here like a tag from the legal phraseology of suits for annulment of marriage on grounds of impotence; such as that brought by the Countess of Essex against her husband. And "*plus quam satis*" might possibly be a (? comic) variation of "*nunquam satis*". It certainly looks as if the two phrases were connected; and the general associations in the passage of Ford are at all events sufficiently obvious. It is however not quite clear whether in modern punctuation the comma after *satis* should stand or no.

32. *pursnets*: bag-shaped nets, the neck of which was drawn tight by a cord: hence in general "trap", "snare".

33. *Oh women, as the Ballet lives to tell you*: the ballad in question seems to live no longer. At least the nearest approach I can find to it is "A Warning to Wives" (1629), printed in H. E. Rollins, *A Pepysian Garland* (1922), (in a note on which the editor refers to this passage of Webster as proof of the existence of an earlier ballad with a similar refrain). The "Warning" is merely an account of a woman who murdered her husband with a pair of shears; but I cannot forbear to quote a specimen verse:

> This was about the houre of tenne
> or rather more that night,

> When this was done, whereof my Pen
>   in tragicke stile doth write;
> The manner of's death most strange appeares,
> Being struck ith' neck with a pair of sheares.
> Oh women,
> Murderous women,
> Whereon are your minds?

Lines 5–6 are superb. The last three form the refrain of the whole ballad. I would suggest that the refrain of the earlier ballad which Webster is quoting, was actually "Oh women, Monstrous women"; for a hitherto unnoted allusion to it occurs also in T. May, *The Heir*, v. (Hazlitt's *Dodsley*, xi. 573): "O women, monstrous women! little does her father know who has married her". *The Heir* was printed in 1633—"As it was acted by the Company of the Revels, 1620". This is important for the dating of our play (for another possible parallel, see on iii. 3. 199 above); and there is a very interesting letter from Chamberlain to Carleton on Feb. 12th 1619–20 (cf. *Cal. State Papers (Domestic)*, cxii. 123; Nichols, *Progresses of James I*, iii. 588): "Our Pulpits ring continually of the insolence and impudence of Women; and to help forward, the Players have likewise taken them to task, and so to the Ballads and Ballad-Singers: so that they can come nowhere but their ears tingle. And if all this will not serve, the King threatens to fall upon their husbands, parents, or friends, that have or should have power over them, and make them pay for it". Chamberlain had indeed already mentioned this subject a year earlier in a letter of Feb. 20th 1618–9 (James I had been questioning Sir George Calvert about his lady): "This, and some other passages of this kind, seem to show that the king is in a great vein for taking down high-handed women". It is clear from the context that Chamberlain has particularly in mind Lady Lake, who had recently disgraced herself in a famous law-case (see p. 215) and Lady Hatton, whose wars with her husband, Sir Edward Coke, are probably alluded to in *A.Q.L.* v. 1. 229–30.

41. *Commenc't*: note the capital letter for the technical term. "To commence" is to take one's degree at the University (cf. "incept", the modern Cambridge term). For the common figurative use, cf. Massinger, *Emp. of the East*, ii. 1:

> How hath he commenced
> Doctor in this so sweet and secret art
> Without our knowledge?

42. *Pewe*: in a wider sense than now. Cf. Evelyn, *Diary*, Feb. 3rd 1644: "one side is full of pewes for the Clearkes of the Advocates".

44. *dry-foundred*: "lamed from inflammation of the hoof"; and so "worked to a break-down".

46. *Non-resident Subsumner!* Ariosto is outraged by Sanitonella's application of pompous professional and ecclesiastical language to

himself—a mere lawyer's hack, a "sub-summoner". As *Commenc't* above is taken from the University, so *Non-resident* comes from the phraseology of the Church (we have to remember the connection between "clerk" and "cleric"). It was applied to priests who held a plurality of livings or benefices and were accordingly non-resident in all but one of them (cf. Milton, *Apol. Smect.*: "non-resident and plurality-gaping prelates"). It is not clear whether a comma should be inserted after *Non-resident.*

46. *Subsumner*: not in *N.E.D.* A summoner was a menial officer who delivered summonses to appear in court, especially ecclesiastical courts. It will be remembered that Chaucer's specimen is not a very agreeable creature; and "*sub*-summoner" is clearly meant to convey the extremity of contempt.

47. *Libell*: written statement of plaintiff's case. Cf. *D.M.* II. 3. 55.

48. *By vertue of the Clergie*: perhaps with an ironic stress on "vertue", since Sanitonella's term "Non-resident" was associated with a grave scandal of the church. Thus "Martin Mar-prelate" exclaimed that "Non-residences have cut the throte of our church".

Perhaps also there is a play on the phrase "by *benefit* of clergy", used of those who escaped the extreme penalty of the law for a capital felony (like Jonson, for instance, after killing Gabriel Spencer) by reading their "neck-verse " (generally *Psalm* li. 1) and so proving that they were "clerks" (*i.e.* able to read). "Benefit of Clergy" was finally abolished in 1827—an extraordinary example of the power of survival possessed by legal anomalies.

55–7. No one has ever surpassed Webster's power of packing a retort with bitterness.

61. *Winter itch*: *pruritus hiemalis,* an obscure disease tending to re-appear each winter on the sufferer's exposure to cold.

62. *Tetters*: any cutaneous eruption. Cf. *Ind. to Mal.* 66.

The efficacy of ink as a remedy was doubtless due to the presence in it of tannic acid from the oak-galls used in its manufacture: this acid is still employed in the treatment of various ulcers and moist eruptions.

63. *splay*: "spreading outwards" (shortened from "display", Lat. *displicare*).

73. *Night-caps*: the white coifs of the serjeants at law. See on *D.M.* II. 1. 21.

77. *bred*: probably old spelling for *breed*: cf. *W.D.* IV. 2. 225—*breds.*

82. *purchase*: "make money"—see on *D.M.* II. 5. 50.

85. *Of another piece*: of a different type. Cf. "of a piece", "all of a piece".

86. *foule Copie*: *i.e* of the brief, the fair copy of it having been torn up by Ariosto.

91. *saved, he can read*: with allusion to "benefit of clergy". See on 48 above.

92–3. *be the hand...pickt out on't*: in a double sense:—
  (1) From the worst handwriting, something can be made out.
  (2) From the dirtiest hand, some gain can be picked.
98. *Give it a dash*: draw a line through it.
99. *Secretary*: a style of handwriting used chiefly in legal documents from the fifteenth to the seventeenth century. We find French and English "secretary", as distinct from the Italian, Roman, Chancelry, and Court hands.
103. *Court hand* was regularly used in English law-courts from the sixteenth century to the time of George II. It was far from legible.
105. *traded in't*: practised in it. "Trade" is in origin connected with "tread" (*i.e.* "to trade" being "to use the beaten track"). So Nash spoke of Sir John Cheke (Preface to Greene's *Menaphon*) as "supernaturally traded in all tongues".
107. *Hogg-rubber*. Cf. Jonson, *Barthol. Fair*, v. 3, where "Goodman Hogrubber of Pickthatch" (a noted brothel), is a term of abuse at once followed by blows.
118. *pent*: confined, narrow.
122 ff. Thus poetry suddenly springs from the lips of Webster's unlikeliest characters. Cf. *W.D.* v. 6. 67 ff.

IV. 2.

Whole stage.
This is surely one of the vividest scenes in all Elizabethan drama.
11–3. *Hollanders...pepperd*: for this allusion to conflicts with the Dutch in the E. Indies, see Introd. p. 214.
17. *expect*: wait to see.
23. *Palavafini*: probably for *Pallavicini*, a well-known Italian noble family whose name may conceivably have come under Webster's notice in connection with *The White Devil*, since it was in their *palazzo* on Lake Garda that the Bracciano of history died. Members of the family, however, also had direct dealings with the English crown—in particular, Horatio Palavicino lent such vast sums to Elizabeth that the fate of England was said at one time to have depended on him. He was knighted, died in 1600 at Babraham, near Cambridge ("Him Death with besome swept from Babram Into the bosom of old Abram"), and left his widow to marry Sir Oliver Cromwell.
30. *Brachigraphy men*: an allusion with special point for an Elizabethan audience. For such shorthand writers used to lurk in the theatre to take down plays surreptitiously, so that they could be pirated by some publisher. To what extent this was really done, it is hard to be sure. The chief evidence we have is Heywood's complaint, in the "Epistle" to *The Rape of Lucrece*, that plays of his had been "copied only by eare" and issued in a garbled form; and again in the prologue to his *If you know not me, you know nobody*—

Some by Stenography drew
The plot: put it in print: (scarce one word trew)

Modern shorthand begins with the *Characterie* of Dr Timothy
Bright in 1588, which was dedicated to Elizabeth and rewarded with
a living in Yorkshire; it was followed in 1590 by Peter Bales's *Writing
Schoolemaster*. The first real success, however, was J. Willis's *Art of
Stenographie* (1602), which had gone through fourteen editions by
1647, apart from numerous imitations. It is a curious fact that the
art was much stimulated by the growing demand for sermons to read,
so that these were even pirated like plays. Cf. Jonson, *Barthol. Fair*:
"What ho, Ralph Shorthand... my stenographical sermon-catcher!"
and J. Phillips, *Satyr against Hypocrites* (1655):

> There Will writes short-hand with a pen of brass,
> Oh how he's wonder'd at by many an asse
> That sees him shake so fast his warty fist
> As if he'd write the Sermon 'fore the Priest
> Has spoke it.

38. *Buckram bagg*: the lawyer's regular appendage, cf. *W.D.* III. 2. 50.
40. *Greene ginger*: the undried root.
41. *Pellitory*: the name is given to two quite different kinds of plant:
(1) "Pellitory of Spain" (Gk. πύρεθρον from πύρ, fire) is so-called,
says Gerard, "by reason of his hot and fiery taste"; and this name
has been extended to some other plants with a similar quality, especially
Masterwort and Sneezewort. (2) "Pellitory of the wall" (Lat.
paries, a wall) is a low, bushy plant growing out of or at the foot of
walls.

Pellitory of Spain, being hot like ginger or peppermint, "easeth
the paine of the teeth, especially if it be stamped with a little Staves-
acre, and hid in a small bag, and put into the mouth, and there
suffered to remaine a certain space". H.D.S. quotes an amusing song
from Lyly's *Midas*, III. 2:

> *Petulus.* O my teeth! deare barber ease me,
> Tongue, tell me why my teeth disease mee,
> O! what will rid me of this pain?
> *Motto.* Some pellitory fetcht from *Spaine*.

45. *Pudding-pye*: a meat-pudding baked in a dish. Doubtless the point
of this somewhat slender episode was the unexpected production of
this object from a bag apparently bulging with its weight of legal
erudition.
51. *after-game at Irish*: *Irish* was a form of backgammon, described
in Cotton's *Complete Gamester* (1680): the *after-game*, or second
game played to retrieve a first, seems to have tended to be particularly
lengthy. Cf. Beaum. & Fl., *Scornful Lady*, v. 4: "longer bearing
than ever after-game at Irish was".
57. *mad...dark*: with allusion to the well-known Elizabethan treatment of lunatics—confinement in the dark, with whipping—which
was based originally on the idea that the mad were possessed by devils.
67. *unequall*: unfair.

73. *discovered*: "revealed" must be the meaning, not "found it out"; for Romelio had himself told her.

74–5. *call My life in question*: *i.e.* bring a capital charge against me.

82. *runnes in a blood*: runs in the blood. H.D.S. compares Jonson, *Staple of News*, v. 1: "An egg of the same nest! the father's bird! It runs in a blood, I see".

84. *An angry fellow*: Ariosto has learnt wisdom since his first unsuccessful adoption of the rôle of a past master in the art of patience (II. 3).

88–9. *East Indy Marchant...spice of pride*: spice being a staple of the E. Indian trade.

102. *as feare*: as to fear.

120–1. Cf. *W.D.* v. 1. 38–9; *D.M.* IV. 2. 141–2.

124. *Æsops Crow*: he means, of course, Aesop's *jackdaw* with the borrowed plumes (Fable 200 B in the Teubner edit.).

131–3. A telescoped simile (cf. *D.M.* I. 1. 82–3 and note). In full it would run: "a kind of saucy pride, which grows most rank when it springs from a mean origin, as mushrooms grow most rank when they spring from dung-hills". Cf. *W.D.* III. 3. 43–5.

134. *The [Fieschi]*: counts of Lavagna, were one of the four great families of Genoa,—the four wild horses by which that state was torn in sunder (the others being the houses of Grimaldi, Doria, and Spinola). The Fieschi were supposed to be descended from three brothers of the house of Burgundy or of Bavaria, one of whom was called Fisco, because he was charged with the collection of the imperial revenue (Lat. *fiscus*). They were allied with most of the royal houses of Europe, and claimed two Popes, Innocent IV and Adrian I, besides more than thirty Cardinals.

134. *Grimaldi*: another famous Genoese family, which like the Fieschi took the Guelf side, while the Doria and Spinola families were Ghibelline. As early as the tenth century Grimaldi I drove the Saracens from Monaco, of which his descendants remained hereditary princes till the eighteenth century. A Grimaldi (and a Doria) fell fighting against us among the Genoese bowmen at Crécy.

134. *Dori[a]*: the best-known of the three families, thanks to Andrea Doria, the great admiral (1468–1560).

It is a curious confusion that Webster should specify these three *Genoese* families as pillars of the state of Naples.

138. *Hedge-sparrow*: one of the favourite victims of the Cuckoo; whence its low Lat. name, *curruca* is used to mean "cuckold".

146. *Gyant in a May-game*. For the "Jack in the Green", the May-day survival of the incarnation of the vegetation-spirit, see Frazer, *Golden Bough* (*Magic Art*, vol. II. 82–3), where is given an amusing account of the ceremony as seen by Dr Rouse at Cheltenham in 1892. Jack in the Green was there played by a chimney-sweep "enclosed in a wooden framework to which leaves were fastened so as to make a thick cone about six feet high, topped with a crown". For the contrast

between the appearance and the real substance of such giants cf.
Puttenham, 165, quoted in Chambers, *Eliz. Stage*, 1. 135³: "these
midsommer pageants in London, where to make the people wonder
are set forth great and uglie Gyants marching as if they were alive,
and armed at all points, but within they are stuffed full of browne
paper and tow, which the shrewd boys underpeering, do guilefully
discover and turne to a great derision".

150. *Chickeens*: zecchins, a gold coin varying in value, in different
Italian states, round about nine shillings.

151. *byth hand.* The earliest and only example of this phrase in *N.E.D.*
is Gurnall, *Christian in Armour* (1659), verse 14, ix. 1: "that they
shall grow rich by the hand". *N.E.D.* renders this "quickly", "forth-
with"; but the sense seems to me rather "by the deal, by the bargain"
(cf. Germ. *Handel, Handlung*). For Gurnall is referring to the bar-
gaining between Shechem and the sons of Jacob (*Genesis* xxxiv),
who offered him and his tribe the right of intermarriage with themselves on condition that the strangers were circumcised. As the sons
of Jacob were rich, Shechem and his fellows hoped to gain "by the
bargain". I have found the phrase again in H. Fitzjeffrey's *Notes
from Blackfriars* (1617), where he says of a prostitute in the audience:
Let her alone! What ere she gives to stand,
Shee'l make her selfe a gayner, *By the Hand.*

Here there is doubtless a double meaning; but one sense is surely
"by the deal". Similarly in *A.V.* iv. 1. 234. H.D.S., who takes the
same view, quotes also "Beaum. & Fl.", *The Faithful Friends*, 1. 2,
Middleton, *Five Gallants*, ii. 3. 147. Even should this not be the
true interpretation, "considerably", "extensively" seems more likely
than the "expeditiously" of *N.E.D.*, which here makes no sense
at all.

154. *Cochineele*: the famous red dye derived from the female of the
Coccus cacti, a tiny insect found on certain plants in Mexico and Peru.

155. *poore John*: dried and salted hake, hence something typically
cheap and worthless. Cf. *Rom. and Jul.* i. 1. 36; Massinger, *Renegado*,
i. 1; *A.V.* iii. 4. 31.

160. *founders*: runs lame, halts.

191. *Without the least of scruple*: unconscious irony. Contilupo means
"without the least *doubt*"; but his words cannot fail to suggest also
his own utter unscrupulousness. For *scruple* = "doubt", cf. Selden,
Illustr. to Drayton's Polyolbion, xi. 189: "as is, without scruple,
apparant (*i.e.* manifest)".

225. *Huswife*: in a double sense—(1) housewife, (2) loose woman
(cf. our "hussy"). There is a similar quibble in *Othello*, ii. 1. 112:
"Players in your housewifery, and housewives in your beds".

227. *study*: used in a wider sense then than now, of any private room
of the master of the house. Cf. its application to the inner stage of the
Elizabethan theatre.

245–6. *makes it up With three quarters of a face*: *i.e.* dresses it up so that it seemed only to have three quarters of a face. Cf. Massinger, *A Very Woman*, I. I (of a lady): "not yet fully made up (*i.e.* attired) Nor fit for visitation"; Dekker in *Satiromastix* speaks of one "made up In sable colours".

250–2. *Gossips...arch-Puritans*: *Gossips* = "god-parents" ("God-sib", one spiritually akin). In the Church of England by a canon (since repealed) parents were forbidden to become god-parents to their own children. The Puritans, on the other hand, objected that it was precisely the child's own parents who ought to be most responsible for its religious training; and in the Genevan form of baptism, instead of there being sponsors, the parents (or other responsible persons) recite the Creed as representing the faith in which they mean to bring up the child.

256. *cases*: with a *double entendre*.

267. *time past, or present*: *i.e. in* time past or present. *N.E.D.* does not notice this adverbial use, though it gives the analogous "time back", "time ago" as provincialisms. Cf. v. 4. 212.

270–1. *and her Councell To inlarge*: *i.e.* and (it is beyond example) *for* her Counsel to enlarge.

271–3. *as much Oratory As ever I did heare them...Defend a guiltie woman*: *i.e.* defend a guilty woman *with*.

278–80. Cf. *D.M.* IV. I. 42–4.

285. *flaw*: breach, quarrel. See on *W.D.* I. 2. 56.

311–2. *loose Her Dower*: in English law Leonora would have been liable to this penalty only if she had gone and lived with her lover (13 Edw. I, c. 34).

322–4. *malice...Powder-Treason*. This suggestion of private vendetta at the bottom of the Gunpowder Plot must refer to Thomas Percy, one of the leading conspirators, who did nurse a personal grudge against James I as having duped him when, in 1602, he was sent to Scotland on behalf of the English Catholics to ask toleration for them in return for their support of James. By his own account he received favourable promises from the King; and when the penal laws against Catholics were after all not at once repealed, he was enraged by the thought that but for this deception they might have taken more drastic action. In May 1603 when Catesby appears to have been first brooding on his plot, Percy rushed into his room exclaiming that he meant to kill the King; and was met with the answer "No, Tom, thou shalt not adventure to small purpose; but if thou wilt be a traitor, thou shalt be to some great advantage".

In the light of this direct allusion, it seems possible that the frequency in Webster and other dramatists of metaphors from under-mining and blowing up may also be partly suggested by the Gun-powder Plot. See *W.D.* IV. 2. 141, *D.M.* III. 2. 187; and cf. *D.M.* II. 3. 15, "This Moale do's undermine me" with Speed, *Hist. of*

Engl. (1611—note date) on the Powder Plot (p. 1232 of the 1632 ed.): "The Moles that first underwent (undertook) these underminings were Robert Catesby, etc." Still it is dangerous work finding such topical allusions; it may end with discoveries like the ingenious Miss Winstanley's, that the Porter in *Macbeth* is no other than Guy Fawkes himself.

331–2. *forsake All naturall example*: *i.e.* to do justice to the infamy of women one must give up comparing them with anything else in Nature, such as the traditional Hyrcanian tigers, crocodiles, pestilences and the like—a precept which the speaker proceeds himself to infringe two lines lower. Cf. Shirley, *Traitor*, II. 1 (in an opposite strain of eulogy):

> Let not fond men hereafter commend what
> They most admire by fetching from the stars
> Or flowers their glory of similitude,
> But from thyself the rule to know all beauty.

338. *seaming lace*: *i.e.* lace used to cover seams. *N.E.D.* quotes (*s.v.* "seaming") from Palliser's *History of Lace*, p. 300 *n.*: "'Seaming' lace and spacing lace appear to have been generally used at this period (under James I) to unite the breadths of linen, instead of a seam sewed. We find them employed for cupboard cloths...shirts etc. throughout the accounts of King James and Prince Charles".

339. *bones*: because small bones used to be employed as bobbins in making what was thence called "bone-lace". Cf. *Twelfth Night*, II. 4. 45:

> And the free maids that weave their thread with bones.

343. *by-slips*: (1) peccadillo; (2) bastard. Here (2).

354–6. *for that womans sinne...consent*. This seems to mean: "*as for* my mother's alleged adultery, to the exact occasion of which you are all so glibly ready to swear, I would never admit it to be true". Here *consent* = "agreement with your *opinion*", cf. "consensus", "assent"; so in *As You Like It*, v. 1. 48: "All your writers do consent that *ipse* is he". This is not very satisfactory: but Romelio clearly seems to be contrasting his own attitude, whatever that is, with the glib precision of his accusers. With this use of *for* cf. *D.M.* II. 4. 20.

362. *my Master*: how could this statement of Contilupo's come as a surprise to Sanitonella, when he had himself drawn up the brief which is Contilupo's sole source of information?

362. *spoyl'd*: ruined.

367. *Don John of Austria*: son of Charles V by Barbara Blomberg of Regensberg; acknowledged by his father in a codicil of his will, and officially recognized by Philip II in 1559.

376. *Battell of Lepanto*: Oct. 7th 1571.

377. *remarkeable*: easily noted.

386. *bagge and baggage*: *i.e.* the attorney with his buckram bag, and the baggage Winifrid. Cf. Middleton, *Fair Quarrel*, IV. 4. 80: "You

may see that by his bag and baggage" (of a Captain retreating with a disreputable woman). Similarly H.D.S. quotes from "Overbury", *Characters*, "A Tinker" (by J. Cocke): "So marches he all over England with his bag and baggage" (*i.e.* doxy). *Baggage* came to mean "worthless trash", thence "a trashy person".

387. *Ore tenus*: *lit.* by word of mouth". *N.E.D.* is hopelessly vague. But the term is used of legal proceedings conducted verbally, without written statements (as *e.g.* sometimes in the Star Chamber): here it apparently means that Winifrid is going to give her evidence "by word of mouth", without a previously written deposition. Or perhaps simply—"Here she is in person".

394. *running*: smoothly tripping. So Nash (*Wks.* ed. Grosart IV. 109) speaks of "merry-running Madrigals".

395. *fidling*: with a *double entendre*.

402. *Pumpes*: close-fitting shoes, with no fastening, and with either low heels or none at all.

404–5. Cf. *W.Ho!* II. 2. (p. 95).

408. *Latin*: a curious reversal of *W.D.* III. 2. 20–1.

412. *Latin*: with a pun on "latten" = "brass" (Fr. *laiton*). Dyce recalls a curious anecdote of Shakespeare's making this pun, in L'Estrange's *Merry Passages and Jeasts* (1650–5) (also quoted in Nares, *Glossary*, *s.v.* "latten"). After much doubt what to give his godchild, Jonson's little boy, at last Shakespeare decided: "I' faith *Ben*: I'le e'en give him a dozen good Lattin spoones, and thou shalt translate them".

414. *ignorant that way*: she means, "of Latin": but we are maybe meant to understand also "of the useful art of supping with the Devil", in which Winifrid was clearly proficient.

415. *Proctor*: "one whose profession is to manage the causes of others in a court administering civil or canon law; corresponding to an attorney or solicitor in courts of equity and common law". (*N.E.D.*)

415. *Commencements*: of the law-terms.

420. *Caudle*: hot drink (Lat. *calidus*); made of gruel, mixed with wine or ale, sugar and spice, and of a strengthening nature.

421. *small drinke*: *small* = "weak in alcohol" or, sometimes, "non-alcoholic"; cf. "small beer" and Phaer, *Regiment of Lyfe*, I. 6: "To abstayne from all kynds of wyne and to use himselfe to smalldrinke".

422. *Julipe*: the name was given to various kinds of sweetened drink, such as barley-water. The point of Ariosto's irony is doubtless that such drinks were often made the vehicle of soothing medicine, so that the word becomes = "a means of removing physical desire". Cf. Massinger, *Parl. of Love*, III. 1: "A coarser julep may well cool his worship".

426. *tester*: canopy.

428–30. A line of policy considered but rejected as inadvisable by Ovid, *Ars Amat.* I. 375 ff.

436. It is a ludicrous touch that this hag finally trips herself up over her vanity about her own age.

441. *from the Byas.* The "bias" being the set (oblique) course of the bowl, "from the bias" or "out of one's bias" was a regular phrase for being out of one's course or, as we say, "off the rails".

443. *two great frosts*: Fleay, with his usual cavalier inaccuracy, says summarily that the frosts must be those of 1564 and 1598. But the frost of 1598 was not nearly so severe as that of 1607–8, when the Thames froze as hard as it had frozen in 1564. Indeed the comparison with 1564 was made at the time. See Stowe's account of these winters. Apparently the Northern European peoples made merry in 1607–8 over the fuss excited in England and France by the occurrence "once in *fifty* years" of the sort of winter they themselves endured annually. Another suggestion made is "1607–8 and 1622": but this is on the face of it quite pointless. Winifrid is trying to extricate herself from the difficulties she has created by pretending to be only forty-six: and she is trying to do this by pretending that she did not really know her own age, and giving circumstantial evidence from frosts and plagues that she is really older after all. But remembering the frosts of 1607 and 1622 would add nothing to her age. And we may compare, in favour of 1564, the other landmarks she gives—the plague of 1563, the fall of Calais in 1558.

443. *three great plagues*: probably those of 1563, 1592–4, 1603 (see Chambers, *Eliz. Stage*, I. 329, IV. 346 ff.). Another suggestion is 1593, 1603, 1613: but 1613 was less severe and the objection again applies that remembering 1593 would not make Winifrid an old woman, which is the whole point.

444. *losse of Callis*: Calais was taken by the Duke of Guise on Jan. 5th 1558. Winifrid chooses her chronological data very cunningly, so that they gradually get earlier and earlier. For the use of the loss of Calais as a means of dating cf. Chapman, *Monsieur d'Olive*, IV. 2. 112, where that boastful personage says his own embassage will become so famous a landmark that "the loss of Calais and the winning of Cales (Cadiz) shall grow out of use".

444–5. *first comming up...great Codpiece.* Here Winifrid appears to fling the reins to her imagination: for the great codpiece was a good century old, having come in from France under Henry VIII. Thus J. Winchcomb, the famous clothier of Newbury (d. 1520) appeared before that king in "slopps, which had a great codpiece whereon he stuck his pins". Cf. Strutt, *Dress and Habits of the English* (1799 ed.), II. 258.

492. *How, a party?* Sanitonella seemed to know quite well how, at 362 above. The explanation may be, I think, that he had not recognized the judge to be Crispiano; but then nothing can explain Sanitonella's conduct as a whole.

492. *fine crosse trickes*: *i.e.* "a fine red herring"—"cross tricks"

being tricks which cut irrelevantly across the progress of the main issue.

499–501. Cf. *Hen. VIII*, III. 2. 455–8.

516. *blea[r]ed him*: thrown dust in his eyes, deceived him (Contilupo). See Text. Note.

527–9. See on II. 1. 13.

535. *honest*: chaste.

537. *daunce lachrimae*: a common Elizabethan phrase, alluding to the musical work of J. Dowland, dedicated to Queen Anne of Denmark (1608) and called *Lacrimae or seaven Teares figured in seaven passionate Pavans*. Hence "to dance *lacrimae*" became as regular a phrase for being whipped as "to dance on nothing" for being hanged. Cf. *F.M.I.* IV. 2. 233–4: "Twice sung *lacrymae* to the Virginalls of a cart's taile". Similarly Massinger, *Maid of Honour*, 1. 1, *The Picture*, v. 3, and many other passages.

541. *your hote liver*: "the hot liver you talked of". The liver was the supposed seat of passion, and a hot one a sign therefore of sensuality. Cf. *A.V.* IV. 1. 255.

545. *arsie varsie*: "backside foremost"; often = "topsy-turvy", but here rather "willy-nilly".

552. *abuse*: deceive.

586. *challenge*: impeach.

593. *Overseer*: executor.

598. It is hard to see why Contarino does not bring in the evidence of his surgeons at this point—probably from a gentlemanly preference of the duel to legal justice.

610–1. Cf. *D.M.* v. 1. 11–3.

634–5. *in the Breach...At Malta*: probably Webster is thinking of the famous repulse of the Turks by the Knights of Malta in 1565, though strictly this would make Ercole and Contarino much too old (*c.* 65) at the supposed date of the play (1610).

637. *your Nation*: Danish, as would appear clearly enough to an audience by Contarino's dress in his disguise. Cf. the s.d. I have added at beginning of this scene, which is based on v. 4. 5.

This tribute to Denmark might be regarded as slightly supporting the idea that these words were written to please the Queen, Anne of Denmark, whose Servants acted the play, and therefore before her death on March 2nd 1619.

644. *throat*: "to lie in the throat" being supposed to express even deeper mendacity than the simple "to lie". H.D.S. quotes *Haml.* II. 2. 609:

> gives me the lie i'the throat
> As deep as to the lungs.

646. *Callis Sands*: a regular duelling-ground for Englishmen, as the nearest place outside the jurisdiction of the English laws against duelling. See on *C.C.* 1. 2. 105.

652. *Knight-Marshall*: an officer of the English royal household, with jurisdiction "within the verge" of the court, *i.e.* for twelve miles round it.

669–73. Clearly a topical allusion: see Introd. p. 215.

672–3. *Mountaines...Vales...* : a favourite antithesis of Webster's, cf. *D.M.* iii. 5. 169; *A.V.* iii. 2. 204.

675–6. *France...strange Law-suite*: Vaughan (*Cam. Hist. Eng. Lit.* vi. 183) suggests an allusion here to the extraordinary trial of Louis Gaufredy as a sorcerer in 1610–1, in which a certain Romillon took a leading part and may, he thinks, have suggested the name of Romelio. For the trial see S. Michaelis, *History of the Passion and Conversion of a Penitent Woman, Seduced by a Magician.* London, 1613; and Michelet, *Hist. de France* (1879), xiii. xix (well worth reading, though the connection with Webster seems to me very doubtful indeed).

Another French trial, however, less remote in date, seems to me a possible subject of allusion—that of *Leonora* Galigai, wife of the murdered Maréchal d'Ancre, whose assassination Webster referred to in the opening he added in 1617 to *The Duchess of Malfi* (see on *D.M.* i. 1. 8). She too was accused of elaborate sorceries and executed on July 8th 1617. But after all some far obscurer case may have been enough of a nine days' wonder at the time to occasion a passing reference like this.

V. 1.

Outer stage? But it is clear that there would be many alternative ways of staging this and the next three scenes. The chief use of alternation here would be to convey that the scene does actually change from one place to another, and drawing the curtain would mark that fact.

10–1. From *Arcadia*, i. (*Wks.* i. 86): "there is nothing more terrible to a guilty hart than the eie of a respected friend". (C.)

17. *taking*: plight. Cf. Pepys, *Diary*, Jan. 12th 1662–3: "the poor boy was in a pitiful taking and pickle".

47. *tumbled*: with a *double entendre.*

48. *for that tricke*: metaphor of a game of cards. Cf. Mabbe's transl. of Aleman's *Don Guzman d'Alfarache*, i. 1: "leaving...to others... to play out that tricke at Cards for me".

V. 2.

Perhaps whole stage. See note at beginning of v. 1.

7–9. The construction is mixed. *Marry this* would naturally lead up to an explanation what the *vild abuse* is; but we are told, instead, the suggested remedy for it, the *new way* to be taken—*that no Proctor ...be tollerated*, etc. What follows makes this clear, I think.

11. *overtaken*: drunk.

12–3. s.d. *Bathanites*: neither Helyot (*Dict. des ordres religieux*) nor Heimbucher (*Orden u. Kongregationen der röm. Kirche*) know of

any order of this name. Stoll (p. 160) identifies them with a Moham-
medan sect he discovered in the *Encicloped. Italiana*, III. 45: "Bateniti,
o Bataniti: setta particolare che si formò fra i mussulmani e che si
componeva di uomini del popolo". This does not seem very helpful;
and my doubt is increased by the statement of the new *Encyclopedia
of Islam* (*s.v. Batiniya*) that the Batinites are *not* a "setta particolare"
at all, since the name is given to all those who seek an exoteric meaning
(*batin*, inner) in the sacred writings, and covers a number of different
sects. In any case what on earth are we to imagine that Webster
thought Moslem mystics could be doing in a convent at Naples?
The name, like so many proper names, is doubtless a corruption,
perhaps of Bethanites (after St Mary or St Lazarus of Bethany) or,
less probably, Bethlemites. For there have at least been Christian
orders so called, though I can find no trace of this alleged custom
before combats.

35–6. *shame...begot*: another of Webster's beloved equivocations.
Jolenta appears to confess incest; she means really that the shame was
thrust upon her by her brother and so "begot" by him in the same
sense as Mr W. H. was the "begetter" of Shakespeare's *Sonnets*. Why
she should play this trick on Ercole is obscure; but we must suppose
her, I think, to be dominated by an almost hysterical desire (cf.
below: "They say shee's a little mad") to get away from the whole
miserable series of entanglements. The reader may sympathize.

v. 3.

Perhaps outer stage. See note at beginning of v. 1.

11. *suborning* seems here to mean simply "aiding and abetting".

v. 4.

Perhaps whole stage. The close of the scene involves the balcony.

5. *the Dane*: the disguised Contarino.

16. *upon returne*: this seems a reference, though it has been ignored by
editors (and *N.E.D.*), to the curious custom practised by Elizabethan
travellers, of gambling on their risks—a kind of inverted insurance.
The traveller paid down a certain sum at his departure; if he failed
to return, the agent kept it; if he did return, he received the amount
of his deposit several times over. Cf. Jonson, *Every Man out of his
Humour*, II. 1: (Puntarvolo) "I do intend...to travel, and...I am
determined to put forth some five thousand pound to be paid me five
for one *upon the return of* myself, my wife, and my dog from the
Turk's court in Constantinople. If all or either of us miscarry in the
journey, 'tis gone; if we be successful, why, there will be five and
twenty thousand pound to entertain time withal". (See on *Tempest*,
III. 3. 65, in Furness's *Variorum Shakesp.*) Hence it grew common

among "bankerruts, stage-players, and men of base condition" to travel abroad merely to make money in this way. Cf. Barnaby Riche, *Faults and nothing but Faults*, 1607 (quoted by Steevens on the *Tempest* passage): "those whipsters, that having spent the greatest part of their patrimony in prodigality, will give out the rest of their stocke, to be paid two or three for one, *upon their return from Rome*". Taylor the Water-Poet attempted to make a little money on this plan; but found great difficulty in getting paid, and had to console himself by writing a satire on the seven hundred and fifty bad debtors who refused to give him anything on his return from Scotland. The odds given seem to imply that the probability of non-return was incredibly high: and yet how great the risks of travel were, may be gathered from such a casual passage as this in a letter from Carleton to Chamberlain (Aug. 12th 1612): "Mr Willoughby and Mr Bowes...are both safely returned (from Jerusalem). Of seven Dutch gentlemen, which made the journey with them, and came back as far as Cyprus, three they buried in that island, and flung the other three overboard, betwixt that place and this". The seventh just survived a long illness. (See also a vast note on the *Tempest* passage in Halliwell's *Shakespeare*; and Fynes Moryson, *Itin.*, 1. 3. 1.)

There is, further, a curious use of "return", as if it had come to mean "wager", in Chamberlain to Carleton, July 31st 1619—a passage interesting in itself: "On St James's Eve, upon a return, or wager, one went from Southwark to Calais, and back again the same day, having almost an hour and a half to spare of his limited time, which was from broad daylight to sunset".

21. *Hung still an arse*: hung back.

26. For this ancient jest, cf. "Beaum. & Fl.", *The Pilgrim*, IV. 3, where there is a joke on a Welshman who

> Ran mad because a rat eat up's cheese.

H.D.S. quotes No. LXXVI of a *Hundred Merry Tales* (1525—*Shakesp. Jest-Books* ed. by W. C. Hazlitt, 1864) in which God grows so weary of the Welsh in Heaven that St Peter is sent to cry "Roast Cheese!" outside the gates of Paradise, and when they have all scampered out to find it, snaps the lock on them for ever.

30. *put in for't*: made his thrusts.

38-9. *anger...sorrow...dry*: with reference to the doctrine of the humours. Cf. Burton, *Anat.* I. 1. 2. 2: "Choler is hot and dry... Melancholy, cold and dry".

43. *Cuckingstoole*: a stool on the end of a swinging pole by means of which scolds were ducked in the village-pond (Lat. *cacare*: perhaps because originally shaped like a close-stool). See Brand, *Pop. Antiq.* p. 641.

57-8. Like a curious mocking echo of Tennyson's last poem. In the lines that follow Webster suddenly recovers some of that eloquence and energy which mark him at his best.

72. *Turne you*: probably "turn yourself round (and look at the opposite supposition—that I were you)". *Turne you* might in itself seem to mean "if I turned into you, became you": but then *were I in your case* becomes the merest tautology.

78–9. *honest man...coward.* Cf. *Char.* "Commander", 7–8. But clearly the idea was a commonplace: *e.g.* H.D.S. quotes Sir Jn. Davies, "In Sillam":

> When I this proposition had defended,
> "A coward cannot be an honest man",
> Thou, Silla, seem'st to be forthwith offended,
> And holds the contrary, and sweares he can.

Cf. too Traherne, *Christian Ethicks*, "Of Courage": "A coward and an honest man can never be the same; a coward and a constant lover can never be the same".

92. *foyle*: (Fr. *fouler*) originally a technical term in wrestling for "a throw not resulting in a flat fall, and so not quite complete". In the common figurative use, however, of such phrases as "to give" or "to take the foil" the sense of incompleteness in the victory disappears.

102. *apprehend*: really understand, form a true conception of.

109. *speake*: *i.e.* the usual speech made by prisoners just before execution.

118–21. A striking parallel to the famous lines in the *Medea* of Euripides (248–51):

> λέγουσι δ᾽ ἡμᾶς ὡς ἀκίνδυνον βίον
> ζῶμεν κατ᾽ οἴκους· ὡς τρὶς ἂν παρ᾽ ἀσπίδα
> στῆναι θέλοιμ᾽ ἂν μᾶλλον ἢ τεκεῖν ἅπαξ.

> Men say we women lead a sheltered life
> At home, while they face death amid the spears:
> Fools! I had rather stand in the battle-line
> Thrice, than once bear a child.

The reference in "A Reverend Judge" (6–7) to the behaviour of the chorus in "ancient Tragedies", the use of a Greek form in *A.V.* I. 1. 135 (see Commentary), and one or two other parallels make it seem possible that Webster may have known some Greek.

129 ff. For this episode cf. *W.D.* v. 4: and for the breaking into octosyllabic recitative (like the Greek choric ode with its excursions into general moralizing in a different metre), cf. Marston, *Antonio's Revenge*, IV. 2 (end).

It all seems strangely inappropriate on Romelio's lips (but cf. II. 3. 110 ff.): yet Webster seems to have thought of his Machiavellian merchant as also having a real streak of poetry in him—a sort of Villon, picking purses at one moment, and at the next composing a poem on his imminent execution.

141. *consequently*: as an inevitable consequence, an inseparable result.

146. *nets...wind*: we may recall Rabelais' picture of pedants who "pitched nets to catch the wind and took cock-lobsters in them".

153. *yonder*: "in the next world"; as, constantly, the Greek ἐκεῖ.
159. *Bandileere*: scarf. To make Julio's remarks intelligible one must imagine some by-play in which he takes the winding-sheet from the coffin and puts it over his shoulder like a scarf; in this pose he wryly compares himself to a felon bound for the gallows and wearing his halter (as in pictures of the Burgesses of Calais).
173. Webster's passion for locking up his characters is extraordinary; cf. Camillo at the beginning of *W.D.*, the Cardinal at the end of *D.M.*
177. *Boson*: boatswain.
184. *and*: as if. Cf. *Mids. Night's Dream*, I. 2. 86: "I will roar you and 'twere any nightingale" (wrongly altered to "as" in Globe edition).
188–9. *'tis that He onely fishes for*: i.e. 'tis only that he fishes for. Cf. on *D.M.* I. I. 33.
192. *mine owne Ballad*: there are perpetual allusions to the doggerel ballads which the condemned criminal had to face as an additional horror. H.D.S. appositely quotes Massinger and Fletcher, *The Lover's Progress*, v. 3:

> I have penned mine own ballad
> Before my condemnation in fear
> Some rhymer should prevent me.

198. *close committing*: (1) committing to prison; (2) committing adultery or fornication. For this obsolete intransitive use, cf. *Lear*, III. 4. 80: "Commit not with man's sworn spouse".
221–2. Cf. *D.M.* II. I. 98.

v. 5.

Outer stage.

2. *Two Tuckets*: trumpet-signals (Ital. *toccata*, a musical prelude). Cf. Markham, *Soldier's Accidence*, 61: "The fourth (trumpet-signal) is, Tucquet or March; Which being hearde simplie of it selfe... Commands nothing but Marching after the Leader". It is used, as here, to introduce a tournament in *Rich. II*, I. 3. 25 (F₁): "*Tucket. Enter Hereford and Harold*".
18. *Champ*: this appears *not* to be an abbreviation for "Champions". The word is regularly used of the lists (*champ clos*): though there seems to be no other example of its personal use, as here. Hazlitt and H.D.S. explain "spectators"; but they were not inside the *champ* or lists; and when we speak to-day of the "field", we mean "the competitors", not the crowd of lookers-on. So here it seems that the other *combatants* take up Romelio's cry.
29–30. This apparently implies Contarino to be paired off in marriage with Leonora, as well as Ercole with Jolenta. It is certainly a strange *dénouement*; and it is even stranger that there should be so much doubt, from the printed text, what the *dénouement* actually is. Though

on the stage of course this obscurity (like that caused by Contarino's Danish disguise) would vanish.

37. *sprung*: "started from their cover"—the correct term. Cf. Lyly, *Midas*, IV. 3. 47–8: "Thou shouldest say, start a hare, rowse the deere, spring the partridge".

38. *Order of Saint Clare*: founded by St Francis of Assisi in A.D. 1212, when St Clara (1194–1253), "the first-born daughter of his Order", was consecrated by him to a religious life.

49. *crimson blood*: the red cheeks of the white races.

62–4. For this terribly lame device cf. Otway's *Orphan*, v. 2 (end):

> You'll in my closet find the story written
> Of all our woes.

66–7. From Montaigne II. 15: "Rareness and difficulty giveth esteeme unto things". (C.)

78. *consort*: concert.

80. *Orlando*: *i.e.* Furioso.

81–2. Cf. *Char.* "Waterman", 17.

94. *vowes breach.* What vow had Jolenta broken to the Monastery? Presumably it is merely that she had disguised herself as a nun. Or had she momentarily taken the veil (cf. III. 3. 221–3, IV. 2. 655–60)?

97–8. *Art...in the Gallies*: as ship's doctors, of course, not as slaves at the oar.

TEXTUAL NOTES
THE DEVIL'S LAW-CASE

For details of editions, see Bibliography. In the notes that follow:

Q = the Quarto of 1623. (Brit. Mus. 644. f. 71.)
D = Dyce.
H = Hazlitt.

In this piece and all those which follow (except *A.Q.L.*, *F.M.I.*, and the *Characters*), where the present text differs from the original, the change is due to Dyce, if not otherwise assigned; where it differs both from the original and from Dyce, the present editor is responsible.

THE ACTORS NAMES

C[o]ntilupo] *Cantilupo* Q.
Woma[n]] *Womar* Q.

TO THE JUDITIOUS READER

5. [et]] *&* Q.

I. I.

1–3. In Q the lines end—*wealth* | *Merchant* | *substance*.
13. *Fortunate Young Man*] *fortunate Youngman* Q.
19. *Baptist[a]'s*] *Baptisto's* Q.
32–3, 48–9. One line in Q.
61. *Intend to travell*] ends 60 in QD.
63–5. Two lines in Q, ending—*of the* | *rate*.
83–4, 86–7. One line in Q.
122. *Exit Romelio.*] Q places one line higher.
141–6. In Q four lines ending—*favours* | *of it* | *fly in* | *breath*: in D lines end—*to you* | *you* | *got* | *breath*.
158–62. In Q four lines ending—*your* | *on me* | *Summer* | *Leafe*.
189. D and H destroy some of the sense by omitting the comma after *steale it*, which emphasizes the separateness of the two ideas; for the portrait must be taken (1) as if unawares; and (2) while she is praying.
*218. *pearch'd* Q (by-form of *pierc'd*): On what...perch'd D: perch'd on H (both taking *pearch* = *perch* (of a bird): but it is a *rara avis* that *perches* on treasuries). I at first conjectured *purchas'd*; but no change is needed.
218. *I hope*] begins 219 in Q.
225–6. One line in Q.
226–8. D prints as prose.

I. 2.

3–9. In Q lines end—*coffin* | *looke you* | *greets you* | *me?* | *now*.
15–7. In Q two lines ending—*my* | *selfe*.
20. *mad?*] *mad;* QD.
40. *in...Fortune.*] separate line in QD.

41–2. One line in Q.
58. *to*] begins 59 in Q.
*89. *our Choyce ∧ here, noble Ercole!* D: *our Choyce. Here noble Ercole.* Q: *? our Choyce—here, noble Ercole!* (*i.e.* if we imagine Romelio seizing his sister's hand and offering it to Ercole. Cf. 144).
105–10. In Q four lines ending—*you* | *soule* | *please* | *nobly.*
116. *Intended*] ends 115 in Q.
123. *Now Ile teach*] begins 124 in Q.
128–30. In Q two lines ending—*regarded* | *appearance:* in D three, ending—*Lord* | *Maidenheads* | *appearance.*
133–4. Prose in Q: in D verse, with lines ending—*you* | *her.*
135–8. In QD two lines ending—*fashionable* | *heartie.*
141. *The*] ends 140 in Q: D moves *the like* to end 140.
180. *Exit Ercole.*] opposite 179 in Q.
184–5. One line in Q.
202. *Nor*] D moves to end 201.
205. *Why sir?*] *Why, sir,*— D.
212. *Chaperoones*[*s*]] *Chaperoones* Q (altered for clearness).
235–6. One line in Q.
240. *th*[*r*]*ee*] *thee* Q.
260. *so.*] *so?* Q.
263. [*m*]*y*] *by* Q.
272. I have added the stage direction: it is clear, I think, from the next lines that this is what happens.
277–9. Two lines in Q, ending—*breath'd* | *opinion.*
278. *monkey* Q: *monkeys* D. This is easier: but Winifrid *may* be still referring to Contarino only—she is clearly rather in love with him herself. In which case a dash must be put after *monkey*, as in the text (Q has a comma).
302. [*Exit Waiting Woman.*] As she has been dismissed, she had better go: though D and H leave her on the stage.
304–5. One line in Q.
307–8. One line in QD.
309–13. In QD seven lines ending—*Ercole?* | *guiltlesse* | *selfe* | *Mother?* | *women* | *married* | *union.*
318. *copartaments shewes* Q: *copartiments show* D.

II. I.

7–8. D prints as prose. Perhaps rightly: but cf. 10–1, 17–8.
28. *p*[*l*]*easure*] *peasure* Q.
35. *c*[*a*]*me* D: *come* Q. The present might just possibly stand, with its more general tone. But cf. III. 3. 37.
48. [*not*] H: QD omit.
49. *swallow*['*d*] D: *swallow* Q.
53–4. One line in Q.
56. *as familiar*] begins 57 in Q.
58. *Wenching?*] *Wenching!* D: so in 70—Q, *Curres?*: D, *Curres!*
95. Ends in Q with *talks with,* in D with *Romelio.*
103. *What*['*s*] D: *What* Q.
123–6. Verse in Q, with lines ending—*question* | *action* | *merry* | *tidings.*
140–1. D makes lines end—*leave* | *first.*
159–60. Prose in D.
169–72. Verse in Q with lines ending—*great* | *officers* | *spent* | *allowance.*

177–8. Verse in Q, with lines ending—*drunkard* | *it* | *Wardrobe.*
180–1. Verse in Q, with lines ending—*stockings* | *anckles.*
188–9. Verse in Q, with lines ending—*velvet* | *netherlands.*
208–9. Verse in Q, with lines ending—*hands* | *heads.*
215. *Exit Ar.*] One line lower in Q.
217–8. Verse in Q, with lines ending—*Barber* | *tongue.*
227–9. Prose in Q.
245. Ends with *hartie* in D. (Very possibly rightly.)
261. Ends with *you* in Q.
264. Ends with *heaven* in Q.
279–80, 302–3. One line in Q.
307. In Q ends with *terrible.*
343–4. In Q lines end—*greatest* | *Sea.*
347–8. One line in Q.

II. 2.

48–9. D prints as one line: as, metrically, they indeed are. But the pause may
be meant.

II. 3.

3–6. In Q two lines ending *doe not* | *but am.*
16–17. In Q end—*else* | *Julio.*
32. Q ends this line with *?*, 34 with full stop.
43–5. Prose in Q.
59. *and*] in QD begins 60.
63. *The Great*] in QD begins 64.
66–7. In QD end—*thinke* | *meane.*
72–3. In Q end—*of them* | *for't.* In D—*made them* | *hansell.*
87–8. In Q end—*thus?* | *understand.*
95. *s*[*o*]*d* D: *seed* Q.
99–100. In Q end—*Contarino* | *combat*; in D—*Ercole* | *slaine.*
*104. *dead lazy march*] ? *lazy dead-march* (the earliest example of *dead-
march* in N.É.D. is dated 1603).
112. *of*[*t*]*, somewhat* D: *of somewhat* Q.
124. Q ends with full stop.
156. D ends with comma, Q with *?* (= *!*)
167. *Yet*] ? *Yes.* Cf. on *D.M.* II. 5. 73.
183. *I meane*] in Q begins 184.

II. 4.

s.d. [*A street.*]] D has: *A room in the monastery of Saint Sebastian.* But it is
easier to imagine some undetermined scene out of doors. The same "street"
will then serve for III. 1 and III. 2 also.
1–4. Prose in Q.
5. *I do looke*] separate line in D.
17. [*S*]*icil*] *Cicil* Q.
18–9. One line in Q.
45–7. In Q two lines, ending—*worke* | *Devill.*
50. *Gordi*[*a*]*n.*] *Gordion* Q.
secund[*us*]] *secundi* Q (a confusion with *Finis Actus secundi*).

III. 1.

1–3. In Q two lines, ending—*promise* | *clouded.*
10. *has* Q: *have* D. But such singular forms with plural subjects are too well established in Elizabethan English to be lightly altered.

III. 2.

S.D. [*before a Surgeon's house.*]] Q, not marking a new scene, has nothing: D *Before the lodging of Contarino.* But in III. 3. 382 Leonora alludes to the affair as "at the Surgeons'".
5. *on*[*e*]] *on* Q.
28. [*incision*] D—an almost certain conjecture. A word has dropped out in Q.
41. *Why*...*wil*] in Q begins 42.
41. *Rom*[*elio*]] *Rom.* Q.
70–1. Here Q has simply *Contarino in a bed*, which I have worked into the S.D. in the text.
89. *Besides this*] *Besides, this* Q.
**90–2. *why, should*...*shall*,] QDH read:

> why should this great man live
> And not enjoy my sister, as I have vowed
> He never shall?

Yet it should surely have been clear that this makes complete nonsense. We should expect, if anything, since Romelio is examining his own reasons for killing Contarino: "Why should *not* this great man live and enjoy my sister?" The mistake has arisen through a failure to see that *should this great man live* is not a question at all, but a conditional clause—"*If* Contarino recovered and were then refused my sister's hand—why then he might alter at pleasure this will he has made in her favour" (cf. IV. 2. 595–6). *Why* is merely an interjection.
100. *Pigs*] ends 99 in Q.
102. [*that*] D adds. Cf. *W.D.* II. 1. 28.
119–20. One line in Q.
130–1. One line in D.
151–3. Prose in Q.
166–9. Two lines in Q, ending with *putrifaction* | *lively.*

III. 3.

17–9. D alters lines to end—*have* | *falne* | *us?*
25–6, 35–6. One line in Q.
37. *kn*[*e*]*w* D: *know* Q.
48. *Excellent worke*] separate line in D.
59. *So—then*] *So then* Q (with the same intention: but ambiguous). It is clearly Webster's common use of *so* as an interjection.
61–5. Three lines in Q ending—*time* | *like* | *it.*
101. *Of my owne*] ends 100 in Q.
102–5. Prose in Q: D ends 104 with *unnaturall.*
128. *him*] begins 129 in Q.
141–3. D makes lines end—*undergone* | *Coward* | *by.* But Q may stand. Scan:

> How came *you* | by this wret|ched know|ledge? His Sur|geon overheard | it.

144, 147, 239. *Surgeon*] *Surgeons* D (not absolutely necessary, I think).

154–6. In QD two lines, ending—*loved* | *money*.

172–3. In Q three lines ending—*us* | *health* | *him*: in D two, ending—*us* | *health*.

187–8. One line in D.

191. D omits semicolon, altering the sense.

194–5. Prose in Q.

196–7. One line in Q.

207. *Ile get one*] separate line in D.

208–10. Four lines in Q, ending—*sorrow* | *enough* | *coat* | *passions*.

217–9. Two lines in Q, ending—*law-case* | *fiend*.

*219. *fiend*] *feud* might be suggested (so Deighton): but *fiend* carries on the *devil* of the last line but one; though it might be argued that this was precisely what caused the printer to make a mistake. *Tweene* is certainly awkward after *fiend*. But cf. *D.M.* I. I. 345.

233. *For...misfortunes*] ends 232 in QD.

238. *Can skip*] ends 237 in QD.

243–4. As prose in Q.

254. *without*] begins 255 in Q.

256. *you are troubled*] begins 257 in QD.

258. The [*aside*], though not in D, is clearly needed.

262–4. Two lines in QD, ending—*Contarino* | *heire*.

264. *sister is*] if 264 is to be taken as metrically one with 265, it would be easier to read *sister's*:

> My sist|er's his heire. | I will make *you* | chiefe mour|ner, beleeve | it.

276. *to affect*] in QD begins 277.

308–9. Three lines in Q, ending—*hearted* | *man* | *me*.

314. *world*] begins 315 in Q.

320. *Say sir?*] *Say sir.* QD. But it is clearly an agonized question. Cf. *W.D.* IV. 2. 77.

323–4. One line in Q.

336–7. One line in QD.

*338. *comfort*] This should perhaps be *consort*; *vowed comfort* is a slightly queer phrase: and *consort* is like enough to Leonora's *comfort* to make the necessary quibble.

339–40. Prose in Q. D makes 339 end with *man*.

375. *fellow! In his loyaltie* D: *fellow in his loyaltie*. Q.

379–80. One line in Q.

382. *Surgeons'* D: *Surgeons* Q (which *generally* omits such apostrophes). Some might prefer *Surgeon's*, though there were actually two. Cf. 144 and Text. Note.

*404. *So one secret shall bind* ∧ *another*] (H, I find, has anticipated this change): *So one secret shall bind one another* QD. This is rather a queer phrase: and if *each* revealed a secret, there would be two secrets, not one.

405. *instru[ct]'st*] *instru'st* Q.

Act[us] Terti[us]] *Acti Tertii* Q.

IV. I.

D. [*The antechamber of a Court of Justice.*] D has *A room in the house of Ariosto*; changing at 83 to *the house of Contilupo.* He does however suggest that the scene may take place in a hall adjacent to the real court. It is clear that this is the case and that the full court-scene in IV. 2 is introduced merely by drawing the traverse of the inner stage. Cf. *W.D.* III. 1–2.

1. *Belly*] begins 2 in Q. D ends this line with *that*.

13. Ends with *cheese* in Q.

*27. D quite alters the sense by omitting the comma at the end of this line. The meaning of Q is clearly *Enow of Overseers*; not *Presentations of Overseers*. But D *may* be right.

46. *Non-resident Sub-sumner!*] *Non-resident, Sub-sumner!* D. It does not seem certain that the change is needed, though it makes good sense. The difference is slight.

52. *So long*] ends 51 in QD.

53–4, 57–8. One line in QD.

91. *to see*] begins 92 in QD.

94–5. One line in QD.

100–1. One line in Q.

107. *tother* Q: *other* D. But *the tother* is found in English of the period.

112–3, 114–5. One line in Q.

118. *Aud[i]ence*] *Audence* Q.

119–20, 126–7. One line in Q.

128. *against him*] in D begins 129.

IV. 2.

6–7. *Enter...disguised.*] In Q misplaced opposite 4–5.

*8. [*Contarino as a Dane.*]] I have added this on the strength of v. 4. 5; 637 below is incomprehensible without it.

19. In Q ends with *borne*.

23. *Palavafini*] D, probably rightly, queries *Pallavicini* (*Palavicini* is also found as a variant, and involves less alteration).

37. [*no*]] *not* Q.

41–2. Three lines in D, ending—*Spaine | better | them*.

51–2. s.D. D alters so that all the persons enter at one or other of two "bars". But it is surely clear that the Judge enters from the centre (*i.e.* of the inner stage) and the opposing advocates from doors at opposite sides. Obscurity is caused by the only stops in Q being commas, throughout the stage direction.

58–60. Prose in Q.

70–1. One line in QD.

78. *This favour*] ends 77 in Q.

90–1. One line in Q.

98. *confident*] Q has no stop, thus exactly inverting the sense. D ends the line with this word.

103–4. One line in Q.

108. *Lordsh[ip]*] *Lordsh.* Q.

134. [*Fieschi*]] *Fliski* Q.

134. *Dori[a]*] *Dori* Q: *Dorii* D. D may well be right, though *Dorii* is a wrong form: *e.g.* we find the equally wrong *Baptisti* in *F.M.I.* II. 4. 88.

156–7. One line in Q.

173–5. In Q two lines, ending—*mother | side*.

177–9. Prose in Q.

186. *Fra[nc]isco*] *Franscisco* Q.

194–5, 218–9. One line in Q.

238. *f[r]ight*] *flight* Q.
254–6. Prose in Q.
275. *so[n]nes*] *soones* Q.
275. *undoing?*] *undoing*: QD.
279. *Tween* Q: *Between* D.
279–81. D makes four lines, ending—*ligitimate* | *nay* | *sir* | *Suite*.
289. Ends in D with *hapt*.
300. Ends in D with *privately*.
306–7. One line in Q.
321. *me but*] *me: but* Q.
329. *growes*] *grow* D.
331. *m[a]n*] *men* Q.
331–3. In Q lines end—*one* | *example* | *mercy*.
338–40. Prose in Q.
360. Ends with *in?* in Q.
371. *And be sure*] begins 372 in QD.
373–4. One line in QD.
376–9. In Q lines end—*one* | *in't* | *pleasure* | *of the*: in D—*one* | *in't* | *lye* | *there* | *mother*.
381–2. Prose in Q.
384–5. One line in QD.
389–90. Verse in Q, first line ending with *dealt*.
394–5. Verse in Q, first line ending with *Violl*.
397–400. Verse in Q, with lines ending—*Lord* | *side* | *busines* | *shooes*.
404–21. As verse in Q, with lines ending—*slippers* | *noyse* | *house* | *there* | *slippers* | *Latin* | *Court* | *-house* | *Office* | *one* | *Devill* | *way* | *abroad* | *him* | *businesse* | *leave* | *her* | *appoyntment* | *refuse* | *drinke*.
422. *Julipe.*] D adds question-mark.
425–7. As verse in Q, with lines ending—*Lord* | *extreamely* | *bed*: the rest of the speech Q puts in prose, as here.
**427–30. *thrust money in my hand; and once...dealing with mee; which I tooke he thought 'twould be the onely way...*] Q has a comma after *mee* and a semicolon after *tooke*: D keeps these, but makes *and once...with mee*, a parenthesis between dashes, so that *which I tooke* refers back to *money*. This is very awkward; and why should Winifrid, however shameless, so unnecessarily stress the fact that she had taken a bribe? And the young lover's thoughts were after all only a matter of surmise to her. So that I prefer, with Hazlitt, to consider *tooke* = "supposed" and punctuate as above, even if Winifrid's grammar thereby becomes no better than it should be. For of course *'twould* should be *would*; H prints *would*; but the change seems hardly needed. It is an easy slip of speech.
434. *Lordsh[ip]*] *Lordsh.* Q.
442–6. Verse in Q, with lines ending—*elder* | *plagues* | *up* | *Codpiece* | *then*.
448. Ends with *Hare* in D.
451–2, 456–7. One line in Q.
467. Ends in D with *time*.
470. In QD ends with *face*.
505. *Sir*] D makes separate line.
*516. *blea[r]ed*] *bleated* QD, which seems quite meaningless. For *blear* = "hoodwink", "deceive"; cf. Heywood, *Golden Age*, IV. (*Wks*. III. 67):

thou hast done inough
To bleare yon Beldams.

Cf. too *A.Q.L.* i. i. 85. And *t* for *r* is of course one of the easiest of corruptions. *Him* in that case is Contilupo.

A possible alternative is *baited* (cf. II. i. 192).

537–8. One line in Q.

540. *slip*[*per*]*s*] *slips* Q. I can find no authority for *slips* = "slippers"; but of course Q *may* be right.

544–53. Verse in Q, with lines ending—*thing* | *businesse* | *fortie* | *you* | *twentie* | *-flower* | *teeth* | *Farrier* | *age* | *woman* | *thus*.

560. The question-mark, omitted by QD, seems required.

569. Ends in Q with *impose*.

572–3. One line in Q.

578–9. One line in QD.

595. *from*] Some copies of Q omit. (D.)

605. *Such a thing*] separate line in D.

610. *Shee*] in D ends 609.

614. Ends with *move you* in Q, with *be* in D.

617. *Oh, it bore*] separate line in D.

619. *When*] in D ends 618.

*626. [*turning to Rom.*]] it seems to me that either this direction must be inserted, or else *approve* altered to *disprove*. The first is much easier.

633–6. In Q lines end—*sweat* | *Malta* | *Nation*; in D—*I* | *Malta* | *Nation*.

647–50. In D three lines, ending—*scoure it* | *Defendant* | *there*.

654. [*risen*]] *rissen* Q.

665. *in Ercoles*] begins 666 in Q.

676. *yet but, for*] *yet, but for* QD. I have moved the comma, which in QD misleads the eye to take *but for* together, whereas really *say but* = "deny that".

676. *Law-suite*] begins 677 in Q

Act[*us*] *Quart*[*us*].] *Acti Quarti* Q.

<h1 style="text-align:center">V. 1.</h1>

5–6. One line in QD.

11. [*Then*]] *Than* D: *As* Q (as if "*so* terrible" had preceded).

12–3. One line in Q.

15. [*First of your*]] *Of your first* Q. D, having made the change, transfers [*First*] to end 14.

46. *rough*] *salt* some copies of Q. (D.) Cf. IV. 2. 595. Both passages occur in sig. K of Q: and as the Brit. Mus. copy gives the corrected reading there, presumably it gives it here too.

50–1. One line in Q.

<h1 style="text-align:center">V. 2.</h1>

11–2. Verse in Q, first line ending with *overtaken*.

37. *incestious*] *incestuous* D; but the other form is not uncommon. See *N.E.D.*

38–9. One line in Q.

<h1 style="text-align:center">V. 3.</h1>

15. *Mistris*] begins 16 in Q.

22–3. One line in Q.

25. *Tell*] in D ends 24.

27–8. One line in Q.

28. [*as for*]] *for as* Q.
28. [*Mistris*]] M*ris* Q.

v. 4.

1–3. Prose in Q.
7. *ignom*[*in*]*iously*] *ignomiously* Q.
24. [*a*] *goes*] *goes* QD. Some pronoun is needed.
66–7. One line in Q.
72–3. In Q lines end—*case* | *shadow*: in D—*laugh* | *you.*
73. *o*[*w*]*ne* D: *one* Q.
75–6. One line in QD.
92–3, 101–2. One line in Q.
104. *Say?* is not Q: *Say, is not* D (a needless change, I think). *Say?* is so common in Webster = *What do you say?*
*130–45. It seems at first sight a mistake that these charming octosyllables should be given to Romelio, instead of being sung by Leonora or someone behind the scenes. The text however has every sign of being right. Romelio calls Leonora's exhibition a "dumbe Pageant" (149); and he has already himself delivered one passage of similar rhymed octosyllables in II. 3. 115 ff. We may compare, for these curious recitations, Marston, *Antonio's Revenge*, IV. 2, where a song is proposed and explicitly rejected in favour of an "antic rhyme"; and *Span. Trag.* II (end):

> I'll *say* his dirge; singing fits not this case.

155–6. S.D. *to his mother*] opposite 151–2 in Q.
160. If this is meant for verse, *in a scarfe* should probably make a fresh line.
170–1. Q's stage direction is simply—*Lockes him into a Closet.*
180. *wisht* ∧ *he*] *wisht him he* QD; *him* may be a relic of an alternative version—*I would have wisht him to have jogg'd it a little.*
187. *I, I,*] separate line in D.
199–200. D marks here a new scene: but Leonora and the Capuchin simply re-appear on the balcony above the inner stage, as Romelio goes out.
212. *time*] D queries *in time.*
223–5. Prose in Q.

v. 5.

9. [*la*]] *le* Q.
9, 17–8. [*Victoire*]] *Victory* Q.
qu[*i ont*]] *que* Q.
15. *them*] *him* D (needless: R. is speaking very hastily.)
31–4. In Q three lines ending—*too* | *Honor* | *abused.*
73. *receiving*] begins 74 in Q.
89. *Th*[*o*]*rough*] *Through* Q.

DATE DUE

FEB 1 2 '88			
APR 8 '88			
GAYLORD			PRINTED IN U.S.A.